The Other Nation

The Other Nation

THE POOR IN ENGLISH NOVELS OF
THE 1840s AND 1850s

SHEILA M. SMITH

CLARENDON PRESS · OXFORD
1980

Oxford University Press, Walton Street, Oxford OX2 6DP

OXFORD LONDON GLASGOW
NEW YORK TORONTO MELBOURNE WELLINGTON
KUALA LUMPUR SINGAPORE JAKARTA HONG KONG TOKYO
DELHI BOMBAY CALCUTTA MADRAS KARACHI
NAIROBI DAR ES SALAAM CAPE TOWN

Published in the United States by
Oxford University Press, New York

British Library Cataloguing in Publication Data

Smith, Sheila M
  The other nation.
  1. English fiction — 19th century — History and
  criticism 2. Labor and laboring classes in
  literature 3. England — Social conditions
  I. Title
  823'.8'0932   PR830.L3   79-41317

  ISBN 0-19-812642-5

Printed in Great Britain by
Billing & Sons Limited.,
Guildford, London and Worcester

ACKNOWLEDGEMENTS

I welcome the opportunity to express my thanks to the many people who have helped me in writing this book, especially to Kathleen Tillotson at the beginning of my work and to Raymond Williams near its close. Of the many friends who read all or part of the book in its various stages of composition I owe a special debt of gratitude to Charles Parker, Michael Slater, Ruby Meager, Stephen Gill, Brian Lee, John Nicoll, Harold Osborne, and Bob Coats. Tom Craig, Judy Egerton, and Christopher Wood gave me generous assistance in assembling the illustrations. Roy Palmer drew my attention to many of the Preston ballads. Also, I should like to thank the staff of the British Library, the Bodleian Library, the Cambridge University Library, the University of London Library, the University of Nottingham Library, the University of Edinburgh Library, the Birmingham Public Libraries, the Nottingham Central Library, the Manchester Local History Library, the Oldham Local History Library, and Trinity College Library, Cambridge, for their help and expertise.

My thanks are due to the University of Nottingham for allowing me two terms' sabbatical leave to complete my work and a subvention towards the cost of publishing the illustrations; also to James Kinsley, Head of the English Department, University of Nottingham, for his help and encouragement. And I should like to thank Gwen Parker and Rosemary Bagley for their impeccable typing.

Some of the material in this book appeared as part of a doctoral thesis submitted at the University of London.

Nottingham, May 1979.

CONTENTS

LIST OF PLATES

between pp. 14–15

1. 'Lazarus and the Rich Man', 1830. Reproduced by permission of The Trustees of The British Museum.

2. William Henry Fox Talbot's photograph, 'The Straw Stack', 1844. Photo. Science Museum, London.

3. Thomas Shotter Boys (1803–74), 'London Bridge from Southwark Bridge', *Original Views of London as it is*, 1842. Reproduced by permission of the British Library.

4. 'The Rookery, St. Giles's'. Illustration to *Picturesque Sketches of London, Past and Present*, 1851, by Thomas Miller. Reproduced by permission of the British Library.

5. Gustave Doré (1832–83), 'Dudley Street, Seven Dials', *London. A Pilgrimage*, 1872. Reproduced by permission of the University of London Library.

6. Photograph of an old clothes shop, Seven Dials, 1877. Reproduced by courtesy of B. T. Batsford Limited.

7. The hanged man woodcut (right), versions of which were commonly used in broadside ballads of murder. From the British Library collection, *Broadsides on Criminal Trials and Executions 1801–58*. Reproduced by permission of the British Library.

between pp. 62–3

8. Philip James de Loutherbourg (1740–1812), 'Coalbrookdale by Night', 1801. Oil on canvas, 68 × 106.75 cm. Photo. Science Museum, London. The monochrome print gives little idea of the lurid glare affecting every surface in the original.

9. Paul Sandby Munn (1773–1845), 'Bedlam Furnace, Madely Dale, Shropshire', 1803. Water-colour, 32.4 × 54.9 cm. Private owner.

10. Vincent van Gogh (1853–90), 'Head of a Peasant Woman in a White Cap', 1885. Oil on canvas, 44 × 36 cm. Kröller-Müller National Museum, Otterlo, Holland.

11. Vincent van Gogh, 'Interior with Weaver', 1884. Oil on canvas, 61 × 93 cm. Kröller-Müller National Museum, Otterlo, Holland.

12. John Constable (1776–1837), 'Old Sarum', 1834. Water-colour, 30 × 48.7 cm. Victoria and Albert Museum, London.

13. 'Merry England', 1831. Reproduced by permission of The Trustees of The British Museum.

14. John Leech (1817–64), 'The Home of the Rick-Burner', *Punch* 7 (1844), 17.

between pp. 110–11

15. Twentieth-century photograph of Birmingham Gaol, now Winson Green Prison. Reproduced by courtesy of Birmingham Public Libraries, Local Studies Department.

16. John Leech, 'The Game Laws', *Punch* 7 (1844), 197.

17. 'John Rutherford Addressing the Miners', *Jane Rutherford; or, The Miners' Strike*, the *True Briton*, 9 June 1853, p. 785. Reproduced by permission of the British Library.

18. 'Lord Westerland and the Colliers', *Jane Rutherford; or, The Miners' Strike*, the *True Briton*, 14 July 1853, p. 865. Reproduced by permission of the British Library.

19. Sarah Burge, admitted to Dr Barnardo's Home 5 January 1883. Barnardo Photo Library.

20. 'E. Moses and Son's Ready Made Department, Aldgate', *Pictorial Times* 9 (1847), 68.

21. 'Pattern for Shawls.—a Card', *Punch* 7 (1844), 221.

22. John Leech, 'Almanack for March—"Bubbles of the Year. Cheap Clothing" ', *Punch* 8 (1845), 3.

23. 'Capital and Labour', *Punch* 5 (1843), 49.

between pp. 158-9

24. John Leech, 'The Poor Man's Friend', *Punch* 8 (1845), 93.

25. 'The Reconciliation', *Punch* 7 (1845), 123.

26. 'Horrid Murder'. From *Collection of Ballads, Chiefly printed in London by Catnach, J. Pitts and others, mostly between 1800 and 1870, but with a few of earlier date and with a few prose broadsides. Collected by the Rev. Sabine Baring Gould. With manuscript indexes*, I (i), 72. Reproduced by permission of the British Library.

27. 'Horrid Murder'. From *Broadsides 1677-1840.* Reproduced by permission of the British Library.

28. Gustave Doré, 'The Angel and the Orphan', *London. A Pilgrimage*, 1872. Reproduced by permission of the University of London Library.

29. Richard Dadd (1817–86), 'Crossing Sweeper', after 1864. Water-colour, 60.3 × 43.2 cm. Broadmoor Hospital. Photo. Paul Mellon Centre for Studies in British Art, London.

30. W. P. Frith (1819–1909), 'The Crossing Sweeper', 1863. Oil on panel, 18.1 × 14.3 cm. Private owner. Photo. National Portrait Gallery, London.

between pp. 206–7

31. Henry Wallis (1830–1916), 'The Stonebreaker', 1857. Oil on panel, 61.87 × 77.5 cm. By courtesy of Birmingham Museums and Art Gallery.

32. Gustave Courbet (1819–77), 'Les Demoiselles de Village', 1851. Oil on canvas, 54 × 65.4 cm. City Art Gallery and Temple Newsam House, Leeds.

33. Gustave Courbet, 'Les Demoiselles de Village', 1851. Oil on canvas, 195 × 261 cm. The Metropolitan Museum of Art, New York.

34. Gustave Doré, 'Scripture Reader in a Night Refuge', *London. A Pilgrimage*, 1872. Reproduced by permission of the University of London Library.

35. 'Distribution of Her Majesty's New Year's Alms on the 1st of January, 1846.' *Pictorial Times* 7 (1846), 1.

36. Interior of Columbia Market. *Builder*, 27 (1869), 147. Reproduced by courtesy of Birmingham Public Libraries, Science and Technology Department.

37. Boy recorded as 'Reynolds', admitted to Dr Barnardo's Home 18 April 1882. Barnardo Photo Library.

between pp. 222–3

38. William Daniels (1813–80), 'Two Children Selling Matches', 1851. Oil on canvas, 47 × 34.3 cm. Alexander Gallery, London.

39. The Wakling children, admitted to Dr Barnardo's Home 30 January 1891. Barnardo Photo Library.

40. A. E. Mulready (died after 1905), 'A London Crossing Sweeper and Flower Girl', 1864. Oil on canvas, 97.8 × 50 cm. Museum of London. Photo. John R. Freeman and Co. (Photographers) Limited.

41. Albert Martin, admitted to Dr Barnardo's Home 19 June 1902. Barnardo Photo Library.

42. Louisa Butin, admitted to Dr Barnardo's Home 6 July 1882. Barnardo Photo Library.

43. Minnie Reynolds, admitted to Dr Barnardo's Home 29 June 1886. Barnardo Photo Library.

44. Children recorded as 'The Holders', admitted to Dr Barnardo's Home June 1874. Barnardo Photo Library.

45. Emma Cook, admitted to Dr Barnardo's Home 5 July 1887. Barnardo Photo Library.

46. 'The Emigrant', *Howitt's Journal of Literature and Popular Progress*, 1 (1847), 323.

47. Gustave Doré, drawing for an illustration to Thomas Hood's poem 'The Bridge of Sighs' (published 1844). Indian ink, heightened with white, 24.7 × 18.3 cm. Victoria and Albert Museum.

ABBREVIATIONS

Baring-Gould, *Ballads*	*A Collection of Ballads . . . mostly between 1800 and 1870*, collected by the Revd. Sabine Baring-Gould, 10 vols.
Birmingham *Report*	*Report of the Commissioners appointed to inquire into the Condition and Treatment of the Prisoners confined in the Birmingham Borough Prison, and the Conduct, Management, and Discipline of the said Prison; together with the Minutes of Evidence.* P.P. Session 1854 (XXXI)
Carlyle, *Works*	Carlyle, *Collected Works*, Library edn., 30 vols., 1870
CEC, I	*Children's Employment Commission, First Report of the Commissioners, Mines*
CEC, I, Appendix, 1	*Children's Employment Commission, Appendix to First Report of Commissioners, Mines. Part I. Reports and Evidence from Sub-Commissioners*
CEC, I, Appendix, 2	*Children's Employment Commission, Appendix to First Report of Commissioners, Mines. Part II. Reports and Evidence from Sub-Commissioners*
Chadwick's *Report*	Chadwick, *Report on the Sanitary Condition of the Labouring Population of Great Britain*, 1842, ed. M. Flinn, Edinburgh, 1965
Charles Kingsley, Letters and Memories	*Charles Kingsley, His Letters and Memories of his Life*, ed. his wife, 2 vols., 1877
Gaskell, *Letters*	*The Letters of Mrs Gaskell*, ed. J. A. V. Chapple and A. Pollard, Manchester, 1966
Hansard	*Hansard's Parliamentary Debates*, Third Series
Leicester *Report*	*Report of the Commissioners appointed to inquire into the Condition and Treatment of the Prisoners confined in Leicester County Gaol and House of Correction; together with the Minutes of Evidence.* P.P. Session 1854
Nonesuch *Letters*	*Letters of Charles Dickens*, ed. W. Dexter, 1938

P.P.   Parliamentary Papers

Reports on Agriculture,   *Reports of Special Assistant Poor Law Com-*
1843   *missioners on the Employment of Women*
                              and Children in Agriculture. P.P. Session
                              1843 (XII)

Ruskin, *Works*   *The Complete Works of John Ruskin,*
                              ed. E. T. Cook and A. Wedderburn, 39 vols.,
                              1904–12

Taylor, *Tour*   William Cooke Taylor, *Notes of a Tour in*
                              the Manufacturing Districts of Lancashire in
                              a Series of Letters to His Grace the Arch-
                              bishop of Dublin, 2nd edn., 1842

TEXTUAL NOTE

Texts used:

Sybil, the Bradenham Edition, 1927, with an introduction by Philip Guedalla.

Yeast, the first edition, 1851, except when reference is made to the serialized version in *Fraser's Magazine*, July–December 1848.

Alton Locke, the first edition, 1850, 2 vols., because Kingsley made slight subsequent alterations to the novel, primarily to accord with his changing ideas about life at Cambridge University; to facilitate reference in cheap later editions I have given chapter headings.

Mary Barton, the Knutsford Edition, 1906, ed. A. W. Ward.

It is Never Too Late to Mend, the first edition, 1856, 3 vols., because some subsequent editions omit Reade's judgement of Hawes in the final chapter; to facilitate reference in other editions note that vol. i consists of chapters 1–20; vol. ii of chapters 1–32; vol. iii of chapters 1–33.

Sketches by Boz, the first edition, 1836, First Series, 2 vols., and Second Series, 1837, because some subsequent editions group the sketches under new headings although the titles of individual sketches remain the same.

Hard Times, the Norton Critical Edition, ed. George Ford and Sylvère Monod, New York 1966, the only modern authoritative text.

The text used for Dickens's other writings is the New Oxford Illustrated Dickens. References to John Forster's *Life of Dickens* follow the edition published by Chapman and Hall, 2 vols., 1908, based on the 1876 edition. All books cited are published in London, unless otherwise specified.

In references to Parliamentary Papers, apart from the *Report on the Sanitary Condition of the Labouring Population of Great Britain* (1842), ed. M. Flinn (Edinburgh, 1965), I have used the collection in the British Library (previously the British Museum Library) and, when using Reports which have been paginated subsequently in ink by hand I have followed this pagination of volumes arranged for the House of Commons. The *Report on Birmingham Gaol*, P.P. Session 1854 (XXXI), has MS pagination until p. 47 (printed p. 7) but no further. For this Report I have used the printed pagination; also in my references to the *Report on Leicester Gaol*, P.P. Session 1854 (XXXIV), the second of two Reports bound into one volume, with no MS pagination.

All the Preston ballads, quoted pp. 189ff. are from the Madden Collection, XVIII, Cambridge University Library.

INTRODUCTION

The novel's subject is society, life in a particular time and place lived by real men and women; this is what distinguishes it from romance. Being in prose and of considerable length it can analyse, discuss, and exhort; and, as the eighteenth-century novelists showed, it has great potential for experiment in form, new subject-matter demanding further experiments. Kathleen Tillotson in *Novels of the Eighteen-Forties* (1954) argues that the novelists of that period who transmitted their society's urgent problems into fiction helped give the novel a new seriousness, relevance, and direction. She describes this fiction as belonging 'to the no-man's-land on the frontier between the two nations' (p. 124), that is, between the rich and the poor. For one of the facts of life in Britain of the 1840s was the poor, whether crowded into the new and rapidly expanding industrialized towns or providing labour in a countryside experiencing an equally fundamental change. Raymond Williams, whose studies of these changes and their effect on literature have contributed significantly to our understanding and appreciation of the Victorian novelists, writes:

The problem of the knowable community, with its deep implications for the novelist, is . . . clearly a part of the social history of early nineteenth-century England and of the imaginative penetration and recoil which was the creative response. But what is knowable is not only a function of objects—of what is there to be known. It is also a function of subjects, of observers—of what is desired and what needs to be known. A knowable community . . . is a matter of consciousness as well as of evident fact . . . it is to just this problem of knowing a community—of finding a position, a position convincingly experienced, from which community can begin to be known—that one of the major phases in the development of the novel must be related. (*The English Novel from Dickens to Lawrence*, 1970, p. 17.)

In this instance Williams's study of the subject is wide-ranging and necessarily somewhat generalized. What I hope to do in my book is to scrutinize in detail a selection of novels in the 1840s and 1850s which recreate their authors' consciousness of a particular and significant part of the Victorian 'community', the poor. I am not trying to survey all the novels written about the poor during the period but to examine selected novels treating different aspects of poverty and with different degrees of aesthetic achievement. I have chosen this period because in the 1840s discussion of the 'two nations' played a major part in the 'condition of England' question as the poor became an increasingly evident by-product of Britain's rapid transformation into the leading industrialized country of the world, and as the early Blue books (reports commissioned by the Government, so called because bound in stiff blue paper) revealed to the public details about the state of the poor. Several of the novelists used this evidence in their fiction. Moreover, the novelists who described the poor at this period met a new and enormous demand for novels, and included the first important novelists since Scott and Jane Austen; they contributed to an intellectual and imaginative resurgence which marks the beginning of Victorian culture. And in the 1850s, the apparently secure period of solid commercial and mercantile prosperity built on the chaotic early years of the so-called Industrial Revolution, with Chartism dead and the 1848 year of political revolutions safely past, the continuation of poverty in a powerful and wealthy nation is a persistent theme. Repudiating Dives's insistence, in the popular ballad, that 'Thou'rt none of my brothers, Lazarus', these novelists demonstrated their kinship in fiction of varying imaginative power. I am concerned with the 'fact' of the poor as it appears in the 'consciousness' created in the novels; with how the appearance accords with verifiable reality and what this reality can tell us of the imagination which created that fiction; how the consciousness is affected by and affects the aesthetic standards and conventions of the period; with the novelists' struggle to shape images adequate to their response to the poor, the difficulties, both social and artistic, with which they had to contend.

That these writers could even contemplate the poor as central, individualized characters—the 'poor man', John Barton, Elizabeth Gaskell explained, was meant to be the 'hero' of *Mary Barton* (1848)—establishes the period. Romantic writers such as Blake, Crabbe, Scott, Clare, Burns, and Wordsworth had extended, in their different ways, the artist's consciousness, not only to include the poor, but also to make them of central importance. Victorian writers—particularly the novelists—developed this tradition. Their response to the poor can also be related to Romantic feeling, generated by the senses and revealing a vital truth unknown to reason; this truth could be shared by others by recreating the feeling. Moreover, imaginative response to phenomena apprehended by the senses, and the confidence in achieving reality by this activity can be traced not only in novels about the poor and in other arts such as Pre-Raphaelite painting and photography, but also in much contemporary scientific, philosophical, historical, political, and economic thought. These novels should be set not only in their artistic context but also in a wider social context.

My subject is the extent to which the poor could be 'known', to use Williams's word, by these novelists of the 1840s and 1850s, and the nature of their imaginative response to this persistent fact of Victorian society.

I

THE TWO NATIONS:
THE NAKED FACT AS IT STANDS

Thou'rt none of my brothers, Lazarus
(Ballad of 'Dives and Lazarus')

Disraeli's *Sybil* (1845) was the second of his three novels on the condition of England in the 1840s—the others were *Coningsby* (1844) which, Disraeli said in the General Preface to the collected edition (1870–1), concentrated on 'the origin and condition of political parties', and *Tancred* (1847), describing 'the duties of the Church as a main remedial agency in our present state'. The subject of *Sybil* was 'the condition of the people'. This being so, Disraeli in this novel had perforce to consider the poor, for 'In the spring of 1842, the Home Secretary reported that almost 1,500,000 people in England and Wales were paupers and receiving poor relief. The total population then was about 16 million.' (Steven Marcus, *Engels, Manchester, and the Working Class*, New York, 1974, p. 26 n.)

The period covered by the novel is from 1837 to 1844. The years 1837 and 1842 were two of the worst for economic depression since the end of the Napoleonic Wars in 1815 and, like the other slumps of the period, they produced acute political protest, in this case the beginning and the climax of the Chartist agitation. Together with *Coningsby*, *Sybil* embodies the ideas of Young England, active from 1842 to 1846, a small group of Tory MPs including Lord John Manners and George Smythe, led by Disraeli, forty years old in December 1844, and, having unsuccessfully sought office in Peel's government, increasingly in opposition to the Prime Minister. Young England attacked the Utilitarians and looked back with nostalgia to an idealized feudal system in which Church and aristocracy combined to protect the rights of the people. Beginning with *Vivian Grey* in 1826, Disraeli had written many romantic novels, two, *Vivian Grey* and *The Young Duke* (1831), having political themes. Indeed, the latter, like *Sybil*, traces a wealthy young aristocrat's gradual acceptance of responsibility to society. But in 1837 Disraeli, at the fifth attempt, succeeded in becoming an MP, and the Young England trilogy is the fruit of his practical experience in politics. *Coningsby* and *Sybil* reassert, in fiction, his claim in *A Vindication of the English Constitution* (1835) that the Tory party was 'the national party; it is the really democratic party of England. It supports the institutions of the country, because they have been established for the common good, and because they secure the equality of civil rights, without which, whatever may be its name, no government can be free, and based upon which principle, every government, however it may be styled, is, in fact, a Democracy.' (p. 182.)

The respective heroes of the two novels, Coningsby and Egremont, are both manifestations of the aristocratic ideal of leadership revived in the 1820s (see Harold Perkin, *The Origins of Modern English Society 1780–1880*, London, 1969, pp. 237–52), and possibly Disraeli lays particular emphasis on this ideal in opposition to the attacks on aristocracy made by the Anti-Corn Law League, founded 1839, but Egremont is seen specifically as the representative of the one 'Nation' coming to terms with the other. His 'education' begins when a stranger challenges him with the idea that Queen Victoria reigns over

Two nations; between whom there is no intercourse and no sympathy; who are as ignorant of each other's habits, thoughts, and feelings, as if they were dwellers in different zones, or inhabitants of different planets; who are formed by a different breeding, are fed by a different food, are ordered by different manners, and are not governed by the same laws.
    'You speak of ——' said Egremont, hesitatingly
    'THE RICH AND THE POOR.' (Bk. II, ch. 5.)

With a typical rhetorical flourish, Disraeli emphasizes in capitals the idea which had become a common subject for discussion, as the novel's reviewers pointed out. For example, the *Athenaeum* commented

On the whole, whatever, as artistic critics, we may think and feel of the expediency of thus mixing up the philosopher's subjects of observation, and the politician's objects of effort, with the mere novelist's tinsel,— 'Sybil' . . . is welcome, if taken as a sign of the times—a sign that the relations of rich and poor—the enlargement of the former's sympathies and the amelioration of the latter's misery,—are becoming matters of interest. Even if benevolence, and generosity, and liberality, are traded in (as the most simple cannot but suspect), the very fact that they are marketable, says something for the health and progress of Mankind. (*Athenaeum*, No. 916 (May 1845), 179.)[1]

Disraeli's reassertion of the aristocratic ideal in the novel should be considered in the context of the labouring people's increasing bitterness at what Carlyle in *Chartism* (1839) describes as 'the abdication on the part of the governors' and Perkin calls 'the demand of landed rulers for power without responsibility' (op. cit., p. 192), characterized during the early years of the century by their refusal to regulate wages, their prevention of the working people from negotiating a living wage in the Combination Acts 1799 and 1800, their passing of the Corn Laws to protect their rents, and their attack on the poor laws in the years immediately after the Napoleonic Wars. (I am indebted for these details to Perkin. For his full discussion of the question see op. cit., pp. 183–95.) The age-old split between rich and poor manifested itself in a more positive, active way in the second decade of the nineteenth century. Perkin discusses the formation of a class society in these years and sees the working class coming into existence with the Parliamentary Reform movement from 1816 to 1819. He argues that 'the essence of class is not merely antagonism towards another class or classes but organized antagonism with a nation-wide appeal to all members of one broad social level' (op. cit., p. 209). I am not equating the working class with the poor, but the identification of this class at the beginning of the nineteenth century largely depended on its struggle for a subsistence wage. Chartism, despite some of its prominent members, such as Ernest Jones, coming from middle-class families, was an organization of the kind described by Perkin; and Chartism, as Joseph Rayner Stephens insisted in 1838, was a 'knife and fork question . . . a bread and cheese question'.

The idea of the poor as a different 'Nation' was created by working-class resentment of aristocratic power without responsibility, and by the alienation of labour from capital in a rapidly developing industrialized society. The theme of the Two Nations was particularly appropriate when Disraeli wrote *Sybil* at a time of recent agricultural riots for better wages, Chartist disturbances,

---

[1] See also *Ainsworth's Magazine*, 7 (1845) 543, and the *Morning Chronicle*, 13 May 1845. I discuss the novel's reception in the introduction to *Mr. Disraeli's Readers*, Nottingham, 1966.

and economic depression in the factory towns. In the novel he countered middle- and upper-class fear of anarchy among the distressed lower orders with the hope of wise government by an aristocracy educated into responsibility. He imposed a romantic, colourful form on an image which had been at the centre of a long-standing debate. Discussion of the idea that the British nation was split in two by increasingly manifested poverty had been a 'sign of the times' for some years. In *Sybil* Disraeli owes much to Cobbett's thought; in 1829 Cobbett argued that the Reformation had created in a hitherto unified and wealthy society 'that state of things which sees but two classes of people in a community, masters and slaves, a very few enjoying the extreme of luxury, and millions doomed to the extreme of misery' (*A History of the Protestant Reformation* (first published in parts 1824–6), 2 vols., 1829, i, Letter V, 149).

Carlyle, three years before Victoria ascended the throne, analysed the ills of English society by quoting the fictitious philosopher Teufelsdröckh who echoed Cobbett's slave image and divided the community into Dandies and Poor Slaves: 'one attracts hourly towards it and appropriates all the Positive Electricity of the nation (namely, the Money thereof); the other is equally busy with the Negative (that is to say the Hunger), which is equally potent' (*Sartor Resartus*, Bk. III, ch. 10, Carlyle, *Works*, i. 276).

From the tangible and visual evidence of such division Engels argued that the development of commerce and manufacture in the rapidly expanding industrialized towns split these communities into rich and poor: 'it is an undenied and easily explained fact that the numerous petty middle-class of the "good old times" has been annihilated by manufacture, and resolved into rich capitalists on the one hand and poor workers on the other' (*The Condition of the Working Class in England*, Leipzig, 1845, English translation introduced by E. Hobsbawm, London, 1969, p. 55).

Another German visitor, the historian Frederick von Raumer, came to England in 1841, and published his impressions of English life. In his discussion of Chartism he comments: 'In no country in the world is there such a striking contrast, so defined a partition, so easy and fearful a comparison between the rich and poor, as in England' (*England in 1841*, trans. by H. E. Lloyd, 2 vols., 1842, i. 106).

Although the writers and speakers quoted differ widely in political persuasion and intention, they all agree that a sharp division between rich and poor is one of the facts of British society. Consciousness of this fact informs the novels I discuss in this book; all of them undertake to transmute a social reality into fiction and unless the resultant work is to be dry thesis or ephemeral propaganda, like Harriet Martineau's *Poor Laws and Paupers* (1833) in which characters and events are merely illustrations of her Utilitarian theories, the imagination must be a mode of perceiving the real, as the earlier Romantic writers believed it was. P. F. Strawson writes that imagination, as conceived at the end of the eighteenth century and the beginning of the nineteenth, 'is the image-producing faculty, the faculty, we may say, of producing actual representatives (in the shape of images) of nonactual perceptions' ('Imagination and Perception', *Experience and Theory*, ed. L. Foster and J. W. Swanson (Mass., 1970), pp. 31–54 (p. 41)). He analyses a faculty of the imagination which he describes as perception of innovation in the image, the sudden revelation which brings insight (we think of Wordsworth seeing 'into the life of things' or Keats's words, 'The Imagination may be compared to Adam's dream—he awoke and found it truth'):

Thus, beginning from such simplicities as seeing a cloud as a camel or a formation of stalagmites as a dragon . . . we may move on to very diverse things: . . . to a natural (or even a social) scientist seeing a pattern in phenomena which has never been seen before and introducing, as we say, new concepts to express his insight; to anyone seeing Keble College, Oxford, or the University Museum or Balliol Chapel as their architects meant them to be seen; to Blake seeing eternity in a grain of sand and heaven in a wild flower . . . In connection with any item in this rather wild list the words 'imaginative' and 'imagination' are appropriate, though only to some of them is the idea of an image coming into contact with an impression appropriate. (Op. cit., p. 50.)

In my study of the early Victorian novelists who described the Other Nation, the poor, I am concerned with their creation of 'images which come into contact with impressions', what the images tell us of their impressions and how appropriate they are to the verifiable reality. My subject is the novelists' re-creation of the physical actuality of the poor, what I shall call 'truth about' the Other Nation: their physical attributes, the 'fact' of their external reality, verifiable by the labour of documentation, evidence, and analysis; and the strength or weakness of their perception of the essential reality of the Other Nation, what I shall call 'truth to' the poor, which is achieved by imagination as the Romantics defined it, and which physical reality can only partially suggest. Keats used the term 'empathy' to describe the going out from himself into the identity of another, even into so humble a creature as a sparrow pecking on the gravel, so as to perceive, to understand its being. Could the novelists so imagine the poor that they, and their readers, could achieve this empathy?

To begin with the physical reality of the poor: there is plenty of documentary evidence to provide the 'truth about' the existence of the Other Nation in Britain in the first half of the nineteenth century. The poverty and destitution which existed in the leading industrialized nation of the world, steadily growing richer and more powerful, are described by a variety of observers. James Kay, later Sir James Kay-Shuttleworth, Elizabeth Gaskell's friend, was an untiring sanitary reformer and educationalist; as secretary of the Manchester Board of Health, formed as a result of the 1830 cholera crisis, he produced a report on that city's housing conditions which G. M. Young described as 'one of the cardinal documents of Victorian history' (*Victorian England*, 1936, p. 26). As a young medical student in 1825, Kay realized that the terrible destitution he found in the Old Town of Edinburgh was part of a social evil which could not be cured by his ministrations. He wrote in his manuscript autobiography:

At the bottom of the valley the Cowgate formed a common approach running northwards towards the Grassmarket. On every side these houses had once been inhabited by the wealthier citizens of Edinburgh, and some of them by the Scottish gentry or higher aristocracy, but they were now almost universally converted into barracks, in the separate rooms of which lodged the poorest and most suffering portion of the Scotch and Irish poor. Climbing from a street which had formerly been a scene of great historic interest, it was not uncommon to find, in rooms which had decorated fireplaces and ceilings, a family in the worst extremities of poverty and disease stretched on sacks and straw five or six stories above the street. It was from such narrow and foul abodes that patients suffering from acute disease, or from the fatal typhoid and typhus of the Old Town, had to be carried to the Royal Infirmary or the Fever Hospital. There were no paid nurses, and in the worst extremities of destitution critical maladies had to be treated in these close and foul rooms . . . I came to know how

almost useless were the resources of my art to contend with the consequences of formidable social evils. It was clearly something outside scientific skill, or charity, which was needed for the cure of this social disease.
This thought was burned into me by daily experience. (*The Autobiography
of Sir James Kay Shuttleworth*, ed. B. C. Bloomfield (University of London, Institute of Education, 1964), Education Libraries Bulletin, Supple-
ment 7, pp. 3–5.)

William Cooke Taylor, whom Perkin describes as an 'optimistic supporter of industrialism' (op. cit., p. 160), was an Irish
lawyer. He toured Lancashire in 1842, a miserable year of riots
and strikes for better wages, and was confronted by 'the naked
fact' of the Two Nations:

Take the naked fact as it stands: the producers of this enormous wealth—
for the whole of it is absolutely the produce of skill and industry—are not
allowed to be its consumers; are not permitted even to retain so much of it
as would afford them a bare subsistence. How the fact may be explained I
have no wish to speculate about, but its reality is proved by the stern evidence of my senses ...
    I have seen misery in many forms; I have been in the huts and hovels of
Ireland, when my native land was visited with the fearful scourge of
cholera; I have visited the cellars of Liverpool where existence assumes an
aspect which ceases to be human; I have penetrated into the wynds and
vennels of Glasgow, localities which would try to the uttermost the
hardest of hearts and the strongest of stomachs;—but nowhere have I seen
misery which so agonized my very soul as that which I have witnessed in
the manufacturing districts of Lancashire. And why? Because the extreme
of wretchedness was there, and there only combined with a high tone of
moral dignity, a marked sense of propriety, a decency, cleanliness, and
order, the elements which produced the vast wealth I have described, and
which do not merit the intense suffering I have witnessed ... We are not
stocks and stones: I am as firmly persuaded as I am of my own existence,
that, if the noble and wealthy had witnessed the scenes which I have gone
through, they would fling all prejudices and selfish interests to the winds,
they would stretch forth eager hands to raise the sufferers, pour oil and
wine into the wounds they have inflicted, and devote the whole of their
energies, heart and soul, to prevent the recurrence of such misery. (Taylor,
Tour, pp. 38–40.)

The effusion at the end of the passage might suggest the
warmth of Taylor's heart rather than the hardness of his head,
but the impression made upon him by what he has experienced
is so strong that he cannot believe that all men, even those
whom he thinks responsible for this misery, will not respond as
he has done. In 1842 conditions in the manufacturing towns

were indeed desperate. In a footnote Marcus cites Donald Read's *Press and People, 1790–1850*, 1961:

In 1842, probably the most distressed year of the whole nineteenth century, it was estimated that in Leeds at least twenty thousand people were living on incomes averaging only 11¼d. per week. Conditions were as bad in Manchester and in Sheffield. 'The picture which the manufacturing districts now present', wrote the *Manchester Times*, 'is absolutely frightful. Hungry and half-clothed men and women are stalking through the streets begging for bread.' (Op. cit., p. 87 n.)

Nor was the social problem of human misery and bitter poverty confined to the industrial towns. In assessing the benefits brought by the Industrial Revolution to the different sections of English society Perkin adopts 'a dynamic model of a new industrial system growing like a vortex within the old, and gradually pulling into its orbit of production and demand circle after circle of producers and consumers' (op. cit., p. 141): he consigns to 'the outermost circle of all . . . the farm labourers, especially those of the counties remotest from industrial towns' (ibid., p. 147), that is, where the factories did not compete for the available labour. In the northern industrial areas agricultural wages rose, but elsewhere there was hardly any increase in real wages (that is, the command of money wages over goods and services); the system of boarding unmarried labourers in farmhouses declined, encouraging early marriages and more children to feed; enclosures, while often providing more employment in occupations such as hedging and ditching, raising root crops and the increased number of other crops now possible in a four-year period, and tending the larger numbers of animals supported by the new fodder crops, also deprived the labourer of grazing rights and fuel, and made accommodation more difficult to get; and declining domestic employment for wives and children, whose work was increasingly lost to the factories, made rural families dependent on agricultural labour for their existence (ibid., p. 126 and p. 147). Perkin agrees with J. Burnett (see *Plenty and Want: a Social History of Diet in England from 1815 to the Present Day*, 1966, p. x and ch. 2) that the agricultural labourer was 'the worst fed of all workers in the nineteenth century' (op. cit., p. 147), and with R. E. Prothero (see *Pioneers and Progress in English Farming*, 1888, p. 224) that he was also the worst housed. As a reviewer of *Mary Barton* wrote, 'Lazarus lies at the gate of Dives . . . by the park palings of the square as well as on the hall-steps of the cotton lord.' (*Edinburgh Review*, 89 (1849), 434.) *The Assistant Poor Law Commissioners' Reports on the Employment of Women and Children in Agriculture*, 1843, reveal the substantial fact behind the metaphor. Sidney Godolphin Osborne, rector of Bryanston, near Blandford, Dorsetshire, and brother-in-law to Charles Kingsley, contributed evidence:

I have now, for more than 11 years, been actively engaged as a clergyman in agricultural districts; for seven years I have acted as a magistrate and *ex-officio* guardian; my opportunity for observation in the matter has thus been great . . . To say nothing of the physical injury done to himself [the labourer] and family from the want, in most instances, of anything like proper drainage without his dwelling, and the foul air which they are compelled to breathe from the too confined space of the dwelling within, from infancy to puberty his children for the most part sleep in the same room with his wife and himself; and whatever attempts at decency may be made . . . still there is the fact of the old and young, married and unmarried, of both sexes, all herded together in one and the same sleeping apartment. Within this last year I saw, in a room about 13 feet square, three beds: on the first lay the mother, a widow, dying of consumption; on the second two unmarried daughters, one 18 years of age, the other 12; on the third a young married couple, whom I myself had married two days before. A married woman of thorough good character told me, a few weeks ago, that on her confinement, so crowded with children is her one room, they are obliged to put her on the floor in the middle of the room, that they may pay her the requisite attention. (*Reports on Agriculture*, 1843, p. 87 and p. 37.)

Carlyle summed up the situation in *Past and Present* (1843):

Why dwell on this aspect of the matter? It is too indisputable, not doubtful now to anyone. Descend where you will into the lower class, in Town or Country, by what avenue you will, by Factory Inquiries, Agricultural Inquiries, by Revenue Returns, by Mining-Labourer Committees, by opening your own eyes and looking, the same sorrowful result discloses itself: you have to admit that the working body of this rich English Nation has sunk or is fast sinking into a state, to which, all sides of it considered, there was literally never any parallel. (Bk. I, ch. 1, Carlyle, *Works*, xiii. 5 f.)

Perkin comments upon the dire poverty of many domestic outworkers throughout the century—those who worked in their own homes at weaving, hosiery, chair-making, tailoring, dressmaking and at the manufacture of boots and shoes (op. cit., p. 146); and of the unskilled and casual labourers, beggars, criminals, and street-folk of the great towns. He refers to Charles Booth's study of London's poverty in the 1880s and to B. S. Rowntree's survey of urban poverty in the 1890s and concludes: Clearly this huge segment of the working class had not yet benefited from industrialism, except in the crude sense that greater numbers of them had been kept alive to suffer the same life of misery and frustration. Their release from the frozen grip of poverty had to wait for the twentieth century with its disproportionate rise of unskilled wages and of the Welfare State.' (Op. cit., pp. 146-7.)

Certainly, in the 1850s, when Dickens wrote *Hard Times* and Reade *It is Never Too Late to Mend*, the beginning of the 'High Victorian' period marked by Britain's increasing commercial expansion and prosperity, the Two Nations still existed. That the poor were not only outworkers, unskilled labourers, beggars or criminals is suggested by the remarks of the Census reporter, Horace Mann, summarizing in 1851 the reasons for the alienation of the working class from all churches, not only the Anglican: 'The masses, therefore of our large and growing towns—connected by no sympathetic tie with those by fortune placed above them—form a world apart, a nation by themselves; divided almost as effectively from the rest as if they spoke another language or inhabited another land.' (Quoted Perkin, op. cit., p. 202.)

Thomas Hughes, Kingsley's friend and fellow advocate of Christian Socialism, wrote with an air of discovery in 1850, 'the noblemen and gentlemen of England are beginning to feel that the heart and sympathies of man are too large for Belgravia and Mayfair; that in the hovels of St. Giles's, in the plague-lanes of Bermondsey, there are living in wretchedness for which history can find no parallel, thousands of our brethren' (*Tracts on Christian Socialism*, No. 2, p. 9).

A review of *Alton Locke* commented on the paradox of the continuing existence of the Other Nation while Britain's power and wealth increased:

Our civil history during the last thirty years of peace resembles nothing which the world has yet seen, or which can be found in the records of civilisation. The progress which has been made in the mechanical sciences is of itself almost equivalent to a revolution. The whole face of society has been altered . . .

Statistical books are written to demonstrate how enormously we have increased in wealth; and yet . . . you will find pamphlets containing ample and distinct evidence that hundreds of thousands of our industrious fellow-countrymen are at this moment famishing for lack of employment, or compelled to sell their labour for such wretched remuneration that the

1. 'Lazarus and the Rich Man', 1830

2. William Henry Fox Talbot, 'The Straw Stack', 1844

3. Thomas Shotter Boys, 'London Bridge from Southwark Bridge', 1842

4. 'The Rookery, St. Giles's', 1851

5. Gustave Doré, 'Dudley Street, Seven Dials', 1872

6. Old clothes shop, Seven Dials, 1877

LIFE TRIAL, CONFESSION, AND EXECUTION

OF F. B. COURVOISIER, for the MURDER

OF LORD WILLIAM RUSSELL,

and the rest of the Family, with good advice to all Persons in trust.

Farewell Letter to his Parents, Sister, and the rest of the Family, with good advice to all Persons in trust.

Attention give to bold and young,
Of high and low degree,
Think while this mournful tale is sung,
Of my sad misery.
I've slain a master good and kind,
To me has been a friend,
For which I must my life resign,
My time is near an end.

Oh, hark! what mean that dreadful sound,
It is the deed in my soul,
It is the bell that sounds my knell,
How solemn is the toll,
See thousands are assembled,
Around this fatal place,
To gaze on my approaching fate,
And witness my disgrace.

There are so many sympathising hearts,
Who feel another's woe,
Even now appears in sorrow,
For my sad overthrow.
Think of the aged man I slew,
Where I sat at ease,
Iroblied him of property and life,
And the poor man at a friend.

Let pilfering passions not intrude,
For to lead you astray,
From step to step it will delude
And bring you to dismay.
Think of the wretche Courvoisier,
Who thus died on a tree,
A death of shame, I've brought to shame,
But my own dishonesty.

Mercy on earth I'll not implore,
To crave it would be vain,
My hands are died with human gore,
None can wash off the stain.
But the merits of a Saviour,
Good Christians pray, as thus I die,
I may his pardon have.

7. The hanged man woodcut (right)

pauper's dole is by many regarded with absolute envy. Dives and Lazarus elbow one another in the street; and our political economists select Dives as the sole type of the nation . . .

These are stern realities—grim facts which it is impossible to gainsay. (*Blackwood's Edinburgh Magazine*, 68 (1850), 594.)

At the end of the decade, in 1858, William Gilbert, father of W. S. Gilbert, presented his facts of the life of the London poor by means of conversations with his medical friend Morton, who describes Gilbert's own experiences. A large part of the book is a savage attack on the 1834 Poor Law and the way in which it is administered: 'The amount of demoralisation and misery occasioned by the present system is beyond belief, yet nothing seems to awake the apathy of the Government to the state of the case.' (*Dives and Lazarus*, 1858, ch. 7.)

He took his title from the Biblical parable which, according to Elizabeth Gaskell, haunted the minds of the poor[2] as an image of the gulf between them and the rich. It recurs, in various forms throughout the early part of the century. A cartoon of 1830 (BM Satires 16047; see Plate 1) shows a starving labourer confronting the Duke of Wellington, gorging himself with food; it is entitled 'Lazarus and the Rich Man'. 'Dives and Lazarus' is also a very powerful ballad, first mentioned in the sixteenth century (see *The Oxford Book of Carols*, 1928, pp. 118 f.) and sung in the new industrial towns of the nineteenth. It was collected by Miss Jewsbury among the carols sung in the neighbourhood of Manchester and presented in a volume to Mary Howitt, wife of the Quaker Radical journalist, William Howitt. William mentions the gift and quotes part of 'that singular old ballad of Dives and Lazarus' in his *Rural Life of England*, 2 vols., 1838, ii. 213. A version of the carol 'Come all you worthy Christians', which includes the story of Dives and Lazarus, and probably dates from the 1820s, is among the Political Broadsides (No. 15) in Birmingham Public Libraries, Local Studies Department, printed mid-century and sold for a penny to help support unemployed workmen tramping the streets. A slightly different version of the carol, probably printed earlier, under the title 'Job, the Patient Man', is among the broadsides in the British Library. It includes the lines:

Come all you worthy Christians
That are so very poor,

[2] See *Mary Barton*, ch. 9.

Remember how poor Lazarus
Sat at the rich man's door,
Begging for the crumbs of bread,
Which from his table fell,
The Scripture doth inform us,
In Heaven he now doth dwell.
(Baring-Gould, *Ballads*, v. 5.)

(I am indebted to Martha Vicinus for the dating of these ballads.)

Thomas Hughes felt that the destitution and wretchedness in which the Other Nation lived, and about which the upper classes and middle classes knew so little, was a new phenomenon—'there are living in wretchedness for which history can find no parallel, thousands of our brethren'; a comment which echoes Carlyle's words, 'a state, to which . . . there was literally never any parallel'. It was not simply a question of the poor being always with us. In the new industrial towns the poor lived in greater concentration than ever before, and the old parable of Dives and Lazarus took on a more intense meaning, expressing the resentful consciousness of the gulf between the rich and the poor, the injustice this implied and the vengeful consolation that Lazarus would enjoy the delights of Heaven after death while Dives was tortured in Hell. It was an appropriate image of the new class antagonism, particularly that associated with political reform, which Perkin describes as developing in the second and third decades of the century (op. cit., p. 28). Ironically, the great gulf set between the rich man and the poor in the after-life is one that Dives strives to pass, not Lazarus: 'Abraham said, Son, remember that thou in thy lifetime receivedst thy good things, and Lazarus in like manner evil things: but now here he is comforted, and thou art in anguish. And beside all this, between us and you there is a great gulf fixed, that they which would pass from hence to you may not be able, and that none may cross over from thence to us.' (Luke 16:25-6.) The ballad based on the parable perfectly expresses the bitter feeling that grew up among the lower classes in the early years of the nineteenth century that there were indeed Two Nations, and that one was being repressed and exploited to the advantage of the other. The resentment at the frightened reactionary measures of the post-war Government, and particularly at Wellington, is reflected in the cartoons of the period; Malthus's philosophy which informed the 1834 Poor Law, was resisted, particularly in the industrial towns, as an attempt by the one Nation to exterminate and cripple the Other (Dickens gives fictional expression to this feeling in *The Chimes*, 1844, in which Alderman Cute determines to 'Put Down' the poor; Toby Veck's sin is that he allows the Alderman to convince him that the poor are 'Born bad. No business here!'); and in London and the rapidly expanding industrial towns there was resentment that the masters were growing rich on the labour of the work-people whose wages they kept as low as possible in order to increase their profits and get a good return on their capital. Ernest Jones, striving to keep alive the spirit of militant Chartism, put this idea in an extreme form:

Now a word with reference to this identity of 'interests':—It is the interest of the employer, as he confesses, to buy cheap and sell dear—but the terms 'cheap' and 'dear' are relative, and you will find it is his interest to sell *cheaper* and buy *cheaper*. For it is cheapness that forces a market for him in his competition with the foreigner and with his competitor at home.

Now, how can he sell cheaply? By buying *more* cheaply. What does he buy? Raw material *and labour*—wool, cotton, flax *and human flesh*.

Low wages, therefore is a necessity for the employer. Working men! are your interests identical with his? But to *keep lowering wages* is another of his 'interests'. Why? Because as competition in manufacture continues increasing abroad, the market becomes more and more artificial, and must be *forced* more and more by under-selling. And, of course, this must be done by lowering wages . . .

Now what say you to 'identity of interests'? My friends I'll tell you plainly how the interests really lie:

IT IS YOUR INTEREST TO RUIN THEM

AND IT IS THEIR INTEREST TO RUIN YOU.

(*The People's Paper*, 13 Nov. 1852, quoted G. D. H. Cole and A.W. Filson, *British Working Class Movements. Select Documents 1789-1875*, 1951, pp. 418 f.)

But twelve years earlier a working man who was no Chartist, who did not 'mix [himself] up with these matters, because they are unprofitable, unsatisfactory, and irritating to my somewhat quiet and studious disposition', wrote to Charles Dickens:

The master claims all the obligation; believes it, I have no doubt; and throws it in the workman's teeth continually. He fixes a certain rate of profit—competition ensues—the new-beginner holds out a lower figure—he that is established meets the market to save his business, *and beats down his men to meet the level of his loss* . . . It is but a few months since that a case came under my own eyes, in my own work, where the reduction was five-and-twenty *per cent* at once, which of course enabled the master to reduce it to his customer ten *per cent*, and still pocket the same profit, while he increased his business. What is a working man to do? His hands can work no faster; his body can hold out no more hours . . . He thinks; and his thoughts tell him from his knowledge, that there is not work for him elsewhere, he consequently leans to the poor man's consolation that 'half a loaf is better than no bread', and submits. But is any one on earth foolish enough to suppose that he is content; that he is ignorant, with such practical inoculation of wisdom; or that his discontent and robbery will not revenge itself in the best way it can?[3]

There is, therefore, plenty of evidence to attest to the 'truth about' the fact of the existence of the Other Nation in Britain in the 1840s and 1850s, and the resentment and despair which some of the lower classes felt at the gulf between them and the privileged classes. In all the novels of the period which I want to examine is found, in differing degrees, concern with 'truth about' this fact. It seems to me that these novels become more intelligible if they are seen not in isolation but in terms of the period's total artistic endeavour. Kingsley, in *Alton Locke* (1850), the fictional autobiography of a Chartist tailor turned Christian Socialist, is very convincing when, in the first person, he describes the working-class boy's excited response to books and especially to poetry as throwing a new light upon his narrow, ugly world. He discovers Tennyson's poetry:

what endeared Tennyson especially to me, the working man, was, as I afterwards discovered, the altogether democratic tendency of his poems. True, all great poets are by their office democrats; seers of man only as man; singers of the joys, the sorrows, the aspirations common to all humanity; but in Alfred Tennyson there is an element especially democratic, truly levelling; not his political opinions, about which I know nothing, and care less, but his handling of the trivial every-day sights and sounds of nature. Brought up, as I understand, in a part of England which possesses not much of the picturesque, and nothing of that which the vulgar call sublime, he has learnt to see that in all nature, in the hedgerow and the sand-bank, as well as in the alp peak and the ocean waste, is a world of true sublimity, —a minute infinite,—an ever-fertile garden of poetic images . . . This is what I call democratic art—the revelation of the poetry which lies in common things. And surely all the age is tending in that direction: in Landseer and his dogs—in Fielding[4] and his downs, with a host of noble fellow-artists

---

[3] John Overs, the carpenter, 20 July 1840, commenting on Carlyle's *Chartism*. For the text of this important letter and my commentary on it, see my article 'John Overs to Charles Dickens: a Working-Man's Letter and its Implications', *Victorian Studies*, 18 (1974), 195–217.

[4] Anthony Vandyke Copley Fielding (1789–1855), a fashionable teacher, was well known for his landscapes in water-colour, and was President of the Water-Colour

—and in all authors who have really seized the nation's mind, from Crabbe and Burns and Wordsworth to Hood and Dickens, the great tide sets ever onward, outward, towards that which is common to the many, not that which is exclusive to the few. (Vol. i, ch. 9 'Poetry and Poets'.)

Leaving aside his assessment of individual artists, the importance of this passage for my argument lies in its expression of the artist's increasing interest in ordinary things, of the belief that imaginative perception of common phenomena induces significant vision, and that that vision is possible to everybody who can feel. Kingsley is really testifying to the change, since the late eighteenth century, of the conception of the artist and his subject matter in Western Europe and, consequently, of the way of perceiving the environment. Scott, despite his conservative politics, brought about a revolution in the conception of history because in his finest novels, such as *The Heart of Midlothian* and *Old Mortality*, he saw it in terms of the ordinary lives of humble folk. James Kay in 1825, for all his sympathy with the Edinburgh poor, felt they were no part of history; when they swarmed into the once grand houses these places lost their 'historic interest'. But nearly twenty years later Carlyle, the implacable opponent of democracy, insisted that the twelfth century came alive in the glimpses Jocelin's *Chronicle* afforded of the ordinary people: 'the image of these justly offended old women, in their old wool costumes, with their angry features, and spindles brandished, lives forever in the historical memory' (*Past and Present*, Bk. II, ch. 5, Carlyle, *Works*, xiii, 80 f.).

For Jocelin has produced for the modern reader 'truth about' the life lived centuries ago in the Abbey of St. Edmundsbury 'For King Lackland *was* there, verily he; and he did leave these *tredecim sterlingii*, if nothing more, and did live and look in one way or the other, and a whole world was living and looking along with him! There, we say, is the grand peculiarity; the immeasurable one; distinguishing, to a really infinite degree, the poorest historical Fact from all Fiction whatsoever.' (Ibid., Bk. II, ch. 1, Carlyle, *Works*, xiii. 59.) And these facts make an appeal because they are noted and recounted with feeling and

Society 1831-55. 'Space is one of the qualities Fielding obtained in his pictures; he delights in distances, extensive flats, and rolling downs.' (Richard and Samuel Redgrave, *A Century of British Painters*, ed. Ruthven Todd, 1947, p. 446.)

therefore awake a responsive feeling in the reader, so that he can recreate this medieval life and find in it something akin to his own:

Readers who please to go along with us into this poor *Jocelini Chronica* shall wander inconveniently enough, as in wintry twilight, through some poor stript hazel-grove . . . perpetually hindering the eyesight; but across which, here and there, some real human figure is seen moving: very strange; whom we could hail if he would answer;—and we look into a pair of eyes deep as our own, *imaging* our own, but all unconscious of us. (Ibid., Bk. II, ch. 2, Carlyle, *Works*, xiii. 64.)

This is the feeling response to phenomena which induces vision —here, historical vision.

Alton mentions Crabbe and Wordsworth as exponents of 'democratic art'. They both considered the poor a serious subject for the artist, as did Scott, although the ways in which they represented the Other Nation are very different. Scott was primarily interested in the philosophy of history, in the interaction between individual humble lives and momentous social changes and developments; Crabbe was concerned with the details of individual lives which denoted moral attitudes and a relationship to a wider human society; Wordsworth idealized his humble figures into mythical characters embodying the fundamental passions of the human heart—paternal and maternal love, courage, grief—and despised Crabbe's poetry as trivial and uninspired. He wrote to Samuel Rogers, 29 September 1808, 'The sum of all is, that nineteen out of 20 of Crabbe's Pictures are mere matters of fact; with which the Muses have just about as much to do as they have with a Collection of medical reports, or of Law Cases.'[5] But, in their different ways, they all three helped encourage that concern for 'the poetry which lies in common things'. In the late 1830s, the 1840s, and 1850s the liveliest novelists were transferring that poetry to prose. Carlyle early argued the Romance of the reality of contemporary nineteenth-century Britain:

if through this unpromising Horn-gate, Teufelsdröckh, and we by means of him, have led thee into the true Land of Dreams; and through the Clothes-Screen, as through a magical *Pierre-Pertuis*, thou lookest, even for moments, into the region of the Wonderful, and seest and feelest that thy daily life is girt with Wonder, and based on Wonder, and thy very blankets

---

[5] Quoted M. L. Peacock, *The Critical Opinions of W. Wordsworth* (Baltimore, 1950), p. 235.

and breeches are Miracles,—then art thou profited beyond money's worth. (*Sartor Resartus*, Bk. III, ch. 9, Carlyle, *Works*, i. 260.)

Manchester, with its cotton-fuz, its smoke and dust, its tumult and contentious squalor, is hideous to thee? Think not so . . . Hast thou heard, with sound ears, the awakening of a Manchester, on Monday morning . . . ten-thousand times ten-thousand spools and spindles all set humming there, it is perhaps, if thou knew it well, sublime as a Niagara, or more so. (*Chartism*, ch. 8, Carlyle, *Works*, x. 397.)

Dickens shares Carlyle's attitude to his environment when, in *Oliver Twist*, he determines to write of the criminal underworld as he has experienced it, rather than repeat the exotic criminal characters created by Gay or Ainsworth. In all his writings Dickens is concerned with 'the romantic side of familiar things', as he put it in the preface to *Bleak House*. Carlyle, in the passages quoted above, argues that the Romantic processes of perception—acute sensuous response to the data of experience—should be applied to the common things of life and to the new forms created by an industrial society: 'seest and feelest that thy daily life is girt with Wonder'; 'hast thou heard, *with sound ears*'. And the reward of such heightened response is the vision of the Romantic artist—'thou lookest . . . into the region of the Wonderful'; 'it is perhaps, if thou knew it well, sublime as a Niagara, or more so'. To describe the effect of this possible vision he uses the word 'sublime', a keyword in the vocabulary of Romantic sensation since the publication of Burke's essay *A Philosophical Enquiry into the Origin of Our Ideas of the Sublime and Beautiful* (1757). Carlyle is asking his reader to perceive life about him as the Romantics defined perception, that process of feeling response to environment which provides every man with knowledge of life and, in an intensified form, gives the artist that knowledge, that vision, which is the substance of his creation. 'To know it well' is the aim of the sentient man and of the artist, but the artist has to shape forms to communicate his knowing.

Raymond Williams writes: 'In the late 1830s and especially in the 1840s everything seems to start at once, in a quite newly experienced world.' (Op. cit., p. 26.) Part of the 'new experience' of the novels of this period which deal with the Other Nation is the evocation of this life in terms of sight, sound, touch, and smell. This is an important distinction between Victorian novels exploring social problems and those written at the end of the eighteenth century, such as William Godwin's *Caleb Williams* (1794) and Robert Bage's *Hermsprong* (1796), which deal with large abstract ideas of Reason, Justice, and Government; as in Carlyle's writing his philosophy of history is expressed by focusing on the ordinary details of the lives of ordinary or particular men, so the contemporary novelists discussed the problems of social justice and the organization of society by establishing what they considered to be 'truth about' lower-class life. As Elizabeth Gaskell wrote of *Mary Barton* to Eliza Fox, 29 May 1849, 'I told the story according to a fancy of my own; to really SEE the scenes I tried to describe, (and they WERE as real as my own life at the time).' Her words are strikingly similar to those of Joseph Conrad who, at the end of the nineteenth century, was concerned with shaping the novel into a subtle art capable of exploring the fundamental crises of human life. He wrote, in the preface to *The Nigger of the Narcissus* (1897): 'My task which I am trying to achieve is, by the power of the written word to make you hear, to make you feel—it is before all, to make you see. That—and no more, and it is everything.' This is the Romantic aesthetic fully accepted by the novelist; the novel has become an 'art' like poetry. The early Victorian novelists who directed the attention of their readers to the Other Nation contributed to the development of the novel as a serious art form. When *Sybil* was published the reviewer of the *Athenaeum* felt that the 'mere novelist' should concern himself with his proper material, 'tinsel', and not meddle with serious ideas. By 1856 George Eliot was writing, 'The greatest benefit we owe to the artist, whether painter, poet, or novelist, is the extension of our sympathies.' ('The Natural History of German Life', *Westminster Review*, 66 (1856), quoted Thomas Pinney, *Essays of George Eliot*, 1963, p. 270.) And, in the same essay, 'Art is the nearest thing to life; it is a mode of amplifying experience and extending our contact with our fellow-men beyond the bounds of our personal lot.' (p. 271.) The novelist is accepted without question as being an artist, and his art is not concerned with fantasy, but with 'life'. She continues,

All the more sacred is the task of the artist when he undertakes to paint the life of the People. Falsification here is far more pernicious than in the more artificial aspects of life. It is not so very serious that we should have false ideas about evanescent fashions—about the manners and conversation of beaux and duchesses; but it *is* serious that our sympathy with the perennial joys and struggles, the toil, the tragedy, and the humour in the life of our more heavily-laden fellow-men, should be perverted, and turned towards a false object instead of the true one.

The novels in which I am interested contributed to establishing 'the life of the People' as a fitting and serious subject for the novelist; also, it was their concern to present a 'true object' and not a false one. Moreover, these novelists' aim to extend their subject matter and to enlarge their readers' sympathies by means of a sensuous response to people and objects not previously scrutinized for the purposes of fiction, relates not only to artistic activity of the late 1830s and 1840s concerned with the extension of consciousness by means of 'true objects', facts apprehended by the senses, but also to social, philosophical, and scientific endeavour. The pursuit of 'truth about' physical fact is outstanding in this period. If, for Carlyle, History is the pursuit of factual details of a bygone age to the point at which 'some real human figure is seen moving', Philosophy is the continual battle against Custom, which dulls men's senses and makes them unaware—'Am I to view the Stupendous with stupid indifference, because I have seen it twice, or two-hundred, or two-million times?' (*Sartor Resartus*, Bk. III, ch. 8, Carlyle, *Works*, i. 250.) 'Strange enough how creatures of the human-kind shut their eyes to plainest facts; and by the mere inertia of Oblivion and Stupidity, live at ease in the midst of Wonders and Terrors.' (Ibid., Bk. I, ch. 8, Carlyle, *Works*, i. 54.)

For the Victorians the outstanding philosopher who, by patient observation, opened men's eyes to the 'plainest facts' of Nature, thereby removing prejudice, the dulling effect of 'Custom', learning Nature's principles and so harnessing them to man's use, was Francis Bacon. In the year of Queen Victoria's accession Macaulay wrote a long review of Basil Montagu's new edition of Bacon's works. 'He knew', wrote Macaulay, 'that all the secrets feigned by poets to have been written in the books of enchanters, are worthless when compared with the mighty secrets which are really written in the book of nature, and which, with time and patience, will be read there' (*Edinburgh Review*, 65 (1837), 99). For him, Bacon's kind of thinking had made the material achievements of the nineteenth century possible:

it has spanned great rivers and estuaries with bridges of form unknown to our fathers . . . it has lighted up the night with the splendour of day . . . it has multiplied the power of the human muscles; it has accelerated motion; it has annihilated distance; it has facilitated intercourse, correspondence, all friendly offices, all despatch of business; it has enabled man to descend to the depths of the sea, to soar into the air, to penetrate securely into the noxious recesses of the earth, to traverse the land in cars which whirl along without horses, and the ocean in ships which sail against the wind . . . it is a philosophy which never rests . . . Its law is progress. (Ibid., pp. 82 f.)

Bacon did not deal in cant or illusion,

In his opinion . . . he was . . . a mere common man. And it was precisely because he was so that his name makes so great an era in the history of the world. It was because he dug so deep that he was able to pile high. It was because, in order to lay his foundations, he went down into those parts of human nature which lie low, but which are not liable to change, that the fabric which he has reared has risen to so stately an elevation, and stands with such immovable strength. (Ibid., p. 83.)

In like spirit, and with similar arguments, the hero of Kingsley's *Yeast* (1848) tries to shake his cousin's conviction that Roman Catholicism is the true faith. He defends 'English Civilization' against 'Romish Sanctity':

'I take my stand on fact and nature; you may call them idols and phantoms; I say they need be so no longer to any man, since Bacon has taught us to discover the Eternal Laws under the outward phenomena . . . . When *we* "draw bills on nature", as Carlyle says, "she honours them,"—our ships do sail; our mills do work; our doctors do cure; our soldiers do fight. And she does not honour yours; for your Jesuits have, by their own confession, to lie, to swindle, to get even man to accept theirs for them. So give me the political economist, the sanitary reformer, the engineer; and take your saints and virgins, relics and miracles. The spinning jenny and the railroad, Cunard's liners and the electric telegraph, are to me, if not to you, signs that we are, on some points at least, in harmony with the universe; that there is a mighty spirit working among us, who cannot be your anarchic and destroying Devil, and therefore may be the Ordering and Creating God.' (Ch. 5.)

Among the influential philosophers of the period Auguste Comte was particularly concerned with the apprehension of phenomena to produce a social philosophy. He considered this to be the *positive* state of man's apprehension of reality; that is, a development from the theological and metaphysical stages. R. K. Webb writes, 'From explaining phenomena by reference to supernatural agency . . . man progressed to explanation in terms of abstract entities, and finally emerged into the clear light of a scientific, positive approach—an examination of phenomena, not in terms of ultimate explanations but in terms of the laws which can be discovered controlling them.' (*Harriet Martineau*, 1960, p. 305.) He had a profound influence on George Eliot's belief that the novelist's moral vision resulted from a scrutiny of the minutiae of ordinary existence, and his optimism in the social illumination which results from apprehension of the facts of social behaviour can be compared with the vision which Romantic writers thought to be the result of the imaginative perception of ordinary or familiar things, or the confidence with which Macaulay heralded the material progress brought about by Bacon's scrutiny of phenomena and his apprehension of the laws it revealed. This is the imagination which is shared by scientist, social scientist and poet, discussed by Strawson above (p. 9).

Kingsley mentions in *Yeast* the political economist and the sanitary reformer whose quest is 'truth to' Nature's laws. During the 1830s, 1840s, and 1850s appeared some of the most important pioneering reports and social surveys of the Victorian period, for example, the Report by Inspectors of Factories made to Government (1839); Edwin Chadwick's *Report on the Sanitary Condition of the Labouring Population of Great Britain* (1842); the *First Report of Commissioners for inquiring into the Employment and Condition of Children in Mines and Manufactories* (1842) and the *Second Report of the Commissioners (Trades and Manufactures)* (1843); the *Reports of Special Assistant Poor Law Commissioners on the Employment of Women and Children in Agriculture* (1843); the *First Report of the Commissioners for Inquiring into the State of Large Towns and Populous Districts* (1844); *Minutes of Information collected with reference to Works for the Removal of Soil Water, or Drainage of Dwelling-houses and Public Edifices, and for the Sewage and Cleansing of the Sites of Towns* (1852). These inquiries purported to reveal the facts about various aspects of contemporary society, facts derived from the observation and experience of the sub-commissioners and reporters. Even the official, neutral language in which they record their evidence betrays the importance of sensuous experience in assessing the facts of the unfamiliar lives they were describing: ' "One of the most disgusting sights I have ever seen," says the Sub-Commissioner [J. C. Symons], "was that of young females, dressed like boys in trousers, crawling on all fours, with belts round their waists, and chains passing between their legs, at day pits at Hunshelf Bank [Yorkshire]."' (*CEC*, I. P.P. Session 1842 (XV), 88.)

J. L. Kennedy, visiting a pit near Bolton, Lancashire, uses the image of Hell familiarly associated with the coal and iron of heavy industry (see below, p. 75 and Plates 8 and 9):

At one pit I visited there was a furnace in the bottom of the engine-shaft, and we descended through the smoke, as it were, down a chimney. On approaching the bottom, figures became visible, flitting to and fro about the furnace. The darkness around us, and the deep-red flames seen through the smoke, together with the shrieks and voices of the people below, gave a forcible idea of a descent into Pandemonium. (*CEC*, I, Appendix ii. P.P. Session 1842 (XVII), 157.)

Kennedy was learning to know Bolton as Engels learnt to know Manchester—by his senses. As Steven Marcus says of Engels, 'He learned to read it with his senses, the chief inlets, as Blake almost said, of mind in the present age.' (Op. cit., p. 99.)

And we have seen that William Cooke Taylor, not collecting evidence for an official report but trying to supply the Archbishop of Dublin with the facts of destitution among the Lancashire factory operatives in 1842, appealed to 'the stern evidence of my senses' to establish the reality of 'the naked fact as it stands: the producers of this enormous wealth . . . are not allowed to be its consumers; are not permitted even to retain so much of it as would afford them a bare subsistence'. Carlyle was right to express doubts about the facts apparently revealed by the newly discovered tool, statistics (the Royal Statistical Society began in the Cambridge meeting of the British Association, 1833). Statistics in early Victorian times was an inexact science. But his criticism was almost certainly prompted by the traditional belief that poverty should be dealt with in moral terms—the poor should be persuaded to be more disciplined and more provident—rather than by means of scientific investigation. And his contemptuous dismissal of statistics and the reports in which they are found—'We have looked into various statistical works, Statistic-Society Reports, Poor-Law Reports, Reports and Pamphlets not a few, with a sedulous eye to this question of the Working Classes and their general condition in England; we grieve to say, with as good as no result whatever' (*Chartism*, ch. 2, Carlyle, *Works*, x. 332)—is too sweeping. For they, too, despite their faults, were part of the battle against Custom. Perkin points out that the Statistical Societies were pioneers of empirical sociology and were among the first to attempt an objective study of the poor. The first was set up in Manchester in 1833 to improve the conditions of the manufacturing population, and in May and June 1834, in the wake of the 1832 depression, the Society made the first recorded house-to-house social survey, supervised by James Kay, in two of the town's central districts. (Op. cit., p. 165.)

In the arts of the period there is a similar concern with the sensuous apprehension of familiar objects to increase the sense of reality, to bring the spectator closer to the actuality of experience. The great artistic discovery of the 1840s, based on the kind of scientific observation which Macaulay admired in Bacon's work, was photography. In 1844 H. Fox Talbot, publishing his first series of photographs ('they are the sun-pictures themselves, and not, as some persons have imagined, engravings in imitation'), described his camera as a seeing eye which could translate the actuality of a scene to the retina, and so to the consciousness: 'It may be said to make a picture of whatever it *sees*. The object glass is the *eye* of the instrument—the sensitive paper may be compared to the *retina*.' (*The Pencil of Nature*, 1844, notes to Plate III.) This transferred image can make the spectator aware of things he had not noticed previously, it can extend his consciousness, make him more aware of his environment, show him a significant detail which will reveal the scene's essential reality. The scientific record of 'truth about' a scene can help him recreate its imaginative reality. Like George Eliot later in Chapter 17 of *Adam Bede* (1859), Talbot relates such scenes to Dutch painting of domestic subjects, and insists that the photographer can produce arresting pictures from his vision of ordinary, familiar objects. In his notes on Plate VI, 'The Open Door', showing a heavily-studded wooden door open with a shaft of sunlight through it, a besom broom leaning in the entrance, a bridle hanging up to the left of the door, a lantern to the right, Talbot writes: 'We have sufficient authority in the Dutch school of art, for taking as subjects of representation scenes of daily and familiar occurrence. A painter's eye will often be arrested where ordinary people see nothing remarkable.'

Obviously he refers to Dutch masters of the seventeenth and eighteenth centuries, such as Vermeer, Cuyp, and Ruisdael. Talbot writes delightedly that photography can reproduce something of the *substance* of actuality for the spectator:

One advantage of the discovery of the Photographic Art will be, that it will enable us to introduce into our pictures a multitude of minute details which add to the truth and reality of the representation, but which no artist would take the trouble to copy faithfully from nature.

Contenting himself with a general effect, he would probably deem it beneath his genius to copy every accident of light and shade; nor could he do so indeed, without a disproportionate expenditure of time and trouble, which might be otherwise much better employed.

Nevertheless, it is well to have the means at our disposal of introducing these minutiae without any additional trouble, for they will sometimes be found to give an air of variety beyond expectation to the scene represented.

In other words, the photographer's art reveals an interest in the scene which previously had not been apparent; the image of the ordinary, of Custom, is replaced by one revealing its reality and therefore its unsuspected interest. The photograph prompting Talbot's comments quoted immediately above is 'The Haystack', Plate X (entitled 'The Straw Stack' in the Fox Talbot Collection at the Science Museum, London). The spikiness, the bristling quality of the stack, its texture, is established because the camera has defined the multitude of straws which make it up; the logs piled near it are emphasized as different in texture because they, too, are defined by the camera. The shadow of the ladder thrown on the stack emphasizes the different appearance of straw in sunlight and in shadow, and provides two visual images which contribute to the spectator's knowledge of its substance. The emphasis on texture helps to recreate the feel of objects as well as their appearance. (See my Plate 2.)

This excitement at the possibility of capturing the substance, the physical reality of objects perceived, can also be found in the early discussions and writings of the Pre-Raphaelite Brotherhood, founded in 1848. They wanted to make the people who saw their pictures look afresh at objects, particularly the details of Nature, undulled by artistic conventions. They sought fresh vision. Millais's son later described their programme, quoting from Kipling's poem 'The Seven Seas' to express their aim:

They must go back to earlier times for examples of sound and satisfactory work, and, rejecting the teaching of the day that blindly followed in his

[Raphael's] footsteps, must take Nature as their only guide. They would go to her, and her alone, for inspiration; and, hoping that others would be tempted to join in their crusade against conventionality, they selected as their distinctive title the term 'Pre-Raphaelites'.

'Each for the joy of the working, and each in his separate star,
    Shall draw the Thing as he sees It for the God of Things as They Are.'
(John Guille Millais, *The Life and Letters of Sir John Everett Millais*, 2 vols., 1899, i. 49.)

He goes on to quote his father's statement in 1896, magisterial, as befits the newly-elected President of the Royal Academy: 'The Pre-Raphaelites had but one idea—to present on canvas what they saw in Nature.' (Op. cit., p. 55.) Hunt reacted with excitement to the first volume of Ruskin's *Modern Painters* (1843), particularly to the injunction 'Go to Nature, selecting nothing and rejecting nothing', because he felt the book accorded with his own ideas on painting.

Even Rossetti, the other most important member of the Brotherhood and the most imaginative, whose ideals and aims in art, as Millais realized, were quite different from his and from Hunt's, went to Ford Madox Brown for tuition because Brown insisted on painting what he had observed rather than reproducing the conventional images demanded by contemporary art pundits: 'the study of anatomy had not helped, for this was never, either at Sass's[6] or the Royal Academy Schools, related to life; but in Brown's studio there were drawings made from living models in such a way that they became part of the intricate structure of the picture without losing their identity. They all bore witness to a patient observation, a relentless pursuit of attitude, form and action.' (Raymond Watkinson, *Pre-Raphaelite Art and Design*, 1970, p. 34.)

The important phrase in this paragraph is 'related to life'. Because the Pre-Raphaelites related their paintings to life and took as their battle-cry 'truth to Nature', Ruskin, who championed their endeavours even though he admonished and

---

[6] Henry Sass (1788-1844) painter and teacher of painting. He found the artist's profession unprofitable so he opened a school of drawing for young artists prior to their entering the Royal Academy Schools. Established in 1818, in a house at the corner of Charlotte Street and Streatham Street, Bloomsbury, Sass's was the first school of its kind in England. Sass was its director until 1842 when, because of ill-health, he relinquished it to Francis Stephen. Millais and Frith were among his pupils.

criticized them, compared them with a painter much greater than they—Turner.

I wish it to be understood how every great man paints what he sees or did see, his greatness being indeed little else than his intense sense of fact. And thus Pre-Raphaelitism and Raphaelitism, and Turnerism, are all one and the same, so far as education can influence them. They are different in their choice, different in their faculties, but all the same in this, that Raphael himself . . . and all who preceded or followed him who ever were great, became so by painting the truths around them as they appeared to each man's own mind, not as he had been taught to see them, except by the God who made both him and them. (Ruskin, *Works*, xii. 385.)

In his appreciative but not uncritical letter on the Pre-Raphaelites' painting to *The Times*, 13 May 1851, Ruskin wrote 'that as studies both of drapery and of every minor detail, there has been nothing in art so earnest or so complete as these pictures since the days of Albert Dürer'; and remarked that these young painters 'will draw either what they see, or what they suppose might have been the actual facts of the scene they desire to represent, irrespective of any conventional rules of picture-making'. In the first volume of *Modern Painters* (Ruskin, *Works*, iii. 136) he stated, confidently, 'the representation of facts . . . is the foundation of all art'; and in the third volume (1856) (ibid., v. 174) he praised Turner because 'nobody had ever given so many hard and downright facts'. By 'facts' he evidently means sensuous perception of substance in paint, not mechanical repetition of conventional colours and shapes. Turner's own angry reaction to adverse criticism of 'Snowstorm: Steamboat off a Harbour's Mouth' (1842) shows his intense concern with making his painting true to his own experience of natural phenomena: 'He brooded on a critic's description of the paint as soap suds and whitewash: "What would they have? I wonder what they think the sea's like? I wish they'd been in it." ' (Lawrence Gowing, *Turner: Imagination and Reality*, New York, 1966, p. 10.)

'The frontiers between art and photography' are certainly 'confused and disputed', as Tristram Powell remarks in his discussion of portrait photography prefacing the catalogue of the Arts Council exhibition of early photography, 'From Today Painting is Dead' (Victoria and Albert Museum, 1972). But the Pre-Raphaelites' pursuit of truth to Nature and the early photographers' delight in capturing the physical reality of a scene or a face at a particular moment in time are related, although perhaps William Bell Scott, friend of the Pre-Raphaelites, especially Rossetti and Hunt, over-simplified the relationship when he recalled the period nearly fifty years later: 'Every movement has its genesis, as every flower its seed; the seed of the flower of Pre-Raphaelism [*sic*] was photography. The seriousness and honesty of motive, the unerring fatalism of the sun's action, as well as the perfection of the impression on the eye, was what it aspired to.' (*Autobiographical Notes*, 2 vols., 1892, i. 251.) But both the early photographers and the PRB were preoccupied with intense scrutiny of physical actuality, particularly of the commonplace and familiar, to induce a vision of the 'truth', which, I would argue, is characteristic of much of the imaginative and intellectual activity of the period and which can be seen as a development of the Romantic belief in 'truth' proceeding from intense sensuous apprehension of phenomena. For Ruskin great painters 'became so by painting the truths around them as they appeared to each man's mind, not as he had been taught to see them'. Intense response to people and Nature and the ability to recreate this response so that it can be shared was, for Keats, the mark of the artist. For the Romantics imagination was intensified perception, a perception undistorted by obsessions preventing a total and spontaneous response to an environment which included both people and Nature. As William Blake (on 23 August 1799) wrote to the stolid Dr Trusler who complained that his work was too spiritual,

I know that This World Is a World of imagination & Vision. I see Every thing I paint In This World, but Every body does not see alike. To the Eyes of a Miser a Guinea is more beautiful than the Sun . . . The tree which moves some to tears of joy is in the Eyes of others only a Green thing that stands in the way. Some See Nature all Ridicule & Deformity, & by these I shall not regulate my proportions; & Some Scarce see Nature at all. But to the Eyes of the Man of Imagination, Nature is Imagination itself. (*The Letters of William Blake*, ed. Geoffrey Keynes, 1956, p. 35.)

This joyful recognition of a life or form of a creature or object outside the spectator's life but related by means of this responsive joy is at the heart of the aesthetic expounded by Blake, Keats, Wordsworth, and Coleridge, despite their differences as poets. When Coleridge is self-obsessed he is incapable of such joy and the vision of Nature's beauties fades—'We see, not feel, how beautiful they are.' ('Ode on Dejection'.)

So that the quality of the imaginative response to perceived physical attributes determines the 'vision'. A simple enumeration of the physical phenomena cannot produce the 'vision'. P. B. Medawar criticized Bacon's inductive method: 'Baconian experimentation is not a critical activity but a kind of creative play' (*The Art of the Soluble*, 1967, p. 119), and defined induction as a 'logically mechanized process of thought which, starting from simple declarations of fact arising out of the evidence of the senses, can lead us with certainty to the truth of general laws' (pp. 118 f.). Hypothesis, on which the deductive method of scientific discovery of truth depends, Medawar defined as 'our imaginative preconception of what might be true that gives us an incentive to seek the truth and a clue to where we might find it' (p. 143). Although he finds scanty evidence that Bacon was aware of the need for hypothesis in scientific discovery, he points out that Coleridge in *On Method* (1818) argued that he was and might very well have convinced later nineteenth-century thinkers of this. The Romantics' joyful response to the nature of phenomena, which results in the truthful vision which others can share, is closely related to an 'imaginative preconception of what might be true that gives us an incentive to seek the truth and a clue to where we might find it'. Indeed, Medawar's book is partly an exploration of the similarity between scientific and artistic creative imagination. Strawson's comparison of Blake's 'vision' and the scientist's perception as imaginative processes is relevant here. The novelists' 'truth about' the fact of the Other Nation in the 1840s and 1850s depends, to a certain extent, on at least sympathy with the scientific imagination which deduced the results of bad housing, overcrowding, general physical deprivation, upon the poor (Charles Kingsley was particularly concerned with the implications of the discovery that cholera was not an act of God but carried by sewage-contaminated water, and severely castigated those who made 'Providence' the excuse for what Carlyle described as the 'mere inertia of Oblivion and Stupidity'); and this attack on comfortable and comforting Custom was shared by the liveliest social reformers, philosophers, and artists of the period.

Custom, indeed, decreed that the poor should be consigned to oblivion, thus creating Two Nations but experiencing only one. Engels, in his exploration of Manchester in 1844, pointed out that the city was built in such a way that the prosperous and mercantile citizens could go about their business or pleasure totally unaware of the poverty and destitution of the Other Nation: 'one is seldom in a position to catch from the street [main thoroughfare] a glimpse of the real labouring districts' (op. cit., p. 80).

Dr Hector Gavin, lecturer on Public Health at the Charing Cross Hospital and member of the Health of Towns Committee, argued that the inhabitants of the West-end did not see the horrors of life in Bethnal Green and therefore remained unaware of them (*Sanitary Ramblings. Being Sketches and Illustrations, of Bethnal Green. A Type of the Condition of the Metropolis and Other Large Towns*, 1848, pp. 3 f.), and Chadwick in his *Report on the Sanitary Condition of the Labouring Population* wrote of Glasgow and Edinburgh, 'We have found that the inhabitants of the front houses in many of the main streets of those towns and of the metropolis, have never entered the adjoining courts, or seen the interior of any of the tenements, situate at the backs of their own houses, in which their own workpeople or dependents reside.' (Chadwick's *Report*, p. 397.)

The inability or the refusal of one Nation to see the Other persisted throughout the nineteenth century. Part of the eccentricity of A. J. Munby, the Victorian civil servant with poetical aspirations and a taste for London literary society, was that he actually looked at, drew and photographed women of the lower classes, the Other Nation. He went so far as to marry one of them, Hannah Cullwick, a kitchen maid, although he kept the marriage secret. After the marriage Hannah came to live with him at Fig Tree Court, Inner Temple, ostensibly as his servant, but when she could she assumed her part as his wife. Munby's diary makes it clear that the ordinary middle-class and upper-class Victorian simply did not see the poor, who performed the dirty or menial tasks of their society, however close, physically, they happened to be to them. On one occasion he found that a friend who called and discovered Hannah doing the household chores in her housemaid's dress 'took no more notice of her presence there than if she had been a dog' (A. J. Munby's diary, 19 April 1874, quoted by Derek Hudson, *Munby Man of Two Worlds*, 1972, p. 365).

Eighteen years earlier Wilkie Collins, confined by illness to a second floor front bedroom in 'Smeary Street' (that is, Tottenham Court Road) in London observed the three unfortunate maids-of-all-work hired successively by Mrs Glutch, his landlady, during the three weeks of his stay. She treated them not as dogs but cats: 'Mrs. Glutch screams at them all indiscriminately by the name of Mary, just as she would scream at a succession of cats by the name of Puss.' 'Number One' is astonished to find that he regards her as a human being:

She looks very much surprised, poor creature, when I first let her see that I have other words to utter in addressing her, besides the word of command; and seems to think me the most eccentric of mankind, when she finds that I have a decent anxiety to spare her all useless trouble in waiting on me . . . Life means dirty work, small wages, hard words, no holidays, no social station, no future, according to her experience of it. No human being ever was created for this. No state of society which composedly accepts this, in the cases of thousands, as one of the necessary conditions of its selfish comfort, can pass itself off as civilized, except under the most audacious of all false pretences. These thoughts rise in me often, when I ring the bell, and the maid-of-all-work answers it wearily. I cannot communicate them to her; I can only encourage her to talk to me now and then on something like equal terms. ('Laid up in Two Lodgings. Second.—My London Lodging', *Household Words*, 13 (1856), 517–23 (p. 521).)[7]

Even if the Victorian poor were not repulsively dirty, like 'Number One' ('always covered from head to foot with powdered black, which seems to lie especially thick on her in the morning') and therefore nasty to contemplate; or living at a distance in a smelly rural hovel or a hideous city slum which it would be dangerous to visit for fear of attack, robbery or disease; or in a community separated from the rest of society by reason of the type of work done, such as a mining community,[8] the classes above them simply did not see them. In *Dombey and Son* (1848) Dickens, brilliant at epitomizing a contemporary attitude in a particular scene, describes this middle-class blindness to the Other Nation in Mr Dombey's encounter with Mr Toodle, who

[7] Perkin comments on the increasing number of servants (600,000 in 1801; 1,300,000 in 1851, 2,000,000 in 1881): 'a clear indication that the rich could afford to buy more of the labour of the poor, and so of the widening gap in income distribution' (op. cit., p. 143). They were a clear indication of the Two Nations in Victorian Society.

[8] See particularly the report of J. R. Leifchild, the Sub-Commissioner collecting evidence for the Children's Employment Commission (*CEC* I, Appendix, 1) BL P.P. Session 1842 (XVI), 527–9.

is trying to express his sympathy with Mr Dombey's grief at the death of Paul:

During the bustle of preparation at the railway, Mr. Dombey and the Major walked up and down the platform side by side; the former taciturn and gloomy, and the latter entertaining him, or entertaining himself, with a variety of anecdotes and reminiscences, in most of which Joe Bagstock was the principal performer. Neither of the two observed that in the course of these walks, they attracted the attention of a working man who was standing near the engine, and who touched his hat every time they passed; for Mr. Dombey habitually looked over the vulgar herd, not at them; and the Major was looking, at the time, into the core of his stories. At length, however, this man stepped before them as they turned round, and pulling his hat off, and keeping it off, ducked his head to Mr. Dombey.

'Beg your pardon, Sir,' said the man, 'but I hope you're a doin' pretty well, Sir.'

He was dressed in a canvass suit abundantly besmeared with coal-dust and oil, and had cinders in his whiskers, and a smell of half-slaked ashes all over him. He was not a bad-looking fellow, nor even what could be fairly called a dirty-looking fellow, in spite of this; and, in short, he was Mr. Toodle, professionally clothed.

'I shall have the honour of stokin' of you down, Sir,' said Mr. Toodle. 'Beg your pardon, Sir. I hope you find yourself a coming round?'

Mr. Dombey looked at him, in return for his tone of interest, as if a man like that would make his very eyesight dirty. (Ch. 20.)

Dickens embodies the violence of Dombey's reaction, which denies that he and the stoker are of the same kind and savagely repulses the workman's sympathy for the loss of his only son, by describing Toodle as he would have appeared to an impartial spectator—'He was dressed in a canvass suit abundantly besmeared . . . He was not a bad-looking fellow' and contrasting this with Dombey's extreme viewpoint—'looked at him . . . as if a man like that would make his very eyesight dirty'. When Dombey is forced physically to look at the stoker he rejects him.

Nearly half a century later Hardy's Jude also found that the undergraduates at Christminster did not see him because he was wearing workman's clothes:

Every day, every hour, as he went in search of labour, he saw them going and coming also, rubbed shoulders with them, heard their voices, marked their movements. The conversation of some of the more thoughtful among them seemed oftentimes, owing to his long and persistent preparation for this place, to be peculiarly akin to his own thoughts. Yet he was as far from them as if he had been at the antipodes. Of course he was. He was a young workman in a white blouse, and with stone-dust in the creases of his clothes; and in passing him they did not even see him, or hear him, rather saw through him as through a pane of glass at their familiars beyond. Whatever they were to him, he to them was not on the spot at all; and yet he had fancied he would be close to their lives by coming there. (*Jude the Obscure*, 1896, Part Second, ch. 2.)

There were many reasons for this mental attitude of the superior Victorian Nation towards the Other, contempt for manual work and pride in belonging to a class which got its money without such labour being an obvious one. Although there was a certain amount of movement between the classes, and although Queen Victoria, in her diary, could praise the achievement of Joseph Paxton who rose from being a 'gardener's boy' to the designer of the Great Exhibition's buildings, yet in the ordinary routine of life class hierarchy was clearly defined; each class consorted with its 'familiars', and the familiars of the middle classes and upper classes did not include the Toodles and the Judes. Some even gave God's sanction to this rigid social division; Mrs Alexander's hymn of 1844, which includes the verse

> The rich man in his castle
> The poor man at his gate
> He made them high and lowly
> And ordered their estate

expresses a contemporary social attitude and counters the bitter Dives and Lazarus ballad by condoning the Dives and Lazarus relationship in this life while remaining prudently silent about the kind of behaviour it generates. The immutable law of political economy was also invoked to sanction the blatant individualism of *laissez-faire*, so that the plight of the Other Nation could be accepted as inevitable and therefore ignored. As K. S. Inglis remarks, 'For most of the nineteenth century, Englishmen looked at poverty and found it morally tolerable because their eyes were trained by evangelical religion and political economy.' (*Churches and the Working Classes in Victorian England*, 1963, pp. 250 f.) Perkin comments: 'Distress . . . commanded the attention of politicians and others, though in the climate of thought increasingly dominated by the classical economists and their denial of the possibility of overproduction or underconsumption there was little that could be done about it beyond the humanitarian charity frowned on by Malthus.' (Op. cit., p. 165.)

David Ricardo, in his *Principles of Political Economy* (1817), argued that labour is a commodity and its price is regulated by the laws of supply and demand; wages must necessarily fall if too many labourers are looking for too few jobs. Wages must not be artificially raised; slumps and financial disasters are an inevitable part of the ordained pattern, but in a country where there is freedom to trade and no restrictions on individual enterprise, things would find their own level. But, in the period of discussion before the hard-won Factory Act, 1819, restricting children's labour in cotton-spinning mills to twelve hours a day, Coleridge argued that although this policy increased the power and prosperity of the nation, it was also responsible for a great deal of poverty:

Persons are not *Things*—but Man does not find his level . . . After a hard and calamitous season, during which the thousand Wheels of some vast manufactory had remained silent as a frozen water-fall, be it that plenty has returned and that Trade has once more become brisk and stirring: go, ask the overseer, and question the parish doctor, whether the workman's health and temperance, with the staid and respectful Manners best taught by the inward dignity of conscious self-support, have found *their* level again! Alas! I have more than once seen a group of children in Dorsetshire, during the heat of the dog-days, each with its little shoulders up to its ears, and its chest pinched inward—the very habit and *fixtures*, as it were, that had been impressed on their frames by the former ill-fed, ill-clothed, and unfuelled winters. (*The Collected Works of Samuel Taylor Coleridge*, vol. vi, *Lay Sermons*, ed. R. J. White (London and Princeton, 1975), pp. 206–7.)

A comfortable optimism concerning political economy as an infallible science allied to the laws of Providence informs Harriet Martineau's *Illustrations of Political Economy*. *The Rioters* (1827) is her first short story and was published in the year following her father's death. He was a textile manufacturer who lost much of his money in the 1825 depression. The family was financially ruined in 1829 (see Ivanka Kovačević, *Fact into Fiction*, Leicester/Belgrade, 1975, p. 212). Kovačević quotes her avowal that she knew nothing of political economy when she wrote her story (p. 213), which purports to be a description of the Manchester hand-loom weavers attempting to destroy the power-looms which they believed to be the cause of their low wages. She expresses sympathy with the starving work-people yet writes:

While I went about from place to place, looking only on the sorrows before my eyes, I might well feel heart-sick: but when I remembered whose hand had inflicted these miseries, I remembered also that in that hand evil is the instrument of greater good; that though *sorrow may endure for a night, joy cometh in the morning*; and that, under his all-wise government, *they who sow in tears shall reap in joy*. (*The Rioters; or, a Tale of Bad Times* (Wellington, Salop, 1827), p. 25.)

It was a powerful argument against agitating for better wages, and small wonder that, after the success of *The Rioters*, a group of Nottingham and Derby manufacturers asked her to write a tale on wages: *The Turn-Out* (1829).

Thomas Hodgskin, a follower of Ricardo, expressed his confident belief in the alliance between God and the political economists in the last of four lectures given in 1825 at the London Mechanics' Institute; they were published as a book in the year of the publication of *The Rioters*. The last sentence reads:

The laws regulating the production of wealth are a part of the creation, in which generally we trace only benevolence in the design and harmony in the execution; . . . and I therefore can have no doubt that the science of Political Economy, which, from being imperfectly known, has thrown doubt, dismay, and terror over the minds of men, will be found when perfectly known, if I may apply to it the language of our most sublime poet, to— 'Justify the ways of God to man.'[9]

Hodgskin was later the chief colleague of James Wilson, founder and first editor of *The Economist*, the first number of which appeared 2 September 1843. This journal's supreme confidence in *laissez-faire* found expression in its opposition to the establishment of the Board of Health in 1847 (see the violent attack on Chadwick, *The Economist*, 5 August 1854); to the Ten Hours Bill; and to a system of State Education.

The laws of Providence and of political economy could provide a respectable mask for self-interest, and self-interest was the greatest cause of the blindness which afflicted the middle classes when regarding the Other Nation. During the discussions of the revelations made by the *Children's Employment Commission (Mines)* 'a most respectable gentleman, a clergyman' had made it clear that he could contemplate with equanimity a child deformed by its work in the mine because this very deformity indicated that it was an efficient instrument in extracting coal. He was quoted by Lord Francis Egerton (in whose pits in the

---

[9] Quoted Scott Gordon, 'The London *Economist* and the High Tide of Laissez Faire', *Journal of Political Economy*, 63 (1955), 470. This article is the source of my comments at this point on Hodgskin and *The Economist*.

Worsley district, according to the miner Samuel Walkden,[10] 'women work . . . common enough, and little girls, too, heaving up with a belt and chain') in the debate on the Commissioners' *Report* and on Ashley's demand for legislation to prevent women, girls, and young boys from working underground in the mines:

> With respect to the ages at which children should begin to labour, he was not sure that his noble Friend had selected quite the proper terms. However, that was a matter to be afterwards discussed; but in the meantime, he could not help stating to the House some information which he had received on this subject, and which was communicated to him by a most respectable gentleman, a clergyman, who had been long conversant with such subjects. This gentleman stated, unwillingly, but conscientiously, that he feared that the peculiar bend of the back, and other physical peculiarities requisite to the employment, could not be obtained if children were initiated at a later age than twelve. (*Hansard*, 63, column 1356.)

And the Annual Register for 1842, reporting the second reading of Ashley's Bill in the House of Lords, recorded that 'The Earl of Radnor objected to all legislative interference with the labour market.' (p. 173.) As the reviewer in the *North British Review*, discussing Charles Kingsley's work, particularly *Alton Locke*, and J. S. Mill's *Political Economy*, pointed out, the middle classes were often prepared to turn a blind eye to the needs of their fellows in lower classes while there was money to be made:

> That something or other steels them to evils patent to every medical man, the present state of London proves; and even the best of them, in the hurry of business and the unceasing struggle of competition, now becoming daily more and more demoralized by puffery and adulteration, are too apt to thrust out of their sight and mind any investment of capital but those which promise the most immediate returns. The whole modern habits of the middle-classes in great cities tend to make them live from hand to mouth; to forget foresight for present gain; to be yearly more and more swayed by individual or trade-interests, less and less alive to corporate ones, least of all to the interests of those classes below them, whose welfare, however surely, yet still only indirectly and invisibly affects their own. (*North British Review*, 15 (1851), 239.)

This single-minded concentration on profits, to the exclusion of all other considerations, is summed up by Peter Ainsworth, MP for Bolton, Lancashire, debating the *Children's Employment Commission* and Ashley's Bill in the Commons, 5 July 1842,

> A gentleman in his own neighbourhood had declared to him that the coal-masters cared not much about the bill; as long as they got their mines

[10] Aged 64, working at the Low Side Mine, near Oldham; he had worked there for eighteen to twenty years. See *CEC* I, Appendix, 2, P.P. Session 1842 (XVII), 850.

worked, they were indifferent as to the sufferings of their workmen; it
was, in fact, a labourer's question. The effect of the bill would be to
deprive many boys of work, and to reduce the wages of the rest 50 per
cent . . . This question had been very properly termed the poor man's
question—it was one which did not affect the rich, or one in which they
took little interest. (*Hansard*, 64, columns 1000-1.)

The Two Nations, the Rich and the Poor; 'the Poor' in this
context range from those who are destitute and starving to
those who live insecure lives because their wages are either very
low or fluctuating. Henry Mayhew, beginning his great study of
poverty in London, based on interviews with those who suffered
it, divided the poor into the honest poor who 'will work' or
'can't work' and the dishonest poor who 'won't work' (see
'Labour and the Poor; the Metropolitan Districts', Letter I, the
Morning Chronicle, 19 October 1849). R. M. Hartwell, in *The
Long Debate on Poverty* (1972), points out the difficulties of
arriving at a definition of poverty and indicates the need for
introducing the concept of relativity into study of poverty in a
particular period; if poverty is defined as 'an insufficiency of
basic needs' or 'receipt of real wages below an accepted norm of
a reasonable standard of living' it must be remembered that
what were considered 'basic needs' changed from one period to
another, and that what would have been considered 'reasonable'
in eighteenth-century England would not have been so a hundred
years later (pp. 11 f.). He quotes S. Mencher's comment, 'Thus,
poverty, particularly in the advanced industrial democratic
nations where the bare physical wants have been met, is a matter
of deviation from social and economic norms.' ('The Problem of
Measuring Poverty', *British Journal of Sociology*, 18 (1967),
12.) But this definition seems to me to ignore two important
factors. One is the class issue; at any period in Britain in the
nineteenth century, people of the middle classes and upper
classes accept as 'reasonable' standards of living which they
would not accept as reasonable for themselves. As Cobbett
wrote in 1832, 'Brougham and Birkbeck, and the rest of the
Malthusian crew, are constantly at work preaching *content to
the hungry and naked*. To be sure, they themselves, however,
are not content to be hungry and naked.' (*Rural Rides*, 2 vols.
(1885 edn.), ii. 365.) This is the attitude expressed in 1830 by
the cartoonist who, in 'Lazarus and the Rich Man', represented

Wellington eating heartily and demanding of the ragged man who cries that starvation stares him in the face, 'Starvation! who the Devil's he?' It is the attitude of the Marquess of Londonderry, righteously indignant at the exaggerations he detects in the reports on the Durham and Northumberland collieries in the *Children's Employment Commission* and presenting, in the House of Lords, a petition against it from the owners of coalmines in the area and others interested in these collieries; he remarked of the trappers, very young children employed to sit by the trap-doors of the underground passages and close them after the wagons had gone through so as to maintain the ventilation and prevent explosions in the mine, 'As the trappers only remain in the pit during the time of drawing coals, they are rarely more than ten hours in the pit, except on the main rollyways, or horse roads, where they necessarily remain during the time the pit is working, which seldom exceeds twelve hours.' (*Hansard*, 64, column 542.) And Wilkie Collins, as we have seen, castigated the society 'which composedly accepts this', that is, life which means for another human being 'dirty work, small wages, hard words, no holidays, no social station, no future . . . in the cases of thousands, as one of the necessary conditions of its selfish comfort'. The Two Nations have two different sets of social and economic norms.[11]

The other consideration noticeably absent from these comfortably academic definitions of poverty, which stress the relativity of the concept, is that the state of a man's being unable to provide food and shelter for himself and his family is absolute not relative, in whatever period it occurs. This was the state of

[11] See Charlotte Elizabeth Tonna's comment on Sunday in an industrial town: 'Considering the vast profits realized by their [the factory children's] means, the masters might be supposed to set apart a fair proportion of such gains, for the erection of a place of worship, and the support of faithful teachers; and as regards the little children, for a very effective system of Sunday-school instruction. Considering the intense anxiety that they manifest for the proper education of their own families, and the horror with which they would recoil from the bare idea of leaving one of them in utter ignorance, we may picture to ourselves their christian solicitude to see their little labourers making the most of the only day allowed them for the acquisition of even the first rudiments of the most common instruction: but everybody knows that such expectations are perfectly absurd, save only where one stands out, in despised notoriety, from the great mass, and devotes himself to a cause utterly overlooked, yea, scorned by the generality of his brethren.' 'The Little Pin-Headers', *The Wrongs of Woman* (1843–4), reprinted Ivanka Kovačević, op. cit. (pp. 313–57), pp. 321–2.

some of the labourers in the Upper George's-road district of Manchester from 1840 to 1842:

The greatest distress abounds in this district. It is not confined to any one class of labourers exclusively, but appears to be most felt among the poor hand-loom weavers, as their earnings do not afford more than two meals a day when labouring fourteen hours a day; so when they are out of work two or three weeks together, as they often have been lately, they are literally starving. Some whom I know to be sober and industrious have assured me that they have passed two days without food. (Joseph Adshead, *Distress in Manchester*, 1842, pp. 33 f.)

He quoted this from the records of the Town Mission, the result of an inquiry instituted August 1841.

In some areas it was the plight endured by the rural poor. Robert Gittings writes of Thomas Hardy's relatives in Dorsetshire, 'Though the Sparks and the Antell families were in the craftsman class, poverty was never far off; the former in particular, for all their family industry, never had a spare penny. Among real labouring families, the young Hardy saw worse than poverty; in the 1840s he actually knew a shepherd boy who died of starvation.' (*Young Thomas Hardy*, 1975, p. 15.)

All the novels of the 1840s and 1850s which I have chosen to discuss in detail deal with different types of the poor, with varying aspects of the Other Nation. It is important to discuss a novel by Dickens, arguably the greatest Victorian novelist; I have concentrated on *Hard Times* (1854) because it is the only novel in which he is concerned with contemporary, rapidly-industrialized society. It has been described as 'the most central of Dickens's works to an understanding of his attitude to society' (K. J. Fielding and Anne Smith, '*Hard Times* and the Factory Controversy. Dickens vs. Harriet Martineau', in *Dickens Centennial Essays*, ed. Ada Nisbet and Blake Nevins (California, 1971), p. 22). The poverty at its centre is the material and spiritual poverty which, he considers, such a society generates. Of the others, *Mary Barton*, written by a good but not great novelist, examines the poverty which drives men to become Chartists; *Alton Locke* has the same theme but is written by a polemical writer with a sharper axe to grind; I chose *Yeast* because it is one of the few novels of the period which deal with the life of the agricultural, as opposed to the urban, poor, and scrutinizes the cliché of the idyllic life of rural England; *Sybil* is written by

a different kind of polemicist who aims at surveying English
society as the Two Nations and at providing the means to
bridge the gulf between them; *It is Never Too Late to Mend*
(1856) translates a contemporary public scandal into fiction to
examine the 'justice' meted out to the poor in an overtly Christian society. They are all concerned with poverty as Mencher
defines it, 'a matter of deviation from social and economic
norms', with a state of human existence widely separated from
the Christian virtues and the material progress accepted as
characteristic of contemporary society. I also discuss several
minor novels, particularly Augustus Mayhew's *Paved with Gold*
(1858) because parts of it are based on the facts he collected for
his brother Henry Mayhew's *London Labour and the London
Poor*; and *William Langshawe, the Cotton Lord* (1842) by Elizabeth Stone, rumoured to be the author of *Mary Barton* when it
first appeared.

All the novelists give their readers physical facts about the
material lives of the Other Nation, what I have called 'truth
about' the poor. The questions which my book tries to answer
are, Can these middle-class novelists, concerned with commenting on the Two Nations in their society, extend their consciousness to include the life of the Other Nation so that their readers
imaginatively experience it? Can they make one Nation 'see' the
Other? Can 'truth about' the Other Nation create imaginative
truth, the essential reality which commands Lear's reaction to
Poor Tom, 'Thou art the thing itself'? Or, to quote Dickens and
Wilkie Collins,[12] do they achieve 'the Art that . . . strikes to the
Soul like Reality'?

[12] 'Doctor Dulcmara, M.P.', *Household Words*, 19 (1858), 52.

HOW THE OTHER HALF LIVES

In our wisdom we have improved on the proverb, 'One half of the world does not know how the other half lives,' changing it into 'One half of the world *does not care* how the other half lives.' Ardwick knows less about Ancoats than it does about China, and feels more interested in the condition of New Zealand than of Little Ireland.[1] (Taylor, *Tour*.)

Yet nothing is more difficult than to get a room that looks something like a room, although the painter can easily enough produce waterfalls and flaming volcanoes. (August Strindberg, Preface to *Miss Julia*, 1888.)

THE LONDON POOR, BY BOZ

The most compelling images in Engels's survey of the English working class in 1844 are those of their physical life: the cellars of Long Acre 'out of which puny children and half-starved ragged women emerge into the light of day' (op. cit., p. 61); Little Ireland in Manchester where 'The cottages are old, dirty, and of the smallest sort, the streets uneven, fallen into ruts and in part without drains or pavement' (p. 93); the cow-stable in Salford inhabited by an old man, 'He had constructed a sort of chimney for his square pen, which had neither windows, floor, nor ceiling, had obtained a bed-stead and lived there, though the rain dripped through his rotten roof.' (p. 96.)

Similarly, in the novels under discussion, an immediately obvious aspect of what Raymond Williams calls the 'consciousness' of the Other Nation is their physical life apprehended by the senses of those brave enough to approach it. In this chapter I examine 'truth about' the Other Nation in these novels, and compare examples of the physical reality of the poor evoked in fiction with that provided by documentary evidence and historical fact. My intention is not to make an exhaustive study of all

[1] Ardwick: a wealthy suburb of Manchester; Ancoats: a very poor working-class area of Manchester; Little Ireland: Irish immigrant district of Manchester.

the sources used in the novels discussed, which would be both monotonous and repetitious, but to examine a representative selection of excerpts to give a fair example of the novelists' sensuous reactions to the poor, of the attitudes implied by their descriptions, the power and quality of their observations, and their part in the context of each novel.

The early Victorian novelist who wanted imaginatively to re-create the Other Nation for his readers had to evoke, convincingly, the physical details of an alien way of life. Its alien quality was part of the romance of the reality of the poor. Where did they live? What were their homes like? What did they eat? What was their work? How much did they earn? What did they wear? By the time that Harriet Beecher Stowe visited England in 1853, such novels had become popular and 'fashionable', supplanting the novels of 'high life'. She wrote:

Fashionable literature now arrays itself on the side of the working classes. The current of novel-writing is reversed. Instead of milliners and chambermaids being bewitched with the adventures of countesses and dukes, we now have fine lords and ladies hanging enchanted over the history of John the Carrier, with his little Dot, dropping sympathetic tears into little Charlie's wash-tub, and pursuing the fortunes of a dressmaker's apprentice, in company with poor Smike, and honest John Brodie [*sic*] and his little Yorkshire wife.[2] (*Sunny Memories of Foreign Lands*, 1854, p. 185.)

Inevitably she mentions Dickens as the novelist who opened the eyes of his readers to the lives of the poor, particularly the London poor. As P. A. W. Collins points out in his essay 'Dickens and London' (*The Victorian City*, ed. H. J. Dyos and M. Wolff (London and Boston, 1973), ii. 537–57), earlier writers such as Defoe, Fielding, Theodore Hook, and Pierce Egan had written about the London poor. However, despite the social concern of Defoe, Fielding, and Hogarth, their poor characters are types rather than individuals, and Defoe, as well as Hook and Egan, exploits the sensational adventures possible in the territory of the poor who are beyond the pale of respectable society. Boz's originality, as Richard Ford noticed in his review of *Oliver Twist* (*Quarterly Review*, 64 (June 1839), 90) was the detail with which he described the poor and their environment. 'Boz

---

[2] *The Cricket on the Hearth* (1845) is the story of John the Carrier and his wife Dot; Charlie is the bailiff's child, left alone to look after the other children when her father is arrested, in *Bleak House* (1853); Smike and John Browdie are in *Nicholas Nickleby* (1839).

sketches localities, particularly in London, with marvellous
effect; he concentrates with the power of a camera lucida.'
Sketches by Boz, the first series in two volumes published in
1836, the second in one volume in 1837, is, as the title tells
us, 'Illustrative of Every-day Life and Every-day People', and
includes descriptions of 'Gin Shops', 'The Pawnbroker's Shop',
'Criminal Courts', and 'A Visit to Newgate'.

Dickens's work which most concerns me in this study is *Hard
Times*, but his descriptions of the London poor are important
to this part of my argument because at least two of the novels
which I discuss owe a heavy debt to them. 'Our great cities',
commented the *Edinburgh Review*, 'have extended with a rapi-
dity wholly unexampled.' (77 (1843), 193.) The greatest was
London, consolidating its position as mercantile and commercial
centre of the world. P. J. Keating writes, 'London increased
phenomenally from under 1 million in 1801 to 4½ million a
century later, when it contained approximately 14 per cent of
England's population.' (*The Working Classes in Victorian Fiction*, 1971, p. 11.) Here the Two Nations were particularly evident, for those who had eyes to see them. As Dickens writes in
Nicholas Nickleby, 'wealth and poverty stood side by side;
repletion and starvation laid them down together' (ch. 32).
John Forster writes, of the period when Dickens's family moved
from Chatham to London in 1821:

he managed gradually to transfer to London all the dreaminess and all the
romance with which he had invested Chatham . . . To be taken out for a
walk into the real town, especially if it were anywhere about Covent
Garden or the Strand, perfectly entranced him with pleasure. But, most of
all, he had a profound attraction of repulsion to St. Giles's. If he could
only induce whomsoever took him out to take him through Seven Dials,
he was supremely happy. 'Good Heaven!' he would exclaim, 'what wild
visions of prodigies of wickedness, want, and beggary, arose in my mind
out of that place!' (*The Life of Charles Dickens*, i. 15.)

Ironically, Seven Dials began as an elegant piece of late-
seventeenth-century town-planning, providing seven avenues
where the London citizens could enjoy their walks; the avenues
converged on a central column faceted with sun-dials. But by
the time Dickens arrived in London it was a notorious slum,
situated in the parish of St. Giles, which shared its reputation.
He describes it in one of the Sketches:

The peculiar character of these streets, and the close resemblance each one bears to its neighbour, by no means tends to decrease the bewilderment in which the unexperienced wayfarer through 'the Dials' finds himself involved. He traverses streets of dirty, straggling houses, with now and then an unexpected court, composed of buildings as ill-proportioned and deformed as the half-naked children that wallow in the kennels. Here and there, a little dark chandler's shop, with a cracked bell hung up behind the door, to announce the entrance of a customer, or betray the presence of some young gentleman in whom a passion for shop tills, has developed itself at an early age . . . long rows of broken and patched windows expose plants that may have flourished when 'the Dials' were built, in vessels as dirty as 'the Dials' themselves; and shops for the purchase of rags, bones, old iron, and kitchen stuff, vie in cleanliness with the bird-fanciers' and rabbit-dealers', which one might fancy so many arks, but for the irresistible conviction that no bird in its proper senses, who was permitted to leave one of them, would ever come back again. Brokers' shops, which would seem to have been established by humane individuals, as refuges for destitute bugs, interspersed with announcements of day schools, penny theatres, petition-writers, mangles, and music for balls or routs, complete the 'still life' of the subject; and dirty men, filthy women, squalid children, fluttering shuttlecocks, noisy battledores, reeking pipes, bad fruit, more than doubtful oysters, attenuated cats, depressed dogs, and anatomical fowls, are its cheerful accompaniments. ('Seven Dials', *Sketches by Boz*, Second Series, 1837.)

He reports the adventures of 'the unexperienced wayfarer'; an important part of his duties describing London, to use Bagehot's phrase, 'like a special correspondent for posterity', was to reveal the strange wonders of life in the Other Nation. Because of the division between its members and his readers, it had to be described as a foreign country. This passage is remarkable for its conscious reference to painting, to 'still life'; for the recreation of life in Seven Dials in terms of sight, particularly, but also of smell, hearing and touch (the insistence on 'dirty', 'squalid', 'filthy'); for the profusion of details and the individual fancy with which some of the details are given special prominence, such as the association of the pet-shops with arks and the meditation on the improbability of any escaped dove returning to them; the lack of solemnity; and the way in which all the people in the scene are described in general terms—'half-naked children that wallow'; 'dirty men, filthy women, squalid children'—compared with the detailed examination of things.

Likewise, his evocation of 'the Rookery' of St. Giles's, the crowded, squalid area defined by W. Weir as 'the triangular space bounded by Bainbridge Street, George Street, and High

Street, St. Giles's' ('St. Giles's, Past and Present', *London*, ed.
Charles Knight, 6 vols., 1841-4, iii (1842), 264), through which
New Oxford Street was later driven. This passage, for example,
begins with the attempt to establish a bridge between the Two
Nations:

The filthy and miserable appearance of this part of London can hardly be
imagined by those (and there are many such) who have not witnessed it.
Wretched houses, with broken windows patched with rags and paper, every
room let out to a different family, and in many instances to two, or even
three: fruit and 'sweet-stuff' manufacturers in the cellars; barbers and red-
herring venders [*sic*] in the front parlours; cobblers in the back; a bird-
fancier in the first floor, three families on the second; starvation in the
attics; Irishmen in the passage; a 'musician' in the front kitchen, and a
charwoman and five hungry children in the back one—filth everywhere—a
gutter before the houses and a drain beind them—clothes drying at the
windows, slops emptying from the ditto; girls of fourteen or fifteen, with
matted hair, walking about bare-footed, and in old white great coats, almost their only covering; boys of all ages, in coats of all sizes, and no coats
at all; men and women, in every variety of scanty and dirty apparel, loung-
ing about, scolding, drinking, smoking, squabbling, fighting, and swearing.
('Gin-Shops', *Sketches by Boz*, i. 1836.)

The delight in the chaotic confusion of objects in 'Seven
Dials'—'announcements of day schools, penny theatres, petition-
writers, mangles, and music'; 'rags, bones, old iron, and kitchen
stuff'—here extends to the people: 'fruit and "sweet-stuff"
manufacturers in the cellars; barbers and red-herring venders in
the front parlours; cobblers in the back'.

Keating, commenting on 'the external nature of Dickens's
London', remarks on 'his special power of investing the ordinary
and the mundane with an air of mystery and strangeness; employing the London streets to reveal a life with which everyone
was familiar but which no one actually knew'. And he quotes
Gissing's comment on *Sketches by Boz*, 'Never had been known
such absorbing interest in the commonplace.' (Op. cit., p. 17.)
'*Sketches by Boz*', says Keating, 'did much to establish the pattern of one kind of semi-fictional urban exploration.' (Ibid.,
pp. 36 f.) Charles Kingsley admits as much when describing
Mackaye, the bookseller who befriends Alton Locke—'By-the-
by, I have as yet given no description of the old eccentric's
abode—an unpardonable omission, I suppose, in these days of
Dutch painting and Boz.' (*Alton Locke*, vol. i, ch. 6, 'The Dul-
wich Gallery'.) This defines the kind of 'still life' to which

Dickens refers his description of Seven Dials and links his 'absorbing interest in the commonplace' with Fox Talbot's endeavours in photography and his statement 'We have sufficient
authority in the Dutch school of art, for taking as subjects of
representation scenes of daily and familiar occurrence.' By the
time Engels wrote his description of the English working class
St. Giles's rookery had become 'famous' (op. cit., p. 60).
Dickens was partly responsible for making it so. Engels, in his
description of St. Giles's, emphasizes the same details as does
Dickens, 'the narrow courts and alleys . . . the walls are crumbling, doorposts and window-frames lost and broken . . . heaps of
garbage and ashes', but he lacks the vigorous imagination which
makes Dickens's details so arresting. In fact, Dickens was so
successful in making writers look at the London poor with his
eyes that they stopped looking with their own.[3] He created a
literary fashion for descriptions of London life, and provided
an excellent example of what Oscar Wilde later described as
Nature imitating Art rather than Art imitating Nature. It is
uncertain how much of Dickens's work Disraeli read, although
to judge by his late satiric portrait of him as Gushy in *Endy-
mion* (1880) he liked the popular novelist far this side of
idolatry. However, it would be strange if he had not read
Sketches by Boz which, Forster remembered, 'were much more
talked about than the first two or three numbers of *Pickwick*' at
a period when Disraeli was bent on establishing himself in the
literary and fashionable London circles, and when both he and
Dickens were numbered among the 'Gore House set', the group
of writers, artists, and politicians who enjoyed Lady Blessing-
ton's hospitality and wit at Gore House, Kensington Gore.
Among the friends they had in common in this group were
Maclise and Bulwer-Lytton. Certainly the passage in *Sybil*, in
which the heroine goes to warn her father of the police trap set
for the Chartist meeting, is reminiscent of the *Sketches*. She is
directed to 'go up St. Martin's Lane to a certain point, and then

[3] Dickens's *Sketches* made a great appeal because they were both idiosyncratic
and accorded with the growing self-consciousness which marks the 1830s and 1840s.
For a contrasting late Regency vision of London, lively, gay, and imposing, see
Thomas Shotter Boys's volume of lithographs, *Original Views of London as it is*
(1842). Even 'London Bridge from Southwark Bridge', close by the territory of Fagin
and his gang, reveals clean golden stretches of sand along the river, and the few tall
smoking chimneys add formal interest rather than pollution (see Plate 3).

you will get into Seven Dials; and then you'll go on . . . you must find your way. Hunt Street, going out of Silver Street, No. 22.' (Bk. V, ch. 5.) Her fear and the danger which she risks for her father's sake are expressed in the description of the slum streets; Disraeli exemplifies his sub-title 'The Two Nations' by making Sybil, like the 'unexperienced wayfarer' in Dickens's 'Seven Dials', feel that she is penetrating into unknown territory:

The houses, the population, the costume, the manners, the language, through which they whirled their way, were of a different state and nation from those with which the dwellers of the dainty quarters of this city are acquainted. Now dark streets of frippery and old stores, now market-places of entrails and carrion, with gutters running gore, sometimes the way was enveloped in the yeasty fumes of a colossal brewery, and sometimes they plunged into a labyrinth of lanes teeming with life, and where the dog-stealer and the pick-pocket, the burglar and the assassin, found a sympa-thetic multitude of all ages; comrades for every enterprise, and a market for every booty.

The long summer twilight was just expiring; the pale shadows of the moon were just stealing on; the gas was beginning to glare in shops of tripe and bacon, and the paper lanterns to adorn the stall and the stand. They crossed a broad street which seemed the metropolis of the district; it flamed with gin palaces; a multitude were sauntering in the mild though tainted air; bargaining, blaspheming, drinking, wrangling; and varying their business and their potations, their fierce strife and their impious irrever-ence, with flashes of rich humour, gleams of native wit, and racy phrases of idiomatic slang. (Bk. V, ch. 6.)

Keating comments on the 'mood of urgency and rush' gener-ated by Dickens's descriptions of London, and quotes the reviewer of *Sketches* in the *Spectator*, 26 December 1836: 'Reading Boz's Sketches is like rattling through the streets of London in a cab: the prominent features of the town strike upon the eye in rapid succession, new objects perpetually effacing the impression of the last; all is bustle and movement, till the jerk of the stoppage announces that the "fare" or the "sketch" is ended.' (Op. cit., p. 16.) Sybil is driven in a cab through these strange streets which frighten her; and certainly the passage has this quality of rush, of the details being seen and swept away. The people are generalized, as in 'Seven Dials', and to make the reader experience the place Disraeli appeals to at least four senses—'yeasty fumes'; 'gas beginning to glare'; 'the mild though tainted air'; 'bargaining, blaspheming . . . wrangling'. But Dickens's passionate delight in the scene has gone, and his vigorous response. The prose has a tired quality. There are no visual images with profounder implications, like Dickens's 'buildings as ill-proportioned and deformed as the half-naked children'. Nor has the passage any wit, it is very solemn; and it lacks the latent humour which denotes Dickens's aesthetic joy in recreating the scene—'more than doubtful oysters . . . anatomical fowls'. The alliteration of Disraeli's 'gutters running gore' over-emphasizes the phrase and dissipates the 'attraction of repulsion' implied in Dickens's scene; it calls attention to itself rather than to the street it is meant to describe.

Possibly Disraeli's contrast between the glare of the gin-palace and the dark filth and squalor of the area is also a memory of Dickens's description:

You turn the corner. What a change! All is light and brilliancy. The hum of many voices issues from that splendid gin-shop which forms the commencement of the two streets opposite and the gay building with the fantastically ornamented parapet, the illuminated clock, the plate-glass windows surrounded by stucco rosettes, and its profusion of gas-lights in richly-gilt burners, is perfectly dazzling when contrasted with the darkness and dirt we have just left.

Boz describes what Brian Harrison calls 'a new phenomenon' of the 1830s, 'the "gin-palace"—with plate-glass windows, richly ornamented façade, gilded lettering and brilliant lamps' ('Pubs', *The Victorian City*, i. 170). He explains the occurrence of this phenomenon: 'In the early 1830s the publican had every reason to follow the fashion for enriching shop façades which had gripped London in the 1820s, for the Beer Act of 1830 [which established beer-houses forbidden to sell spirits] had created a new rival for his custom.' The new gin-palaces literally outshone their rivals. Dickens's description is again remarkable for the particularity and accuracy of its detail. He not only mentions the plate-glass windows, but also their stucco rosettes; he comments on the profusion of gas-lights, and their 'richly-gilt burners' so that the typical scene becomes particular and visualized. His observant eye notices the palace's position—'that splendid gin-shop which forms the commencement of the two streets opposite', illustrating Harrison's point, 'Pubs occupy strategic positions in the Victorian slum. Of the 160 pubs in the area bounded by Bethnal Green Road/Commercial Street/Whitechapel Road/Cambridge Road . . . 131 were situated on corners

or opposite road junctions.' (Op. cit., p. 169.) These details help
to explain why we see Dickens's gin-palace with such clarity,
but have only a vague idea of Disraeli's.

The gin-palace was regarded by middle-class philanthropists
as the prime tempter and destroyer of the Other Nation—see
George Cruikshank's etching 'The Gin-Juggernath, or, The Worship of the Great Spirit of the age' (*My Sketch Book*, 1834-6,
printed in the catalogue to the exhibition, 'George Cruikshank',
Victoria and Albert Museum, London, 1974, Arts Council,
p. 23), and his popular series of prints, 'The Bottle' (1847) and
its sequel, 'The Drunkard's Children' (1848). In a review of 'The
Drunkard's Children' for the *Examiner* Dickens pointed out the
absurd crudity of its moralizing, despite the power of the pictures—the lure of the gin-shop is the effect of lack of education
and recreation for the lower classes; crime and immorality
amongst the poor cannot be traced solely to gin. It is typical of
his early sympathy with the very poor that Dickens suggests, in
Sketches, the gin-shop's attraction as it stands, bright and warm,
in the cold, dirty street. Kingsley, writing later in a period of
sterner moral exhortation, represents the gin-shop as Cruikshank
does, as a monstrous place of dire temptation. He has Mackaye
exhort Alton, ' "Look at the jaws o' the monsters, how they
open and open, and swallow in anither victim and anither. Write
aboot that." "What jaws, Mr. Mackaye!" "They faulding-doors
o' the gin shop, goose." ' (Vol. i, ch. 8, 'Light in a Dark Place'.)
Alton has been writing a poem about a South Sea Island, and is
hauled off by Mackaye to confront his real subject: 'he seized
me by the arm, and hardly giving me time to put on my hat,
marched me out into the streets, and away through Clare Market
to St. Giles's'. The passage which follows is heavily indebted to
Dickens:

It was a foul, chilly, foggy Saturday night. From the butchers' and green-
grocers' shops the gas-lights flared and flickered, wild and ghastly, over
haggard groups of slip-shod dirty women, bargaining for scraps of stale
meat and frostbitten vegetables, wrangling about short weight and bad
quality. Fish-stalls and fruit-stalls lined the edge of the greasy pavement,
sending up odours as foul as the language of sellers and buyers. Blood and
sewer water crawled from under doors and out of spouts, and reeked down
the gutters among offal, animal and vegetable, in every stage of putrefaction. Foul vapours rose from cowsheds and slaughter-houses, and the door-
ways of undrained alleys, where the inhabitants carried the filth out on

their shoes from the back yard into the court, and from the court up into the main street; while above, hanging like cliffs over the streets—those narrow, brawling torrents of filth, and poverty, and sin—the houses with their teeming load of life were piled up into the dingy choking night. A ghastly, deafening, sickening sight it was. Go, scented Belgravian! and see what London is! and then go to the library which God has given thee—one often fears in vain—and see what science says this London might be!

Here are Boz's sensuous details to make the one Nation aware of the Other, but the exemplum is more crudely drawn and more emphatically displayed. It is the fictional equivalent of Thomas Hughes's *Tract on Christian Socialism*, quoted above, p. 14.

The key-note is horror and repulsion. Again, Dickens's fascination and delight, the wit and the humour consequent upon them, have gone. Also, some of the disgusting details do not bear scrutiny because they bombard us into submission to the writer's argument rather than allow an active, imaginative response to the scene. Obviously, we are meant to be repelled by the 'haggard groups of slip-shod dirty women, bargaining for scraps of stale meat and frostbitten vegetables, wrangling about short weight and bad quality', but surely the fact that they objected to short weight and bad quality shows both sense and discrimination? Kingsley is the only one of the three writers who mentions God and relates his moral judgements of the scene to God. Dickens is the only one who suggests the prostitution in these slums, but very discreetly: 'girls of fourteen or fifteen, with matted hair, walking about bare-footed, and in white great-coats, almost their only covering'.

St. Giles, largely because of the verbal skill and imaginative power of Dickens, became a literary and artistic set-piece to describe the Other Nation. Engels uses it as typical of the division between rich and poor: 'St. Giles is in the midst of the most populous part of the town, surrounded by broad, splendid avenues in which the gay world of London idles about, in the immediate neighbourhood of Oxford Street, Regent Street, of Trafalgar Square and the Strand.' (Op. cit., p. 60.) It is indicative of the increasingly social consciousness of the time that Engels emphasizes its social context; Dickens, in the *Sketches*, despite an occasional comment such as that at the end of 'Gin-Shops' when he insists that hunger and distress send the poor to the gin-palaces and that Temperance Societies would

do well to cure these rather than preach temperance, was more
interested in the details than in their social relevance. (Also,
these 'dark' Sketches are very much in the minority in the
series.) In 1851, a year after the publication of *Alton Locke*,
Douglas Jerrold published his novel on the Two Nations, although he set the period back into the eighteenth century; he
chose two areas of London to represent them, *St. Giles and St.
James*.[4] In the same year Dickens got his friend Inspector Field
to take him through St. Giles's and again wrote a description of
his visit:

How many people may there be in London, who, if we had brought them
deviously and blindfold, to this street, fifty paces from the Station House,
and within call of Saint Giles's church, would know it for a not remote
part of the city in which their lives are passed? How many, who amidst
this compound of sickening smells, these heaps of filth, these tumbling
houses, with all their vile contents, animate and inanimate, slimily over-
flowing into the black road, would believe that they breathe *this* air? How
much Red Tape may there be, that could look round on the faces which
now hem us in—for our appearance here has caused a rush from all points
to a common centre—the lowering foreheads, the sallow cheeks, the brutal
eyes, the matted hair, the infected, vermin-haunted heaps of rags—and say,
'I have thought of this, I have not dismissed the thing. I have neither blus-
tered it away, nor frozen it away, nor tied it up and put it away, nor
smoothly said pooh, pooh! to it when it has been shown to me?' ('On
Duty with Inspector Field', *Household Words*, 3 (1851), 265–70; *Reprinted Pieces*, pp. 514 f.)

Collins writes that although Inspector Bucket of *Bleak House* is
not Inspector Field 'some prominent features of Bucket were
very clearly derived from Field' (*Dickens and Crime*, 1962,
p. 207). Indeed, it is clear from the passage that the ideas of the
novel, begun in November that year, dominate Dickens's mind,

[4] This became an accepted term for the Two Nations. Baring-Gould collected a
copy of a broadside, 'St. James' and St. Giles's'. One verse runs
> In St. James's with calling the morning is spent,
> In St. Giles's the landlord he calls for his rent;
> In St. James's the Queen holds a drawing-room gay
> In St. Giles's Joe Smith holds a garret all day,
> In St. James's the togs are got out very bright,
> In St. Giles's they're got out [from pawn] on Saturday night
> In St. James's they sleep on down pillows and snore,
> In St. Giles's the same, but its down on the floor.
Disraeli is associated with St. James's literary aspirations:
> In St. James's the Authors, when the Muses inspire
> Dash off with a touch of D'Israeli's fire.
> (Baring-Gould, *Ballads*, vi. 108.)

particularly the reference to 'Red Tape' to signify Governmental irresponsibility towards grave social problems. There are great differences between Dickens's account of St. Giles's in the *Sketches* and his later one in *Household Words*, which is more generalized, lacking the precise, acutely-perceived details which evoke strong visual images of the scene. Even the thieves' kitchen lacks individuality:

Saint Giles's church strikes half-past ten. We stoop low, and creep down a precipitous flight of steps into a dark close cellar. There is a fire. There is a long deal table. There are benches. The cellar is full of company, chiefly very young men in various conditions of dirt and raggedness. Some are eating supper. There are no girls or women present. Welcome to Rats' Castle, gentlemen, and to this company of noted thieves! (*Reprinted Pieces*, p. 515.)

But the greatest difference is the lack of sympathetic wit and humour. There is 'attraction' as well as 'repulsion' in the early scenes. But in this later piece the people have ceased to be people and are criminal types with 'lowering foreheads' and 'brutal eyes'; they have become a Social Problem to which the Government should pay attention. Dickens here allies himself with the Law, and he describes the scenes illuminated by the policeman's bull's-eye lantern:

Rogers to the front with the light, and let us look!
      Ten, twenty, thirty—who can count them! Men, women, children, for the most part naked, heaped upon the floor like maggots in a cheese! (Ibid., p. 517.)

He is, in fact, recording a 'slumming' expedition, like those of Pierce Egan's *Life in London* (1821). In 1855 Edmund Yates, the journalist, enjoyed a similar adventure with him. Yates, then a young man of twenty-four, recorded the adventure in his autobiography:

the first of very many subsequent delightful nights, passed among odd scenes in close intimacy with him. We went on what would nowadays be called a 'slumming' expedition, quite original in those days, but long since done to death. A friend of Dickens's, a certain M. Delarue, a banker in Genoa, who was on a visit to Tavistock House, had a great desire to see some of the low life of London; and Dickens accordingly arranged with the police for a party of us, of which I was one, to dine early together, and then 'go the rounds' of the thieves' quarters in Whitechapel, the sailors' and German sugar-bakers' taverns in Ratcliff Highway, the dens of the Mint, &c. It was a curious experience, but the interest of it to me was greatly increased by the fact that I was in the company of the man whose genius I had worshipped so long and so ardently; and when he called me into the cab, and we returned alone together, he chatting freely and charmingly, I wondered whether Fate could have in store for me greater distinction or delight. (*Edmund Yates: his Recollections and Experiences*, 1884, i. 284.)

Dickens did the same circuit 'On Duty with Inspector Field'.

Obviously, a part of the acute pleasure Dickens felt as a small boy 'if he could only induce whomsoever took him out to take him through Seven Dials' was that of seeing the horrors of evil and destitution in the safety of an adult's protection. The thrills of life in the Other Nation could be enjoyed without personal danger. It was like going to the Zoo, where the lions were safely behind bars. This pleasure Dickens provided for the readers of the *Sketches*, albeit with an imaginative sympathy and interest in these alien creatures, and he himself experiences it as an adult when moving in the orbit of the all-powerful Inspector Field, who now has the writer's sympathy rather than 'this cellar company':

Yet Inspector Field stands in this den, the Sultan of the place. Every thief here cowers before him, like a schoolboy before his schoolmaster . . . let Inspector Field have a mind to pick out one thief here, and take him; let him produce that ghostly truncheon from his pocket, and say, with his business-air, 'My lad, I want you!' and all Rats' Castle shall be stricken with paralysis, and not a finger move against him, as he fits the handcuffs on! (*Reprinted Pieces*, p. 516.)

Yates experiences the same kind of pleasure, a 'curious experience' of 'odd scenes' in the protection of the great man, who knows his way round these places, and of the great man's friends, the police.

In the same year that Dickens published 'On Duty with Inspector Field', Thomas Miller, boyhood friend of Thomas Cooper, the Leicestershire Chartist who provided some of the characteristics of Kingsley's Alton Locke, published his *Picturesque Sketches of London, Past and Present*. It includes a chapter on St. Giles's which begins: 'By way of contrast, we will stride from splendour to squalor—from St. James's to St. Giles's, whose names Douglas Jerrold has rendered inseparable in his fearless and life-like novel.' He describes the dirt, the smells, the crazy streets, and continues:

The air which now blows through the open windows of the emblazoned carriage in which the diamonded duchess is seated, a few seconds ago swept over the poisonous avenues of Church-street and Carrier-street, and is laden with odours from the sink and sewerage of St. Giles's . . . How essential is it, then, fair lady, for thy own sake, to aid us in cleansing these Augean stables, in purifying these pest-houses of poor humanity. You may build yourself a fine house, my lady, and hem it round with a lofty wall; but you must, while in town, still breathe the poisonous air which they breathe, until these grievous evils are remedied. (Ch. 15.)

This inevitable and gruesome connection of the Two Nations is used to plead the humane connection which should be acknowledged, the connection Carlyle had emphasized in *Past and Present* (1843). From the report of the Edinburgh physician Dr William Pulteney Alison, *Observations on the Management of the Poor in Scotland and its Effects on the Health of the Great Towns* (1840), he took the incident of the poor Irish Widow in Edinburgh who begs 'help from the Charitable Establishments of that City', is refused by them all, dies of typhus and infects seventeen other people who die in consequence. 'The forlorn Irish Widow applies to her fellow-creatures, as if saying, "Behold I am sinking, bare of help: ye must help me!" They answer, "No, impossible, thou art no sister of ours." But she proves her sisterhood; her typhus-fever kills *them*: they actually were her brothers, though denying it! Had human creature ever to go lower for a proof?' (*Past and Present*, Bk. III, ch. 2, Carlyle, *Works*, xiii.)

Dickens thinks along these lines when he asks, in 'On Duty with Inspector Field', 'How many . . . would believe that they breathe *this* air?' and when, in *Bleak House*, small-pox originating in Tom-All-Alone's attacks Esther.

Opposite the description of St. Giles's in Miller's book is an engraving of The Rookery, St. Giles's (see Plate 4). It shows people leaning out of the windows of crazy houses, washing hanging from poles projecting from the walls, wretched stalls in the street, boys fighting, a pig, a dog, babies, and garbage in the gutter. It is the perfect graphic equivalent to the literary stereotype of St. Giles's. The quality of both the engraving and the verbal description is suggested by the book's title: *Picturesque Sketches of London, Past and Present*. From its beginnings in the eighteenth century the picturesque was an attempt to impose on Nature a form which would give the spectator an agreeable sensation. Gilpin said, 'I am so attached to my picturesque rules, that if nature gets wrong, I cannot help putting her right.' (See Carl Paul Barbier, *William Gilpin*, 1963, p. 71, quoted Leslie Parris, catalogue to the exhibition 'Landscape in Britain c.1750–1850', Tate Gallery 1973, p. 59.) Its essence is safely formalized wildness. Uvedale Price in *An Essay on the Picturesque . . . and on the Use of Studying Pictures, for the Purpose of Improving Real Landscape* (1794) wrote:

Among trees, it is not the smooth young beech, nor the fresh and tender ash, but the rugged old oak, or knotty wych elm that are picturesque . . . among horses, it is the wild and rough forester, or the worn-out cart-horse to which the title is applied . . . In our own species, objects merely picturesque are to be found among the wandering tribes of gypsies and beggars; who in all the qualities which give them that character, bear a close analogy to the wild forester and the worn-out cart-horse, again to old mills, hovels, and other inanimate objects of the same kind. (Quoted Parris, op. cit., p. 60.)

In the Victorian period William Bell Scott defined the pleasure of the picturesque for his senior students at Newcastle:

The pleasure it gives is not so much a natural as an artificial or simply artistic one; it is only when painted that we learn to admire those conditions of nature that are picturesque . . . Whatever we would consider undesirable as a personal adjunct or condition, that is what the picturesque painter for the most part covets for his canvas. Wild and gaunt features as well as artless and contented expression, dishevelled tresses or elf-locks, tattered garments, he prefers; beggary is the most picturesque condition of social life. (*Half-Hour Lectures on the History and Practice of the Fine and Ornamental Arts*, 1861, pp. 323 f. The lectures were begun in 1859.)

'Whatever we would consider undesirable as a personal adjunct or condition' is an apt description of the social horrors at a safe distance offered for enjoyment in Dickens's descriptions of St. Giles's and imitated by his followers. Like Uvedale Price, he reduces the people to wild objects producing a frisson of delight in the beholders. His later descriptions of the place lack the detail and vigour of the earlier, but in both he is concerned, like Defoe, with the sensation which can be elicited from reality. Forster's account of the young Dickens's delight in St. Giles's because it afforded him 'wild visions of prodigies of wickedness, want, and beggary' is very revealing. He uses the place and its inhabitants to conjure up his 'wild visions'; this is not so much the romance of reality as romance imposed upon reality. It helped to create a literary 'fashion', as Harriet Beecher Stowe noted, and Margaret Oliphant later in 1862, surveying recent English literature:

Mr. Dickens was one of the first popular writers who brought pictures of
what is called common life into fashion. It is he who has been mainly
instrumental in leading the present generation of authors to disregard to a
great extent the pictorial advantages of life on the upper levels of society,
and to find a counter-picturesqueness in the experiences of the poor . . .
He has made washerwomen as interesting as duchesses. (*Blackwood's
Edinburgh Magazine*, 91 (1862), 574.)

Certainly Dickens exploited the 'counter-picturesqueness' of
slums like Seven Dials, concentrating largely on 'the poor who
won't work', the thieves' kitchens, the rogues' hide-outs. It
comes as something of a shock to learn that Dickens's friend the
cabinet-maker, John Overs, a sober, earnest man if ever there
was one, lived for a time in St. Giles's. According to the birth
certificate, Overs's daughter Harriet was born there, at 10 Crown
Street,[5] on 1 November 1837, before Overs had met Dickens.
It is a measure of the sensational quality of Dickens's descriptions of St. Giles's that it is impossible to imagine Overs in their
context. Also, when Dickens describes the area he concentrates
on the Rookery rather than describing the shabby gentility of a
street like Crown Street, or the gaiety of Monmouth Street,
which according to Weir, was bright with 'hanging gardens' and
singing birds (op. cit., p. 265). In the *Sketches*, his 'Meditations
in Monmouth Street' is mainly concerned with the masses of
old clothes and shoes displayed for sale, and the pathetic or
comic owners which they suggest to him; the inhabitants he
briefly describes, with lumbering facetiousness, as cheerful but
grotesque, a view supported by Cruikshank's illustration. When
a lesser writer like Kingsley imitates Dickens's account of the
slum, the distorted sensationalism is very obvious; it's there in
the relentless accumulation of horrible details—'gas-lights wild
and ghastly'[6] 'haggard groups of slip-shod dirty women', 'stale
meat', 'frostbitten vegetables', 'odours as foul as the language',
'foul vapours', 'undrained alleys'; and also in the extravagance
of the language—'those narrow, brawling torrents of filth, and

---

[5] Crown Street was NW of Seven Dials and ran between the bottom of Tottenham
Court Road and what was then Old Compton Street/New Compton Street, which ran
across the bottom of Crown Street at right angles to it. According to Weir (op. cit.,
p. 264) it formed the western boundary of St. Giles's.

[6] Gas lights could be 'wild and ghastly' or cheerful, according to viewpoint. See,
for example, the scene on Christmas Eve in *A Christmas Carol*: 'The brightness of the
shops where holly sprigs and berries crackled in the lamp-heat of the windows, made
pale faces ruddy as they passed.'

poverty, and sin,—the houses with their teeming load of life were piled up into the dingy, choking night'. Weir's description of the listless hopelessness of the Rookery calls in question the frantic, hectic activity of Kingsley's passage; and Kingsley's assault on the reader induces numbness. Gustave Doré, a great admirer of Dickens's work, and Blanchard Jerrold, the son of Dickens's friend Douglas Jerrold, made their literary and graphic record of London in 1872. Doré was obviously much influenced by Dickens's vision of the London slums. For example, his engraving of Seven Dials in *London. A Pilgrimage* owes much to Dickens's conception of the place (see Plate 5). It is interesting to compare Doré's drawing with a photograph of the district, also taken in the seventies (see Plate 6). The great difference between them is that in Doré's illustration the place looks like hell peopled by monsters brooding on the wrongs done them, whereas in the photograph the district is obviously poor but the people are human beings with whom, we feel, it would be possible to communicate. Picturesque horror, sensationalism feeding on reality, panders to the spectator's pleasurable sensations and enlarges the gulf between the Two Nations rather than appealing to feeling to bridge it.

JACOB'S ISLAND, WODGATE AND COKETOWN

In Thomas Hughes's *Tract on Christian Socialism* (quoted above, p. 14) he links with St. Giles's 'the plague-lanes of Bermondsey' as places in which thousands of the Other Nation live in unprecedented wretchedness. Jacob's Island was a Bermondsey slum on a tidal creek of the Thames where the earliest fatal cases of cholera occurred in the outbreaks of 1832 and 1840. In 1842 J. Saunders described the tidal stream as being used by tanneries in the manufacture of leather, although the mill at the mouth of the channel into the Thames was a lead-mill (see Charles Knight, op. cit., iii. 22). Kingsley and his Christian Socialist friends tried to establish a supply of clean drinking-water there during the cholera outbreak in the autumn of 1849. Kingsley had been inspired to act after reading Henry Mayhew's article, 'The Cholera Districts of Bermondsey', in the *Morning Chronicle*, 24 September 1849. Mayhew showed his readers why cholera bred in Jacob's Island and how petty capitalists oppressed the wretched inhabitants by charging exorbitant rent for derelict accommodation. He traces the district's history from medieval times when running streams turned the monks' flour-mills, to the period when the London citizens enjoyed their ale in gardens beside the clear water, up to the present conditions: 'a tidal sewer, in whose putrid filth staves are laid to season; and where the ancient summer-houses stood, nothing but hovels, sties, and muck-heaps are now to be seen'.

He describes the creek from the Thames which runs into the district: 'This creek was once supplied by the streams from the Surrey hills, but now nothing but the drains and refuse of the houses that have grown up round about it thicken and swell its waters.' Mayhew is good at suggesting physical appearance. He uses a simile and visual details to describe the creek of Jacob's Island, with a certain suggestion of the journalist's relish for horrors: 'The water is covered with a scum almost like a cob-web, and prismatic with grease. In it float large masses of green rotting weed, and against the posts of the bridges are swollen carcases of dead animals, almost bursting with the gases of putrefaction.' Close to this filth people live: 'Across some parts of the stream whole rooms have been built, so that house adjoins house; and here, with the very stench of death rising through the boards, human beings sleep night after night, until the last sleep of all comes upon them years before its time.' In London-street, where 'the cholera first appeared seventeen years ago', the disease had struck during the past autumn with similar virulence: 'As we passed along the reeking banks of the sewer the sun shone upon a narrow lip of the water. In the bright light it appeared the colour of strong green tea, and positively looked as solid as black marble in the shadow—indeed it was more like watery mud than muddy water; and yet we were assured this was the only water the wretched inhabitants had to drink.'[7]

Jacob's Island is described in some detail in *Alton Locke*. Jemmy Downes, once a 'sweater', that is, a sub-contractor of

---

[7] Mayhew reprinted this description of Jacob's Island in his essay 'Home is Home, Be it Never So Homely', *Meliora: or Better Times to Come*, ed. Viscount Ingestre (C. J. C. Talbot), 1852, pp. 258–80. Thomas Beames, preacher at St. James's, Westminster, quotes from Mayhew's article, which he refers to as a 'tract' and entitles 'Jacob's Island; and the Tidal ditches of Bermondsey' (see Thomas Beames, *The Rookeries of London* (1st edn. 1850, 2nd edn. 1852), reissued Frank Cass, 1970, p. 82).

clothes made by cheap labour, has been reduced to doing piece-
work for another 'sweater' at starvation wages. Gin-sodden and
on the point of suicide, he takes Alton back to his lodging in
Jacob's Island, where his wife and children are lying dead of
typhus.

He stopped at the end of a miserable blind alley, where a dirty gas-lamp
just served to make darkness visible, and show the patched windows and
rickety doorways of the crazy houses, whose upper stories were lost in a
brooding cloud of fog; and the pools of stagnant water at our feet; and the
huge heap of cinders which filled up the waste end of the alley—a dreary,
black, formless mound, on which two or three spectral dogs prowled up
and down after the offal, appearing and vanishing like dark imps in and
out of the black misty chaos beyond. (Vol. II, ch. 14, 'The Lowest Deep'.)

As in his account of St. Giles's, Kingsley emphasizes the horror
and disgust of the scene, but here the description is more re-
strained and effective. The details suggest direct observation:
the squalid stillness of everything—'miserable blind alley', no
traffic going through; 'the brooding cloud of fog', 'the pools of
stagnant water', 'the huge heap of cinders'—all give an air of
permanence and hopelessness, further emphasized by the only
movement in the scene, the prowling dogs 'appearing and vanishing', 'in and out' on their sinister quest. Typically, Kingsley
speculates on the reasons for Bermondsey's physical state:

The neighbourhood was undergoing, as it seemed, 'improvements', of that
peculiar metropolitan species which consists in pulling down the dwellings
of the poor, and building up rich men's houses instead; and great buildings,
within high temporary palings, had already eaten up half the little houses;
as the great fish, and the great estates, and the great shopkeepers eat up
the little ones of their species . . .

He sees this as characteristic of contemporary social values and
takes the opportunity to attack the political economists: 'by
the law of competition, lately discovered to be the true creator
and preserver of the universe. There they loomed up, the tall
bullies, against the dreary sky, looking down with their grim,
proud, stony visages, on the misery which they were driving out
of one corner, only to accumulate and intensify it in another.'
    William Gilbert, author of *Dives and Lazarus*, in 1872 pub-
lished an essay, 'The Dwellings of the London Poor',[8] in which
he surveys the 'destruction of the dwellings of the London poor,

    [8] I am indebted to David Rubinstein, Department of Social and Economic History,
University of Hull, for drawing my attention to this article.

8. Philip James de Loutherbourg, 'Coalbrookdale by Night', 1801

9. Paul Sandby Munn, 'Bedlam Furnace, Madely Dale, Shropshire', 1803

10. Vincent van Gogh, 'Head of a Peasant Woman in a White Cap', 1885

11. Vincent van Gogh, 'Interior with Weaver', 1884

12. John Constable, 'Old Sarum', 1834

Stands England where it did

MERRY ENGLAND

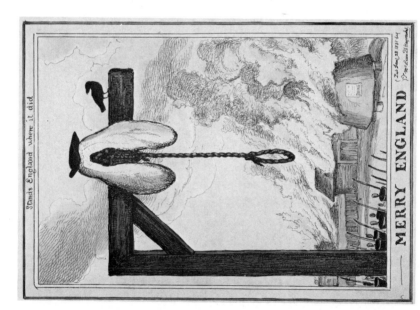

THE HOME OF THE RICK-BURNER.

which has been carried on so energetically for the last forty or fifty years' (*Good Words*, 13 (1872), 458-62). The villain of his piece is the Metropolitan Board of Works which took over from Her Majesty's Office of Works in 1855, five years after the publication of *Alton Locke*, and controlled what J. N. Summerson describes as 'the virtual rebuilding of the central area of the City between 1857 and 1877' before being exposed as inadequate and sinking 'in a morass of scandal' in the 1880s. ('London, the Artifact', *The Victorian City*, i. 315, 310.) But, as Summerson says, 'the transformation had . . . begun much earlier, the chief agents being the great banking-houses and, still more, the competing insurance companies . . .' (ibid., p. 315). This is the period of the demolition of parts of Bermondsey described in *Alton Locke*, although, of course, Bermondsey is not 'the central area of the City', and it is hard to believe that rich men's *houses* were being built in Bermondsey in the late 1840s; the buildings were much more likely to have been warehouses and offices. Kingsley is sometimes careless in the details used to make his social comments, and so the scene loses focus.

Kingsley takes Downes's plight as typical of that to which official policy had brought many of the London poor; the house in which he lives is part of a widespread desolation: 'The house at which we stopped was the last in the row; all its companions had been pulled down; and there it stood, leaning out with one naked ugly side into the gap, and stretching out long props, like feeble arms and crutches, to resist the work of demolition', using the personification of inanimate objects which is such a feature of Dickens's style. Many of the details in Kingsley's description are obviously echoes of Mayhew's article. Kingsley was very impressed by Mayhew's revelations concerning the Other Nation and, in 'Cheap Clothes and Nasty' (1850), which he wrote as one of the 'Tracts by Christian Socialists' to expose the horrors of the sweated tailoring trade, he acknowledges his debt to Mayhew's articles on the subject in the *Morning Chronicle*, 14 and 18 December 1849. The articles also provided him with material for *Alton Locke*. The earlier article on Bermondsey similarly gave his fiction substance. Like the houses mentioned by Mayhew, Downes's room is built over the sewer; Mayhew establishes the presence of the Other Nation's territory by its stench: 'a feeling of nausea and heaviness comes

over any one unaccustomed to imbibe the musty atmosphere';
Alton experiences a similar reaction: 'The first breath I drew
made my heart sink, and my stomach turn.' This is a fictional
situation embodying what Steven Marcus describes as an abrupt
disturbance of the 'advanced middle-class consciousness' of the
1840s, 'the realization that millions of English men, women and
children were virtually living in shit' (op. cit., p. 184). When
Downes demands money for gin Alton refuses it and tactlessly
suggests that he should drink water. Then, as Kingsley and
his friends experienced in Jacob's Island, he finds that it is safer
to drink gin than the sewer water which constitutes their water-
supply. Exciting action develops in these extraordinary sur-
roundings; Downes rushes out on to the balcony over the ditch
at the back of the house to haul up a bucket of water which he
intends to force Alton to drink. Alton, terrified, calls for help;
and Downes, who is very drunk, falls into the ditch. As in
Dickens's slumming excursions, it is the policeman's lantern
which illuminates the details of the scene, which is a more emphatic version of Mayhew's description of the sewer-water:

We rushed out on the balcony. The light of the policeman's lantern glared
over the ghastly scene—along the double row of miserable house-backs,
which lined the sides of the open tidal ditch—over strange rambling jetties,
and balconies, and sleeping sheds, which hung on rotting piles over the
black waters, with phosphorescent scraps of rotten fish gleaming and
twinkling out of the dark hollows, like devilish grave-lights—over-bubbles
[*sic*] of poisonous gas, and bloated carcases of dogs, and lumps of offal,
floating on the stagnant olive-green hell-broth—over the slow sullen rows
of oily ripple which were dying away into the darkness far beyond,
sending up, as they stirred, hot breaths of miasma[9]—the only sign that a
spark of humanity, after years of foul life, had quenched itself at last in
that foul death. I almost fancied that I could see the haggard face staring
up at me through the slimy water; but no—it was as opaque as stone.

To make the disappearance more dramatic Downes drowns at
an improbable speed, without a struggle. But, although some
impact is again lost by accumulating rather too many details,
they are controlled and effective, emphasizing the sustained

---

[9] Miasma: vapour given off by rotting substances. At this date it was not known
that cholera is caught by drinking water contaminated by sewage or eating food
tainted by such water. It was, however, known to have a physical cause connected
with foul water. 'Miasma' was a favourite contemporary term used to describe the
exhalations thought to be responsible for disease, particularly typhus fever, in dirty
localities. See *Yeast*, 'the cool breath of those glittering water-meadows too often
floats laden with poisonous miasma' (ch. 3).

contrast of light and darkness—the light which serves only to reveal horrors, and the darkness which is broken only by lights which bespeak its foulness. The use of the word 'hell-broth' marks the weakest point of the passage and is an example of the sensationalism which could so easily result from the over-emphatic delivery of a social message.

The description of the place prefaces an attack upon the law, with which the chapter ends. Alton returns to the squalid room to find the local women covering the bodies of Downes's wife and children, and talking about his ill-treatment of them while they lived:

And in the midst of all the rout, the relieving officer stood impassive, jotting down scraps of information, and warning us to appear the next day, to state what we knew before the magistrates. Needless hypocrisy of law! . . . Too superstitious to offend its idol of vested interests, by protecting the poor man against his tyrants, the house-owning shopkeepers under whose greed the dwellings of the poor became nests of filth and pestilence, drunkenness and degradation. Careless, superstitious, imbecile law!—leaving the victims to die unhelped, and then, when the fever and the tyranny has done its work, in thy sanctimonious prudishness, drugging thy respectable conscience by a 'searching inquiry' as to how it all happened—lest, forsooth, there should have been 'foul play!' Is the knife or the bludgeon, then, the only foul play, and not the cesspool and the curse of Rabshakeh?[10] Go through Bermondsey or Spitalfields, St. Giles's or Lambeth, and see if *there* is not foul play enough already—to be tried hereafter at a more awful coroner's inquest than thou thinkest of!

Here Kingsley shelters behind his fictional character to make an apostrophe to the authorities (similar in sense but more outspoken than Hughes's in his *Tract on Christian Socialism*), referring to the Old Testament and echoing its language to assume some of the authority of that vengeful text.

J. Saunders, writing on 'Modern Bermondsey' in Charles Knight's collection of essays on London (op. cit., iii. 20), commented: 'All Londoners have heard of the "Rookery" . . . but far less is known of "Jacob's Island" in Bermondsey, though it has been rendered familiar to many by the most successful of

---

[10] See 2 Kgs. 18:27. Rabshakeh is sent by the King of Assyria with an army to besiege King Hezekiah in Jerusalem. Rabshakeh tries to shake the Jews' trust in their God. When those closest to King Hezekiah, to whom Rabshakeh addresses himself, ask him to speak Syrian because they do not understand the Jewish language of the common soldiers, Rabshakeh replies that these are the people he has come to address, to make them eat their own dung and drink their own urine, aristocrats and soldiers in the same plight together, unless they submit to Assyria.

living novelists.' And he included Dickens's description of the
place in *Oliver Twist* because 'the features which this spot
presents are described so vividly, and with such close accuracy,
that we cannot do better than quote the passage'.

Dickens's Jacob's Island exemplifies the existence of the Other
Nation in London; he emphasizes its superlative strangeness:

Near to that part of the Thames on which the church at Rotherhithe
abuts, where the buildings on the banks are dirtiest and the vessels on the
river blackest with the dust of colliers and the smoke of close-built low-
roofed houses, there exists the filthiest, the strangest, the most extraordinary of the many localities that are hidden in London, wholly unknown,
even by name, to the great mass of its inhabitants. (Ch. 50.)

The place proved to be an even more startling example of the
existence of the Two Nations than Dickens originally imagined.
At the first public meeting, on 6 February 1850, of the Metropolitan Sanitary Association, created to galvanize the authorities
into improving the sanitary condition of London, the Bishop of
London took the chair and made the opening speech, in the
course of which he said that 'a survey had been made of a block
of houses (including what is called Jacob's Island) which was
most severely ravaged by cholera', and pointed out that this
report showed that 'the most important sanitary improvements
might be obtained for these houses for an average rate of 1¾d.
a week' so that reform could not be opposed on the grounds of
expense. Dickens spoke to second the Revd Dr John Cumming's
resolution deploring the number of deaths from preventable
disease in London, and declaring that 'this great sacrifice of
human life is accompanied by an amount of physical degradation and mental depravity, which act as effective barriers to the
inculcation either of social obligations or of Christian virtues'.[11]
During his speech Dickens referred to Jacob's Island 'which he
had described in a work of fiction some ten or eleven years ago,
and where the improvements had been made at a cost of less
than the price of a pint of porter or two glasses of gin a week to
each inhabitant'. Shortly after the meeting the Marylebone
Vestry were engaged in discussing the propriety of using rate-
payers' money to provide any education for the pauper children

[11] For the account of this meeting and its outcome, and the text of Dickens's
speech, see *The Speeches of Charles Dickens*, ed. K. J. Fielding (Oxford, 1960),
pp. 104–10.

of the parish when Sir Peter Laurie, Chairman of the Union Bank, Lord Mayor of London in 1832, and prototype of 'Alderman Cute' in *The Chimes*, opposed such a measure and, to pillory misguided and misinformed reformers, read out a passage about Jacob's Island from the Bishop of London's recent speech. ' "The Bishop of London, poor soul", said Sir Peter, "in his simplicity, thought there really was such a place . . . whereas it turned out that it only existed in a work of fiction, written by Mr. Charles Dickens ten years ago (*roars of laughter*)." ' (*Observer*, 11 February 1850, p. 3, quoted K. J. Fielding, op. cit., p. 109.) The vestry highly approved of this comment. In the words of another member, 'It was all very well to listen to the rubbish of Mr. Charles Dickens who sold his work at a very high price, and got a good living out of it . . . All that was cant and humbug.'

In *Oliver Twist* Dickens describes the district as displaying 'every imaginable sign of desolation and neglect' but unlike Kingsley he does not make overt social comments upon it. Jacob's Island appears in *Oliver Twist* primarily as a suitable setting for Sikes's violent death. People who are desperate seek a hiding-place there: 'They must have powerful motives for a secret residence, or be reduced to a destitute condition indeed, who seek a refuge in Jacob's Island.' He gives far fewer details of the horror of the place than does Kingsley:

It is a creek or inlet from the Thames, and can always be filled at high water by opening the sluices at the Lead Mills from which it took its old name. At such times, a stranger, looking from one of the wooden bridges thrown across it at Mill Lane, will see the inhabitants of the houses on either side lowering from their back doors and windows, buckets, pails, domestic utensils of all kinds, in which to haul the water up; and when his eye is turned from these operations to the houses themselves, his utmost astonishment will be excited by the scene before him. Crazy wooden galleries common to the backs of half-a-dozen houses, with holes from which to look upon the slime beneath; windows, broken and patched, with poles thrust out, on which to dry the linen that is never there; rooms so small, so filthy, so confined, that the air would seem too tainted even for the dirt and squalor they shelter; wooden chambers thrusting themselves out above the mud, and threatening to fall into it—as some have done; dirt-besmeared walls and decaying foundations; every repulsive lineament of poverty, every loathsome indication of filth, rot and garbage; all these ornament the banks of Folly Ditch.

Yet some of the details noticed by the 'stranger's' eye give a sudden revelation of the life of the place lacking in Kingsley's passage, for example, the 'poles thrust out, on which to dry the linen that is never there' in which the comfortable image of drying clothes is rudely cancelled by the two bleak words 'never there'.

But, despite Saunders's praise of its 'accuracy', the 'attraction of repulsion' is very strong in the passage. At this point in the novel Dickens needs a suitable meeting-place for the three thieves who have escaped after Fagin's arrest, and a fitting background for the tableau of Sikes's death, stark and melodramatic as the wood-cut on a broadside ballad describing a sensational murder, such as the valet Courvoisier's murder of his master Lord William Russell in 1840 (see Plate 7). Jacob's Island is perfect for both purposes, particularly as it crowds Sikes's pursuers on the bridges, so that the hunt is intensified, and the packed, jumbled houses provide the 'tiers and tiers of faces in every window'. Also, the place sets a trap for Sikes—' "Give me a rope, a long rope. They're all in front. I may drop into the Folly Ditch, and clear off that way." ' But, 'The water was out, and the ditch a bed of mud.' (Such is the excitement of the action that the reader does not query the speed with which the tide has gone out; Sikes, when he comes to the Island shortly before this, says it is in.[12]) Finally, the Ditch provides the horrible detail of the death of Sikes's dog which springs, falls into the ditch and brains itself.

In *Oliver Twist* Jacob's Island is described as a shameful example of neglect and apathy in a prosperous society, but primarily its effect is sensational and macabre. However, the scene makes its mark partly because it connects with the descriptions, developed throughout the novel, of London's squalid underworld. Such is Dickens's imaginative power that he succeeds in creating a fictional world of criminals, with its recklessness, its insecurity and fear of treachery, and its continual menace to the ordered, prosperous, middle-class world. It is such a world which Edward Gibbon Wakefield documents in his *Householders*

---

[12] Compare Thomas Beames's description: 'This district . . . is insulated by a quadrangular *ditch*; the very figure of the island tells you that such reservoirs must be stagnant; and stagnant they are until moved for a while by the tide, which does not at each rising pour fresh water into them, but which at intervals alone, twice or thrice a week, is sparingly introduced, and checked again when enough is supposed to have been done for purposes of those who are concerned in traffic.' (Op. cit., p. 80.)

in Danger from the Populace (1831)—and presupposes a similar conclusion, that all householders should possess a gun. Kingsley's descriptions, on the other hand, are illustrations of his argument, exempla in his sermon; they are not developed, growing in imaginative significance during the novel. In 1857, when Kingsley's *Poems* appeared, he wrote to his friend Ludlow, who had written a flattering review in the *Leeds Express*:

I know I can put into singing words the plain things I see & feel: but all that faculty which Alexander Smith has—(and nothing else)—& which Shakespeare had more than any man—the power of metaphor & analogue— the instinctive vision of a connexion between all things in heaven & earth, which Poets *must* have, is very weak in me; & therefore I shall never be a great poet. (Quoted R. B. Martin, *The Dust of Combat, a Life of Charles Kingsley*, 1959, p. 216.)

Although the passage calls in doubt Kingsley's literary acumen when he accords the shaping spirit of the imagination to Alexander Smith, it wins our respect for his shrewd self-criticism when he denies such a spirit in his own poetry. For all his observation and feeling, the creative imagination does not shape *Alton Locke* as a whole, whereas in *Oliver Twist*, a shapeless novel compared with later works like *Great Expectations* or *Little Dorrit*, the criminal world, ever present and menacing the prosperous society, gives the novel a certain significant structure, so that the social comment is embodied in the imaginative form rather than expressed in exhortations to the reader.

BARBARIC WODGATE AND SAVAGE COKETOWN

We do not get close enough to the inhabitants of Jacob's Island in *Oliver Twist* to find out what they do to live; the impression is of people who 'won't work', of the type in Rats' Castle in St. Giles's. There is no suggestion of work in the tanneries or in the lead-mill mentioned in Saunders's account; or of the longshoremen or coal-porters mentioned in Mayhew's. In Kingsley's description there is the sort of desperate work which is undertaken to ward off starvation. For both novelists the district is alien and savage, and their descriptions emphasize these qualities. The Other Nation is conceived as a nation of savages, a constant reproach to the apparent civilization of the rest of society.

In the novels under discussion certain types of productive

labour are also described in terms of savagery. In *Sybil*, Disraeli's
town of locksmiths

Wodgate . . . was a district that in old days had been consecrated to
Woden, and which appeared destined through successive ages to retain its
heathen character. At the beginning of the revolutionary war, Wodgate was
a sort of squatting district of the great mining region to which it was contiguous, a place where adventurers in the industry which was rapidly
developing settled themselves; for though the great veins of coal and iron-
stone cropped up, as they phrase it, before they reached this bare and
barren land, and it was thus deficient in those mineral and metallic
treasures which had enriched its neighbourhood, Wodgate had advantages
of its own, and of a kind which touch the fancy of the lawless. It was land
without an owner; no one claimed any manorial right over it; they could
build cottages without paying rent. It was a district recognized by no
parish; so there were no tithes, and no meddlesome supervision. It
abounded in fuel which cost nothing, for though the veins were not worth
working as a source of mining profit, the soil of Wodgate was similar in its
superficial character to that of the country around. So a population
gathered, and rapidly increased, in the ugliest spot in England, to which
neither Nature nor Art had contributed a single charm . . . where there
was neither belfry nor steeple, nor a single sight or sound that could soften
the heart or humanize the mind. (Bk. III, ch. 4.)

These are the multiplying poor, dreaded by Malthus and the
architects of the 1834 Poor Law. The Chartist, Walter Gerard,
in conversation with Egremont, compares them with the invasions of the barbarian hordes in the Dark Ages: ' "What are
your invasions of the barbarous nations, your Goths and Visi-
goths, your Lombards and Huns, to our Population Returns!" '
(Bk. II, ch. 16.) The inhabitants of Wodgate are highly skilled
manufacturers of ironmongery, steel-workers, brass-founders,
nail-makers and lock-smiths; 'that squatters' seat . . . soon
assumed the form of a large village, and then in turn soon ex-
panded into a town, and at the present moment numbers its
population by swarming thousands, lodged in the most miserable tenements in the most hideous burgh in the ugliest country
in the world' (Bk. III, ch. 4).

Disraeli might very well have been inspired by the name Wednesbury, derived from Woden, the Saxon god, for his fictitious
town, Wodgate. Wednesbury is in the heart of the Black
Country, between Wolverhampton and Birmingham, to the
east of Willenhall. He found much of his material for Wodgate
in R. H. Horne's report on children's employment in 'the manufacturing district of Staffordshire and the contiguous counties'

printed in *CEC* II, Appendix 2.[13] Disraeli's main reasons for assigning it to heathendom are lack of churches and of a feudal hierarchy. (There was at the time a firm faith in the power of church-building to counteract the heathendom of the lives of the Other Nation. St. Albans, Holborn, was built as a direct result of the impression made upon Lord Leigh by *Sybil*; see my *Mr. Disraeli's Readers* (University of Nottingham, 1966), pp. 63–5.) Although as I have shown in my study of Disraeli's use of Horne's Report, he bases most of the Wodgate details on fact and is not given to wild exaggeration, he chooses one of the worst areas in the Black Country to make a point in his discussion of the nature of aristocracy, so important to the whole novel:

Here Labour reigns supreme . . . The business of Wodgate is carried on by master workmen in their own houses, each of whom possesses an unlimited number of what they call apprentices . . .

These master workmen indeed form a powerful aristocracy, nor is it possible to conceive one apparently more oppressive. They are ruthless tyrants . . . Yet . . . the aristocracy of Wodgate is by no means so unpopular as the aristocracy of most other places.

In the first place, it is a real aristocracy; it is privileged, but it does something for its privileges . . . It is the most knowing class at Wodgate; it possesses indeed in its way complete knowledge; and it imparts in its manner a certain quantity of it to those whom it guides. Thus it is an aristocracy that leads, and therefore a fact. (Bk. III, ch. 4.)

This aristocracy is in ironic contrast with that of the upper classes in the novel, shown to be effete or self-seeking, or both. Egremont, disgusted with the aristocratic life into which he is born, comes to believe in the true aristocracy which accepts its duties as well as its privileges. Like Kingsley, Disraeli uses his descriptions of the living places of the poor (in this case those who serve these tyrannical masters) to support his argument: that in a 'civilized' society there is intolerable savagery which yet reveals skill and organization shaming the orthodox custodians of order and civilization. Wodgate is of a piece with Seven Dials, it represents descent into nightmare. Morley, inquiring his way to Wodgate, is told by the colliers in the Rising Sun pub, ' "If you want to see divils carnal, there's your time of day. They're no less than heathens, I be sure. I'd be sorry to see

[13] See my essay 'Willenhall and Wodgate: Disraeli's Use of Blue Book Evidence', *Review of English Studies*, 13 (1962), 368–84.

even our butty among them, for he is a sort of Christian when he has taken a glass of ale." ' (Bk. III, ch. 1.) And the place he wants is Hell-house Yard, a name which Disraeli took from Horne's report on Wolverhampton. The reader approaches the place through the experience of the exploring stranger, Morley. Disraeli deploys the facts taken from Horne's report, mostly from Willenhall, Wolverhampton and Sedgley, to give a generalized scene of unrelieved squalor and destitution:

As you advanced, leaving behind you long lines of little dingy tenements, with infants lying about the road, you expected every moment to emerge into some streets, and encounter buildings bearing some correspondence, in their size and comfort, to the considerable population swarming and busied around you. Nothing of the kind. There were no public buildings of any sort; no churches, chapels, town-hall, institute, theatre; and the principal streets in the heart of the town in which were situate the coarse and grimy shops, though formed by houses of a greater elevation than the preceding, were equally narrow, and if possible more dirty. At every fourth or fifth house, alleys seldom above a yard wide, and streaming with filth, opened out of the street. These were crowded with dwellings of various size, while from the principal court often branched out a number of smaller alleys, or rather narrow passages, than which nothing can be conceived more close and squalid and obscure. Here, during the days of business, the sound of the hammer and the file never ceased, amid gutters of abomination, and piles of foulness, and stagnant pools of filth; reservoirs of leprosy and plague, whose exhalations were sufficient to taint the atmosphere of the whole kingdom, and fill the country with fever and pestilence. (Bk. III, ch. 4.)

Most of these details can be found in Horne's report. Disraeli compresses them into one short passage to create a horrific, barbarous image. He also deprives the place of church and chapel, although Horne says of Willenhall 'There is one Sunday-school in connexion with the Church, one with the Wesleyans, one with the Baptists, and one with the Primitive Methodists' (*CEC*, II, Appendix 2, P.P. Session 1843 (XV), 611), implying the presence of the Church of England and the three chapels. Moreover, he ignores Horne's comment that 'amidst all this degradation and filth . . . it very frequently happens that the inside of the poorest houses is perfectly clean. If the clothing of the women be mere rags, they keep them clean. It is frequently the same with regard to their children at home who are too young to work; they, also, are as clean as children could be kept in such circumstances.' (Ibid., p. 600.)

As a descriptive passage Disraeli's gives the reader information, with a particular purpose in view, rather than providing him with the kind of sensuous detail which will allow him to recreate for himself the experience of the locality. Incidentally, it provides a good example of a verifiable fact appearing with comic and unconvincing effect because it has not been digested and re-created as fiction, but simply added to the scene: 'infants lying about the road' is justified by Horne's description of the Wolver-hampton children, 'In summer they play and sleep in the dirt' (ibid., p. 573), but the incongruity of the language Disraeli uses suggests absence of mind on the part of the parents rather than destitution!

The same implications of savagery are in Disraeli's description of the Mowbray (Manchester) life which produced Devilsdust (Bk. II, ch. 10), a term given to the cotton-waste[14] which provides his earliest employment at the age of five, and prevents him from starving, and in the comments on 'the subterraneous nation of cellars' in Mowbray (Bk. II, ch. 9), although the sub-human implications of this phrase are somewhat mitigated by the street-market scene which follows. Unlike Kingsley's description of Clare Market, this is a cheerful scene, despite the poverty of the shoppers, as is the later scene in the Temple of the Muses (Bk. II, ch. 10) where the factory workers go to enjoy them-selves.[15]

The heathen, savage quality of working-class life is given its antidote in the account of Trafford's model village and the amenities he provides for those who work at his mill. (Bk. III, ch. 8.) Like the worsted spinners Hindes and Derham at Dol-phinholme, near Lancaster, Trafford organized a community

[14] Another name for it was shoddy. In the series 'Labour and the Poor' the letter on 'The Cloth Districts of Yorkshire' (the *Morning Chronicle*, 3 Dec. 1849) remarks that 'an essential feature' of the cotton town Oldham 'is the spinning and preparing of waste and refuse cotton', that is, Devilsdust's earliest paid work. He worked in the 'wadding-hole'. Wadding was a loose fibrous material used for padding and made from cotton waste. The letter continues: 'To this stuff the name of shoddy is given, but the real and orthodox shoddy is a production of the woollen districts, and con-sists of the second-hand wool manufactured by the tearing up, or rather the grinding, of woollen rags by means of coarse willows, called devils; the operation of which sends forth choking clouds of dry pungent dirt and floating fibres—the real and origi-nal "devil's dust".'

[15] Almost certainly based on the music-saloon the Apollo, in the London-road, Manchester, later described by Angus Bethune Reach in the *Morning Chronicle* 8 Nov. 1849, reprinted in *Manchester and the Textile Districts in 1849*, ed. C. Aspin (Helm-shore Local History Society, 1972), pp. 57-9.

around his mill.[16] Leonard Horner, the factory inspector, wrote of Hindes and Derham in 1838:

The mill is surrounded by the cottages of the workpeople, and they form quite a community of themselves . . . The moral conditions of the people is a great object of attention with the proprietors; they pay eighty pounds a year to a clergyman, have built a chapel and school-house and maintain a schoolmaster. From all I hear, it is a most virtuous and happy little colony. (Quoted C. Aspin, *Lancashire, the First Industrial Society* (Helmshore Local History Society, 1969), pp. 133 f.)

Disraeli approves of Trafford's village because it reasserts the feudal principle in a new form, replacing the anarchy of the 'heathen' Hell-house Yard, chaotic despite the despotism of the aristocracy of labour. Trafford's own house is in the village, in the same way that Mr Arrowsmith's cottage is among those provided for his workers near his mill on the outskirts of Bolton (see C. Aspin, *Manchester and the Textile Districts in 1849*, p. 69). Disraeli writes, 'Trafford . . . comprehended his position too well to withdraw himself with vulgar exclusiveness from his real dependents, but recognised the baronial principle, reviving in a new form, and adapted to the softer manners and more ingenious circumstances of the times.' (Bk. III, ch. 8.) And Sybil in this community is greeted as 'queen'. But it is characteristic of Disraeli's intelligence that he has Caroline tell Mrs Carey that she left Trafford's mill because it was dull in the country and she wanted company, and that she found the insistence on schooling wearisome, ' "And those Traffords had so many schools." ' (Bk. II, ch. 9.) However, her opinion is not given much weight, and it comes long before the glowing account of Trafford's mill, so it does not detract from his glory.

Discussing Disraeli's use of ideas in his fiction, Raymond Williams considers *Hard Times* 'nearer to the methods of Disraeli than any other Dickens novel' ('Dickens and Social Ideas', *Dickens 1970*, ed. M. Slater, 1970, p. 85). *Hard Times* is a novel apart from the rest of Dickens's work because it most obviously advances an argument against the Utilitarians and because in it he makes one of his rare excursions outside London to describe

[16] See also the description of Marshall's flax works at Leeds, described by Fanny Mayne, journalist and novelist: 'We cannot leave the works of Messrs. Marshall, without a word for the well-regulated schools, all conducted at the expense of the proprietors; the neat—more than neat—beautiful church also erected by them; the garden allotments for their work-people, the library and reading-rooms.' ('What I Saw and Heard in the Manufacturing Districts', the *True Briton*, 2 (1853), 257.)

an industrial town. In *The Old Curiosity Shop* (1840) Little Nell and her grandfather pass through part of the Black Country where they encounter 'the clustered roofs, and piles of buildings, trembling with the working of engines, and dimly resounding with their shrieks and throbbings; the tall chimneys vomiting forth a black vapour, which hung in a dense ill-favoured cloud above the housetops and filled the air with gloom; the clank of hammers beating upon iron, the roar of busy streets and noisy crowds' (Ch. 43), and the reader sees darkness fall with the eyes of the terrified child, who has never seen sights like these: 'night, when the smoke was changed to fire; when every chimney spirted up its flame; and places, that had been dark vaults all day, now shone red-hot, with figures moving to and fro within their blazing jaws, and calling to one another with hoarse cries—night, when the noise of every strange machine was aggravated by the darkness; when the people near them looked wilder and more savage' (Ch. 45).

This is a nineteenth-century version of the medieval Hell-mouth, and the literary equivalent to earlier paintings of the new industrial scene, such as 'Coalbrookdale by Night', 1801, by Philip de Loutherbourg, or 'Bedlam Furnace', 1803, by Paul Munn, Nos. 133 and 270 in 'Landscape in Britain c.1750–1850', Tate Gallery 1973 (see Plates 8 and 9). Like Dickens's descriptions of St. Giles's, these lurid scenes are also in the picturesque tradition—in this case, the industrial landscape assimilated into this tradition. Disraeli, in *Coningsby*, describes Manchester in the same way, 'dingy as the entrance of Hades, and flaming with furnaces' (Bk. IV, ch. 1). Marcus comments on the habitual 'association of the early industrial world with the classical infernal regions' (op. cit., p. 39)—even Sub-Commissioners used the image (see above, p. 26)—but does not connect the usage with an established pictorial tradition. As in the treatment of Seven Dials, the picturesque mode protected the spectator from the realities of the scene. See Kovačević on Harriet Martineau's evasion of details of slums and belching smoke in Birmingham and her comments, during a visit to that city in 1851, that 'a full but picturesque account of manufactures [*sic*] and other productive processes might be valuable both for instruction and entertainment' (*Fact into Fiction*, p. 219).

Nell and her grandfather are befriended by one of the savages of the place—'a black figure . . . the form was that of a man, miserably clad and begrimed with smoke . . .'—but a noble savage: 'His voice was harsh by nature, but not brutal; and though his face . . . was overshadowed by a quantity of long dark hair, its expression was neither ferocious nor bad.' (Ch. 44.) He lets them sleep near the furnace fire he tends and, like the Noble Savage who protects Serena in *The Faerie Queene* (VI. iv–vi), sees that they come to no harm in this rude country.

There is another brief glimpse of 'the iron country farther north' in *Bleak House* (1853), published the year before *Hard Times*, when trooper George goes to be reconciled with his brother, the ironmaster. Again, the scene is described through a stranger's eyes: 'As he comes into the iron country farther north, such fresh green woods as those of Chesney Wold are left behind; and coalpits and ashes, high chimneys and red bricks, blighted verdure, scorching fires, and a heavy never-lightening cloud of smoke, become the features of the scenery.' (Ch. 63.) Everything assaults his senses, and what he sees is distorted:

a great perplexity of iron lying about, in every stage, and in a vast variety of shapes; in bars, in wedges, in sheets; in tanks, in boilers, in axles, in wheels, in cogs, in cranks, in rails; twisted and wrenched into eccentric and perverse forms, as separate parts of machinery; mountains of it broken up, and rusty in its age; distant furnaces of it glowing and bubbling in its youth; bright fireworks of it showering about, under the blows of the steam-hammer; red-hot iron, white-hot iron, cold-black iron; an iron taste, an iron smell, and a Babel of iron sounds. (Ch. 63.)

But this is little more than a backdrop to George's family business and a reinforcement of the staunch, practical character of the ironmaster, hitherto in the novel seen away from his own territory. *Hard Times* is the only novel in which Dickens makes an industrial town of central importance. He calls it the 'key-note' of the novel. Coketown is described as 'a great town' and Mr Gradgrind, who had been in 'the wholesale hardware trade', lives in a great house on a moor a mile or two away from it (*Hard Times*, Bk. I, ch. 3). Stephen Blackpool is 'a good power-loom weaver' (Bk. I, ch. 10). Although Mr Gradgrind made hardware, Coketown is a place where most of the factories produce cloth: 'Time went on in Coketown like its own machinery: so much material wrought up, so much fuel consumed . . . so much money made.' (Bk. I, ch. 14.) The type of material is not specified, but as the work-people are sometimes described as being covered in fluff (see Bk. II, ch. 1) it is presumably cotton (confirmed by Dickens's letter, see below). The town is sur- rounded by coal-pits, both used and disused (Stephen falls down a disused shaft), and the railway travels across this country on a viaduct (see the description of Bounderby's country retreat, Bk. II, ch. 7). When Sissy and Rachael go for their country walk, before they discover Stephen, they are a few miles away from Coketown and can see rising hills in one direction and in another 'there was a faint change in the light of the horizon where it shone upon the far-off sea' (Bk. III, ch. 6). All this suggests Preston, which Dickens visited in January 1854 when the town was in the throes of the 1853–4 cotton-mill strike which he wrote up for *Household Words* ('On Strike', 8 (1854), 553–9), or a mixture of Preston and Manchester, rather than Hanley, Staffs., which Bernard Shaw, in characteristic dogmatic fashion, insists, in his preface to the novel, is the real name of Coketown, but without giving any reasons. On 11 March 1854 Dickens himself rebuked Peter Cunningham for suggesting in the *Illus- trated London News* that Coketown is Preston,[17] and insisted that he had thought of the title before he visited the cotton town (Forster's *Life* substantiates this); such a statement 'localizes . . . a story which has a direct purpose in reference to the working people all over England, and it will cause, as I know by former experience, characters to be fitted on to individuals whom I never saw or heard of in my life' (Nonesuch *Letters*, ii. 545).

Some years later he wrote to the actor Fechter after having read Boucicault's play *A Long Strike* based on *Mary Barton*, 'Might it not ease the way with the Lord Chamberlain's Office, and still more with the audience, when there are Manchester champions in it, if instead of 'Manchester' you used a fictitious name? When I did Hard Times I called the scene Coketown. Everybody knew what was meant, but every cotton-spinning town said it was the other cotton-spinning town.' (4 September 1866, ibid., iii. 483.) Obviously, Coketown is not meant to be an accurate physical description of a particular town, but a

---

[17] 'The title of Mr. Dickens's new work is "Hard Times." His recent inquiry into the Preston strike is said to have originated the title, and, in some respects, suggested the turn of the story.' ('Town and Table-Talk on Literature, Art, etc.', the *Illustrated London News*, 24 (1854), 194.)

typical mill-town of the 1850s with enough reference to Preston to give a spice of contemporaneity but not enough to run the risk of a libel action. The long, bitter strike at Preston was a stage in the battle to establish the workmen's right to combine in Trades Unions. G. D. H. Cole and A. W. Filson write:

This was by far the biggest industrial struggle in the cotton trade since the general 'turn-out' of 1842. It affected both spinners and weavers, and was part of a general struggle which extended over a large part of the cotton area. The Unions had been endeavouring to secure a rise in wages, which had been heavily cut in the depression of 1847, and had been supporting strikers at firms paying bad wages out of the funds of their Unions. The employers retorted with a general lock-out, refusing to re-employ workers unless they renounced Trade Union membership. They also launched prosecutions against the Union leaders, whose arrest helped to break the strike—the charges being subsequently abandoned. Funds in aid of the Preston workers were raised in many places, including London, by specially constituted Trades' Committees. (*British Working Class Movements. Select Documents 1789–1875*, 1951, p. 483.)

So, as David Craig shows in his introduction to the Penguin edition of *Hard Times* (1969), Coketown suggests a factory town in an area which saw the beginning of industrialization in England and, more particularly, a town long associated with radicalism and, at the time that the novel was being written, engaged in a bitter struggle which had national implications.

It was also, for Dickens, a symbol of the Two Nations and of the desperate need to bridge the gulf between them. Like Ruskin, Dickens felt that the factory system degraded the operatives to 'hands', depriving them of individuality. In 'The Nature of Gothic' Ruskin argued that, despite the growing humanitarian feeling of the 1840s, the split between the Two Nations was wider than ever because the operative was degraded into a machine by the work he had to do, and so he lost all pleasure in it:

Never had the upper classes so much sympathy with the lower, or charity for them, as they have at this day, and yet never were they so much hated by them: for, of old, the separation between the noble and the poor was merely a wall built by law; now it is a veritable difference in level of standing, a precipice between upper and lower grounds in the field of humanity, and there is pestilential air at the bottom of it. (*The Stones of Venice*, ii, *Works*, x. 194.)

Dickens sounds the same note of warning in *American Notes* (1842) when, describing the well-organized factories at Lowell, U.S.A., where the factory girls enjoy music, reading, and creative writing, and are treated as people, he exhorts his readers 'to pause and reflect upon the difference between this town and those great haunts of desperate misery [the English factory towns]: to call to mind . . . the efforts that must be made to purge them of their suffering and danger: and last, and foremost, to remember how the precious Time is rushing by' (ch. 4).

When describing Lowell he forestalls the inevitable English reaction that the American factory girls are aspiring 'above their station':

In reply to that objection, I would beg to ask what their station is.

It is their station to work. And they *do* work. They labour in these mills, upon an average, twelve hours a day, which is unquestionably work, and pretty tight work too. Perhaps it is above their station to indulge in such amusements, on any terms. Are we quite sure that we in England have not formed our ideas of the 'station' of working people, from accustoming ourselves to the contemplation of that class as they are, and not as they might be?

For Dickens, the scandal was that the Other Nation was not only poor in worldly goods but, inevitably because of the conditions in which they lived, poor in spirit. He had been horrified by the Manchester cotton-mills on his first hasty visit in 1838; he had warmly supported Lord Ashley in his fight for better working conditions for both adults and children in the factories. As Edgar Johnson points out, the factory system, for Dickens, consisted of the exploiters and the exploited and was characteristic of the evils of contemporary industrialized society (see *Charles Dickens, His Tragedy and Triumph*, 2 vols., Boston and Toronto, 1952, ii. 794-5). On receiving a copy of Ashley's speech moving the Children's Employment Commission he wrote to Southwood Smith, one of the Commissioners, that he 'could not forbear . . . cursing the present system and its fatal effects in keeping down thousands upon thousands of God's images' (15 December 1840, Pilgrim *Letters*, ii. 165). And in *Household Words*, April 1854, the same month in which *Hard Times* began its serialization in that journal, appeared John Morley's horrifying article 'Ground in the Mill' attacking those mill-owners who defied the law and saved the expense of fencing dangerous machinery regardless of their workpeople's hazards.

The first metaphor Dickens uses to describe Coketown is that of a savage. 'It was a town of red brick, or of brick that would have been red if the smoke and ashes had allowed it; but as matters stood it was a town of unnatural red and black like the painted face of a savage.' (Bk. I, ch. 5.) The metaphor is not repeated, although the novel is punctuated by evocations of the town, but it establishes the pervasive red-brick and coal-dust of the place, and the associated images 'serpents of smoke' and 'the head of an elephant in a state of melancholy madness', the steam-engine's piston going up and down, are images of the jungle which continue the idea of savagery.

Six months before he began *Hard Times* Dickens published an essay, 'The Noble Savage', in *Household Words* (7 (1853), 337-9). It makes startling reading. Dickens is always an emotional writer; that is his strength and his weakness. But in this essay he writes with uncontrolled hysteria.

I consider him a prodigious nuisance, and an enormous superstition. His calling rum fire-water, and me a pale face, wholly fail to reconcile me to him. I don't care what he calls me. I call him a savage, and I call a savage a something highly desirable to be civilised off the face of the earth. I think a mere gent (which I take to be the lowest form of civilisation) better than a howling, whistling, clucking, stamping, jumping, tearing savage. It is all one to me, whether he sticks a fish-bone through his visage, or bits of trees through the lobes of his ears, or bird's feathers in his head; whether he flattens his hair between two boards, or spreads his nose over the breadth of his face, or drags his lower lip down by great weights, or blackens his teeth, or knocks them out, or paints one cheek red and the other blue, or tattoos himself, or oils himself, or rubs his body with fat, or crimps it with knives. Yielding to whichsoever of these agreeable eccentricities, he is a savage—cruel, false, thievish, murderous; addicted more or less to grease, entrails, and beastly customs; a wild animal with the questionable gift of boasting; a conceited, tiresome, bloodthirsty, monotonous humbug.

He is indignant that anyone should suggest that there is anything to regret in the passing of the savage's way of life or that it reveals any 'blemishes' in civilization, and indulges in sadistic fantasies when he thinks of the Bushmen who have been exhibited in England: 'I have never seen that group sleeping, smoking, and expectorating round their brazier, but I have sincerely desired that something might happen to the charcoal smouldering therein, which would cause the immediate suffocation of the whole of the noble strangers.'

To say that this complacent prejudice is of the period is not to deny its danger, or its hindrance to rational thought or imaginative sympathy. Dickens's essay has the same kind of narrow-minded arrogance as Carlyle's 'The Negro Question' (later, 'The Nigger Question') which had appeared nearly four years earlier in *Fraser's Magazine*; and it might well be that his friendship with, and admiration for, Carlyle encouraged him in this reactionary attitude, which contrasts so sharply with his admiration for the Red Indian chieftain whom he met on his first visit to America (see *American Notes*, ch. 12) 'as stately and complete a gentleman of Nature's making, as ever I beheld' who showed up some of the deficiencies of 'civilized' society. Certainly Carlyle influenced him to join the defenders of Eyre, Governor of Jamaica, who in 1865 put down a negro rebellion with great severity. Overtly, Dickens's description of Coketown as a savage's face is an image of sympathy for the people who live there. The savage is uncivilized, murderous; the work-people are subjected to a life which destroys them. But to describe their place of living and working in such terms insidiously associates them with the ideas evoked by these images. As G. D. Carnall has pointed out ('Dickens, Mrs Gaskell and the Preston Strike', *Victorian Studies*, 8 (1964), 31–48) it contrasts strongly with Dickens's description of the sober, rational behaviour of the Preston cotton operatives in the essay 'On Strike'. The arresting image in the fiction parts company with the actuality rather than illuminates it. To describe the Other Nation as savages, or their life as associated with savagery, as Disraeli, Kingsley, and Dickens, in their different ways, do, creates a curiosity that distances these people, emphasizes their strangeness and separateness. Dickens's simple, crude reaction to the industrial towns can be seen in the ways he repeats, in *The Old Curiosity Shop*, *Bleak House*, and *Hard Times*, the three facts of smoke, flame, and sounding machinery. The repetition indicates his limited imaginative reaction to the region. He never gets beyond the state of simple, physical distaste. It is revealing that he uses the metaphor of the savage to describe Coketown because the simple distaste he feels for the savage is his basic reaction to the industrial town and the people who live there. He wrote to John Forster from Preston, 29 January 1854, 'I am afraid I shall not be able to get much here. Except the crowds at the street-corners reading the placards pro and con; and the cold absence of smoke from the mill-chimneys; there is very little in the streets to make the town remarkable . . . . It is a nasty place (I thought it was a model town).' (Nonesuch *Letters*, ii. 538.)

And in 1867, during his readings, he wrote to Mary Angela Dickens from Leeds, 'This is a beastly place, with a very good hotel. Except Preston, it is one of the nastiest places I know.' (Nonesuch *Letters*, iii. 506.) I am not arguing that Dickens should have liked either Preston or Leeds. My point is that prejudiced physical distaste is not likely to produce the empathy needed to recreate the essential life of a place, 'truth to' the cotton town.

But Stephen Blackpool is to be seen not as a savage but as a poor, decent, ordinary man whose great sorrow is his drunken wife and whose idea of greatest happiness is marriage with Rachael, the work-girl who is loving, compassionate, moral, and domestic. The description of Stephen's lodging is completely different in kind from the metaphoric, symbolic description of Coketown:

His home, in such another street as the first, saving that it was narrower, was over a little shop. How it came to pass that any people found it worth their while to sell or buy the wretched little toys, mixed up in its window with cheap newspapers and pork (there was a leg to be raffled for to-morrow night), matters not here. He took his end of candle from the shelf, lighted it at another end of candle on the counter, without disturbing the mistress of the shop who was asleep in her little room, and went upstairs into his lodging.

It was a room, not unacquainted with the black ladder [the under-taker's ladder for getting the coffin out of the window of houses where the stairs were narrow] under various tenants; but as neat, at present, as such a room could be. A few books and writings were on an old bureau in a corner, the furniture was decent and sufficient, and, though the atmosphere was tainted, the room was clean. (Bk. I, ch. 10.)

The muddle in the shop window is not exuberant, as in the Seven Dials description in *Boz*, but dreary, and, far from being dwelt on with delighted humour, 'matters not here'. There are few details to help the reader particularize the scene, which is general, neutral and, compared with descriptions of Bounderby's house or Gradgrind's, dull. But the description extends the panoramic view of Coketown—'It contained several large streets all very like one another, and many small streets still more like one another, inhabited by people equally like one another, who all went in and out at the same hours, with the same sound upon the same pavements, to do the same work' (Bk. I, ch. 5)—with its suggestion of routine, to the more personal routine of an individual character. The monotony of Coketown's lay-out embodies the spiritual vacuity of the operatives' lives. Stephen's lodging implies a way of life as neither Bounderby's house nor Gradgrind's does. But this is one of the very few passages in the novel describing the pattern of the weaver's personal, ordinary existence and it exists uneasily with the exuberant imaginative passages associating the red and black of Coketown with a savage's war-paint or conceiving Mr Bounderby's dwelling as an extension of his personality—'a red house with black outside shutters, green inside blinds, a black street door, up two white steps, BOUNDERBY (in letters very like himself) upon a brazen plate, and a round brazen door-handle underneath it, like a brazen full-stop' (Bk. I, ch. 11). This ironic writing is the staple of *Hard Times*; the attempt to see Stephen 'straight', as demonstrated by the description of his lodging, deliberately protects him from Dickens's invigorating wit, and, while this suggests Dickens's seriousness of purpose and his fear of misrepresenting Stephen's life, it makes his image of the man solemn, not serious, and diminishes him. The metaphysical description of Bounderby, in its intensity, implies the essence of the character. The neutral description of Stephen suggests that he has no essence, no arresting characteristic. Ironically, Dickens, like Bounderby, suggests that he is a 'hand'. His exceptional, protective treatment of Stephen implies condescension rather than understanding.

MANCHESTER'S POOR, AS SEEN BY ELIZABETH GASKELL

Asa Briggs has described Manchester as 'the shock city' of the 1840s, forcing 'to the surface problems of "class", of the relations between rich and poor'. He comments, 'It was just as difficult to be neutral about it as it was to be neutral about Chicago in the 1890s or Los Angeles in the 1930s.' (*Victorian Cities*, 1963, pp. 92–3.) Elizabeth Gaskell came to live in Manchester when she was twenty-two, the bride of a Unitarian Minister. *Mary Barton* is her fictional picture of the 'shock city', split into the Two Nations. Neutrality is a poor quality for a novelist, and in her depiction of Manchester Elizabeth Gaskell is not neutral; but she is level-headed. She is particularly successful in suggesting the routine of the Other Nation's life, its process. When, in *North and South* (1855), her second Manchester novel,

written to give a fair picture of the mill-owners, she uses the
familiar device of a stranger reporting his experience of an industrialized society and describes Margaret Hale's reaction to
Heston, the sea-side place near Milton (Manchester), the details
given are more telling than those noted by Little Nell or George
in Dickens's Black Country, or the sights assailing Morley as he
seeks out Hell-house Yard, because they express a credible
routine of lives in their entirety, not the more spectacular evidence of work at an unfamiliar trade:

> everything looked more 'purpose-like.' The country carts had more iron,
> and less wood and leather about the horse-gear; the people in the streets,
> although on pleasure bent, had yet a busy mind. The colours looked greyer
> —more enduring, not so gay and pretty. There were no smock-frocks, even
> among the country-folk; they retarded motion, and were apt to catch on
> machinery, and so the habit of wearing them had died out . . . the shop-
> men . . . if they had any leisure from customers . . . made themselves busi-
> ness in the shop—even, Margaret fancied, to the unnecessary unrolling and
> re-rolling of ribbons. (Ch. 7.)

The added dimension comes from the sense of life continually
going on and shaping the appearances which can be caught at
one particular moment; it is typical that we are told how the
shopmen occupy themselves when they are not actually selling.
It could be also argued, as does John Lucas (*Tradition and
Tolerance in Nineteenth-Century Fiction*, 1966, pp. 192–3) that
Elizabeth Gaskell's interest in evoking the life of the new industrial areas sometimes subdues her interest in creating character;
the reasons for the absence of smock-frocks come from her consciousness rather than Margaret's; although it is possible to
accept that the passage denotes Margaret's lively reactions to
the landscape—she has been asking intelligent questions during
the journey, in contrast to her mother's despairing passivity.

In *Mary Barton* no observant stranger leads the enquiring
reader into Manchester life. The novel begins with a group of
work-people walking in the fields which are still close to Manchester and follows them to their homes. Despite its melodramatic plot, this immediate contact with the physical facts, ordinary
routine and custom of the lives of the work-people in the
greater part of the novel is the source of its strength. And, although in her brief description of Liverpool, where Mary goes
to try to prevent Will Wilson from sailing before he has given his
vital evidence in Jem's trial, she succeeds in differentiating, as

few Victorian novelists do, between the kinds of Victorian cities, suggesting that the great seaport is different in appearance and nourishes a different kind of labour from that of the manufacturing city, her vision is centred on Manchester. She succeeds in her object 'to really SEE the scenes I tried to describe' because her sympathetic understanding directs her choice of details to recreate for the reader the process of that life. And so she produces 'a room that looks something like a room', to use Strindberg's words, not the 'flaming volcanoes' of Dickens's and Doré's Seven Dials, or Disraeli's Wodgate, or Kingsley's Jacob's Island. She discerns the interest of Mrs Barton's 'house-place' without making for it the apology of the picturesque:

The room was tolerably large, and possessed many conveniences. On the right of the door, as you entered, was a longish window, with a broad ledge. On each side of this, hung blue-and-white check curtains, which were now drawn, to shut in the friends met to enjoy themselves. Two geraniums, unpruned and leafy, which stood on the sill, formed a further defence from out-door pryers. In the corner between the window and the fireplace was a cupboard, apparently full of plates and dishes, cups and saucers, and some more nondescript articles, for which one would have fancied their possessors could find no use—such as triangular pieces of glass to save carving knives and forks from dirtying table-cloths. However, it was evident Mrs. Barton was proud of her crockery and glass, for she left her cupboard door open, with a glance round of satisfaction and pleasure. On the opposite side to the door and window was the staircase, and two doors; one of which (the nearest to the fire) led into a sort of little back kitchen, where dirty work, such as washing up dishes, might be done, and whose shelves served as larder, and pantry, and store-room, and all. The other door, which was considerably lower, opened into the coal-hole—the slanting closet under the stairs; from which, to the fire-place, there was a gay-coloured piece of oil-cloth laid. The place seemed almost crammed with furniture (sure sign of good times among the mills). Beneath the window was a dresser, with three deep drawers. Opposite the fire-place was a table, which I should call a Pembroke,[18] only that it was made of deal, and I cannot tell how far such a name may be applied to such humble material. On it, resting against the wall, was a bright green japanned tea-tray, having a couple of scarlet lovers embracing in the middle. The fire-light danced merrily on this, and really (setting all taste but that of a child's aside) it gave a richness of colouring to that side of the room. It was in some measure propped up by a crimson tea-caddy, also of japan ware. A round

---

[18] Small four-legged table with two folding flaps. See the mention of 'a rather handsome mahogany Pembroke' in the description of one 'of the better class houses in Hulme' in the third letter on Manchester in the series 'Labour and the Poor', the *Morning Chronicle*, 25 Oct. 1849.

table on one branching leg, ready for use, stood in the corresponding
corner to the cupboard; and, if you can picture all this, with a washy, but
clean stencilled pattern on the walls, you can form some idea of John
Barton's home. (Ch. 2.)

Elizabeth Gaskell rarely 'brings on' the poor as exhibits or
exempla as Kingsley, Disraeli, Reade, and Dickens often do. She
establishes herself as the curious visitor but sympathetic, familiar with the scene, not the bewildered, assaulted stranger in
Coketown, or Kingsley's hero appalled at his first sight of Bermondsey; and she acts as mediator with her reader—'if you can
picture all this'. She maintains this relationship with the Other
Nation throughout the novel. Here she implies a routine of hospitality at a time when wages are good, and of care for the
home in which Mrs Barton delights to entertain her friends.
Details suggest how life is lived day by day—washing-up is done
in the little back kitchen, where Mrs Barton stores her food; the
oil-cloth implies a habit of passing backward and forward from
the closet to put coal on the fire. The wider routine of life as a
factory hand is also suggested, its underlying insecurity. The
many pieces of furniture show that times are good; it will have
to be sold when wages fail. These people are well acquainted
with poverty, but not always poor. The comfortable quality of
pleasure in ordinary things, the reassuring solidity of life's common routine, are set against the possibility of desolation when
the routine is broken and the familiar objects disappear. There
are two hints of condescension in the passage quoted above, surprise that Mrs Barton should have owned a device for keeping
carving cutlery off the tablecloth, with the suggestion that such
refined behaviour is remarkable in this context, and the patronizing remark that the taste for gay colours is childish although
appropriate; but Elizabeth Gaskell is remarkable for the respect
she gives to a routine of life which is not her own.

A further distinguishing characteristic in her depiction of the
lives of the poor is her use of local names. Kingsley in *Alton
Locke* also uses the names of real places, Battersea, Bermondsey,
Covent Garden; Alton as a child envisages *Pilgrim's Progress* in
terms of London: 'the Wicket of the Way of Life I had strangely
identified with the turnpike at Battersea-bridge end; and the
rising ground of Mortlake and Wimbledon was the Land of
Beulah—the Enchanted Mountains of the Shepherds' (vol. i,

ch. 1, 'A Poet's Childhood'). Alton begins work as a tailor at
'Mr. Smith's shop, in a street off Piccadilly' (vol. i, ch. 2, 'The
Tailor's Workroom'). When he prevents Jemmy Downes from
flinging himself off Waterloo Bridge the desperate man drags
him 'off towards the Surrey side' and turns 'down Stamford-
street' (vol. ii, ch. 14, 'The Lowest Deep'). Then he dashes
'across the broad, roaring thoroughfare of Bridge-street, and,
hurrying almost at a run down Tooley-street', plunges 'into
the wildernesses of Bermondsey'. But, despite these detailed
references, they give a strange impression of being detached
from the characters who are supposedly acting out their lives in
these localities. *Mary Barton* is remarkable for the particularity
of its references to localities in Manchester, so that not only is it
possible to chart the main characters' addresses on a contemporary map of the city, and their movements during the
action, but the references arise from the accustomed lives of the
characters and reinforce the sense of day-to-day existence in the
descriptions of working-class domestic interiors. John Barton's
house is not far from Green Heys Fields; Alice Barton lives in a
cellar 'under 14, Barber Street'. But the fields near Manchester
are 'well known to the inhabitants as "Green Heys Fields" ',
and she is 'our Alice', in Alice's brother's words, and in John
Barton's 'she lives just right round the corner'. This kind of
reference, often given in the characters' Manchester idiom,
establishes the reality of the city as the workpeople's home in
the way that Alton's neutral speech and the more generalized
references of Kingsley's novel fail to do. Elizabeth Gaskell uses
this very old narrative technique as traditional storytellers still
do, to establish verisimilitude and a familiar relationship with
the hearer to convince him of the narrative's actuality. When
recording storytellers in Shetland I noticed that many name
the places where marvellous or exciting events occurred; for
example, one describing a miraculous escape from shipwreck
said 'And the boy climbed up the cliff just where the Post
Office is now, maybe you saw it as you came along.' Because
the hearer can see the place where the event happened his
imagination is given the aid of verifiable actuality in recreating
the marvellous event.

In 1859, when Elizabeth Gaskell was an established novelist,
she wrote to her daughter Marianne some advice on novel-writing

which was to be passed on to Herbert Grey, whose novel *The Three Paths* had just been published:

I think you must observe what is *out* of you, instead of examining what is *in* you . . . certainly—whether introspection be morbid or not,—it is not \a/ safe {for a nov} training for a novelist. It is a weakening of the art which has crept in of late years. Just read a few pages of De Foe &c—and you will see the healthy way in which he sets *objects* not *feelings* before you. I am sure the right way is this. (After 15 March 1859, Gaskell, *Letters*, p. 541.)

Objective description, which nevertheless implies emotion, is the staple of *Mary Barton*; very different from the densely metaphoric style of most of *Hard Times*, or the shrill insistence of *Alton Locke*, or Disraeli's witty rhetoric in *Sybil*, or Reade's hectoring tone in *It is Never Too Late to Mend*. For example, she gives her readers information about the notorious Manchester cellars when John Barton and Wilson go to try to help Davenport, who has no work and is ill of typhoid. His home is in Berry Street, off Store Street. Berry Street

was unpaved; and down the middle a gutter forced its way, every now and then forming pools in the holes with which the street abounded . . . As they passed, women from their doors tossed household slops of *every* description into the gutter; they ran into the next pool, which overflowed and stagnated. Heaps of ashes were the stepping-stones, on which the passer-by, who cared in the least for cleanliness, took care not to put his foot. Our friends were not dainty, but even they picked their way till they got to some steps leading down into a small area, where a person standing would have his head about one foot below the level of the street, and might at the same time, without the least motion of his body, touch the window of the cellar and the damp muddy wall right opposite. You went down one step even from the foul area into the cellar in which a family of human beings lived. It was very dark inside. The window-panes were many of them broken and stuffed with rags, which was reason enough for the dusky light that pervaded the place even at mid-day. After the account I have given of the state of the street, no one can be surprised that on going into the cellar inhabited by Davenport, the smell was so foetid as almost to knock the two men down. Quickly recovering themselves, as those inured to such things do, they began to penetrate the thick darkness of the place, and to see three or four little children rolling on the damp, nay wet, brick floor, through which the stagnant, filthy moisture of the street oozed up; the fire-place was empty and black; the wife sat on her husband's chair, and cried in the dank loneliness. (Ch. 6.)

Here Elizabeth Gaskell establishes the 'truth about' the physical details of life for the Other Nation in the Manchester cellars, appealing to the senses of sight, smell and touch to re-create the experience for the ignorant reader. Stephen Gill, in his introduction to the Penguin edition of *Mary Barton* (1970), suggests that the novelist tones down this description for middle-class consumption, and contrasts Joseph Adshead's *Distress in Manchester* which emphasizes the squalid overcrowding in the cellars. But her description tallies almost exactly with two drawings of the exterior and the interior of a Manchester cellar of the 1840s which appeared in the *Pictorial Times* (2 (1843), 172, reproduced as plate 29 in C. Aspin's *Lancashire, The First Industrial Society*). James Kay came to Manchester in 1827 and practised as a doctor. In his autobiography he recalls: 'many thousands of the population lived in basement or cellar dwellings below the level of the street. These were often so imperfectly drained that the floors were either damp or covered with water, and I have had to make my way to the bedside of patients by stepping on bricks placed in the water of the flooded floors.' (Op. cit., pp. 6 f.)

By the 1840s, as Engels shows, the Other Nation in Manchester was still living in such places. Early in 1840 over 12,000 poor families in Manchester were investigated at the instigation of gentlemen who had undertaken to administer nearly £4,000 which, as Adshead says, 'the benevolent portion of their fellow-townsmen had provided, for the alleviation of the physical sufferings of a large mass of our working population'. Adshead directed the investigation. Under the heading 'General Conditions of the Poor' he records that 10,132 families in Manchester received relief from the fund, and that one-fifth of those included in the return, and relieved, live in cellars: 'They are most of them neither drained nor soughed. They are consequently damp,—are always liable to be flooded,—and are almost entirely without the means of ventilation, having rarely but the outlets of door and window at the one side, and these almost hid below the level of the street.' (Op. cit., p. 14.) So Elizabeth Gaskell uses some if not all the details given of cellar dwellings by Adshead. One could argue that her reticence, what Ruskin called 'the right concealment of things', makes her description all the more convincing because it leaves the reader's imagination something to work on.

In 1846 John Ruskin expounded his theory of the right representation of detail in a composition. Typically, he links painting with poetry, in this case the poetry of one of the greatest Romantics. His comments on painting can be compared with Elizabeth Gaskell's descriptive methods in *Mary Barton*:

The fact is, that both finish and impetuosity, specific minuteness and large abstraction, may be the signs of passion, or of its reverse; may result from affection or indifference, intellect or dulness . . . Now both the finish and incompletion are right where they are the signs of passion or of thought, and both are wrong, and I think the finish the more contemptible of the two, when they cease to be so . . . On the whole, I conceive that the extremes of good and evil lie with the finishers, and that whatever glorious power we may admit in men like Tintoret, whatever attractiveness of method in Rubens, Rembrandt, or, though in far less degree, our own Reynolds, still the thoroughly great men are those who have done everything thoroughly, and who, in a word, have never despised anything, however small, of God's making. And this is the chief fault of our English landscapists, that they have not the intense all-observing penetration of well-balanced mind; they have not, except in one or two instances, anything of that feeling which Wordsworth shows in the following lines:

> 'So fair, so sweet, withal so sensitive;—
> Would that the little flowers were born to live
> Conscious of half the pleasure which they give,
> That to the mountain daisy's self were known
> *The beauty of its star-shaped Shadow, thrown*
> *On the smooth surface of this naked stone.*'

That is a little bit of good, downright foreground painting—no mistake about it; daisy, and shadow, and stone texture and all. Our painters must come to this before they have done their duty; and yet, on the other hand, let them beware of finishing, for the sake of finish, all over their picture. The ground is not to be all over daisies, nor is every daisy to have its star-shaped shadow; there is as much finish in the right concealment of things as in the right exhibition of them; and while I demand this amount of specific character where nature shows it, I demand equal fidelity to her where she conceals it . . . but the rule is simple . . . if the artist is painting something that he knows and loves, as he knows it, because he loves it . . . he is all right; but the moment he does anything as he thinks it ought to be, because he does not care about it, he is all wrong. He has only to ask himself whether he cares for anything except himself; so far as he does he will make a good picture; so far as he thinks of himself, a vile one. (*Modern Painters*, i, Ruskin, *Works*, iii. 176–8.)

For Ruskin the image is the embodiment of passion and thought; image and feeling coincide. When Elizabeth Gaskell later came to know him personally she greatly admired him. They both believed in the moral seriousness of art, and Elizabeth Gaskell's concern for objectivity in a novel, the respect for the object perceived—'I think you must observe what is *out* of you, instead of examining what is *in* you' coincides with Ruskin's definition of arresting vision in painter's or poet's work—'so far as he [cares for anything except himself] he will make a good picture; so far as he thinks of himself, a vile one'. Also, Ruskin's insistence on the choice and representation of detail guided by feeling for the subject, 'the intense all-observing penetration of well-balanced mind', so that concern for the subject results in its effective re-creation in art, accords with Elizabeth Gaskell's desire to make her reader see what she describes. In her letter to Marianne she says that the novelist should set objects not feelings before the reader, as Defoe does. The great strength of her descriptions of the places where the poor live, the quality which distinguishes her from the other Victorian novelists who treated the same subject, is their directness in describing 'something that' she 'knows and loves', to quote Ruskin. She never despises 'anything, however small, of God's making', in other words anything which denotes human activity. She is the only Victorian whose depiction of the poor has anything of the substance of Van Gogh's paintings, such as 'Peasant Woman in a White Cap' (1885) and 'Interior with Weaver' (1884) (Plates 10 and 11). With the significant difference that she never describes the Manchester factory operatives at their work, her approach to these people is, like Van Gogh's, direct and humble, with the humility of someone patiently seeking the truth. Van Gogh's paintings have a powerful effect because from his alert reaction to his subjects' faces and clothes, the man's dim cottage and his skill at the complicated loom, he creates poetry. He depicts them so that they suggest human dignity and ability, and the interest of an individual way of life. Here is Wordsworth's poet, 'a man . . . being possessed of more than usual organic sensibility' seeing 'into the life of things'. On the rare occasions when Elizabeth Gaskell suggests outrage or disapproval, moral or aesthetic, a jarring note enters her description. For example, the suggestion that the scarlet and green tea-tray in the Bartons' home implies childish taste (one thinks of the hectic colours of Holman Hunt's paintings), or the outraged italics 'household slops of *every* description', or the offended fastidiousness implied in the self-conscious literary phrase 'damp, nay wet, brick floor', in the account of Davenport's cellar, destroy the objectivity which releases the reader's reaction, 'the intense all-observing penetration of well-balanced mind' embodied in the rest of the passage. At her best she depicts objects, observed with care, to re-create feelings; a process which can be compared in kind, if not in degree, with the finest poetry of Wordsworth, Coleridge, and Keats. In Chapter 2 of *Mary Barton* the factual information she gives about the streets through which the Bartons and their friends make their way home is like that found in many contemporary accounts of Manchester, James Kay's, Peter Gaskell's, both of which were used by Engels, Joseph Adshead's. The prose remains pedestrian and generalized: 'the party proceeded home, through many half-finished streets'; 'they turned out of one of these innumerable streets into a little paved court, having the backs of houses at the end opposite to the opening, and a gutter running through the middle to carry off household slops' until she remarks that the women who lived in the court were taking in their washing strung on low lines across the court so that 'if our friends had been a few minutes sooner, they would have had to stoop very much, or else the half-wet clothes would have flapped in their faces' when the particular detail conveying sensation re-creates the experience of crossing the courtyard as nothing earlier has done. Ruskin's discussion of the use of natural details can be extended to include physical details. Elizabeth Gaskell knows the washing in the courts and 'loves' it in the way an artist does, that is, does not approve or disapprove of it, but apprehends it, her imagination 'seizes upon' it, to use Keats's phrase, and so it becomes 'truth' because she sensuously re-creates it and, consequently, the way of life it suggests. This, in a small detail, is the imaginative 'truth' which proceeds from 'truth about'.

Elizabeth Gaskell often depicts objects in such a way as to identify herself with the people who have to live in such an environment, as in the description of Davenport's cellar, 'It was very dark inside. The window-panes were many of them broken and stuffed with rags, which was reason enough for the dusky light that pervaded the place even at mid-day.' Set this beside Adshead's description of a similar cellar as being 'almost entirely without the means of ventilation, having rarely but the outlets of the door and window at the one side, and these almost hid below the level of the street' (op. cit., p. 14), and it is obvious how the choice of detail of the broken window and the stuffing of the holes helps the reader to enter imaginatively into the cellar-dwellers' lives rather than simply assent rationally to information about them. She gives the reader the kind of information which makes imaginative participation possible.

Also, she chooses the physical details which will allow the reader to share the consciousness of a particular character. The black, empty fireplace in Davenport's cellar suggests his wife's mental and emotional condition, and the fact that she sits 'on her husband's chair' as she cries 'in the dark loneliness' perfectly embodies the disorder of her household. Similarly, in the description of John Barton's reaction to his wife's death:

He tried to realise it—to think it possible. And then his mind wandered off to other days, to far different times. He thought of their courtship; of his first seeing her, an awkward beautiful rustic, far too shiftless for the delicate factory work to which she was apprenticed; of his first gift to her, a bead necklace, which had long ago been put by, in one of the deep drawers of the dresser, to be kept for Mary. He wondered if it was there yet, and with a strange curiosity he got up to feel for it; for the fire by this time was well nigh out, and candle he had none. His groping hand fell on the piled-up tea-things, which at his desire she had left unwashed till morning— they were all so tired. He was reminded of one of the daily little actions, which acquire such power when they have been performed for the last time by one we love. He began to think over his wife's daily round of duties: and something in the remembrance that these would never more be done by her, touched the source of tears, and he cried aloud. (Ch. 3.)

His unreasoning action in getting up to look for the necklace suggests the automatic, detached behaviour of a man shocked out of contact with ordinary existence, and engages the reader's sympathy with his pathetic worry about the gift while establishing his bewildered state of mind. It has been kept in 'one of the deep drawers of the dresser'; these details help actualize the furniture, the room and the customs of the people who live in it. The fact that John has to grope for it because the fire has gone out and he has no candle imaginatively realizes his situation, and his blundering hand knocking against the dishes suggests his bewilderment and lack of direction which, now his wife is dead, is not simply physical. The stacked dishes imply Mrs Barton's orderliness—she left the dishes only at John's wish because they were so tired after the party. The dishes now lack their mistress, and their disorder, like the unusual occurrence of Mrs Davenport sitting in her husband's chair, suggests the disturbance in John's life now that his wife is gone, despite the fact that his home and all his possessions are solid about him. His realization that their ordinary familiar routine of life is broken for ever, and his despair at the sundering of his relationship with his wife, are sudden and terrible, and perfectly expressed by the accidental contact with the stacked dishes. Carefully chosen physical details express psychological reality.

Elizabeth Gaskell never achieved Dickens's power in his mature novels of extending an image of environment with psychological and spiritual implications so that it gives an organic structure to the novel—the prison in *Little Dorrit*, the Court of Chancery in *Bleak House*, Mr Dombey's house in *Dombey and Son*—but she structures the early part of the book by recalling the previous comfort of the Bartons' home when John had work and Mrs Barton was alive; this emphasizes his desolation and despair after the 1839 Chartist petition to Parliament has failed and he is refused work because he is a known Trades Unionist:

> The smart tea-tray, and tea-caddy, long and carefully kept, went for bread for her father. He did not ask for it, or complain, but she saw hunger in his shrunk, fierce, animal look. Then the blankets went, for it was summer time, and they could spare them; and their sale made a fund, which Mary fancied would last till better times came. But it was soon all gone; and then she looked around the room to crib it of its few remaining ornaments. To all these proceedings her father said never a word. (Ch. 10.)

John Barton's plight she represents as typical of the working-class despair in Manchester of the 1840s. Joseph Adshead wrote:

> That the mind of a man who has been long unsuccessfully struggling against the inroads of poverty, and suffering from the bitter trials of grinding penury, should become debased and weakened, can excite no surprise . . . his spirits are broken; and feeling that he has no domestic comforts to lose—that he cannot descend lower in the scale of social existence . . . his wretchedness drives him to despair, and he sinks at last into a state of mental apathy, or plunges into reckless improvidence. If, again, the depressing influences of hopeless poverty should not have the effect of hardening his feelings and blunting his sensibility, his accumulated miseries—the sight of his house without furniture, without food, without fire, and his children perhaps crying for bread, will probably have the effect of impelling him to crime or depriving him of reason; and the termination of his career . . . may be sought in a prison or a lunatic asylum. (Op. cit., p. 52.)

And John's indignant response to Mary's question why he does not apply for relief, ' "I don't want money, child! Damn their charity and their money! I want work, and it is my right. I want work" ', dramatizes the Lancashire workman's pride and self-respect noted by William Cooke Taylor: 'the operative is far more thankful for employment than for alms: if he could obtain the one, he would look upon the offer of the other as an insult' (Taylor, *Tour*, p. 45.)

Elizabeth Gaskell's method is to dramatize John's despair by reference to the details of a physical environment and to give it a more than personal application. His plight is seen as an instance of the reason why men become Chartists, the word terrifying the middle classes in the 1840s.[19] She agrees with Cooke Taylor when he writes that the Chartist movement was not instigated by sinister plotters against the State, but 'was commenced by those who feared suffering, and was swelled by the vast tide of those who are actually suffering . . . By rather a bold personification, indeed, Want of Employment, Distress, and Famine, may be described as the conspirators; and I believe that few will object to *their* being sentenced to transportation.' (Ibid., p. 319.)

But Elizabeth Gaskell's weakness is that she does not reach out far from the description of places and the people in them to put them in their historical or political context. The descriptions are important in embodying her argument, in this case that hunger breeds Chartism and that her contemporaries should understand this, while condemning the violent activities of Chartists, but no questions are raised as to how Manchester came to be the city it is, or who is responsible for building courts like the one inhabited by the Bartons. Disraeli gives a sketchy history of Wodgate and through his description of the place suggests his ideas about organizing men into a community —obviously, he prefers a feudally structured society: Kingsley says why so many of the houses near Jemmy Downes's lodging are being pulled down and deplores this philosophy of municipal 'improvements' which increase the wealth of the rich at the expense of the poor; Reade's oppressive Gothic castle of a

---

[19] In *Mary Barton*, Chapter 15, Elizabeth Gaskell writes, 'John Barton became a Chartist, a Communist, all that is commonly called wild and visionary.' By 'Communist' she means 'Owenite'. For the hysterical hatred which the Owenites aroused see the Bishop of Exeter's attack on them in the House of Lords, 24 Jan. 1840; his motion (3 Feb.) praying that 'steps be taken to prevent the diffusion of blasphemous and immoral doctrines'; and the accounts of attacks both physical and verbal on Owen during that year, all mentioned in the Pilgrim *Letters of Charles Dickens*, ii. 100, 2 n.

prison is an image of an oppressive, unjust penal code; for Dickens Coketown's monotonous streets embody the *laissez-faire* philosophy which achieves technical miracles, makes money, pollutes the river and reduces people to 'hands'. Elizabeth Gaskell is accurate in placing the Carsons' grand house two miles from the centre of Manchester. When Wilson goes to beg an infirmary order for Davenport he 'had about two miles to walk before he reached Mr. Carson's house, which was almost in the country' (ch. 6). But she fails to set this piece of geography in the context of the increasing prosperity of Manchester's trade which altered the physical features of the city, some of which emphasized an increasing split between the Two Nations. This point is made in the second edition (1842) of Lowe and Burton's guidebook, *Manchester as it is*: 'Within the last few years Mosley Street contained only private dwelling houses: it is now a street of warehouses. The increasing business of the town is rapidly converting all the principal dwelling-houses, centrally situated, into mercantile establishments, and is driving most of the respectable inhabitants into the suburbs.' (Quoted Asa Briggs, op. cit., p. 103.)

In *Hard Times* Bounderby also acquires a country residence 'about fifteen miles from the town', and Dickens remarks,

The bank had foreclosed a mortgage effected on the property thus pleasantly situated, by one of the Coketown magnates, who, in his determination to make a shorter cut than usual to an enormous fortune, overspeculated himself by about two hundred thousand pounds. These accidents did sometimes happen in the best regulated families of Coketown, but the bankrupts had no connexion whatever with the improvident classes. (Bk. II, ch. 7.)

Dickens's shrewd last sentence reveals the gulf between the Two Nations in the factory town and the overbearing moral censure which the prosperous middle classes felt they had a right to direct at the lower. To reveal the psychological and spiritual relationships of a community by reference to a geographical detail is not within the scope of Elizabeth Gaskell's imagination, nor has it the intensity which can create from a landscape an image of human despair, as Marcus Clarke does in his description of the Australian bush in his study of convict life *For the Term of his Natural Life* (1874) or as Dickens does in his evocation of the machines and streets of Coketown.

THE RURAL POOR, AS SEEN BY KINGSLEY AND DISRAELI

Perkin classes agricultural labourers among the last to receive material benefits from the new, expanding industrial system of the nineteenth century (see above, p. 12). In northern England, in the neighbourhood of new industries competing for labour, agricultural wages began to rise in the late eighteenth century and continued in the nineteenth, but in the south and east wages were static and desperately low (in Wiltshire, for example, wages were 7s. a week in both 1770 and 1850). Certainly the agricultural labourer in these regions was of the ranks of the Other Nation and existed permanently on the edge of starvation. 'It was not until after 1870, when the exodus from the country-side became rapid, money wages rose, and real wages rose sharply with the great price fall, that the southern farm labourers at last joined the outer fringe of those who benefited from in-dustrialism.' (Perkin, op. cit., p. 148.)

Sidney Godolphin Osborne wrote in 1839: 'Paint the situation of the cottager in what colours you will, and many are the fanciful portraitures made of him and his home,—the real truth will ever be, that his life must be one of much trial, his home a scene of much privation.' (*Hints for the Amelioration of the Moral Condition of a Village Population*, p. 82.) *Yeast, Alton Locke*, and *Sybil* are outstanding novels in their period because they claim to give something of 'the real truth' of the agricul-tural labourer's life. I have examined fictional embodiments of the physical reality of the urban poor. With what success did these novelists create the physical details of life lived by the rural poor? Osborne had a profound influence on *Yeast* and *Alton Locke*. He was one of those many unfortunate men in the nineteenth century who were forced into the Church by paren-tal pressure although they felt they had no vocation. His real interests were surgery, medicine, and microscopic investigation. He was a conscientious if controversial parson, and he applied his flair for scientific observation to social investigation. In the early 1840s, when Kingsley was in his first curacy at Eversley, Hampshire, Osborne had encouraged the younger man in his concern for his rural parishioners. Osborne lived in the county from which the Tolpuddle Martyrs had been transported in 1834 for attempting to form a union to fight for a living wage,

and where the shepherd boy known to Hardy died of starvation in the 1840s. Osborne fought a long, hard battle for better
wages and better housing for the Dorsetshire agricultural
labourers, sometimes in the many letters he wrote to *The Times*
signed 'S.G.O.'. His protest against the 'fanciful portraitures' of
the country labourer is similar to Will Fern's desire to

hear the real Truth spoke out for once . . . Gentlefolks, I've lived many a
year in this place. You may see the cottage from the sunk fence over yon-
der. I've seen the ladies draw it in their books, a hundred times. It looks
well in a picter, I've heerd say; but there an't weathers in picters, and
maybe 'tis fitter for that, than for a place to live in. Well! I lived there. How
hard—how bitter hard, I lived there, I won't say. Any day in the year, and
every day, you can judge for your own selves. (*The Chimes*, Third Quarter.)

By the time he wrote *Yeast* Kingsley was established as Rector
of Eversley and, with his friends F. D. Maurice, the theologian,
John Ludlow, a barrister, Charles Mansfield, a chemist, and
Thomas Hughes, then a barrister who later achieved fame as the
author of *Tom Brown's Schooldays*, was busy preaching Christian Socialism to working men as a sound alternative to Chartism,
which had virtually collapsed after the fiasco of the presenta-
tion of the Charter to Parliament 10 April 1848. *Yeast* had been
designed for the penny weekly *Politics for the People* edited by
Maurice and Ludlow and aimed at the working people, but publication ceased in July 1848 and Kingsley serialized *Yeast* in
Fraser's Magazine (see R. B. Martin, *The Dust of Combat*,
pp. 78–92). In it he was concerned to describe the poverty and
hard-living of the rural labourer in southern England and to
scrutinize the traditional picturesque representations of rural
life, the persistent pastoral myth of the beauty and innocence
of the country contrasted with the dirt and vice of the town.
The buildings erected by the new thriving manufacturers gave
added point to this contrast. Robert Southey's conversations
between Montesinos (Southey himself) and the Ghost of Sir
Thomas More, *Sir Thomas More, or Colloquies on the Progress
and Prospects of Society*, appeared in two volumes in 1824,
were reprinted in 1829 and 1831, and again, in one volume, in
1837. In describing the cottages built for the operatives in the
(presumably) water-powered mills of Cumberland, he emphasizes
the idyllic life of the agricultural peasantry:

By this time we had reached the bank above Applethwaite . . . Here, and in
the adjoining hamlet of Millbeck, the effects of manufactures and of

agriculture may be seen and compared. The old cottages are such as the poet and the painter equally delight in beholding. Substantially built of the native stone without mortar, dirtied with no white-lime, and their long low roofs covered with slate, if they had been raised by the magic of some indigenous Amphion's music, the materials could not have adjusted themselves more beautifully in accord with the surrounding scene; and time has still farther harmonized them with weather stains, lichens and moss . . . the hedge of clipt box beneath the windows, the rose bushes beside the door . . . the bee-hives, and the orchard with its bank of daffodils and snow-drops . . . indicate in the owners some portion of ease and leisure, some regard to neatness and comfort, some sense of natural and innocent and healthful enjoyment. The new cottages of the manufacturers, are . . . upon the manufacturing pattern . . . naked, and in a row. (*Sir Thomas More: or Colloquies on The Progress and Prospects of Society*, 1829, pp. 173 f.)

The effect is achieved by following the picturesque painter in describing at a distance the peasant's cottage in a charming setting. The reader is never allowed to get near the rural labourer, see him at his work or in his home.

Similarly, in Susan Ferrier's novel *Marriage* (1818), in which she contrasts the pure simple life of the country with the corruption and affectation of London, the Scottish fisherman and shepherd, and their dwellings, are also seen from afar and so 'picturesque':

the sun shone out in all his splendour, shedding life and beauty even over the desolate heath-clad hills of Glenfern. But, after they had journeyed a few miles, suddenly emerging from the valley, a scene of matchless beauty burst at once upon the eye. Before them lay the dark blue waters of Loch Marlie, reflecting, as in a mirror, every surrounding object, and bearing on its placid transparent bosom a fleet of herring boats, the drapery of whose black suspended nets contrasted with picturesque effect the white sails of the larger vessels, which were vainly spread to catch a breeze. All around, rocks, meadows, woods, and hills, mingled in wild and lovely irregularity.

On a projecting point of land stood a little fishing village; its white cottages reflected in the glassy waters that almost surrounded it. On the opposite side of the lake, or rather estuary, embosomed in wood, rose the lofty turrets of Loch Marlie Castle; while here and there, perched on some mountain's brow, were to be seen the shepherd's lonely hut, and the heath-covered summer sheiling.

Not a breath was stirring, not a sound was heard save the rushing of a waterfall, the tinkling of some silver rivulet, or the calm rippling of the tranquil lake; now and then, at intervals, the fisherman's Gaelic ditty chanted, as he lay stretched on the sand, in some sunny nook: or the shrill distant sound of childish glee. (Ch. 15.)

The details of the scene are carefully selected to give exquisite

pleasure to the observer's refined sensibility, trained to respond
to the picturesque. The people, their activities and homes are
simply the component parts of a decorative effect; and no
awkward questions are asked about why the Scottish hills are
so desolate and deserted. Such a passage is the literary equivalent to many contemporary paintings depicting the rural
labourer's life. For example, John Constable's 'Morning in
Dedham Vale' (1811, see catalogue of 'The Shock of Recognition', Tate Gallery, 1971, Plate 3; Suffolk was an area of great
rural poverty and the scene of bread riots in 1816, see A. J.
Peacock, *Bread or Blood; the Agrarian Riots in East Anglia:
1816*, 1965), in which the labourers and their cattle provide
'foreground interest' to the study of light on a broad, peaceful
landscape; or 'The Vale of Dedham' (1814, see catalogue of
'Primitives to Picasso', Royal Academy, 1962, exhibit 184); or
the later watercolour 'Old Sarum' (1834, see catalogue of 'The
Romantic Movement', Tate Gallery and Arts Council Gallery,
1959, exhibit 643), in which the shepherd with his flock moves
at the edge of the picture of which the central interest is the
sublimely desolate sky lowering over an ancient, awe-inspiring
landscape (Plate 12). This perspective on the rural labourers had
been popular since the late eighteenth century, for example in
Thomas Gainsborough's 'Cornard Wood', 1748, catalogue of
'The Shock of Recognition' Plate 30. Here the labourers and
their activities provide decorative points of interest in the
peaceful landscape.

Both the novels and the drama of the 1840s foster the image
of rural idyllic innocence and beauty; to do this they have to be
vague about the factual details of rural life and labour. Typical
is Edward Lancaster's melodrama *Ruth* (1841) in which the
heroine declaims: 'I will once more seek my own dear village
home. Who would dwell in cities, where our days are passed in
obscurity; whilst here each rustic belle has the chance of becoming a rural queen! Ah, my own village home before a palace.'
She then sings a song, 'My Own Village Home',[20] emphasizing

[20] Possibly the song 'My Village Home', printed as a street ballad. The second
verse runs:

> The village church, the village church,
>   I see it 'mid the trees,
> Again I hear its merry bells,
>   Upon the passing breeze;

her sentimental words and gesture with music. Thomas Frost's
novel *Paul the Poacher* (1848), although it makes some cur-
sory reference to Radical agitation, distances this by setting
the action of the novel in the time of Castlereagh and Sid-
mouth, and presents the rural characters in terms of the picturesque painter and the melodramatist. Here is Paul, having
broken prison, to which he is condemned for shooting and
killing a gamekeeper, walking through the woods to join the
gipsies:

The dark clouds, which had for a time threatened a storm, had now passed
over, and the moon shone clear and full above the wood, throwing her
silvery radiance over the upper branches of the trees, which contrasted in
a picturesque manner with the dark shadows below . . . The clumps of
shrubs, the deep recesses, the lighter foliage hanging over the darker, and
here and there a holly branch, with its clusters of red berries, illuminated
by the moonbeams, made up a picture which would have delighted a
Poussin or a Claude . . . There is an indescribable charm in rambling by
moonlight through the sylvan scenery of a wild forest . . . and Paul Copley,
despite the dangers which environed him, experienced its influence as he
strode through the Mistletoe Wood, with his gun under his arm, and Ponto
by his side, and more than once caught himself humming a distich of the
old poaching ballad—
> 'It's my delight of a moonlight night,
> In the season of the year!' (Ch. 20.)

The generalized, picturesque impression of the countryside is
reinforced by reference to Claude and Poussin, and the unrealis-
tic glamour of the social outcast in Gay's *Beggar's Opera* or
Ainsworth's *Rookwood* is transferred to the rural scene. Thomas
Miller's *Gideon Giles the Roper* (1841) gives a better idea of the
privations of rural life but it, too, is primarily concerned with a
terrific melodrama, Gideon's rescue of his daughter Ellen from
the gamekeeper Banes who tries to abduct her to satisfy the lust
of the local squire, Sir Edward Lee. This suggests the kind of
demands made by contemporary fiction because Miller was a
countryman, born in Gainsborough, and six years later published
*Pictures of Country Life, and Summer Rambles in Green and
Shady Places* in which he described the factual details of rural

> The valley green the silver brook,
>   Are all belov'd by me;
> But those I prized above them
>   I never more shall see.
>   (Baring-Gould, *Ballads*, vii. 137.)

life conflicting with the picturesque view of a charming landscape:

to draw a true picture of village life, as it really is in the present day, cannot be done without depicting much poverty, and many hardships.

Nature is ever lovely; and in no country has she been more bountiful
in scattering her beauties than in our own; but the carol of the lark, the
hum of the bee, and the fragrance of hawthorn hedges and flowery
fields, mingled with the aroma of old woods in summer walks, along peaceful foot-paths, are not found—

'Within the huts where poor men lie.'

The country has not the same charm for these, as it has for those who
with plenty come to retire there; and to the accumulated savings, gathered
by years of successful commerce in the city, bring that keen appetite for
change, which is pleased with every thing that differs from what they have
been accustomed to. To the peasant, the scene is just the same: he looks
on the fields, and they recall years of ill-paid labour; he has toiled in them,
early and late, and is not a shilling the richer than, when twenty years ago,
he first became a tiller of the soil. The woods but remind him of short
days and reduced wages, when he bound faggots or made hurdles, and the
cold pierced to his very bones. ('English Villagers', *Pictures of Country
Life*, 1847, p. 136.)

Even a serious writer like William Howitt, in his *Rural Life of
England* (1838) which purported 'to present to the reader a
view of the Rural Life of England at the present period, as seen
in all classes and all parts of the country', hovers uncertainly
between the realistic and the picturesque view of the countryside and its inhabitants.[21] Unlike Susan Ferrier's distant and
rapturous view of a Scottish cottage, his is closely observed and
factual, albeit he and his wife 'came upon it after wandering
through the delicious fairyland of birch woods that clothe . . .
Loch [Echilty, Rosshire] in the very romance of picturesque
beauty . . .' (*Rural Life of England*, 1838, 2 vols., ii. 134). Yet
oatcakes and tea are all that can be provided for them, ' "There
was," said our hostess, "a great cry in the country for food!" ',

[21] Elizabeth Gaskell came to know William Howitt and his wife Mary. Admiration for their description of rural life and scenery prompted her to write to them in
1838. 'Habits, Amusements, and Conditions of the People', Part VI, Chapter 16 of
Rural Life of England in the later editions owes something to her; she provided information of the Knutsford custom of sprinkling red sand and making flower patterns
in white sand upon it in front of a house where a joyful event, such as a wedding, was
to be celebrated. Howitt also published her account of a day spent at Clopton House
in *Visits to Remarkable Places* (1840), and her first published prose tale, 'Life in
Manchester: Libbie Marsh's Three Eras', appeared in *Howitt's Journal of Literature
and Popular Progress*, 5, 12, and 19 June 1847. Mary Howitt, in her *Autobiography*,
claims that William encouraged Elizabeth Gaskell to write *Mary Barton*.

and there is a constant battle to protect their crops from the on-slaughts of the preserved game. He describes the typical Scottish cottage: 'a little, low, long building of mud, or rough stones; the chimney composed of four short poles wrapped round with hay-bands; a flat stone laid upon it to prevent the smoke being driven down into the hut by the tempestuous winds from the hills; and another stone laid upon that, to keep it from being blown away. The roof is thatched with bracken, with the roots outermost . . . A little window of perhaps one pane of thick glass, or of four of oiled paper. The door . . . is so low that you must stoop to enter; and the smoke is pouring out of it faster than it ascends from the chimney.' (pp. 132 f.) As the Howitts leave in the morning they look at 'the primitive cheese-press, consisting of a pole, one end of which was thrust into a crevice of a rock, and the other weighted with a huge stone . . . We could not avoid feeling how far was all this from the cottage-life of England.' (pp. 136 f.) He continues:

This is a scene in the scale of comfort far below the general run of la-bourers' houses in England; but yet how far, infinitely far lower, do many of our working people's abodes sink. What dens have we in manufacturing towns! What little, filthy, dismal, yet high-rented dens! What cabins do some of our colliers and miners inhabit! What noisome, amphibious abodes abound in our fishing villages, such as Crabbe has painted! (p. 137.)

And, like Southey, he uses the manufacturers' housing to provide a foil for the beauty of 'our English cottages':

Where manufacturers have not introduced their red, staring, bald brick houses, and what is worse, their beershops and demoralization: where, in fact, a more primitive simplicity remains. There, on the edges of the forests, in quiet hamlets and sweet woody valleys, the little grey-thatched cottages, with their gardens and old orchards, their rows of beehives, and their porches clustered with jasmines and roses, stand . . . and give one a poetical idea of peace and happiness which is inexpressible . . . these rustic abodes must inspire us with ideas of a peace and purity of life, in most soothing contrast with the hurry and immorality of cities . . . There are thousands of them, inhabited by woodmen, labourers, or keepers, that are fit dwellings for the truest poet that ever lived; and it is the *ideal* of these picturesque and peace-breathing English cottages that has given origin to some of the sweetest paradises in the world—the cottages of the wealthy and the tasteful. What most lovely creations of this description now abound in the finest parts of England, with their delicious shrubberies, velvet lawns, hidden walks, and rustic garden-huts. (pp. 138–40.)

Both Southey's and Howitt's descriptions exemplify the

familiar protest against industrial capitalism by using the nostalgic image of pastoral innocence and beauty which masks the
unpleasant reality of agrarian capitalism.[22] Howitt's sentimental
effusion, concluding with the unintentionally ironic praise of
labourers' dwellings for providing a pattern for the homes of the
wealthy (among which he includes Wordsworth's cottage at
Rydal) both ratifies Miller's criticism of the wealthy who
enthuse over country life and sharply contrasts with his own
preceding description of the Scottish cottage. The oiled-paper
window, 'the roof thatched with bracken, with the roots outermost', the pole and huge stone which serve as a cheese press, are
observed details which not only suggest the physical appearance
of the cottage, but the nature of its inhabitants' life and labour.
To support his description of the English cottage he quotes
from the poetry of John Wilson, 'Christopher North', including
'An Evening in Furness Abbey' which he describes as 'a poem
flushed all over with the violet hues of poetry'. Wilson's descriptions are just as generalized and distanced as Howitt's—phrases
such as 'sylvan gloom', 'verdant slopes', 'low coppice', 'hundreds
of huts' are common. Howitt plainly is not looking at the English cottage as he looked at its Scottish counterpart, but is
simply repeating what the poets have told him. In another chapter of *Rural Life of England* he praises the illustrator, Thomas
Bewick, laments that there is no one to rival his keen observation of Nature, and comments 'Our artists, like the poets, have
forsaken nature herself, to study and imitate one another.'
(ii. 54.) He himself demonstrates this in his description of the
English cottage.

'In many of the southern counties', writes Howitt, 'but I
think nowhere more than in Hampshire, do the cottages realize,
in my view, every conception that our poets have given us of
them.' (ii. 139.) Charles Kingsley's parish, Eversley, is in Hampshire. In *Yeast*, in which he tried to enlighten his readers on the
reality of the agricultural labourer's life, the country described
is a combination of Hampshire and Dorsetshire. Early in the
novel Kingsley evokes the expected idealized description of the
country:

---

[22] This has been explored in detail by Raymond Williams in his illuminating book
The Country and the City (London and Toronto, 1973).

Of all the species of lovely scenery which England holds, none, perhaps, is more exquisite than the banks of the chalk-rivers—the perfect limpidity of the water, the gay and luxuriant vegetation of the banks and ditches, the masses of noble wood embosoming the villages, the unique beauty of the water-meadows, living sheets of emerald and silver, tinkling and sparkling, cool under the fiercest sun, brilliant under the blackest clouds. (Ch. 3.)

Then comes the questioning note:

There, if anywhere, one would have expected to find Arcadia among fertility, loveliness, industry, and wealth. But, alas for the sad reality! the cool breath of those glittering water-meadows too often floats laden with poisonous miasma. Those picturesque villages are generally the perennial hotbeds of fever and ague, of squalid penury, sottish profligacy, dull discontent too stale for words. There is luxury in the park, wealth in the huge farm-steadings, knowledge in the parsonage: but the poor? those by whose dull labour all that luxury and wealth, ay, even that knowledge, is made possible, what are they? We shall see, please God, ere the story's end.

Kingsley liked to think of himself as an aristocrat and delighted to trace back his family's ancient lineage. During a pub meeting of working men in 1849 he inaccurately described himself as a Chartist because, like Disraeli, he believed in the ancient alliance between aristocrat and labourer. *Sybil* sought to revive the aristocratic ideal in political terms. Lancelot Smith, the hero of *Yeast*, combines in his name the chivalric knight and the common man. He is an aristocrat finding a new sense of direction in the socially responsible Church, no longer the preserve of privilege and exclusion, and in the new scientific observation revealing God's aims afresh. These concerns create a new image from the sense impressions of the rural landscape:

they paced on past lonely farm-yards, from which the rich manure-water was draining across the road in foul black streams, festering and steaming in the chill night air. Lancelot sighed as he saw the fruitful materials of food running to waste, and thought of the 'over-population' cry: and then he looked across to the miles of brown moorland on the opposite side of the valley, that lay idle and dreary under the autumn moon, except where here and there a squatter's cottage and rood of fruitful garden gave the lie to the laziness and ignorance of man, who pretends that it is not worth his while to cultivate the soil which God has given him. 'Good heavens!' he thought, 'had our forefathers had no more enterprise than modern landlords, where should we all have been at this moment? Everywhere waste! Waste of manure, waste of land, waste of muscle, waste of brain, waste of population—and we call ourselves the workshop of the world!' (Ch. 13.)

The scene gives insight into the wastefulness of the apparently opulent Victorian society. And, like Kingsley's description of

Jacob's Island, or Disraeli's Wodgate, or Dickens's Coketown, these rural scenes illustrate arguments and propagate ideas. Often such scenes are based on printed evidence as well as on personal experience, like Lancelot's encounter with the woman in Ashy:

'No wonder you have typhus here,' said Lancelot, 'with this filthy open drain running right before the door. Why can't you clean it out?'

'Why, what harm does that do?' answered the woman, peevishly. 'Beside, here's my master gets up to his work by five in the morning, and not back till seven at night, and by then he an't in no humour to clean out gutters. And where's the water to come from to keep a place clean? It costs many a one of us here a shilling a-week the summer through to pay for fetching water up the hill. We've work enough to fill our kettles. The muck must just lie in the road, smell or none, till the rain carries it away.'

Lancelot sighed again. (Ch. 13.)

This closely follows the report made by Alfred Austin, one of the Assistant Poor Law Commissioners, on the Dorsetshire labourers' housing conditions:

In the village of Stourpain, in Dorsetshire, there is a row of several labourers' cottages, mostly joining each other, and fronting the street, in the middle of which is an open gutter. There are two or three narrow passages leading from the street, between the houses, to the back of them. Behind the cottages the ground rises rather abruptly; and about three yards up the elevation are placed the pigsties and privies of the cottages. There are also shallow excavations, the receptacles apparently of all the dirt of the families. The matter constantly escaping from the pigsties, privies, &c., is allowed to find its way through the passages between the cottages into the gutter in the street, so that the cottages are nearly surrounded by streams of filth. It was in these cottages that a malignant typhus broke out about two years ago, which afterwards spread through the village . . . I hardly visited a cottage where there were any attempts at draining. The dirt of the family is thrown down before or behind the cottage; if there is any natural inclination in the ground from the cottage, it escapes; if not, it remains till evaporated. (*Reports on Agriculture*, 1843, pp. 36 f.)

Such facts helped Kingsley give a startling close-up of the picturesque cottage and its inhabitants. However, the 'consciousness' of the rural poor in *Yeast* is that permitted by Lancelot's quest to discover himself and his vocation. The latter-day knight remains metaphorically on horseback and we see the Other Nation as they come into focus at his stirrup. Tregarva, the gamekeeper, comes from the Other Nation and understands them, but is not of them. Because of his intelligence and industry he has raised himself to a position somewhat above the struggle for bread which occupies the Other Nation and so can guide Lancelot who is so far above the struggle that he feels obliged to help those below. When Tregarva takes Lancelot to the village fair at Bonesake (a self-consciously fictional name) to show him 'what the poor are like', Lancelot remains the centre of attention:

Lancelot . . . entered the village fair, and was a little disappointed at his first glimpse of the village-green. Certainly his expectations had not been very exalted; but there had run through them a hope of something melodramatic, dreams of May-pole dancing and athletic games, somewhat of village-belle rivalry, of the Corin and Sylvia school; or failing that, a few Touchstones and Audreys, some genial earnest buffo humour, here and there. But there did not seem much likelihood of it. Two or three apple and ginger-bread-stalls, from which draggled children were turning slowly and wistfully away to go home; a booth full of trumpery fairings, in front of which tawdry girls were coaxing maudlin youths, with faded southernwood in their button-holes; another long low booth, from every crevice of which reeked odours of stale beer, and smoke, by courtesy denominated tobacco, to the treble accompaniment of a jigging fiddle and a tambourine, and the bass one of grumbled oaths and curses within. (Ch. 13.)

Kingsley rejects the stereotype which the contemporary stage offers as the reality of rural life ('melodramatic'); together with the pastoral ('Corin and Sylvia') and literary ('Touchstones and Audreys') conventions. But the corrected vision he offers is no clearer. The prejudice the scene embodies is evident in its lack of precision and curiosity. William Howitt and Elizabeth Gaskell would have asked questions about it. Southernwood is a shrub with a delicious fragrance; another name for it is 'lad's love'. Why did the boys wear it in their buttonholes? Was it a sign of serious courtship? What were the tunes they were playing? Local tunes? Were they dancing? If so, what were the dances? 'Tawdry girls' and 'maudlin youths' give no more precise a picture than 'Corin and Sylvia' or 'Touchstones and Audreys'. The passage relies heavily on S.G.O.'s description of the 'Statute Fairs' in *Reports on Agriculture*, 1843:

Let me now call your attention to one of the most destructive sources of evil to which the character of the young female is exposed in the agricultural districts. In many counties it is the custom to hire lads and girls for farm-work at what are called 'Statute Fairs', known amongst the poor as 'Staties', 'Mops', or 'Wakes'. Some second-rate country town is in general the scene of these assemblages: a few shows, a few stalls for the sale of toys, &c.; a good many itinerant singers and sellers of ballads, many of which are of the most obscene character; a certain number of fiddlers in a certain number of public-houses and beer-shops, comprise the chief attractions of the fair. The business part of it consists in the exhibition of a large number of young lads and girls, dressed in all the finery they can muster, that they may be seen, as they think, to the best advantage, and be hired on the spot by those masters or mistresses who come to such places to seek for servants . . . Those only who have witnessed them can form any idea of the scenes of vice which these fairs become late in the day: I know of no language of reproach too strong to apply to them, and I think one of the first duties of the legislator, who seeks to throw the protection of the law over the moral character of the young in country districts, will be either to put an end to, or at least appoint some efficient superintendence over, these fairs. (Op. cit., p. 91.)

The final comment is echoed by Tregarva: ' "It's a pity these fairs can't be put down. They do a lot of harm ruin all the young girls round . . . The parson here, sir, who is a God-fearing man enough, tried hard to put down this one, but the innkeepers were too strong for him." ' (Ch. 13.)

Kingsley tempers the disapproval slightly by having Lancelot reply: ' "To take away their only amusement, in short. He had much better have set to work to amuse them himself" ', and to think to himself 'that if Tregarva's brain had been a little less preponderant, he, too, might have found the need of some recreation besides books and thought'; but this does little to lessen the distaste with which the whole episode is described. The strength of this distaste can be gauged if Kingsley's account is compared with Howitt's much more sympathetic description of statute fairs, to which the servants look forward because

They furnish occasion for a holiday. They are for the time their own masters, having left, or being about to leave their places, and either to re-engage themselves, or to seek new ones . . .

It is a true country scene, to see all these rude sons of the soil collected together from their farm-yards, and solitary fields . . . and the girls that have been scrubbing, churning, and milking, and occasionally helping in the hay or corn fields, here dressed out in their rustic finery, and shewing such robust forms and rosy faces as might astonish our over-delicate citizens . . . These matters [the hirings] all satisfactorily disposed of . . . away go the farmers . . . and leave the lads and lasses to a day of jollity and fun . . . the afternoon is spent in eating, flirting, drinking and dancing, and then, all separate their several ways, for at least another year. (*Rural Life of England*, ii. 248–50.)

Although Kingsley takes so much from S.G.O.'s account of the fair—the few poor stalls, the beer-drinking, the obscene ballads, the labourers' tawdry finery—he belittles the festivities witnessed by Lancelot by describing not a country town's hiring fair where a countryman would go on the serious errand of securing a job, but a village wake, a local parish feast such as was the original festivity at St. Giles's, Oxford, which during the nineteenth century grew to be a great fair. Sally Alexander, in her history of St. Giles's Fair, quotes reminiscences of it in the early years of the century when it must have been very like the wake described by Kingsley:

the fair had scarcely 'extended half way up one side of St. Giles's', and had 'consisted of two or three fruit and gingerbread stalls and a display of toys';

'of the smallest possible extent, being confined to the space from St. John's College to the Lamb and Flag on the east side; gypsies with their snuff-boxes and drinking booths occupying the west side of the street.' (*St. Giles's Fair, 1830-1914*, History Workshop Pamphlet 2, Oxford 1970, p. 4, n. 5 and 4.)

Certainly there are 'snuff-box gypsies' at Bonesake. As Lancelot and Tregarva are about to go into a booth:

'What upon earth is that?'
'I say, look out there!'
'Well, you look out yourself!'
    This was caused by a violent blow across the shins with a thick stick, the deed of certain drunken wise-acres who were persisting in playing in the dark the never very lucrative game of three sticks a-penny, conducted by a couple of gipsies. Poor fellows! there was one excuse for them. It was the only thing there to play at, except a set of skittles; and on those they had lost their money every Saturday night for the last seven years each at his own village beer-shop. (Ch. 13.)

Sally Alexander quotes Lord George Sanger's account of this game of chance in his *Seventy Years a Showman* (1927):

'Big sticks—"livetts" they were termed—[hurtled] towards the knives and snuff-boxes which formed the prizes for skilful shots, and were placed on tall ash rods, stuck into baskets full of mould, ranged against a canvas background. That was before the day of the "roll, bowl or pitch", with a ball, for coco-nuts. The latter were then rather costly rarities, and iron snuff and tobacco boxes, with cheap knives . . . were put up at two shies a penny to tempt onlookers to try their luck with the "livetts".' (Sally Alexander, op. cit., p. 54.)

The Oxford civic authorities no more approved of the game than did Kingsley, and in 1838 they tried to expel the 'snuff-box gypsies' from the fair.

    Kingsley makes what George Eliot called a 'diagram' of the village wake; he uses it to further his argument of the ignorant

brutishness of the agricultural labourers and to demonstrate its
effect on Lancelot's thought and action; he does not re-create
a closely observed and deeply felt rural scene. His concern for
argument rather than observation, his lack of the sympathy
which would bring him understanding of the scene, are apparent
if we compare his prejudiced view of the wake with Howitt's.
Like Kingsley, Howitt is concerned that the wake shall not be a
disorderly, immoral occasion. 'Let them root out cruelty and
rudeness, and drunkenness, as they have done already in a great
degree—for where now are bull-baitings, bear-baitings, dog-fights,
and cock-fights, which twenty years ago were the invariable
accompaniments and great attractions of these wakes?' (*Rural
Life of England*, ii. 248.) But he observes, with evident pleasure,
that the wake, celebrating the dedication of the church, 'fur-
nishes a certain point in every year, in every individual parish,
to which the rural people can look forward as a point of rest
and mutual rejoicing' (ii. 245), and he remarks that the village
feasts 'are times of pleasant exchange of hospitalities and
renewals of simple friendships. Out of doors there are stalls of
toys and sweetmeats, and whirligigs for the children; within,
there is, for once, plum-pudding and roast beef, and an infinity
of such talk as best pleases their tastes.' (ii. 247.)

Howitt and S.G.O. (followed by Kingsley) create different
images of the same kind of fair because their impression of it is
determined by prejudice. S.G.O. and Kingsley adopt the moral
tone of disapproving Anglican clergymen, albeit liberal ones.
Howitt is more interested in the human activity of the fair, and
in the experience and feelings of the people involved in it. Kingsley writes with conviction of the rural labourer's home and
labour when his argument generates passion. His most impressive
passage on the subject occurs in *Alton Locke* when Alton is
sent from London to attend a meeting of half-starved agricultural labourers to propagate Chartism and to find out how far
the men will go in the effort to raise their wages. The date is
1845. His destination is 'a knot of thatched hovels, all sinking
and leaning every way but the right, the windows patched with
paper, the door-ways stopped with filth', 'in the midst of a
dreary, treeless country, whose broad brown and grey fields
were only broken by an occasional line of dark doleful firs'
(vol. ii, ch. 7 'The Men who are Eaten'.) Apparently this is

15. Winson Green Prison (formerly Birmingham Gaol)

THE GAME LAWS;

OR, THE SACRIFICE OF THE PEASANT TO THE HARE.

16. 'The Game Laws', 1844

"THE PURITY OF THE PRESS, THE SAFEGUARD OF SOCIETY."

No. 49. JUNE 9, 1853.   PRICE ONE PENNY.   Vol. I. New Series.

JONATHAN RUTHERFORD ADDRESSING THE MINERS.

17. 'John Rutherford Addressing the Miners'

"THE PURITY OF THE PRESS, THE SAFEGUARD OF SOCIETY."

No. 54. JULY 14, 1853.   PRICE ONE PENNY.   Vol. I. New Series.

LORD WESTERLAND AND THE COLLIERS ON MAG'S HILL.

18. 'Lord Westerland and the Colliers'

19. Sarah Burge, 1883

E. MOSES AND SON'S READY MADE DEPARTMENT, ALDGATE.

20. E. Moses and Son's Ready Made Department, Aldgate,
1847

PATTERNS FOR SHAWLS.—A CARD.

Mr. PUNCH presents his compliments to wholesale dealers, and other practical philanthropists, who are wont—"regardless of expense"—to give to their serfs of the needle sixpence for the working of eighty flowers (see the late case of ESTHER PIERCE), that he has just completed a series of the most beautiful and significant Shawl Patterns, peculiarly illustrative of the benevolence of the employers and the comforts of the employed.

Mr. PUNCH has misery in every phase, and worked in all colours. Death's heads and broken hearts are most tastefully blended with roses and amaranths,—and picturesque starvation set off by gilliflowers and carnations.

Ladies who have a passion for great bargains, will find these Shawl Patterns peculiarly to their taste, inasmuch as they so beautifully and so truly illustrate the certain results of hard dealing.

Mr. PUNCH begs to submit the subjoined to the inspection of wholesale dealers, and to the gentle sex, assuring them that he has a great variety on hand.

21. Mr Punch's Shawl Patterns, 1844

Bubbles of the Year. – Cheap Clothing.

22. 'Bubbles of the Year. Cheap Clothing', 1845

CAPITAL AND LABOUR.

23. 'Capital and Labour', 1843

Cambridgeshire, like Suffolk an area of great rural poverty where rick fires had been started by the labourers in the 1830s and where incendiarism continued in the 1840s (see E. J. Hobsbawm and George Rudé, *Captain Swing*, 1969, p. 135 and p. 327). 'D' seems to be in Cambridgeshire (see *Alton Locke*, vol. i, ch. 13 'The Lost Idol Found'). The place where the meeting is to be held is near 'D' (see vol. ii, ch. 6 'The Plush Breeches Tragedy').

Alton's host, the shoemaker, enlightens him on

the custom of landlords letting the cottages with their farms, for the mere sake of saving themselves trouble; thus giving up all power of protecting the poor man, and delivering him over, bound hand and foot, even in the matter of his commonest home comforts, to farmers, too penurious, too ignorant, and often too poor, to keep the cottages in a state fit for the habitation of human beings. Thus the poor man's hovel, as well as his labour, became, he told me, a source of profit to the farmer, out of which he wrung the last drop of gain. The necessary repairs were always put off as long as possible—the labourers were robbed of their gardens—the slightest rebellion lost them not only work, but shelter from the elements; the slavery under which they groaned penetrated even to the fireside and to the bedroom.

In the preface to his novel *The Pageant; or, Pleasure and its Price. A Tale for the Upper Ranks of Society* (1843), which, in the wake of the Children's Employment Commission, exposed the privations of young seamstresses and milliners, the Revd Francis Paget quotes the remark of 'one who has had abundant opportunities of judging: "... there is nothing like a stay in the City of London, in the house of an active clergyman, for opening one's eyes to the *depths* of human misery. The so-called poor people of my own dear Kent, are, I see clearly now, the actual originals of the shepherds and shepherdesses of the Golden Age." '

Kingsley describes Alton enduring the horrors of sweated labour in London but also shows that the rural labourers endure comparable misery. Alton and his guide, on their way to the meeting, encounter not the shepherds and shepherdesses of the Golden Age but the sheep-tenders of the Iron Age:

Not a house was to be seen for miles, except the knot of hovels which we had left, and here and there a great dreary lump of farm-buildings, with its yard of yellow stacks. Beneath our feet the earth was iron, and the sky iron above our heads ...

We trudged on, over wide stubbles, thick with innumerable weeds; over wide fallows, in which the deserted ploughs stood frozen fast; then over clover and grass, burnt black with frost; then over a field of turnips, where we passed a large fold of hurdles, within which some hundred sheep stood, with their heads turned from the cutting blast. All was dreary, idle, silent; no sound or sign of human beings. One wondered where the people lived, who cultivated so vast a tract of civilised, over-peopled, nineteenth-century England. As we came up to the fold, two little boys hailed us from the inside—two little wretches with blue noses and white cheeks, scarecrows of rags and patches, their feet peeping through bursten shoes twice too big for them, who seemed to have shared between them a ragged pair of worsted gloves, and cowered among the sheep, under the shelter of a hurdle, crying and inarticulate with cold.

'What's the matter, boys?'

'Turmits is froze, and us can't turn the handle of the cutter. Do ye gie us a turn, please!'

We scrambled over the hurdles, and gave the miserable little creatures the benefit of ten minutes' labour. They seemed too small for such exertion: their little hands were purple with chilblains, and they were so sore-footed they could scarcely limp. I was surprised to find them at least three years older than their size and looks denoted, and still more surprised, too, to find that their salary for all this bitter exposure to the elements—such as I believe I could not have endured two days running—was the vast sum of one shilling a week each, Sundays included. 'They didn't never go to school, nor to church neither, except just now and then, sometimes—they had to mind the shep.'

I went on, sickened with the contrast between the highly-bred, over-fed, fat, thick-woolled animals . . . and the little half-starved shivering animals who were their slaves. Man the master of the brutes? Bah! As society is now, the brutes are the masters—the horse, the sheep, the bullock, is the master, and the labourer is their slave. 'Oh! but the brutes are eaten!' Well; the horses at least are not eaten—they live, like landlords, till they die. And those who are eaten, are certainly not eaten by their human servants . . . and after all, is not the labourer, as well as the sheep, eaten by you, my dear Society? (Vol. ii, ch. 7 'The Men who are Eaten'.)

Despite the 'Bah!', Kingsley's favourite exclamation of disgust, this is a powerful passage, challenging both the pastoral and the picturesque treatment of the countryside. 'Corin and Sylvia' are absent. Sheep are no longer the decorative accompaniment to idyllic tales of love but evidence of a lucrative type of farming which can denude the countryside and oppress the labourer. The thatched cottages, with trim gardens and bee-hives, are replaced by 'the knot of hovels'.

Again, the facts Kingsley uses can be found in *Reports on*

Agriculture, 1843. One of the medical officers of the Blandford Union, Dorsetshire, testified:

With regard to the children, they are generally sent out to work at the ages of eight or nine, and some as young as seven years of age. They assist occasionally in ploughing, but more generally in bird-keeping [scaring the birds from the crops], attending cows, pigs, and horses, when at field. The labour of these *infants* is seven days a-week . . . The consequence is, they seldom, if ever, enter a place of worship . . . Morally speaking, I should say it is a miserably bad system to prevent these children from attending daily and Sunday schools, and the church . . . Physically speaking, I think it does, in children so young, produce severe chills and colds, &c., &c., which occasionally terminate in other diseases which prove injurious in after-life . . . They are, during the most severe weather, constantly exposed to its vicissitudes, and at an age much too young. (P.P. Session 1843 (XII), 97.)

A less sympathetic medical officer of St. Thomas's Union, Exeter, commented:

I observe that boys are employed very early in life; generally when seven or eight years old. They begin by getting in wood for the house, gathering turnips together for cattle . . . Their work, however, is favourable to their health; it seems to have the effect of establishing it. Chilblains appear to be the only things boys suffer from, which might be avoided if the farmer would take care and provide proper things for them; but the spring always cures them. (p. 110.)

There are several references to young boys minding sheep. In Lincoln the boys 'are much occupied with the sheep, and more still when the snow is on the ground' (p. 272). According to a bailiff of an estate near Dorking, Surrey, 'On the turnip-lands some farmers . . . will have the turnip taken up from the ground to feed the sheep through the winter. The turnip is in this case pulled and dressed, and the cutting-machine turned by boys. Boys of eight years old are occasionally hired for this, at 2*s*. or 2*s*. 6*d*. a-week.' (p. 210.) This is double the wages quoted by Kingsley, but in the *Reports* there are several instances of young boys being paid much less, for example, in Dorsetshire young boys in their first job of scaring birds from the crops got 1*s*. to 1*s*. 6*d*. a week. This sum was considered 'the average pay' for boys aged 8 to 12 in this county (p. 48).

Kingsley's indignant address to 'Society', which gives the chapter its title, seems to have been inspired by S.G.O.'s summary of the hardships endured by the agricultural labourer but unknown to the public, including 'the manner in which he often sees the welfare of the beast he drives more valued than his

own' (p. 92). And it might be an echo of Carlyle: 'There is not
a horse willing to work but can get food and shelter in requital;
a thing this two-footed worker has to seek for, to solicit occasionally in vain.' (*Chartism*, ch. 4, Carlyle, *Works*, x. 345.)
Kingsley's prose in this episode is at once both more precise and
more evocative than that describing Ashy in *Yeast*. 'A great
dreary lump of farm-buildings' well suggests the occasional
looming dark shapes on the bare sky-line, and in its economy
and directness echoes the Shetlanders' phrase to describe a huge
menacing wave, 'a great lump of water'; Kingsley's use of the
word 'lump' also implies a threat. The outstanding colour
yellow—'its yard of yellow stacks'—serves to emphasize the
otherwise total dinginess and drabness of the scene. Also, there
is, for Kingsley, an unusually subtle use of rhythm in 'Beneath
our feet the earth was iron, and the sky iron above our heads'
emphasizing repetition of the kind ballad writers use[23] to evoke
the monotony of the landscape and, with similar linguistic
economy, suggesting in 'iron' colour, oppression, and inflexi-
bility. The passage is a rare example of Kingsley's perceiving a
landscape with such imaginative intensity that it achieves
symbolic significance. Truth about the physical facts of the
landscape establishes the imaginative truth of the desolation and
desperation of the labourers who try to get their living in it.
This imaginative extension of the particular scene is paralleled
by its logical extension from the particular to the general condition of England: 'One wondered where the people lived, who
cultivated so vast a tract of civilised, over-peopled, nineteenth
century England.' The desolation results from the depopulation
of that district because of the type of farming favoured, mecha-
nization and the consequent migration of people into town to
find a living.

As in *Yeast* the description both implies argument and re-
inforces it, but is more powerful because what Alton sees and
experiences makes him argue as he does, and these sights and
experiences are re-created for the reader so that he shares them
and the arguments. The images of the landscape both cause his
indignation and express it. The scenes are not merely general

---

[23] Compare the verse in 'Van Diemen's Land', the ballad on transportation, which
repeats 'blue' to suggest the wearying monotony of the journey from England to
Australia: 'Beneath us one blue water / And above us one blue sky.'

support for preconceived ideas; 'illustration', to use Raymond Williams's word ('Dickens and Social Ideas', p. 85). When the reader ceases to enter imaginatively into Alton's experience, but is asked to believe that Alton's faith in Chartism is shattered by Eleanor's flimsy arguments, the novel falters and dies.

Disraeli also presents argument and challenge of conventional representations of the English rural scene in his description of Marney, in *Sybil*:

The situation of the rural town of Marney was one of the most delightful easily to be imagined. In a spreading dale, contiguous to the margin of a clear and lively stream, surrounded by meadows and gardens, and backed by lofty hills, undulating and richly wooded, the traveller on the opposite heights of the dale would often stop to admire the merry prospect that recalled to him the traditional epithet of his country. (Bk. II, ch. 3.)

Here is the picturesque prospect seen from afar and apparently ratifying the description 'Merry England', according to the Oxford English Dictionary, first used in the fourteenth century with the suggestion that the country was a place of feasting and sport, and employed repeatedly by successive writers, including Spenser in his national epic *The Faerie Queene* (see I. x. 61). 'Beautiful illusion! For behind that laughing landscape, penury and disease fed upon the vitals of a miserable population.' This ironic exposure of the reality of 'Merry England' echoes Peacock, whom Disraeli admired and who asserted that the phrase 'must be a mirifical puzzle to any one who looks for the first time on its present most lugubrious inhabitants' (*Misfortunes of Elphin*, 1829, Halliford edition, ed. H. F. B. Brett-Smith and C. E. Jones, 10 vols., 1924–34, iv. 110). It also closely resembles Cobbett's line of argument in his *History of the Protestant Reformation*, published in book form the same year as Peacock's novel:

my chief object is to show, that this alteration [the Reformation] made the main body of the people poor and miserable, compared with what they were before; that it impoverished and degraded them; that it banished, at once, that 'Old English Hospitality,' of which we have since known nothing but the name; and that, in lieu of that hospitality, it gave us pauperism, a thing, the very name of which was never before known in England. (I, Letter I, §36.)

In *Chartism* Carlyle used 'Merry England' with an irony similar to Disraeli's. Commenting on the pamphlet *The Possibility of Limiting Populousness* by one 'Marcus', who advocated that working people should practise infanticide to prevent the number of their children from exceeding three, he writes, 'What a black, godless, waste-struggling world, in this once merry England of ours, do such pamphlets . . . betoken!' (Ch. 10, Carlyle, *Works*, x. 422.) For Engels, who owed a good deal to Carlyle, it was a phrase pregnant with meaning in the struggle between the Two Nations. In his chapter 'The Industrial Proletariat' he writes of the great manufacturing towns: 'here the morals and customs of the good old times are most completely obliterated; here it has gone so far that the name Merry Old England conveys no meaning, for Old England itself is unknown to memory and to the tales of our grandfathers' (op. cit., p. 56).

It was, in fact, a common phrase in the 'Condition of England' debate and Disraeli's use of it makes his description part of that debate. In the *Reports on Agriculture*, 1843, the Vicar of Calne, Wiltshire, concluded his assessment of the rural labourers' condition: 'the best way of relief is by emigration, by education, and by improving the system of agriculture, so as to compel the farmers to employ more men. Only give us a little present relief, that we may have time to raise the character of the rising generation and we may still see Merry Old England once more.' (P.P. Session 1843 (XII), 73.) And Pugin, whose vision of society is clearly apparent in *Sybil*, and whose *Contrasts* demonstrates the difference between Merry Old England and the dismal new Utilitarian kingdom, uses the same phrase in arguing the social virtues of medieval monasteries: 'humbler guests partook of their share of bounty dealt to them by the hand of the almoner beneath the groined entrance of the gatehouse. Catholic England was merry England, at least for the humbler classes.' (*The True Principles of Pointed or Christian Architecture*, 1841 (reprint from 1853 impression, Oxford, 1969, p. 51).)

Disraeli, also, is nostalgic for a lost 'Merry England' and associates its joy with the social responsibility of the Roman Catholic Church. Marney (possibly based on Ripon) reveals the harsh reality of the present:

The contrast between the interior of the town and its external aspect was as striking as it was full of pain. With the exception of the dull high street, which had the usual characteristics of a small agricultural market town, some sombre mansions, a dingy inn, and a petty bourse, Marney mainly consisted of a variety of narrow and crowded lanes formed by cottages built of rubble, or unhewn stones without cement, and, from age or badness of the material, looking as if they could scarcely hold together. The gaping chinks admitted every blast; the leaning chimneys had lost half their original height; the rotten rafters were evidently misplaced; while in many instances the thatch, yawning in some parts to admit the wind and wet, and in all utterly unfit for its original purpose of giving protection from the weather, looked more like the top of a dunghill than a cottage. Before the doors of these dwellings, and often surrounding them, ran open drains full of animal and vegetable refuse, decomposing into disease, or sometimes in their imperfect course filling foul pits or spreading into stagnant pools, while a concentrated solution of every species of dissolving filth was allowed to soak through, and thoroughly impregnate, the walls and ground adjoining. (Bk. II, ch. 3.)

Like Kingsley describing the Ashy landscape, Disraeli destroys the prospect of Marney as seen by 'that gentlemanly spy upon Nature, the picturesque traveller', to use Lamb's words, by coming in close to the place. It lacks the immediacy and imaginative intensity of Alton's encounter with the sheep-tenders. It has the neutral effect of some of Elizabeth Gaskell's descriptions of Manchester, in which she enumerates features, rather than recreating them for the reader. There are no imaginatively selected details, such as Kingsley's 'great dreary lump of farm-buildings' or the 'deserted ploughs' standing frozen fast in the stubblefields to help the reader both visualize and experience the scene. Disraeli's details are, in fact, lifted bodily from Edwin Chadwick's *Report* in which he quotes the Revd Dr Gilly, vicar of Norham and canon of Durham, on labourers' cottages: 'built of rubble or unhewn stone, loosely cemented; and from age, or badness of the materials, the walls look as if they would scarcely hold together . . . The chimneys have lost half their original height, and lean on the roof with fearful gravitation. The rafters are evidently rotten and displaced.' (pp. 95 f.)

The one outstanding detail of Disraeli's description is the thatch which 'looked more like the top of a dunghill than a cottage'. The visual image implies the community's squalor and discomfort, also the waste involved, men's lives are being squandered, flung on a dunghill. But the imagination which seizes upon this detail is the Revd Dr Gilly's, not Disraeli's: 'and the thatch, yawning to admit the wind and wet in some parts, and in all parts utterly unfit for its original purpose of giving protection from the weather, looks more like the top of a dunghill

than of a cottage' (p. 96). The rest of Disraeli's description also
leans heavily on Chadwick's *Report*, sometimes quoting directly,
for example, the evidence of Mr W. J. Gilbert collected at Tiver-
ton when Assistant Poor Law Commissioner for Cornwall and
Devon: 'The open drains in some cases ran immediately before
the doors of the houses, and some of the houses were surrounded
by wide open drains, full of all animal and vegetable refuse'
(p. 80), and 'Some have neither windows nor doors sufficient to
keep out the weather, or to let in the rays of the sun, or supply
the means of ventilation; and in others the roof is so constructed
or so worn as not to be weather tight. The thatch roof frequently is saturated with wet, rotten, and in a state of decay,
giving out malaria, as other decaying vegetable matter.' (pp. 80 f.)

Disraeli's passage, incorporating the contemporary belief in
'exhalation' causing malaria, runs: 'These swarming walls had
neither windows nor doors sufficient to keep out the weather,
or admit the sun, or supply the means of ventilation; the humid
and putrid roof of thatch exhaling malaria like all other decaying vegetable matter.' (Bk. II, ch. 3.) Or his description is close
to Dr Barham's evidence of conditions in Truro: 'gutters forming pits here and there . . . a concentrated solution of all sorts of
decomposing refuse being allowed to soak through and thoroughly impregnate the walls and ground adjoining'[24] (p. 82).

Like Kingsley, Disraeli ascribes the desolation of the rural
scene to agricultural policy:

This town of Marney was a metropolis of agricultural labour, for the
proprietors of the neighbourhood having for the last half-century acted on
the system of destroying the cottages on their estates, in order to become
exempted from the maintenance of the population [that is, paying the
poor-rates], the expelled people had flocked to Marney, where, during the
war, a manufactory had afforded them some relief, though its wheels had
long ceased to disturb the waters of the Mar. (Bk. II, ch. 3.)

He is concerned to establish the causes of the squalor he has
described:

Deprived of this resource, they had again gradually spread themselves over
that land which had, as it were, rejected them; and obtained from its churl-
ish breast a niggardly subsistence. Their re-entrance into the surrounding

---

[24] For Disraeli's use of Chadwick's *Report* in the description of Marney I am in-
debted to J. M. Blom, The English and American Institute, University of Nymegen,
Holland, who produced an unpublished paper on this topic for one of my seminars.
He generously allowed me to use this material.

parishes was viewed with great suspicion; their renewed settlement opposed by every ingenious contrivance. Those who availed themselves of their labour were careful that they should not become dwellers on the soil; and though, from the excessive competition, there were few districts in the kingdom where the rate of wages was more depressed, those who were fortunate enough to obtain the scant renumeration had, in addition to their toil, to endure, each morn and even, a weary journey before they could reach the scene of their labour, or return to the squalid hovel which profaned the name of home. To that home, over which malaria hovered, and round whose shivering hearth were clustered other guests besides the exhausted family of toil, Fever, in every form, pale Consumption, exhausting Synochus, and trembling Ague, returned, after cultivating the broad fields of merry England, the bold British peasant, returned to encounter the worst of diseases, with a frame the least qualified to oppose them; a frame that, subdued by toil, was never sustained by animal food; drenched by the tempest, could not change its dripping rags; and was indebted for its scanty fuel to the windfalls of the woods. (Bk. II, ch. 3.)

The style is ponderous, self-conscious, and remote, but the passage is based on factual evidence. 'Never sustained by animal food' is a pardonable exaggeration for emphasis. The *Reports on Agriculture*, 1843, reveal that most agricultural labourers lived on bread and potatoes, with very occasional bacon and cheese. Also, a collection of reminiscences of rural life in the 1840s provides evidence to support Disraeli's assertion. True, they were used to propagate the idea of Free Trade at the beginning of this century, but the insight they provide into the daily life of the early Victorian agricultural labourer is none the less valuable. An old woman remembered her life as a farm-labourer's child in Dorset:

'The family lived on flatcakes, about an inch thick, made of coarse barley flour, and baked in a little black iron crock with three legs . . .

Treacle they used instead of sugar, as it was cheaper. Beef and mutton they were unable to purchase; but on Sundays, perhaps, the father and mother would have a rasher or two of bacon, whilst the children looked on with longing eyes and whispered to each other . . . that when they "grew up" they also would have their rasher!' (*The Hungry Forties*, Mrs Jane Cobden Unwin, 1904, pp. 160 f.)

A ploughman's boy brought up on a farm near Stanfield Hall, Norfolk (the scene of the Rush murders, which so interested Dickens), recollected:

'You would never guess the dainties my father's seven shillings provided for us, and it has been the mystery of my life how my mother eked it out. I have a very distinct recollection of dumplings made of barley meal, and it was with some difficulty I got my teeth through them. Then we had some potatoes, and sometimes we found a swede in the road, having fell off the farm cart. That was a treat indeed! This was our usual weekday fare. But Sunday came, and with something extra for dinner. Meat? Oh no! A simple herring between five of us constituted our Sunday dinner, and the tail, I remember, was my share as a rule.' (Ibid., pp. 88 f.)

The individual details of the 'flatcakes . . . baked in a little black iron crock with three legs' and of 'a swede in the road, having fell off the farm cart' expose the pompous, official tone of Disraeli's 'never sustained by animal food'. Disraeli has caught the tone of the reporting Commissioners rather than that of the people giving evidence.

The *Reports on Agriculture*, 1843, ratify Disraeli's contention that the agricultural labourer has little bodily stamina because of the poor quality of his food: 'Generally speaking the labouring population is healthy; but it appears that when grown-up women are attacked by diseases of certain descriptions, the low quality of their food is unfavourable to their recovery.' (p. 34.) Also, they make the point reiterated by the novelist: 'The clothing of women employed in field-labour would appear to be inadequate for their work, but the deficiency is not complained of by them. [Their acceptance of their lot as inevitable is one of the most appalling aspects of the Reports.] A change of clothes seems to be out of the question.' (p. 38.)

The women come home, go to bed so that their clothes can dry, but have to put them on wet the next morning. 'It does not appear that any ill consequences to the health have been observed by medical men to arise from this cause, unless rheumatism be partly attributable to it.' (p. 38.)

This comfortable conclusion shows how the official prose can remove the reader from the reality of the life described. One of the witnesses, Mrs Smart, wife of a Calne stonemason, brings him nearer its substance:

I went out leasing (gleaning) this autumn for three weeks, and was very lucky: I got, six bushels of corn. I got up at two o'clock in the morning, and got home at seven at night. My other girls, aged 10, 15, and 18, went with me . . . I have had 13 children, and have brought seven up. I have been accustomed to work in the fields at haytime and harvest . . . Often, out of the hay-fields, myself and my children have come home with our things quite wet through: I have gone to bed for an hour for my things to get a little dry, but have had to put them on again when quite wet. (pp. 81 f.)

Sybil is a novel of political debate; discursive, in the tradition of Henry Brooke's *The Fool of Quality* (1766-70), which discusses the education and the attributes of a gentleman, or Robert Plumer Ward's *Tremaine* (1825), which debates the existence of revealed truth as opposed to rational enquiry. Together with *Coningsby* and *Tancred*, it extends and develops the political thinking which had always been important in Disraeli's novels, from *Vivian Grey* onwards. His own personality and voice are prominent in his novels, and in *Sybil* he uses visual scenes, such as the descriptions of Marney, like a politician making his case in the House of Commons. A skilful debater, he repeats the ironic 'Merry England' to taunt the hated Whigs, particularly about their 1834 Poor Law which even an Assistant Poor Law Commissioner considered partly responsible for the rural labourers' plight.[25]

His description of Marney in 1837 ends with the agitation of Lord Marney and Sir Vavasour Firebrace at the previous night's rick-burning; in the next chapter one of the labourers appears. He has a walking-on part with one sentence to speak:

'And what do you think of this fire?' said Egremont to the hind.
   'I think 'tis hard times for the poor, sir.'
   'But rick-burning will not make the times easier, my good man.'
   The man made no reply, but with a dogged look led away the horse to his stable. (Bk. II, ch. 4.)

'The hind', like Kingsley's anxious villager, is a 'diagram', in this case to demonstrate Egremont's blindness and his need to be educated into the life of the Other Nation.

History supports Disraeli's fiction. After the agricultural labourers' riots of the winter 1830-1, rick-burning had continued each winter. It had been particularly frequent in the winter 1843-4, preceding the publication of *Sybil*. So Disraeli uses it to establish his period and to comment on contemporary conditions. The 1830-1 riots had been put down with great savagery

---

[25] 'The present state of the labour-market, combined with the effect of the New Poor Law, in throwing the labouring classes mainly on their own resources [it discouraged outdoor relief, and forced those applying for help to enter the workhouse], almost compels the parents to take their children from school as soon as they can earn anything in the fields.' Evidence of Stephen Charles Denison on conditions in Suffolk, Norfolk and Lincoln, *Reports*, 1843, p. 233. Also the remark of the Revd T. Attwood, Framlingham, Suffolk, 'The New Poor Law had a visible effect on education, in making children used as earners at an earlier age.' (p. 254.)

(see J. L. and Barbara Hammond, *The Village Labourer, 1760–1832* (first published 1911), 2 vols., 1948, ii. 123) so the continuation of rick-burning and machine-smashing, under the leadership of the mythical Captain Swing, suggests how desperate the labourers were. A cartoon published 28 January 1831 (see Plate 13) exposes, as Disraeli did later, the hollowness of the phrase 'Merry England' applied to a countryside of burning ricks and overshadowed by the judge's black cap, the noose and the gallows. In the same year Edward Gibbon Wakefield published *Swing Unmasked; or, The Causes of Rural Incendiarism*, the results of his investigations into the plight of the Suffolk agricultural labourers. Like Disraeli, he explodes the pleasant fiction expressed in the phrase 'the bold peasantry of England', with its ironic echoes of Goldsmith's 'Deserted Village'. All peasants, says Wakefield, are paupers 'for the words are synonymous'. He concludes his pamphlet: 'Such, then, is the nature of *Swing* incendiarism, that the crime is not to be stopped, either by hanging, or by exhortation, or by execration, or by a tax on landlords and parsons, or by charitable subscriptions, or by martial law, or even by spring-guns. The first main cause of the crime is misery.' (p. 45.)

Leech's cartoon, 'The Home of the Rick-Burner', *Punch* (7 (1844), 17) (see Plate 14), is the graphic equivalent of Wakefield's argument. It could be argued that both the pamphlet and the cartoon are more effective than Disraeli's ponderous fiction; both show that Disraeli, in his description of the 'peasant' as in that of 'Merry England', appeals to arguments and images long familiar. And it is fitting that his description of the Marney peasants should end in abstractions—Fever, 'pale Consumption, exhausting Synochus, and trembling Ague'. The actuality of rural life is dimmed in an idealized significance. Disraeli has no business with the barley cakes baked in the black crock, or the one herring.

THE POOR IN GAOL, AS DESCRIBED BY READE

Previously in this chapter I have described the novelists' descriptions of the domestic dwellings and physical environment of the poor. To conclude it I want to consider Reade's description of a place which the poor were often forced to inhabit—prison.

Reade's objective is different from that of the other novelists I have been discussing in that he is not describing a whole society, a community of the poor, but rather the injustice which poor individuals were liable to suffer. In this case, the norms of society which failed to apply to the Other Nation were the norms of justice. This is important to my argument because the insistence that the Law divides the Two Nations, there being one Law for the poor and another for the rich, is a persistent theme in the period both in popular ballads, such as 'The Rich and the Poor; or, The Gentleman and the Brick-layer',[26] and in middle-class writing—'alas! as respects the most numerous class of her people . . . her boasted laws of equal right and privilege are a farce', wrote Charlotte Elizabeth Tonna in 1843 (see 'The Little Pin-Headers', based on evidence in the *Children's Employment Commission*, reprinted Ivanka Kova-čević, p. 345). Stephen Morley, initiating Egremont's social education, insists that the Two Nations 'are not governed by the same laws' (*Sybil*, Bk. II, ch. 5).

The Utilitarians, disciples of Bentham, had long urged penal reform. The new prisons of the 1830s, 1840s, and 1850s were physical manifestations of a social philosophy; they applied science to penology as statistics and Royal Commissions applied science to government. Cleanliness, industry, and order were to supplant the dirt and chaos of the old eighteenth-century prisons. The criminal was forced to accept the work ethic of the increasingly earnest society; labour was to be the remedy for his disease, crime, and he was to be kept away from the contamination of other criminals. Hence the development of two rival methods of punishment, the 'separate' system of solitary confinement, with the prisoners hooded when they had to move about the prison, and the 'silent' system in which prisoners were one man to a cell but associated for work and exercise, keeping silence on pain of severe punishment. The Reformed Parliament,

[26] It tells the story of a gentleman and a bricklayer, both tried for murder. The gentleman is judged insane and removed to a comfortable lunatic asylum: ' "Remove him to the madhouse and justice will be done," / But had he been a poor man he'd surely have been hung.' The bricklayer pleads guilty because he cannot afford to pay counsel, and is condemned to death. Finally, the listener is exhorted, '. . . bless the Lord you live in a land where evermore, / There's one law for the rich man and another for the poor.' It was evidently a popular ballad. There are at least two copies in Baring-Gould's collection, one printed in London and the other in Leeds. (See Baring-Gould, *Ballads*, v. 181 and vi. 196.)

1832, established a Royal Commission to revise the whole criminal law; a report was published in May 1837.[27] It was in this year that the Government adopted the separate system as the official penal system. Pentonville, opened December 1842, was designed as the new model 'separate' prison, in which the convicts were to have a rigorous reformatory period of not more than eighteen months, during which they would be taught useful trades, before being transported to Van Diemen's Land.

Both Pugin and Ruskin, although of very different religious persuasions, advocated the Gothic style as the architectural expression of spiritual endeavour and moral health. In *Contrasts*, Pugin attacks modern prisons and workhouses, indicative of the oppressive, materialistic, modern spirit, by contrasting them with the gracious spires and welcoming cloisters of medieval churches and monasteries. In 'The Nature of Gothic' Ruskin urges that Gothic architecture should be considered as an index of 'religious principle'. After the Reformed Parliament had come into being Cobbett noted, in October 1832, that Morpeth, in Northumberland, had 'the disgrace of seeing an enormous new jail rising up in it'. He added, 'From cathedrals and monasteries we are come to be proud of our jails, which are built in the grandest style, and seemingly as if to imitate the Gothic architecture.' (*Rural Rides*, ii. 374.) The new prisons imitated the Gothic not by soaring ecclesiastical spires and arches but by castellar bastions, turrets and frowning walls. They were to be modern Castles of Perseverance, bulwarks against crime, and public symbols of moral endeavour; moreover, such a respectable type of architecture would ensure their acceptance in the districts in which they were built. It continued to be the prison style for many decades; Birmingham Gaol, built as a new model prison in 1850, is an example of it (see Plate 15).

The most solid part of what Reade, in the dedication, described as 'this attempt at a solid fiction', *It is Never too Late to Mend*, is undoubtedly the section, roughly a third of the novel, dealing with the Gaol. It was Reade's first major novel; his first social problem novel; and the first written according to

[27] For a discussion of the reduction of crimes punishable by the death penalty 1832–41 and its relation to the ways in which Bulwer-Lytton and Dickens described the criminal in their fiction of this period, see Keith Hollingsworth, *The Newgate Novel*, Wayne State University Press, 1963, particularly pp. 24–84 and pp. 111–27.

the plan he formulated in June 1853: 'I propose never to guess where I can know.' (See Malcolm Elwin, *Charles Reade A Biography*, 1931, p. 86.) Originally intended to be a romance, *Susan Merton*, it retold the plot of Reade's successful play, *Gold* (first performed Drury Lane, 10 January 1853), with the addition of the prison scenes, and was transformed by Reade's passionate ideas on the penal system. The prison scenes are worked into the plot of the play by having the thief Tom Robinson, one of the original characters, sent to the Gaol before being transported to Australia; but they are not well integrated into the novel as a whole, which splits awkwardly into three separate parts: the love story of George Fielding and Susan Merton; the prison chaplain's defeat of the governor and his system, and his redemption of Tom Robinson; and the adventures of George and Tom prospecting for gold in Australia. John Coleman says that in 1852, at the time when Reade was writing *Peg Woffington* (1853), he was shown over Durham Gaol by the governor, and that a prisoner, Jennins, wrote his autobiography for Reade and was the prototype of Robinson in *Gold* (*Charles Reade As I Knew Him*, 1903, p. 118); also, he cites a jotting in Reade's diary for 17 July, presumably 1853, in which he complains of the droning parson in Reading Gaol chapel and determines to 'say a few words, in my quiet temperate way about this sort of thing' (p. 161). Reade rightly felt that the life of the book was in the prison scenes. Annie Fields quotes the letter he sent his publishers, Ticknor and Fields, changing the novel's title even after advertisement had begun:

The scenes in which she [Susan Merton] figures are the stale and conventional part of the work. The soul of it are [*sic*] the scenes in which a bad man is despaired of and tortured by fools, and afterward not despaired of by a wise and good man, but encouraged, softened, converted. These psychological scenes and the melodramatic scenes that follow, in which the thief's understanding is convinced as well as his heart, are the immortal part of the work. The rest dozens of men and women on both sides the water could have written, and better than I have done them. I stand, therefore, on my ace of spades and not on my nine of hearts, and the title of the work is 'It's Never too Late to Mend.' ('An Acquaintance with Charles Reade', *Century Illustrated Monthly Magazine*, 7 (1884), 70 f.)

But although he had been interested for some time in the treatment of prisoners, his indignation at prison abuses had an immediate cause: the revelation, during the Royal Commission of

Enquiry, August and September 1853, and in the Commissioners'
Report, 1854, of the cruel and illegal punishments inflicted upon
prisoners in Birmingham Gaol by Lieutenant William Austin R.N.
and by his subordinates, with his approval. Austin, who had
been Deputy-Governor of Tothill Fields Prison, Westminster,
which was run on the 'silent' system (see P. A. W. Collins, op.
cit., p. 66), had become Governor of Birmingham Gaol in 1851,
after he had secured the dismissal of the first Governor, Captain
Alexander Maconochie, whom he had served as Deputy.
Maconochie (idealized as 'Captain O'Connor' in Reade's novel)
had been Governor of Norfolk Island, the Australian penal
settlement. He aimed at reforming the criminal and reintegrat-
ing him into society rather than savagely punishing him. He
devised the 'marks system' whereby the length of a prisoner's
sentence was not predetermined but dependent upon the number of 'marks' acquired for good conduct and behaviour. Because
they prevented convicts working together in groups and sharing
responsibility for rewards and punishments he disapproved of
both the 'silent' and the 'separate' systems. Austin, a stern disci-
plinarian, at a period when increasing severity towards criminals
was winning public approval (see P. A. W. Collins, p. 76), gained
the support of the visiting justices who disapproved of Maconochie's ideas, and supplanted him at Birmingham.

Reade, who had been trained as a lawyer, was particularly
indignant at the leniency with which the prison officers were
subsequently treated. Thomas Freer, chief warder since 1852,
who had tried to bully the prisoner John Cartwright, aged
twenty, into saying that a guilty conscience had driven him to
his suicide attempt,[28] who was sullen and evasive during the
Commissioners' questioning and was severely censured by
them,[29] had been dismissed from his job by the visiting magistrates before the inquiry began and no further action was taken
against him. Blount, the prison surgeon, whom three prison officers accused of having ordered salt to be stuffed into a prisoner's
mouth to prevent his crying out when clamped in the punishment jacket, was also strongly censured by the Commissioners

[28] Birmingham *Report*, p. 190.
[29] Mr Welsby, Recorder of Chester, one of the Commissioners, said of Freer, 'I
never saw a witness, in the course of a long experience, from whom it has been more
difficult to extract the truth than from you.' (Birmingham *Report*, p. 159.)

who recorded: 'We are bound also to express our opinion, with respect both to Lieut. Austin and to Mr. Blount, the latter in particular, that much of their evidence before us was given in an evasive, disingenuous, and discreditable manner.' (Birmingham *Report*, p. xxxvi.) He was later acquitted of the charge of ill-treating the prisoner, but found guilty of not keeping entries of punishment in the prison books, as the law required. Sentence was deferred and, in fact, never passed on him.[30] The Commissioners concluded, 'with respect, then, to the case of Edward Andrews [the fifteen-year-old boy whose suicide, by hanging, on 28 April 1853, was the direct cause of the inquiry], we are of the opinion that, by the order and with the knowledge of the governor, he was punished illegally and cruelly, and was driven thereby to the commission of suicide' (ibid., p. xi), and they censured Austin strongly. Later he was found guilty of the charges brought against him with regard to Andrews, and also of having failed to make entries of punishment in the prison books. Sentence was deferred until 24 November 1855 when he was given three months' imprisonment[31] by the Queen's Bench, Mr Justice Coleridge stipulating that during that time he was to 'be kept among the first-class misdemeanants' (see *The Times*, 26 November 1855). Andrews,[32] whose death he had caused, was serving three months, with hard labour, 'for stealing four pounds of beef' (Birmingham *Report*, p. vi). 'He had been twice in the prison before; in September 1851, on a commitment for a month's imprisonment to hard labour, for stealing garden fruit; and in September 1852, under a sentence of fourteen days' imprisonment, for throwing stones in the street.' Reade blamed the Law for its partiality and society for allowing men like Austin to terrorize those, especially the poor and defenceless, whom it had placed in his power. P. A. W. Collins points out that it was the exposure of the Birmingham atrocities—in which Reade's novel played a part—that made people think again about the wisdom of severe punishment for crime.

[30] See John Thackray Bunce, *History of the Corporation of Birmingham: with a Sketch of the Earlier Government of the Town* (Birmingham, 1885), ii. 314.

[31] Not six months, as in P. A. W. Collins's *Dickens and Crime*, p. 66.

[32] The Birmingham *Report* describes him as 'of a thin spare habit of body, about five feet high' and gives the chaplain's description of him, ' "a very ignorant poor boy, very desolate in his circumstances;" "a very neglected desolate child" ' although the governor thought him 'sullen' and 'dogged' (p. vi).

Often when a Victorian novelist has to describe a place in order to expose an abuse the writing is precise and gives an impression of experience in a manner not characteristic of the book as a whole—for example, the description of the factory on a bleak winter morning in Frances Trollope's *Michael Armstrong* (1840), or that of the work-house in the same writer's *Jessie Phillips* (1844), or Charlotte Elizabeth Tonna's description of the interior of the factory in *Helen Fleetwood* (1841). It is as though these places, unusual both to the writers and their readers, command attention and sharpen observation. When Reade describes the place in which Josephs, the fictional counterpart of Andrews, serves his sentence, his writing has a precision which distinguishes it from his vague sketch of the stage-farm in Berkshire, the home of George Fielding in the early part of the novel, or the later descriptions of Australia, compiled from books, his brother's descriptions and the stage representations of 'the diggings' which had so delighted the audiences of *Gold* because of the spectacular mechanical devices in this scene. 'The meadows round Grassmere' are vague enough, but with 'a massive castellated building, glaring red brick with white corner stones' Reade immediately establishes the frowning Gothic architecture of the new Victorian prisons. Both the pretension and the menace of the Gaol are suggested in Reade's description:

Two round towers flank the principal entrance. On one side of the right-hand tower is a small house constructed in the same style as the grand pile. The castle is massive and grand: this, its satellite, is massive and tiny, like the frog doing his little bit of bull . . . There is one dimple to all this gloomy grandeur: a rich little flower-garden, whose frame of emerald turf goes smiling up to the very ankle of the frowning fortress . . . From this green spot a few flowers look up with bright and wondering wide-open eyes at the great bullying masonry over their heads; and to the spectator of both these sparks of colour at the castle-foot are dazzling and charming; they are like rubies, sapphires, and pink topaz, in some uncouth, angular, ancient setting. (Vol. i, ch. 10.)

The visual precision generates a metaphoric intensity. The little house imitating the great castle both mocks the castle's pretensions and suggests that its aggression is repeated, in little, by those who serve it. The few flowers are not only picturesque, 'charming . . . in some uncouth angular ancient setting', but their natural beauty and vigour flourish despite 'the great bullying masonry'—Nature impudently refuses to be daunted by the

walls designed to shut her out. The treatment of prisoners, anachronistic despite its modernity, suggested in the anachronistic
architecture, is emphasized by the first human figure described
in this setting: 'Between the central towers is a sharp arch, filled
by a huge oak door of the same shape and size, which, for
further security or ornament is closely studded with large
diamond-headed nails. A man with keys at his girdle, like the
ancient house-wives, opens the huge door to you with slight
effort, so well oiled is it.' (Ibid.)

The entrance into the prison suggests the springing of a trap,
the inexorable workings of a mechanism it will be difficult to
reverse should the prisoner be proved innocent: 'You slip under
a porch into an enclosed yard, the great door shuts almost of
itself, and now it depends upon the housewifely man whether
you ever see the vain, idle, and every way objectionable world
again.' (Ibid.)

Possibly this section mocks the canting declarations in which
the moralistic regime encouraged prisoners to indulge. Reade
later in the novel satirizes the hypocritical convicts who 'played
the system' so cunningly (see his description of the 'show
prisoner' and 'the multitude of incurable felons who have
swapped texts for tickets-of-leave', vol. ii, ch. 32), as does
Dickens in *David Copperfield* (1850) when he describes Uriah
Heep as a show prisoner (see ch. 61).

The thief, Robinson, whom Reade uses to introduce his
reader into the Gaol, is a perky 'rogue' character, one of the
poor who 'won't work'; he is imprisoned for passing stolen
bank-notes, and sent to the Gaol to await transportation. This
is his first spell in prison for some years and he is horrified at
the new, regimented system in place of the old laxity. He is confronted by the desolate efficiency of his solitary cell:

A bedstead, consisting of the side walls of the apartment; polished steel
staples are fixed in these walls, two on each side the apartment, at an elevation of about two feet and a half. The occupant's mattress (made of
cocoa bark) has two stout hooks at each end; these are hooked into the
staples, and so he lies across his abode. A deal table, the size of a pocket-
handkerchief; also a deal tripod. A water-spout so ingeniously contrived,
that, turned to the right, it sends a small stream into a copper basin, and
to the left, into a bottomless close stool at some distance. A small gas-
pipe, tipped with polished brass. In one angle of the wall, a sort of commode, or open cupboard, on whose shelves a bright pewter plate, a knife

and fork, and a wooden spoon: in a drawer of this commode, yellow soap and a comb and brush. A grating down low for hot air to come in, if it likes, and another up high for foul air to go out, if it chooses. On the wall over table, a large placard containing rules for the tenant's direction, and smaller placards containing texts from Scripture, the propriety of returning thanks after food, &c.; a slate, and a couple of leathern knee guards, used in polishing the room. And that is all. (Ibid.)

The passage is similar to Dickens's description of a cell in the experimental 'separate' system prison, Cherry Hill, the Eastern Penitentiary in Philadelphia, opened in 1830 (see *American Notes*, ch. 7). This is a documentary description of a system which appals him by its unintentional cruelty—he much prefers the 'silent' system. Dickens's lively imagination works upon the prison's physical realities to enter into the prisoner's mind: the details of his agony when 'every now and then there comes upon him a burning sense of the years that must be wasted in that stone coffin'; his imaginings about the prisoners in the adjacent cells—'Day after day, and often when he wakes up in the middle of the night, he thinks of these two men until he is almost distracted.' And then the sure psychological detail: 'He never changes them. There they are always as he first imagined them . . .' which perfectly embodies his mental stagnation. The growing horror of the cell from which he can never escape: 'as the darkness thickens, his Loom begins to live; and even that, his comfort, is a hideous figure, watching him till daybreak'. Then, finally, the fancies fade and in their place the even more horrible, inert resignation: 'Occasionally, the old agony comes back . . . but it does not last long, now: for the world without, has come to be the vision, and this solitary life, the sad reality.'

This is more powerful than anything in Reade's novel. Reade's great defect as a novelist is his melodramatic imagination and his love of sensation. In an earlier essay I showed how Reade in *It is Never Too Late to Mend* slightly but persistently exaggerates the details of the punishments in the prison ('Propaganda and Hard Facts in Charles Reade's Didactic Novels', *Renaissance and Modern Studies*, 4(1960), 135–49) but none the less he achieves an initial impact (often subsequently lost by overemphasis and repetition) by the physical details of the prison—the weight of the crank which must be turned so many times a day in order to escape punishment, the blackness of the dark cell, the physical agony induced by the straitjacket, meant to restrain violent prisoners but used by Austin as a punishment. Although he cannot emulate Dickens's re-creation of the prisoner's experience, Reade's descriptions are not lacking in psychological reality, for example, the precise description of the contents of a cell suggests the neurotic concentration of the occupant to whom these objects will be a world for the duration of his sentence.

Moreover, the descriptions of physical existence in the Gaol establish the philosophy of a penal system 'that severe punishment of mind and body was the essential object of a gaol, and that it was wrong and chimerical to attempt any cures by any other means'. 'Cures' because in the new Victorian penal system the prison 'is intended to be a penal system for diseased and contagious souls' (vol. i, ch. 10). Although there were disagreements as to the ways in which such 'cures' might be effected, the belief in them informed both the 'separate' and 'silent' systems. Even Maconochie, who supported neither, believed that 'Vice is a disease and penal science just moral surgery' (see P. A. W. Collins, op. cit., p. 165; both Dickens and Carlyle came to oppose this view, believing that some criminals were incurable and suggesting increasingly vindictive punishments for crime, see Collins, pp. 17–18). Robinson's cell 'is inviting at first sight', but the clinical cleanliness, which suggests the hospital, is shown to be the result of an insistent, desolating, routine:

he was ushered into a cell white as driven snow, and his housewifely duties explained to him, under a heavy penalty if a speck of dirt should ever be discovered on his little wall, his little floor, his little table, or if his cocoa-bark mattress should not be neatly rolled up after use, and the strap tight, and the steel hook polished like glass, and his little brass gas-pipe glittering like gold, etc. (Vol. i, ch. 10.)

This is cleanliness next to the vengeful godliness of the Old Testament.

There was considerable variety in the regimes known as 'separate', as Reade himself accepts, and, as Collins points out, separatists did usually believe in the corrigibility of criminals through exhortation and training in honest work (see Collins, op. cit., p. 69). The prison scenes in Reade's novel show the dangers of such a system run by unimaginative men shielded from public inspection, and the futility of labour which is

non-productive and used as a punishment rather than construc-
tively as education and preparation for an honest job in society.
Moreover, the unbroken solitude was not only mental torture
(as was recognized when the term of solitary confinement at
Pentonville was reduced in the 1850s from eighteen months to
nine because of the mental deterioration of prisoners subjected
to it, see Collins, op. cit., p. 145) but unfitted the prisoner for
a return to society. Collins suggests (p. 168) that the system
advocated by Reade in which a prisoner has his own cell but is
not allowed to stagnate, being brought to moral understanding
by discussion with a humane and intelligent chaplain, and associating with other prisoners in learning a trade to fit him for the
outside world which he enters gradually, on parole, and finally
is protected by an after-care scheme, is similar to that established in Ireland in the 1850s by Sir Walter Crofton, who was
much influenced by Maconochie's ideas. Collins also shows that
Reade's hopes for a more constructive penal regime were not
realized and that, despite the check given to the increasingly
harsh ideas about the penal system by the revelation of conditions at Birmingham, the Carnarvon Committee Report (1863)
came out against moral reformation of the prisoner and for
vindictive punishment (p. 78).

Reade's attack on the relentless order and isolation of the
Gaol can be related to Disraeli's satire on Utilitarian philosophy
in his description of the lonely young trappers in the mines,
'They endure that punishment which philosophical philanthropy
has invented for the direst criminals, and which those criminals
deem more terrible than the death for which it is substituted.'
(*Sybil*, Bk. III, ch. 1.)[33] Reade's protest is also similar to
Dickens's at the factory system in *Hard Times* in which unvary-
ing routine and dependency on machinery turn men into 'hands'
as in prison they turn men into numbers. The descriptions of
prison exterior, cell and corridor are the finest in Reade's novel;
it is in them rather than in the sensational episodes of punishment

[33] Collins in *Dickens and Crime* shows how Dickens's ideas on the punishment of
criminals gradually became more reactionary and vindictive. He quotes the passage
from *Little Dorrit* (1857) in which the landlady of the Break of Day, talking of
Rigaud's escape, insists 'that there are people who have no human heart, and who
must be crushed like savage beasts and cleared out of the way' (ch. 11). It is interesting that the 'philosophical philanthropy' she repudiates, described in *Hard Times* as
harsh and inhumane, is in this passage associated with 'amiable whitewashers'.

and torture, based on fact but undoubtedly heightened for sensational effect, that the reader experiences something of the
reality of being poor and imprisoned in a society in which privilege is afforded those with money and power. James Fitzjames
Stephen, then a barrister of three years' standing, later a judge,
highly respected, but not distinguished for his imagination,
attacked the novel (along with Dickens's *Little Dorrit* and Elizabeth Gaskell's *Life of Charlotte Brontë*) as an example of the
novelist's irresponsible distortion of fact in the interest of allur-
ing sensation ('The Licence of Modern Novelists', *Edinburgh
Review*, 106 (1857), 124–56). He rightly exposes the exaggerations in Reade's account of life in the Gaol; he gives good legal
reasons why the passing of sentence on Austin should have been
so long deferred, but does not mention that the brutal warder
Freer evaded justice and that the law failed to punish the surgeon Blount; nor does he refer to Mr Justice Coleridge's qualifi-
cation of Austin's sentence, that he should serve it as a first-class
misdemeanant. Stephen's complacent support of the sentence,
that it 'was no doubt lenient, but we think that our readers will
agree with us in feeling that it was anything but illusory, and
that it was one which the Court had a perfect right to pro-
nounce' (p. 151) is a good example of the mental attitude
which Reade attacks in the novel: inflexible support of official-
dom can destroy common sense and humanity. This attitude,
held by the legal establishment, made the Carnarvon Report
inevitable.

Reade was right to underline the irony that the servants of
an inflexible law were treated with great leniency when they
themselves broke it, and to emphasize the helplessness of those
at the mercy of such a system. Stephen's superior jests about
Reade's absurdity in arguing that there was a conspiracy to
protect 'a half-pay lieutenant' who 'had been governor of a gaol'
miss the point that Reade establishes in his descriptions of the
Gaol—that the servants of official policy move together to
protect each other when that policy is attacked. The lawyer
Stephen's anonymous article is itself an example of this. Un-
fortunately, Reade laid himself open to retaliation by his
intemperateness and by his incorrigible delight in melodrama,
although possibly one could argue that the very sense of the
impregnability of the system which he was attacking induced

his over-emphasis and hysteria. Certainly, in his creation of the Gaol, concern combined with factual knowledge and physical impressions to produce descriptions outstanding in a fanciful novel and alien to it. They convey something 'that was there to be known' in Birmingham Gaol in 1853.

3
PROBLEMS, NOT PEOPLE

The evidence of the workpeople themselves is worth more than all the rest. (Lord Ashley, 1842.)

Life escapes; and perhaps without life nothing else is worthwhile. (Virginia Woolf, 'Modern Fiction', 1919.)

BLUE BOOKS AND THE NOVELISTS' CONSCIOUSNESS OF THE POOR

For some middle-class novelists writing about the poor, Blue books were a way of bridging the gulf between the Two Nations, and helped to form their 'consciousness' of the poor, to use Raymond Williams's phrase. In *Yeast, Alton Locke, Sybil* and *It is Never Too Late to Mend* Kingsley, Disraeli, and Reade all use Blue books in an attempt to represent the actuality of the Other Nation. In the previous Chapter I have shown how they use them to describe the physical and material life of the Other Nation, 'truth about' the poor, but what kind of 'consciousness' of the poor did these publications afford them, and how close was it to that more elusive 'life', 'truth to' the Other Nation?

One thing is obvious, that the novelists made little or no use of the personalities and language of the poor who gave evidence in the Reports. Indeed, some of the Reports which provided material for fiction of their very nature contain no comments by the poor upon their lives. Chadwick's *Report* was undertaken in a period of great depression and had its genesis in his 'concern for economy in the face of a rising demand for poor relief expenditure which persuaded him in the first place to publicize some facts about the economic consequences of neglect of elementary public health precautions' (M. Flinn, in his edition of Chadwick's *Report*, p. 43). It therefore consists of the comments of Assistant Poor Law Commissioners, who in turn relied on Poor Law medical officers, local relieving officers, clerks to Boards of Guardians, the Guardians themselves, doctors like the Cornishman Charles Barham (whose remarks on Truro are quoted above, p. 118) and Robert Baker of Leeds who was also a sub-inspector of factories, prison superintendents and prison officers. So any novelist who used the *Report* would begin by being one remove from the poor themselves.

And of those Reports which do print the evidence of the poor, some bring us much closer to their lives than others. On 7 June 1842 Lord Ashley, quoting the evidence of collier women in the *Children's Employment Commission* (1842), said:

I will quote the evidence of one woman who deposes to her own sufferings; and let me here observe, that the evidence of the workpeople themselves is worth more than all the rest; for they know what they suffer, and what the consequences are. I can say for them that I have ever found their statements more accurate, and that I have never met with attempts to mislead in the evidence given by working men of their own condition. (*Hansard*, 63, column 1328.)

One of the Sub-Commissioners was J. R. Leifchild, who at least wanted to reproduce the speech of his informants and was interested in it (*CEC*, I, Appendix, 1. P.P. Session 1842 (XVI), 531); and many of the people who gave evidence were colliers, agreed to be remarkable for their independence, their isolation and their sense of community, so that regional speech is marked. Therefore, despite a certain amount of 'tidying-up', of toning down the language for polite ears, and of transmutation into third-person speech, this *First Report* is a quarry for examples of vigorous vernacular language in various parts of the country ranging from Scotland to Lancashire, whereas the sections on the young dressmakers and milliners in the *Second Report* (which dealt with Trades and Manufactures) one of the few Commissions to which Dickens referred in writing a work of fiction, *The Chimes*, provides hardly any examples of striking vernacular speech in the evidence of the depressed, overworked girls aspiring, presumably, to gentility in their trade.

But the novelists who use the Reports do not make use of the witnesses' speech. Reade shows that the penal system oppresses those who are of no consequence and have no important friends to help them evade it. The prisoners Reade describes are inevitably of the Other Nation, men like William Burton, imprisoned in Leicester Gaol. He told the Commissioners why:

I went from Croxton Park races for gambling. I won a sovereign. They took me up, and I had a month in half an hour,—I had a month in a moment,—I got no trial nor anything. (Leicester *Report*, p. 215.)

This is direct, economical, and forceful; the perfect expression of Reade's theme. 'A month in a moment'—the ease with which a man is deprived of his liberty, without trial, if he happens to be of the Other Nation—all this is expressed by the alliterative phrase; there is, however, no such wit to be found in the speech of Reade's convicts, although Reade knew the Leicester *Report* and used some of its details, for example, descriptions of the crank, in his novel.

Because Edward Andrews's suicide had instituted the inquiry into the government of Birmingham Gaol Reade obviously had no example of his speech in the Birmingham *Report*—the chief witness was of necessity mute. But there is the evidence of John Cartwright, aged twenty, imprisoned for burglary, who had been brought to the point of suicide by the relentless punishments which had driven Andrews to despair. Cartwright was punished for speaking through the ventilator of his cell to other prisoners; while grinding corn, part of his punishment, he stole some of it because he was famished with his bread and water punishment diet. For this he got another three days' bread and water. A fortnight later he again spoke to other prisoners through his ventilator, and was punished with three more days' bread and water, fourteen days' grinding corn, and deprivation of bed and gaslight for the fortnight. At the beginning of this further period of punishment he tried to kill himself. On Friday 26 November 1852:

How did you try to hang yourself?—I knocked a pane in the window, and put my hammock straps round the bar. I got upon my stool to do it . . .
  . . . how were you saved?—
I believe one of the officers found me when he came to fetch my bed out . . .
  Had you lost your senses? . . . Yes . . .
What was the reason you tried to destroy yourself?—Because I was so clammed [starved]. It was very cold weather, and having nothing in my inside, I preferred death before living in that state. (Ibid., p. 190.)

Cartwright's words express growing desperation born of total isolation, and his attempted suicide, described without self-pity, is moving because it leaves the reader's imagination to work on the bare details he gives, unlike the self-conscious rhetoric of the fictional character, Josephs, whose thoughts are set out as monologue before he hangs himself:

'I wonder what Hawes was going to do with me to-morrow. Something worse than all I have gone through,' he said . . . 'He does know how to torture one . . . there is the sky; it is a beautiful place. Who would stay here under Hawes if they could get up there. God lives up there: I am almost afraid he won't let a poor wicked boy like me come where he is. And they say this is a sin too: he will be angry with me but I couldn't help it. I shall tell him what I went through first, and perhaps he will forgive me . . .

'It is hard, but I can't help it . . . Some say it hurts a good deal; some think not. I shall soon know, but I shall never tell. That doesn't trouble me, it is only throttling when all is done; and ain't I throttled every day of my life. Shouldn't I be throttled to-morrow if I was such a spoon as to see to-morrow . . .

'Mr. Evans will be sorry: I can't help it. Bless him for being so good to me; and bless Mr. Eden . . .

'My mother will fret, but I can't help it. O dear! oh dear! oh dear! I hope some one will tell her what I went through first . . .' (Vol. i, ch. 20.)

The spasmodic attempts to indicate lower-class speech by using words like 'ain't', and 'spoon' for 'fool', conflict violently with stilted phrases like 'He does know how to torture one' and reveal the artificiality of the whole. The repeated phrase 'I couldn't help it' insists on the boy's pathetic helplessness; the image of the beaten, suffering poor is prominent in Reade's 'consciousness' of the Other Nation, and in that of the other novelists under discussion.

Reade uses the Blue books on Birmingham and Leicester Gaols to advance an argument against cruelty condoned by society; the prisoners, Josephs, Robinson, Carter, are used as exempla in this argument. He emphasizes the last two sentences of Chapter 7 in the second volume of the novel by printing them in small type: 'Josephs a larcenist and a corpse. The law a liar and a felon.' The next chapter begins: 'Josephs has dropped out of our story. Mr. Hawes has got himself kicked out of our story. The other prisoners, of whom casual mention has been made, were never in our story, any more than the boy Xury in "Robinson Crusoe". There remains to us in the prison Mr. Eden and Robinson, a saint and a thief.' Reade then proceeds with the congenial task of writing a Victorian picaresque romance with a moral flavour, and takes Robinson off to complete his reformation in Australia, and to join George Fielding in his exciting adventures prospecting for gold. Despite the impact of the prison itself in the novel, it is evident that Reade used the Blue books to publicize rather than to re-create the poor.

Similarly, Disraeli uses Blue books to grind his own particular axe rather than imaginatively embody the lives of the Other Nation. In *Sybil* he makes extensive use of the *First Report* of the Children's Employment Commission but makes little use of the witnesses' language recorded there, although he gives his workpeople a self-conscious sprightliness of speech which only serves to emphasize their puppetry:

'Now, now,' said Julia, 'I hate suspense. I like news to go round like a fly-wheel' . . .

'. . . next day is the blackest day in all the week,' said Julia. 'When I hear the factory bell on Monday morning, I feel just the same as I did when I crossed with my uncle from Liverpool to Seaton to eat shrimps. Wasn't I sick coming home, that's all!' . . .

'Chaffing Jack be hanged!' said Mick . . . 'We are going to do the trick, and no mistake. There shan't be a capitalist in England who can get a day's work out of us, even if he makes the operatives his junior partners.' (*Sybil*, Bk. VI, ch. 8.)

As W. R. Greg said in his review of the novel (*Westminster Review*, 44 (1845), 141–52) the working-class characters speak a bastardized Cockney[1]—like the remark made by Tummas, the filer, of Wodgate: 'he's wery lib'ral too in the wittals' (Bk. III, ch. 4) which smacks of watered-down Sam Weller. Very often Disraeli generalizes the evidence of several witnesses in the *Report* and so makes it neutral and uninteresting. Part of the Sub-Commissioners' routine questionnaire was calculated to test the children's knowledge of the Christian religion. Examples of the replies are:

I go to Sunday-school at John Sorby's. I learn Reading made Easy. They don't teach me religion much, I think. They teach me what will happen to me if I am not a good girl. I don't know whose son Christ was, but he's not on earth now; he's in heaven I expect. (Emily Margaret Patterson, 'going 15', at Messrs Stansfeld's and Brigg's Low Bottom Pit, Flockton, 11 May 1841, to J. C. Symons, reporting on the Yorkshire Coal Field; *CEC*, I, Appendix, 1, P.P. Session 1842 (XVI), 288.)

---

[1] 'Their language is what no one who had ever conversed with those classes would have dreamed of putting into their mouths; and the vulgarisms by means of which he endeavours to give an air of life and nature to their conversations, are never those of the provinces, but always either Cockneyisms or Americanisms.' (p. 143.)

Having to pull so hard in the pit makes me poorly sometimes. They teach
me to read in the Testament at the Sunday school. Jesus Christ was the
Son of God, but I don't know what he came on earth for. (Ann Hague, 13,
Webster's pit, Hunshelf Bank Coal Works, 18 February 1841, to J. C.
Symons; ibid., p. 242.)

These answers, and more like them, Disraeli compresses into
the words of Tummas's 'wife', Sue: ' "I be a reg'lar born Christian and my mother afore me, and that's what few gals in the
Yard can say. Thomas will take to it himself when work is slack;
and he believes now in our Lord and Saviour Pontius Pilate,
who was crucified to save our sins; and in Moses, Goliath, and
the rest of the Apostles." ' (Bk. III, ch. 4.)

This supports one of the novel's themes, already discussed,
that the Other Nation consists of barbarians who have to be
civilized by their social superiors (see above pp. 69ff.). Disraeli's
fiction embodies the ideas of Lord Ashley, speaking on the
Children's Employment Commission to the House 7 June 1842:
'Never, I believe, since the first disclosure of the horrors of the
African slave-trade, has there existed so universal a feeling on
any one subject in this country, as that which now pervades the
length and breadth of the land in abhorrence and disgust of this
monstrous oppression'; he called for the removal of 'evils that
are both disgusting and intolerable—disgusting they would be in
a heathen country, and perfectly intolerable they are in one
that professes to call itself Christian. (*Hansard*, 63, columns
1336–7.) He took his cue from the Sub-Commissioners. Of
Patience Kershaw, aged 17, working in Booth Town Pit, Halifax
('the bald place upon my head is made by thrusting the corves
. . .') Samuel Scriven, the Sub-Commissioner, commented: 'This
girl is an ignorant, filthy, ragged, and deplorable-looking object,
and such an one as the uncivilized natives of the prairies would
be shocked to look upon.' (*CEC*, I, Appendix, 2, P.P. Session
1842 (XVII), 110.)

The children's ignorance of the rudiments of the Christian
story was, he believed, demonstrable proof of their pagan state.
But the terrible, unconscious irony of 'I don't know whose son
Christ was, but he's not on earth now . . .'; 'Jesus Christ was the
Son of God, but I don't know what he came on earth for' is
never perceived by Ashley, the Sub-Commissioners or by Disraeli. In fact, nowhere is the gulf between the Two Nations so

apparent as in these confident, set questions about the Christian story and the shocked reactions at the children's evident incomprehension. The Sub-Commissioner J. C. Symons acutely points out that the muddle in the children's minds reflects on the quality of education they receive in the Sunday schools rather than upon the children:

The notion is inveterately implanted in the mind of the great majority of schoolmasters and schoolmistresses, that comprehension is no necessary part of instruction; and others seem to imagine it a matter of intuition, and are astonished that a child has not learnt what it has never had the means of understanding. 'Have I not been preaching justification by faith, by the law of Moses, and setting forth the essence of the Godhead, this very morning?' exclaimed a Calvinist preacher and schoolmaster in a paroxysm of amazement at finding that a group of scholars could not explain who or what Christ was! . . . in the vast majority of cases child and teacher jog on in the established ruts, so ingeniously devised to avoid the exercise of mind and everything in the shape of instruction, save the mere mechanism of memory. (Report by J. C. Symons on the Yorkshire Coal Field, *CEC*, I, Appendix, 1, P.P. Session 1842 (XVI), 208.)

Dickens brilliantly satirizes this mechanical 'education' in the school-room scenes in *Hard Times* where the children are an 'inclined plane of little vessels then and there arranged in order, ready to have imperial gallons of facts poured into them' (Bk. I, ch. 1). J. C. Symons's comments on the bewildered collier children are a humane and intelligent blast against complacency, as are Ashley's words, 'It is a mockery to talk of education to people who are engaged . . . in unceasing toil from their cradle to their grave' (*Hansard*, 63, column 1351)—although this remark reveals the limited nature of Ashley's conception of 'education'. But Blake's earlier perception of the savage irony of teaching the Christian religion to children whose appalling condition results from an un-Christian society which none the less congratulates itself on its Christian values, is totally lacking. Ashley's appeal to the House, quoted above, is illogical. If society is only professedly Christian what hope is there that it will right its wrongs by following Christian precept? If it is really Christian, so that a confident appeal can be made to this precept, how have these terrible conditions come about? There is the same illogicality in *Sybil* when Disraeli uses references to the *Children's Employment Commission* to make such an appeal (see particularly the end of Bk. III, ch. 4).

But for Disraeli politics were always more interesting than

religion, despite his fascination by the history and appeal of the
Jewish religion and his delight in the theatrical quality of the
medieval Church of Western Europe. A close examination of his
use of the section on collieries in the *Report* of the Children's
Employment Commission shows his continual withdrawal from
the people involved to the political argument so important to
his 'consciousness'.

But can we wonder at the hideous coarseness of their language, when we
remember the savage rudeness of their lives? Naked to the waist, an iron
chain fastened to a belt of leather runs between their legs clad in canvas
trousers, while on hands and feet an English girl, for twelve, sometimes for
sixteen hours a day, hauls and hurries tubs of coals up subterranean roads,
dark, precipitous, and plashy; circumstances that seem to have escaped the
notice of the Society for the Abolition of Negro Slavery. Those worthy
gentlemen, too, appear to have been singularly unconscious of the sufferings of the little trappers, which was remarkable, as many of them were in
their own employ.

See, too, these emerge from the bowels of the earth! Infants of four
and five years of age, many of them girls, pretty and still soft and timid;
entrusted with the fulfilment of responsible duties, and the nature of
which entails on them the necessity of being the earliest to enter the mine
and the latest to leave it. Their labour indeed is not severe, for that would
be impossible, but it is passed in darkness and in solitude. They endure
that punishment which philosophical philanthropy has invented for the
direst criminals, and which those criminals deem more terrible than the
death for which it is substituted. Hour after hour elapses, and all that
reminds the infant trappers of the world they have quitted and that which
they have joined, is the passage of the coal-waggons for which they open
the air-doors of the galleries, and on keeping which doors constantly
closed, except at this moment of passage, the safety of the mine and the
lives of the persons employed in it entirely depend. (Bk. III, ch. 1.)

The passage apparently develops ideas and references in
Ashley's speech in the House of Commons, 7 June 1842, when
he presented the *First Report of the Commissioners (Mines)*:

Well might all the charter-masters in Shropshire speak of the system with
horror, and say it was as bad as the African slave-trade. For my part, I
think it quite as bad, if not worse; for, at any rate, slaves have the advantage of working in the night [*sic*, presumably for 'light'] of the open day
. . . These wretched apprentices have committed no crime, and even if they
had so, they would not deserve to meet with such punishment. Only a
few days ago I went over the new prison at Pentonville. Never have I seen
such preparations as are there made for securing a proper degree of comfort to the prisoner. Such care for light, such care for ventilation, such
care that every necessary requirement of the prisoner should be furnished.
He is to have books, tools, instruction—to hear the human voice at least

fourteen times a day. Sir, I find no fault with that; but bear in mind that all this is done for persons who have forfeited their liberty by the laws of their country; but here you have a number of poor children, whose only crime is that they are poor, and who are sent down to these horrid dens, subjected to every privation, and every variety of brutal treatment, and on whom you inflict even a worse curse than this—the curse of dark and perpetual ignorance. (*Hansard*, 63, columns 1346-7.)

Only one detail in Disraeli's passage seems to be an exaggeration—the girl working sixteen hours a day. There might be an isolated example of this in the *Report*; generally children appear to have worked eleven to twelve hours a day. Disraeli is correct in saying that hours of work varied. For example, in Lancashire and Cheshire the normal period was twelve hours, from 5 a.m. to 5 p.m. or from 6 a.m. to 6 p.m. (see *CEC*, I, P.P. Session 1842 (XV), 120), whereas in Oldham a child could work in the pit for as long as fifteen hours; the adults worked nine, ten, eleven hours, ' "and the Children and Young Persons employed in bringing to the pit-bottom the coal which they have hewn, about two hours longer, or 11, 12, and 13 hours, which are sometimes protracted to 14 and 15" ' (ibid., p. 120). So if Disraeli's period of sixteen hours is an exaggeration it is not a very great one; and for his other statements there is plenty of corroboration in the *Report*:

I am nearly 15 years old; and began to work in Webster's pit when I was going on 10 . . . I have hurried all the time. I am the oldest girl there. There are seven regular hurriers, who are girls. I am sure they always hurry the same time, i.e. from six in the morning till two in the afternoon . . . When the corve is loaded, one of us is harnessed with a belt round the waist, and a chain comes from the front of the belt and passes betwixt our legs and is hooked on to the corve, and we go along on our hands and feet, on all fours. I do so myself, and a little boy pushes behind. We wear trousers always as when you saw us. It doesn't tire us very much. (Harriet Morton, 18 February 1841, Hunshelf, Yorkshire, to J. C. Symons; *CEC*, I, Appendix, 1, P.P. Session 1842 (XVI), 241 f.)

I am a hurrier, and help to fill and riddle [that is, filling corves with coal at the coal-face where it is being hewn; sieving the small coal at the coal-face and piling the lumps remaining in the sieve upon the corve]. I have been in the pit five years last July. It tires me enough sometimes, and sometimes not . . . It's hard work going to pit. I care nothing about where I am. I should be worked hard anywhere, I dare say . . . I was poorly with the work when I was at Clarke's pit, for I had to work harder there, often 13 hours . . . The water used to make my feet raw, it was bad water. (Ann Fern, 14, Silkstone, Yorkshire, to J. C. Symons; ibid., p. 266.)

We go at four in the morning, and sometimes at half-past four. We begin
to work as soon as we get down. We get out after four, sometimes at five,
in the evening . . . I know the corves are very heavy they are the biggest
corves anywhere about . . . I am very tired at night. Sometimes when we
get home at night we have not power to wash us, and then we go to bed.
Sometimes we fall asleep in the chair . . . I began to hurry when I was
seven and I have been hurrying ever since. (Ann Eggley, 18, near Barnsley,
to J. C. Symons; ibid., p. 260.)

I'm a trapper in the Gawber pit. It does not tire me, but I have to trap
without a light and I'm scared. I go at four and sometimes half past three
in the morning, and come out at five and half past. I never go to sleep.
Sometimes I sing when I've light, but not in the dark; I dare not sing then.
I don't like being in the pit. I am very sleepy when I go sometimes in the
morning. (Sarah Gooder, 8, to J. C. Symons; ibid., pp. 260 f.)

To come to these children's voices after reading Disraeli's
description is like reversing a telescope after having looked
down the wrong end; distant problems become people. Again
the unconscious irony of their speech is startling and very
moving—largely because it *is* unconscious and not aiming for
effect—'I began to hurry when I was seven and I have been
hurrying ever since . . .' (which is really a poem epitomizing the
Industrial Revolution from the labourer's point of view); 'I care
nothing about where I am. I should be worked hard anywhere,
I dare say . . .' It makes Disraeli's irony at the expense of 'those
worthy gentlemen' seem laboured and over-elaborate. And again
the complete lack of self-pity paradoxically gives a much greater
sense of their sufferings than Disraeli's exclamations—'Yet these
are to be, some are, the mothers of England!' Disraeli's irony is
also at the expense of the Whigs of the first Reformed Parliament (see his attacks on the 'benefits' of the Reform Act, *Sybil*,
Bk. II, ch. 5) who passed the Act to abolish slavery in the
Crown Colonies, 1833, and at the members of the Society for
the Extinction of Slavery formed in 1840. These partisan remarks fix our attention on the debate and the debater, rather
than on the children who are the ostensible subject.

In giving evidence for the Commission one of the collier
women uses a phrase found in Disraeli's description—'bowels of
the earth'—but with a totally different effect. 'See, too, these
emerge from the bowels of the earth', writes Disraeli, of the
little trappers. Jane Peacock Watson, aged forty, a coal-bearer in

a Peebleshire pit,[2] told R. H. Franks: 'I have wrought in the bowels of the earth 33 years.' (*CEC*, I, Appendix, 1, P.P. Session 1842 (XVI), 466.) The phrase, which in Disraeli appears affected periphrasis, partly because of the cumbersome introduction 'See, too, these . . .', inevitably implying a showman's gesture, and partly because of its association with the feeble generalizations, eroded Augustanisms which introduce the section on the mines: 'the swarming multitude', 'troops of youth', in Jane Watson's speech regains its ancient Biblical power, partly because of the expressive rhythm—'I have wrought in the bowels of the earth 33 years'—partly because the nature of the experience described gives her the right to use such terms; here the associations with hell seem appropriate, not lurid. The evidence which follows substantiates this right: 'Have been married 23 years, and had nine children; six are alive, three died of typhus a few years since; have had two dead born; thinks they were so from the oppressive work: a vast of women have dead children and false births, which are worse, as they are no able to work after the latter.'

Despite the falsifying shift from first to third person in this reported speech, its power is evident. And later in her evidence her words give the reader a moment of illumination which 'strikes to the heart' and demonstrates how Disraeli's description of the colliers precludes any such illumination because, by his words, he arranges his characters in a formal tableau preventing change or growth or discovery. Jane Watson says: 'Knows it is bad to keep bairns from school, but every little helps; and even if inclined there is no school nearer than two miles, and it is a fearfu' bad road across the moor in summer, much more winter.' The 'fearfu' road' has the imaginative power and verbal economy found in traditional ballads, the kind of road which took Thomas the Rhymer to Elfland, or the road across the Whinny-muir which the soul of the dead had to pass in 'A Lyke-Wake Dirge'. And by its very reticence and its contact with experience the phrase illuminates the collier children's lives more brightly than the Sub-Commissioners' shocked observations that they could not read or Disraeli's phrase 'the savage rudeness of their lives', and demonstrates the limitations of such reactions.

[2] Harlaw Muir, Coaly Burn, parish of West Linton, Peebleshire, the Revd J. J. Beresford, Leaseholder and Heritor.

Both the *Children's Employment Commission*, aiming to shock Parliament and the nation by revealing horrors to upset contemporary middle-class ideas of religion and womanhood and so pass laws to prevent such atrocities, and Disraeli's novel, which shares the attitude of the Sub-Commissioners and holds out the hope that the new young leaders of the Conservative Party will redress such wrongs, fail to give any idea of good sense and humour among the collier-women, or tell us much about the normal routine of their lives. A. J. Munby's sketches and jottings, even though they were done twenty-seven years after the Commission, give us a better idea of what ordinary life must have been like in these colliery communities.

Undoubtedly, Munby was a strange man. Although his feeling for Hannah Cullwick was strong, and the delay in marrying her was largely caused by his lack of money and dependence upon his family, he was obsessed with what he considered to be servitude's purifying effect on women, with touching working women's hard hands, and with the sight of girls in men's clothes which allowed them the freedom to do hard labour. His attitude both defied the contemporary image of the 'lady' who was frail and protected, and magnified contemporary approval of servitude in those who ministered to the business and comfort of the Victorian middle classes and upper classes. Nevertheless, his repeated visits to the Wigan pits, for example, and his detailed description of his encounters with pit-girls, now no longer employed underground but at the pit-head, let us see a girl like Ellen Grounds going home in her pit-clothes to the house where she lives with her father, mother, and brother. She scours the hearth and the stone-floor, blackleads the grate. She is good-humoured and amiable, exchanging some back-chat with her brother before going upstairs to change into a dress.

Her mother never wrought at pit: but her father had worked below, as a lad, with 14 women, who drew with the belt and chain, and went on four legs like horses, and sweated so that the sweat dropped off their faces as they crawled. Yet they behaved 'decent', said the father; but they were not looked after as they are at brow [that is, on the surface]. (Wigan, August 1870. Munby MSS 97, Notebook No. 4, Trinity College Library, Cambridge.)

When in 1874 Munby returned to Wigan he spoke to Margaret Pallett, 'a stout hearty woman of 45, with a very black face. She worked below ground in the pit, thrutching [drawing] corves, from ten years old to 18, when the women were turned out. When I said, Did you like it? She gave me the usual answer: "Like it? Aye! an' Oi'd gaw dahn again, if tha'd let ma"!' (14 September 1874. Munby MSS 97, Notebook No. 6.) Leaving aside this woman's obvious zest for life and her hearty good nature providing Munby with the answer he wanted, this interchange gives a dimension to colliery life completely lacking in the Commissioners' *Report*. Certainly, as the *Report* shows, many of the women and girls were overwhelmed by their work, but the zest, humour, and sheer determination to exist and have some fun, which Munby describes in the girls he interviews, ring true. Munby, like the Commissioners and the novelist, recorded the evidence to prove his case, namely, that women like hard work work and are capable of it. But although obviously he selected his evidence there is no reason to believe that he falsified it, and his descriptions of collier girls, many of whom he got to know well over the years, and comments such as 'it seems that at Birket Bank pit [where Ellen Grounds worked] many women worked below in disguise after the Act passed' (Ashley's Act, 1842, made it illegal for girls and women to work underground in the pits) reveal deficiencies both in the Commissioners' *Report* which, although its strength is the wealth of working people's evidence, restricts that evidence in the straitjacket of a limited and limiting questionnaire, and in the novel, and make us aware of some of the distortions the life of the Other Nation suffers in their pages.

Disraeli, as might be expected of a politician, among the novelists under discussion relies the most heavily on Blue books for factual evidence about the Other Nation. For *Sybil* he used material from the two *Reports of the Children's Employment Commission*; Chadwick's *Report*; the *Reports on Agriculture* (1843); the *Report of the Commissioners on Handloom Weavers* (1841); the *Report from the Select Committee on the Payment of Wages* (1842); and the *First Report of the Midland Mining Commission (South Staffordshire)* (1843). Obviously he also knew the *First and Second Reports from Commissioners appointed to collect Information in the Manufacturing Districts, relative to Employment of Children in Factories, and as to the propriety and means of curtailing the Hours of their Labour* (1833) and the succeeding Reports by Inspectors of Factories made to Government, for example, in the years 1839, 1840,

1841, and 1842. Material from these and earlier Factory Reports helped him to describe the lives of the factory children in *Sybil*. Facts for Devilsdust's early life occur in many of them. For example, the description of the destitute children who find the factory a haven—Mr John Hall, overlooker of worsted spinning in a Bradford mill, was asked, 21 May 1832, about the children waiting for a chance of work:

Do you think that the children who have been employed in mills, as far as you have observed . . . are better clothed and fed than those employed in other professions, or not?—I cannot say; they may have some comforts; there is the comfort that will arise out of their wages, if their parents are not thrown out of their own employment on that account.

Then they have better wages?—Than those that have no work. (*Report from the Select Committee on the Bill to regulate the Labour of Children in Mills and Factories of the United Kingdom*, P.P. Session 1831-2 (XV), 119.)

The chilling remark that they have better wages than the unemployed perfectly describes Devilsdust's precarious hold on life.

C. R. Fay has remarked that the Tommy-shop scene in *Sybil* is based on the Midland Mining Commission[3] and quotes a typical example of Disraeli's use of a striking Blue book phrase to create a character and suggest a scene:

Diggs, the butty of the novel, is Banks the coal proprietor of the Report. In the novel the people say of Master Joseph Diggs the son: 'He do swear at the women, when they rush in for the first turn, most fearful. They do say he's a shocking little dog'. In the Report, page 93, the miner's wife says: 'He swears at the women when the women are trying to crush in . . . He is a shocking little dog'. (*Life and Labour in the Nineteenth Century*, Cambridge, 1947, pp. 193 f.)

The Tommy-shop was owned by the master, factory-owner or, as in this case, coal-owner, and there his work-people were compelled either to accept goods instead of money for their wages, or to spend a certain proportion of their wages on goods offered for sale in the shop. The work-people complained that they were being defrauded; that either they were given useless goods in return for their work (Fay cites an instance of Bradford woollen manufacturers in 1842 giving their workers pieces of

---

[3] Fay has a curious misreading of a phrase in *Sybil*. He interprets the miner's desire to have 'the young Queen's picture' (Bk. III, ch. 1) as a patriotic longing for her portrait ascribed to him by the royalist novelist. In fact the man is asking for money, coins bearing the Queen's head, rather than the useless goods he is forced to take in the Tommy-shop.

cloth and bundles of rags as part payment of wages) or that
necessities like flour and tea cost more in the Tommy-shop than
elsewhere and were of inferior quality.

It is worth quoting the whole passage which is the source of
the Tommy-shop scene in *Sybil*. The evidence was taken in the
South Staffordshire Coal Field from the wife of a man who
worked in Banks's mine. She was the fourth witness at Bilston,
1 February 1843:

I never went to the [Tommy] shop but there were 12 or 13 standing
round the door in rain, snow, or whatever weather it may be; they do not
allow you to come in. I have seen when it was supposed near 200 were
there when there has not been any flour for some days.

The women will be fighting and tearing to get in. About a month or six
weeks ago, one Thursday, I went from home at 11 o'clock in the day; I
was there certainly before 12, having only called at my mother-in-law's on
the way, and it was 8 o'clock at night before I got home, having only
called to leave some tommy on the road and was not delayed five minutes.

What kept you so long on that occasion?—There was a great crowd to
get flour, and when I got into it I was forced to stay or else I should not
have got anything for my children or husband. He was hurt in the knee,
and his field pay, or most of it, was to be paid in goods; 15s. was paid so
out of 20s. When at last I got into the shop my bonnet was off, and my
apron was all torn, with the women all trying who should get in first.

There were two women carried off who had fainted, and I helped them
to come to themselves and that got me out of my turn and made me
longer. And there was a little boy who wanted a loaf for his mother and
having no dinner, he was quite smothered and I thought he was dead and
the sweat poured off him. They carried him up to bed, but he went home
afterwards. Ah it's cruel work is the tommy shop.

Banks's shop has got much worse of late since young Mr. Charles Banks
came to the shop; he swears at the women when the women are trying to
crush in with children crying in their arms. He is a shocking little dog.
Midland Mining Commission, *Appendix to First Report*, 1843, P.P. Session 1843 (XIII), 249.)

It is not surprising that Disraeli borrows this scene for his novel.
She is a vigorous narrator and tells her tale with economy and
effect. She becomes 'the comely dame' in the novel, who tries
to rescue the fainting boy—Disraeli adopts her phrase that 'he
was quite smothered'.

In the scene he also uses details from the *Report from the
Select Committee on the Payment of Wages*, such as the detail
of adulterated flour sold at the Tommy-shop making women
and children ill: 'I have two children at home ill from their
flour; I have been very poorly myself; one is used to a little

white clay, but when they lay it on thick, it's very grave.' (*Sybil*, Bk. III, ch. 3.)

Thomas Charlesworth, a collier in Barnsley, told the Commission 27 June 1842 that flour he was obliged to buy at the Tommy-shop had been made into bread which had made his wife and children ill (P.P. Session 1842 (IX), 284); and on the same day Daniel Jubb, a collier at Darley Main Colliery, produced a sample of Tommy-shop flour and said that it gave people a bowel complaint (ibid., p. 278). The same *Report* makes the point which Disraeli emphasizes, that work is scarce and therefore the owners have the whip hand because the workpeople are in no position to refuse truck (ibid., p. 136); and it describes the way the colliers move about in search of work— the Revd F. D. Perkins from Sowe, near Coventry, gave evidence 24 June 1842: 'They may only be there a few weeks, or a few months in the year, and then if trade is bad they go into Staffordshire, or they go to Merthyr; those that do not belong to the place.' (Ibid., p. 268.) The *Report* supplies the detail that Merthyr is a favourite place to work: 'the men had rather live in Merthyr, because there is money paid there; or in Pontypool, where there is money paid in that neighbourhood more than others' (Benjamin Morgan, 15 June 1842, works at Cambrian Iron Works, Maisteg, ibid., p. 222). All of which justifies Disraeli in making Diggs say:

'You are Jones' wife, are you? Ticket for three and sixpence out of eighteen shillings wages. Is this the only ticket you have brought? There's your money; and you may tell your husband he need not take his coat off again to go down our shaft . . . Tell him I hope he has got plenty of money to travel into Wales, for he won't have no work in England again, or my name ayn't Diggs.' (*Sybil*, Bk. III, ch. 3.)

As usual, his factual information is correct and can be substantiated. But, as is also usual, the facts are crowded unnaturally into Diggs's speech giving that elusive but unmistakable air of fabrication common to Disraeli's Blue book scenes. As I have shown elsewhere (see particularly 'Willenhall and Wodgate: Disraeli's Use of Blue Book Evidence', the *Review of English Studies*, 13 (1962), 368–84; and 'Blue Books and Victorian Novelists', ibid., 21 (1970), 23–40) he uses Blue book evidence intelligently and eclectically to give substance to the scenes and people he describes and so support the arguments he draws from them. In the Tommy-shop scene, for example, he exemplifies the split between the Two Nations, the gulf between masters and men. When Morley talks with the colliers in their pub they complain about the tyranny of the managers and the middle men, and he asks why they do not complain to the owners and landlords. Nixon, the collier presiding over the pub discussion, replies:

'I take it you be a stranger in these parts, sir, or else you would know that it's as easy for a miner to speak to a main-master as it is for me to pick coal with this here clay [clay pipe]. Sir there's a gulf atween 'em . . . I'll tell you what, sir, that I never knew the people play [strike] yet, but if a word had passed atween them and the main-masters aforehand, it might not have been settled; but you can't get at them any way. Atween the poor man and the gentleman there never was no connection, and that's the wital mischief of this country.' (*Sybil*, Bk. III, ch. 1.)

This discussion, which includes a description of Tommy-shop frauds, serves as a prelude to the Tommy-shop scene a chapter later. Nixon's pronouncement is the novel's theme, and receives dramatic emphasis in the scene with Diggs, the butty, the desperate woman and 'the comely dame'. Egremont, the novel's hero, is to learn that, if the aristocracy shoulder their responsibilities and concern themselves with the Other Nation's welfare, aristocracy and working people will be true allies to build a better future. This is to rise like a phoenix from the smoking ruins of the Chartist rioters but, for the sake of poetic justice and to show sympathy with the people's cause, the rioters, before they are quelled, destroy the Tommy-shop and Diggs in it: 'The glare of the clear flame fell for a moment upon his countenance of agony; the mob gave an infernal cheer; then, some part of the building falling in, there rose a vast cloud of smoke and rubbish, and he was seen no more.' (Bk. VI, ch. 7.)

Disraeli's use of Blue book facts when attempting to represent the elusive actuality of the Other Nation is competent rather than imaginative, as is also the case when he is describing the physical details of their lives, discussed in the previous chapter. His representation of groups—of the colliers in the pub, of the women at the Tommy-shop, of the colliers coming up out of the mine, of the children working underground—lacks imaginative power and distorts their originals, as I have shown, but they are at least appropriate to the panoramic, declamatory style of the whole novel. But when he attempts a close-up of a member of the Other Nation, the result is disaster. For example,

Warner, the handloom weaver (*Sybil*, Bk. II, ch. 13), one of that unfortunate body of men who, after a period of prosperity at the end of the eighteenth and beginning of the nineteenth centuries when they were in demand to weave the yarn produced more easily and cheaply by the newly-invented spinning-machines, sank to desperate poverty in the 1820s, 1830s, and 1840s because of competition for ever lower-paid work in a glutted market and the increasing demand for power-loom goods in place of hand-woven. (For a full discussion of the history of the hand-loom weavers' impoverishment see E. P. Thompson, *The Making of the English Working Class*, Pelican edn., 1968, pp. 297–346.) Disraeli's chapter is based on fact:

'The inference,' says Mr. Austin, in his report on the south-western parts of England, 'from all my evidence is, that the weavers, taken as a body, are out of work one-third of their time, which reduces the income of the master weaver, for one loom, to 8s, instead of 12s. a-week, and that of the journeyman to 7s. instead of 10s.

'Referring to the evidence of a person deputed by me to go from house to house to inspect personally the condition of the weavers, and to obtain from each family a statement of income and expenditure, I find that, "in the 74 houses he has visited to procure this statement, there is great distress. In some of them he was told they had not a bit of bread nor a potatoe in the house, and he believes this to be true." ' (*Report of the Commissioners on Handloom Weavers*, P.P. Session 1841 (X), 299.)

This report from south-west England is a convenient summary of the weavers' plight, although the Commission makes it clear that weavers in the Manchester area were suffering similar hardships—Warner lives in 'Mowbray', a fictional Manchester. Reach, in his description of Ashton-under-Lyne, near Manchester, in the series 'Labour and the Poor' in the *Morning Chronicle*, writes:

In Ashton . . . there lingers on a handful of miserable old men, the remnants of the cotton hand-loom weavers. No young persons think of pursuing such an occupation—the few who practise it were too old and confirmed in old habits, when the power-loom was introduced, to be able to learn a new way of making their bread . . . We repaired . . . to one of the oldest portions of the place, called Charleston. The streets thereabouts were filthy and mean, the houses crumbling . . . The chamber was a large one, but hardly an article did it contain which could be by courtesy denominated furniture. The principal objects were the loom and the bed . . . On a low chair, by the small fire, sat a woman, looking one bundle of dirty tatters . . . busily employed in some job of needlework, while she rocked herself to and fro to lull the child which clung to her bosom . . . By the [loom] stood the weaver. He was a gaunt, big-boned man, with a stony glare in his eyes, and a rigid, unimpassioned looking face, on which was stamped the most unequivocal marks of a stolid, hopeless, apathetic despair. The man was preparing hanks from which to produce a mingled web of linen and wool. He went about it like one half torpid, and who works from mere instinct, without energy and without hope.

I asked him what were his usual wages.

'Not five shillings a week.'

'Your trade is a bad one now.'

He made no reply for a moment, but presently said, in a low drawling tone, and with a sort of strange smile on his face, as if he enjoyed the recital of the very hopelessness of his condition—

'Look here—I'll have to weave eighty yards of cloth in this piece. It will take me eight or nine days, and I shall have seven shillings for it. I walked to Manchester and back to the master's to fetch the yarn, and I shall walk there and back with the cloth when I am paid.'

Here was a journey on foot amounting to nearly thirty miles, and nine days' work at the loom, for seven shillings! . . . Some of the hand-loom weavers are better off, because they have sons and daughters who work in the mills; but, taken all together, they are a wretched and hopeless set. Potatoes and bread, with a little miserably weak tea, form, of course, the only articles of nutriment which they ever taste. (The *Morning Chronicle*, 8 November 1849.)

But in Disraeli's scene the actual physical details of Warner's room, accurately suggesting the destitution of contemporary handloom weavers—'An iron kettle was by the hearth, and on the mantlepiece some candles, a few lucifer matches, two tin mugs, a paper of salt, and an iron spoon', and the desperate shifts to which his wife is put to silence the baby's cries of hunger—' "I have a morsel of crust here . . . moisten it in water, and tie it up in this piece of calico: he will suck it; it will keep him quiet; I can bear anything but his cry" '—are in violent contrast with the Parliamentary debating speeches which Disraeli puts into Warner's mouth:

'Why am I here? Why am I, and six hundred thousand subjects of the Queen, honest, loyal, and industrious, why are we, after manfully struggling for years . . . driven from our innocent and happy homes, our country cottages that we loved, first to bide in close towns without comforts, and gradually to crouch into cellars, or find a squalid lair like this, without even the common necessaries of existence . . .

'It is that the Capitalist has found a slave that has supplanted the labour and ingenuity of man. Once he was an artisan: at the best, he now only watches machines . . .

'If a society that has been created by labour suddenly becomes independent of it, that society is bound to maintain the race whose only property is labour, out of the proceeds of that other property, which has not ceased to be productive.

'When the class of the Nobility were supplanted in France, they did not amount in number to one-third of us Hand-loom weavers; yet all Europe went to war to avenge their wrongs, every state subscribed to maintain them in their adversity, and when they were restored to their own country their own land supplied them with an immense indemnity. Who cares for us? Yet we have lost our estates. Who raises a voice for us? . . . We sink among no sighs except our own. And if they give us sympathy, what then? Sympathy is the solace of the Poor; but for the Rich there is Compensation.' (Bk. II, ch. 13.)

The handloom weaver's few words, quoted in the *Morning Chronicle*, and especially his moment of silence in reply to the journalist's fatuous remark 'Your trade is a bad one now', are much more compelling. The inability of Warner's speech to re-create the actuality of the weaver's plight is most plainly evident if it is compared with the song of the Oldham weaver (see below, pp. 197 ff.), or with descriptions of similar distress in the Rowbottom *Diaries*. These *Diaries* (1787–1830) are preserved in the Oldham Local History Library, and are thought to have been written by William Rowbottom, taken to be a weaver because he records in such detail Oldham's weaving trade. His entry for 31 December 1826 reads:

This misserable year is nearly at an End—the poor people of this Country are in that Miserable state that was it truly Stated futer [future] ages would dout the truth of it the work houses are . . . not sufficient to acomodate the numerous poor, in Chorderton [presumably Chadderton] workhous on the 26th instant, there where [were] 84 souls Dined but some where [were] lodged out, and their dinner . . . Consisted of two pounds of Butchers meat only, wich was stewed or Hashed with pottatoes no dout but there was hundreds all over the Country who could not get any Dinner at all . . . a Deal of poor Children have never a clog shoe or stocing [stocking] put on and have to Encounter the winter Storms Bare leg and Bare foot.

The direct language of that last sentence, the few evocative concrete details—clog, shoe, or stocking—and the strong rhythm pointing the meaning, re-create the sensuous experience of ill-clad poverty in a startling manner. Moreover, the wit in Disraeli's passage is not born of a struggle with circumstances, as it is in the ballad, but is the applied wit of Parliamentary debate—'Sympathy is the solace of the Poor; but for the Rich there is Compensation.' Because of the lack of involvement the wit calls attention to itself, rather than to the weaver's plight—and this is ludicrous in that the words—or thoughts—are meant to be wrung from him in his distress. Warner is represented as displaying himself as an exemplum of the distress of the Other Nation, a suitable case for pity and charity. He is placed in position to give Sybil, the representative of the Church with a social conscience, a chance to pose as ministering angel:

'Lives Philip Warner here?' inquired a clear voice of peculiar sweetness.
   'My name is Warner.'
   'I come from Walter Gerard,' continued the voice. 'Your letter reached him only last night . . .'
   'Pray enter.'
   And there entered SYBIL.

So the chapter ends.

Appropriately enough, Disraeli is most successful in using Blue book facts to create, not a member of the Other Nation, but an aristocrat. As I have shown (see 'Blue Books and Victorian Novelists', op. cit., pp. 32 f.) he uses details in the *Reports on Agriculture* to create the irresponsible, Tory aristocrat of the old school, Lord Marney. He is particularly good at establishing Marney's tone of voice and all that it implies. Here his imagination is engaged in a way in which it is not in his treatment of Warner, because Marney is at the centre of Disraeli's interest in the novel, which pleads the cause of responsible, socially-minded aristocracy as the answer to the nation's problems. Warner is one of these problems.

Dickens certainly knew some of the most important Blue books, particularly those dealing with children's welfare and with sanitary reform. He was given advance information about the Children's Employment Commission of 1842 by one of the Commissioners, Dr Southwood Smith (see letter to Macvey Napier, 8 August 1841, Pilgrim *Letters*, ii. 353 f.) and intended going with Smith in 1841 to see some of the colliery children at work but at the last moment was unable to keep his appointment (see letter to Dr Southwood Smith, 2 June 1841, Pilgrim *Letters*, ii. 290). He admired Smith's work and found Chadwick's *Report* a valuable source of information. In May 1851, speaking at the first anniversary banquet of the Metropolitan Sanitary Association, he linked their names in grateful acknowledgement: 'Twelve or fifteen years ago, some of the first valuable reports of Mr. Chadwick and of Dr. Southwood Smith strengthening and much enlarging my previous imperfect knowledge of this truth [that disease is no respecter of social distinctions], made me, in my sphere, earnest in the Sanitary Cause.' (*The Speeches of Charles Dickens*, ed. K. J. Fielding, Oxford, 1960, pp. 128 f.)

Edgar Johnson suggests that the Blue books gave direction and substance to Dickens's sympathy with the poor:

the reports on child labour and on the hard toil and filth and long hours in the mines and factories that his friend Southwood Smith had put in his hands had broadened his horizons . . . And the hard times that had set in with the forties, the rick-burnings in the south, the labor violence in the industrial north, were ominous signs of the more catastrophic disorders that a ruthless system might generate. (Op. cit., i. 534–5.)

But Dickens never relied on Blue books for the substance of his fiction, as did Disraeli, or Reade, or, to a lesser extent, Kingsley. He uses the revelations about over-worked milliners in the *Second Report* of the Children's Employment Commission to describe Meg's desperate attempts to make a living in *The Chimes*. Characteristically, he does not use material from the *Report* to argue a case, but to create an emotional tableau: 'Meg strained her eyes upon her work until it was too dark to see the threads; and when the night closed in, she lighted her feeble candle and worked on. Still her old father was invisible about her; looking down upon her; loving her—how dearly loving her!' (*The Chimes*, Third Quarter.) As Disraeli summarizes the hand-loom weaver's plight in the character Warner, Dickens here generalizes the facts of the exploitation of the young milliners and seamstresses, their desperately long hours to earn miserable wages, in a pitiful exemplum of the distress caused to the Other Nation. But whereas Disraeli uses the pathos to support a political argument, Dickens rests on the appeal for pity, with which *The Chimes* ends:

O Listener . . . try to bear in mind the stern realities from which these shadows come; and in your sphere . . . endeavour to correct, improve, and soften them. So may the New Year be a happy one to you, happy to many more whose happiness depends on you! So may each year be happier than the last, and not the meanest of our brethren or sisterhood debarred their rightful share, in what our Great Creator formed them to enjoy.

Hard Times, written eleven years after *The Chimes*, has a very different tone, delivers a more urgent message of warning, and is dependent on no Blue book for its material. Indeed, following Carlyle, Dickens is bitingly critical of statistics, tabulated information and their use in Blue books, as in his description of Mr Gradgrind in his study at the beginning of Book I, Chapter 15.

(For a discussion of Dickens's attitude to Blue books implied in the passage, see my 'Blue Books and Victorian Novelists', op. cit., pp. 23-8.)

In *Hard Times* Dickens made no attempt to trace the lives of the Other Nation in Blue books, but used symbols and metaphors to embody stereotypes—the suffering poor, the exploitative factory-owner—confirmed by his earlier reading of documents like the two *Reports* of the Children's Employment Commission.

Kingsley, like Dickens, shared the belief that inspired Ashley and Chadwick and Southwood Smith, that cleanliness had to precede Godliness and that it was useless preaching morality to the Other Nation until they were decently housed, clothed and fed. Co-operation between poet and scientific sanitary reformer which might have pleased Wordsworth, and proof that by 1848 Kingsley had achieved some public acknowledgement as a prophet of the cleanliness necessary to morality, are seen in the prefix to Hector Gavin's *Report on Bethnal Green* (1848)— a quotation from Kingsley's verse drama *The Saint's Tragedy* published that same year:

> I turned into an alley 'neath the wall—
> And stepped from earth to hell.—The light of Heaven,
> The common air was narrow, gross, and dim—
> The tiles did drop from the eaves; the unhinged doors
> Tottered o'er inky pools, where reeked and curdled
> The offal of a life; the gaunt-haunched swine
> Growled at their christened playmates o'er the scraps.
> Shrill mothers cursed; wan children wailed; sharp coughs
> Rang through the crazy chambers; hungry eyes
> Glared dumb reproach, and old perplexity,
> Too stale for words; o'er still and webless rooms,
> The listless craftsmen through their elf-locks scowled.

(Although it is doubtful, always supposing that Wordsworth read *The Saint's Tragedy*, that in these halting lines he saw the realization of his hope expressed in the Preface to the *Lyrical Ballads* that 'the Poet will lend his divine spirit to aid the transfiguration' should the man of science make his discoveries 'manifestly and palpably material to us as enjoying and suffering beings'.)

Kingsley, like Disraeli and Reade, is a debating novelist; and he uses both *Yeast* and *Alton Locke* to preach the kind of Christianity in which he passionately believed. He epitomizes this belief in a letter, 14 July 1853, to his close friend and fellow Christian Socialist, F. D. Maurice, whom he called 'Master'. Maurice had recently published his volume *Theological Essays*, which were to cost him his Chair of Theology at King's College, London, because in one he suggested that after death God did not punish sinners for eternity, and this was regarded as dangerous heresy. Kingsley writes that the book has given him courage to speak more boldly, and that its theme will frighten people, 'especially such an expression of it as that in § 3. P 144. As I read it, I shuddered, to think how here was *the* truth the cardinal truth of my own heart, to preach which I wish to live and die.' (BL MS 41,287.) He refers to the paragraph in Essay VII, 'On the Atonement', which ends describing Christ: 'One who appears as the actual representative of Humanity, cannot be a formal substitute for it. We deny Him in the first character, by claiming the second for Him.' That Christ was God become a physical man and that therefore the Christian church had a social responsibility towards men was the central tenet of Kingsley's religion and of Christian Socialism. 'Jesus Christ— THE MAN' is the foundation of the visionary community at the end of *Yeast*, of which Kingsley remarked, 'I think this will explain a good deal of Maurice.' (*Charles Kingsley. Letters and Memories*, i. 305.)

Kingsley's Christianity controls his use of Blue books. Like Lancelot in *Yeast*, although he reads and uses them, ultimately he abandons them in favour of God. In the previous chapter I showed how he used them to describe the physical conditions of the Other Nation, but there is much less use of detailed Blue book facts in *Yeast* or *Alton Locke* to create a scene or a character than there is in *Sybil*; nor does he make intensive use of a specific Blue book as Reade does of the *Report on Birmingham Gaol*. But he is perhaps more successful than either in taking a detail from a Blue book and giving it imaginative life to express the oppression of the Other Nation, as he does in *Yeast* in making the ravaging hare a symbol of the upper classes' determination to have their sport and protect their game even at the cost of ruining the poor. (See Leech's cartoon, 'The Game Laws; or, The Sacrifice of the Peasant to the Hare', *Punch*, VII (1844), 197; Plate 16.) In the *Report from the Select Committee on the Game Laws* Robert Ackrill, a reporter for the *Worcester*

THE RECONCILIATION;

OR, AS IT OUGHT TO BE.

25. 'The Reconciliation', 1845

THE POOR MAN'S FRIEND.

24. 'The Poor Man's Friend', 1845

HORRID MURDER

AT

Zion Place Aldermanbury

March 2, 1842.

Yesterday, at a quarter to nine o'clock one of the most appalling and tragical events occurred. From the fact's which we were enabled to collect it appears that the house in question, and let out all parts of it but the kitchen and attics, and his family consisted of his wife and three children, namely, George, aged 10, Ann, aged 7, and Alfred, aged 4, and Ann Hammond, the niece of Mr. Lucas, aged 18. It was his custom on every Sunday morning to bring his children down stairs to be dressed preparatory to taking them to church, he asked his wife in the calmest manner if he should go up for the children, and she requested he would. He then proceeded to the attic, and as it appeared, his first victim was the little girl, who he wrapped in a shawl and carried her to he room in which he and his wife slept, and placing her on the front of the bed cut her throat from ear to ear.

He next carried the little boy Alfred to the same place, and placing him on the bed, also cut his throat in the same manner. The eldest son was his last victim, and there is no doubt from the fact of his having one stocking and garter on, that the poor little fellow was in the act of dressing, when his wretched father summoned them to destruction. It would seem here, from the carpet in the passage leading from the room in which he slept, to that of the third room where he was murdered, being rolled up in many places, that the poor little fellow had struggled very hard, and his cries were so loud as to be heard in the next house. However, on getting him inside the door, his wretched father cut his throat, and then his own, and both fell quite close together. An alarm was instantly given, and police-constable Richard Andrews, 185, who was on the beat; and William Henry Wallace, 6, proceeded up stairs, but the fury of the unhappy man had by this time accomplished its object in so determined a manner that death in each case must have been instantaneous.

BIRT, Printer, 39, Great St. Andrew street, Seven Dials

Horrid Murder
Of SEVEN PERSONS.

Good people all I pray draw near,
Of a wholesale murder you shall hear,
The like among savages could not be found,
As did take place near Uxbridge town.
Seem poor souls near Uxbridge fell,
By a murderer's hand, how sad to tell.

At Denham village there did dwell,
A man named Marshall known full well,
With his wife and family as you shall hear,
Together with his aged mother dear.

On Monday, May the twenty third,
To Marshall's cottage there repaired,
Two labourers as we may read,
Who brought to light these dreadful de...

They could not make the inmates hear.
Which fill'd their minds with dread and fear
They forced the door, mark what I say,
And a fearful sight there met their gaze.

Upon the floor covered with wounds,
Mrs. Marshall and her sister found;
The floor in pools was covered o'er,
By the monster, with the victims gore.

In the back room there lay we hear,
The grandmother, and three children dear,
Their heads were smash'd, they were still in
death.

Oh, shame upon that heartless wretch,
Poor Marshall's body they soon found.
Covered with sacks upon the ground,
His poorhead by the monster had been smash'd
With a sledge hammer or an axe.

Marshall's sister was there on that fatal night
Expecting soon to be made a wife,
But by the murderer's hand she died,
And a corpse lay the expectant bride.

That poor soul, 75 years of age.
Could not escape the monster's rage,
To her side one little darling press'd,
Tho' her aged eyes were closed in death.

It was malice caused these dreadful deeds.
Which makes each feeling heart to bleed,
But may we ne'er have again to tell,
Where so many by a murder's hand has fell.

Now the horrid murderer has been found.
At a lodging-house in Reading town,
He is more than fiend, he is not a man,
And deserves to die by the hangman's hand.

These deeds have caused much grief around
The country, as well as Uxbridge town.
For justice one and all do cry,
While tears of sorrow fill each eye.

Disley, Printer, 57, High Street, St. Giles.

28. Gustave Doré, 'The Angel and the Orphan', 1872

30. W. P. Frith, 'The Crossing Sweeper', 1863

29. Richard Dadd, 'Crossing Sweeper', after 1864

Herald who travelled through the countryside to attend the petty sessions at Worcester and Pershore, gave evidence:

I have seen hares upon small allotments doing amazing injury . . .

You state that you have not heard of the cottagers making any complaint; do you know the reason why they do not make complaints?—I think if they were to make any complaints, they would be very likely to find themselves rather awkwardly placed on their allotments; I do not know that Mr. Acton [who owned the land at Egdon, where he had seen the hares] would take away their allotments, but I think there are game preservers in the neighbourhood that would. (*Report from the Select Committee on the Game Laws*, P.P. Session 1846 (IX. i), 673.)

His statement is corroborated by William Elcomb, of Dunford in Heyshott, who held a quarter-acre allotment which had been much damaged by hares and rabbits,

But you would not like to kill a rabbit, for fear of spoiling the game?—It is not allowed.

Did anybody ever tell you that it was not allowed?—No, but we know that the law is very strict, and anybody is afraid to do it now. I never would do it, if I could get a bit of bread anywhere else. (Ibid., p. 871.)

As Thomas Hardy wrote nearly forty years later about the Dorset labourer's condition, which had changed little since Kingsley wrote *Yeast*, 'melancholy among the rural poor arises primarily from a sense of the incertitude and precariousness of their position . . .' ('The Dorsetshire Labourer', *Longman's Magazine*, 2 (1883), 257.)

Also, as the Commons Committee on Game Laws learnt, there was bitter feeling against the Game Laws: 'The chaplains of prisons find they can produce no moral effect whatever upon prisoners under the Game Laws; that they leave the prison only to return, frequently replying to advice by saying, "that game was made for the poor as well as for the rich, and God made the birds of the air and fishes of the sea for all".[4] (Op. cit., P.P. Session 1846 (IX. ii), 37.)

[4] Compare the sentiments expressed in the broadside ballad 'Working Poor of Old England':

> The great landholders are leagued in a band,
>   And who will deny it is so?
> For game preserves, to monopolize the land,
>   That food for the people should grow,
> Cries my lord—'for the starving rabble who cares
>   We'll transport Poachers, who dare to set snares,
> For we think far more of our pheasant's [*sic*] and hares,
>   Then [*sic*] we do for the starving poor of old England.
>
> (Baring-Gould, *Ballads*, vi. 240.)

Kingsley well expresses both this melancholy and this bitterness in the menacing image of the 'merry brown hares' which inexorably 'come leaping' over the hill while the woman whose crops are being destroyed weeps for the death of her poacher husband. But Kingsley, like Disraeli in his treatment of the Chartists, expresses sympathy with the oppressed rural poor, but stays safely on the side of law and order by making the poachers involved in a fight flash chaps from London who want the game to sell, and the local poacher, Crawy, is a snivelling craven, easily overpowered by Tregarva who exerts his authority, despite his criticism of the landlords. (See *Yeast*, Ch. 8.) Robert Ackrill's comments on poachers dispute Kingsley's version of their kind: 'I think, as a general rule, the best poachers are the best labouring men; as far as regards abilities, they have rather a greater share of common sense than their brethren. It requires more tact and ability to make a good poacher than it does to make a common ploughman.' (Op. cit., P.P. Session 1846 (IX. i), 673.)

While querying his assessment of the skill needed by a ploughman, I think his idea of the poacher seems more likely than Kingsley's. Crawy is an exemplum of the wretchedness to which the labouring rural population, in Kingsley's eyes, have been reduced. If Christ were God made man, man was made in God's image; therefore man degraded in physical squalor is blasphemy. In Crawy, Kingsley is inveighing against that blasphemy rather than imaginatively recreating a nineteenth-century poacher.

Similarly, because he fervently believed that an important manifestation of God in human physical life was Christian marriage, he used facts from the Blue books to inveigh against the sexual squalor of the poor. In a period of obsessive reticence about sex, he is remarkable among Victorian novelists in doing this. Alfred Austin wrote in the *Reports on Agriculture*, 1843:

The consequences of the want of proper accommodation for sleeping in the cottages are seen in the early licentiousness of the rural districts [licentiousness which has not always respected the family relationship [typical Blue book euphemism for incest]. It appeared to me that generally the accommodation for sleeping is such as necessarily to create an early and illicit familiarity between the sexes; for universally in the villages where the cottages are the most crowded, there are the greatest number of illegitimate children, and also the greatest depravity of manners generally (Op. cit., P.P. Session 1843 (XII), 40.)

> Our daughters with base-born babies
> Have wandered away in their shame;
> If your misses had slept, squire, where they did,
> Your misses might do the same . . .

Tregarva's ballad is echoed in his remark about Honoria, the squire's younger daughter: 'I think sometimes, if she had been born and bred like her father's tenants' daughters, to sleep where they sleep, and hear the talk they hear, and see the things they see, what would she have been now?' (*Yeast*, ch. 4.)

Hardy warns against judgements made about the rural labourer 'by philosophers who look down upon that class from the Olympian heights of society' ('The Dorsetshire Labourer', op. cit., p. 255), and points out that first impressions after a brief interview change radically if the inquirer takes the trouble and time to live for a period with the family in question. Living, for the agricultural labourer, was precarious, wages were uncertain and low, and food was monotonous and often very scarce, but this shocked insistence on sexual immorality among the poor is part of the familiar argument that they were savages to be civilized and, I suspect, arises largely from a total ignorance of a way of life viewed 'from Olympian heights' and very rapidly for the purpose of getting together a report (Alfred Austin, in the *Reports on Agriculture*, 1843, had only thirty days in which to examine the employment of women and children in agriculture in Wiltshire, Dorsetshire, Devonshire, and Somerset). Also, it seems to me that the shocked reaction of men like Austin and Kingsley to the freedom and realism of sex in country villages was inevitable because they were confronted with communities where the middle-class Victorian reticence and evasion about sex simply could not be maintained. So rather than trying patiently to explore and re-create the reality, they reacted by lamenting that they did not discover their own customs and mores.[5] No doubt there were examples of incest in the villages, and crowded conditions made it impossible for any girl to assume the 'modesty' ideally supposed to adorn Victorian womanhood, but Austin's generalization that crowded cottages

[5] Kingsley himself had very strong sexual feelings and an equally strong belief that they could be expressed beneficially only in Christian marriage. In 1848 he wrote in a letter, 'The highest state I define as that state through and in which men can know most of God, and work most for God: and this I assert to be the married state.' (*Charles Kingsley. Letter and Memories*, i. 190.)

inevitably produce 'depravity of manners' is over-emphatic and suggests the distorting viewpoint of 'Olympian heights'. According to the Police Report in *The Times* 11 October 1843 (see below, p. 176) many of the illegitimate children born to country girls were the result of seductions by locally-billetted soldiers, rather than incest. Or the local gentry were sometimes of the opinion that the poor were fair game. Joseph Ashby, instrumental in forming the Agricultural Workers' Union, was the illegitimate child of a Warwickshire village girl and the local squire. His daughter's biography of him (*Joseph Ashby of Tysoe, 1859–1919: a study of English village life*, Mabel Kathleen Ashby, Cambridge, 1961) describes how his mother reared him in the village to become a highly intelligent man with a large family of distinguished children. The village's attitude to the illegitimacy seems to have been one of common sense and acceptance, but there is no suggestion of 'depravity of manners'. And if we set this account beside the stormy seduction drama in *Yeast*, the shameful story of Colonel Bracebridge and the 'coarse, handsome, showily-dressed' village girl whom Lancelot sees at the village wake (Ch. 13) the fiction seems lurid and rings false.

Kingsley also uses Blue book facts to expose the Other Nation's ignorance of hygiene and its fatal consequences in the encounter between Lancelot and the woman whose child is dying of typhus (Ch. 13). The open drain before her door comes from the *Reports on Agriculture*, 1843 (see above, p. 106); the woman considers it does no harm. But the scene is also a reproach to the squire who allows his tenants to live in such conditions, and is part of Kingsley's campaign to preach man's responsibility for disease such as typhus and cholera; that it was no good resting on the assumption that epidemics were visitations of 'Providence' and that nothing could be done. A clean water supply could conquer such disease, and it was up to the intelligent members of the middle class to see that the whole community was provided with it, and taught how to use it. God's will was worked by man's using his intelligence to trace God's laws in cause and effect.

Kingsley also occasionally uses Blue book facts to provide a pathetic tableau to advance his argument that the middle class should open their eyes and right the wrongs of the poor, as Disraeli does in his tableau of Warner and his destitute family. An example of this is in *Alton Locke*, Ch. 8, 'Light in a Dark Place', in which Kingsley uses the *Second Report* of the Children's Employment Commission to provide the scene of the two over-worked seamstresses in their bare garret, tempted to prostitu-tion in order to survive. The scene emphasizes the dire nature of the poverty and the urgency with which it should be re-dressed. But, like Disraeli, he is concerned with the problem rather than the people.

A plot detail in *Alton Locke*, connected with the scene just mentioned, is taken from another kind of report, one not insti-tuted by the Government but by the tailors themselves who, in 1844, conducted an inquiry into the conditions of their trade. George, Alton's wealthy and ambitious cousin, dies from small-pox caught from a coat made in an infected garret by a sweated tailor. It is the familiar appeal to the selfishness of the upper Nation to do something about the disease of the lower—if nothing is done the upper Nation itself will be contaminated. (The plot of *Yeast* carries a similar warning—Argemone dies from typhus when she goes to nurse the labourer's child.) The Report compiled by the Operative Tailors exposed and con-demned the sweating system. Henry Mayhew quotes from it in his series of letters 'Labour and the Poor: The Metropolitan Districts' to the *Morning Chronicle* which later formed the beginning of *London Labour and the London Poor*: 'MR. French, one of the undersigned medical gentlemen, states that he has seen a garment (which was a few hours afterwards to be forwarded to a person of rank) serving at the time of his visit as a covering to an individual suffering from small pox.'[6] (*Morn-ing Chronicle*, 18 December 1849.)

Sometimes the novelists' omissions in their use of the Blue books are particularly revealing. For example, despite Disraeli's concern with the colliers' lives and the enormity of women and girls working in the mines, he ignores evidence of the colliers' own discussion of the subject:

At a Meeting of above 350 working colliers from the surrounding district, held in the Court-house, Barnsley, on the 25th of March, 1841, before the Sub-Commissioner [J. C. Symons], it was resolved—

---

[6] This extract from the Report, which I have not yet been able to trace, is re-printed in Henry Mayhew's essay 'In the Sweat of Thy Face Shalt Thou Eat Bread', *London Characters*, 1874.

1. That 11 hours is the usual time collieries are actually worked each day on the average.

2. That eight hours is quite sufficient time for both men and children to be in the pits, and that longer hours are injurious to both, considering the atmosphere of mines and the accidents to which they are exposed.

3. That children ought not to be employed in the pits at all before they are 11 years old, but that parents cannot afford to maintain them up to that age without the assistance of their labour; and no legislation ought to take place without provision be made for their maintenance.

4. That the work of hurriers is very laborious for children, and that the work of trappers is wet and cold, and hurtful to the health of young children.

5. That the employment of girls in pits is highly injurious to their morals, that it is not proper work for females, and that it is a scandalous practice. —(Carried with five dissentients only.)

6. That the ignorance of the children of colliers is very great, and the reason is that their wages are not sufficient to enable the colliers to give their children education, and they earnestly desire to have better means of education. The long hours the children work tire them too much to allow them to learn in the evening.

I certify that these resolutions were duly passed by show of hands at the above-mentioned meeting, after full and free discussion, by the colliers there assembled.

> (Signed) W. C. Mence,
> Clerk of the Peace at Petty Session,
> Barnsley.

(*CEC*, I, Appendix, 1, P.P. Session 1842 (XVI), 270 f.)

That the voice of the Other Nation could be the voice of reason is something constantly denied by the Victorians who tried to express that voice in fiction, in Slackbridge, the Trades Union agitator in *Hard Times*, whom Dickens carefully dissociates from the 'safe solid sense' of the working men who are, none the less, swayed by him; in Crossthwaite's hot-headed arguments for the Charter in *Alton Locke* stilled by Eleanor's exposition of Christian Socialism; in the rash talk of Devilsdust and Dandy Mick on behalf of 'what he conceived was the vindication of popular rights' in *Sybil* which ceases when they become capitalists, patronized by Lord Marney; in Fanny Mayne's strike orator in *Jane Rutherford; or, The Miners' Strike* (serialized in the *True Briton* June–October 1853, published in book form 1854); in later novels which also owe a debt to Dickens, such as Gissing's *Demos* and Walter Besant's *All Sorts and Conditions of Men* (1882) in which Dick Coppin's fiery speech at the Stepney Advanced Club calling for the abolition of the House of Lords is followed by the sweet reason of his upper-class, educated cousin, Harry Goslett, who silences Dick. Besant comments: 'as for the people, it had made them laugh, just as Dick's had made them angry; they came to the hall to get these little emotions, and not for any personal or critical interest in the matter discussed; and this was about all the effect produced by them' (Ch. 35). All these scenes embody Carlyle's assertion that the Other Nation needed guidance from those in the classes above them and that they were incapable of helping themselves. The argument is perfectly expressed in illustrations to *Jane Rutherford*. One shows Jonathan Rutherford wildly haranguing the miners; another contrasts Jonathan's uncontrolled fury with the calm good sense of Lord Westerland, coal-owner, who at once assumes command of the situation (see Plates 17 and 18).

Before I complete my discussion of the novelists' debt to documentary evidence assembled to plead a case, I must mention Henry Mayhew's *London Labour and the London Poor* because it provides a unique example of a novelist, Augustus Mayhew, using in fiction material he collected for his brother's survey. Moreover, a comparison between Henry Mayhew's reports on the poor and the Blue books emphasizes his originality as an explorer amongst the Other Nation. He is of his time in applying Bacon's empirical method to social discovery:

Mr. Mayhew is . . . a mere collector of facts, endeavouring to discover the several phenomena of labour with a view of arriving ultimately at the laws and circumstances affecting, and controlling the operation and rewards of the labourer, as well as of showing the importance of the poor and the working classes as members of the state. ('Answers to Correspondents', at the end of *London Labour and the London Poor*, weekly part No. 10, 15 February 1851.)

He sets himself against the political economists:

they have sat beside a snug sea-coal fire and tried to excogitate, or think out the several matters affecting the working-classes—even as Adam Smith, the great founder of the science retired for twelve years to an obscure village in Scotland to dream upon the laws concerning production and producers. And yet it is upon the cobweb philosophy thus spun out that the whole of the legislation of the present day is made to depend! (Ibid., end of No. 15, 22 March 1851.)

These attitudes are familiar enough, but Henry Mayhew was a pioneer in that he saw the importance of contacting the Other Nation and listening to its members telling their stories in their own way, although obviously he and his helpers lacked the equipment accurately to record what they heard, and, again, we can never be quite sure how much the material has been tidied up for publication. But he was right to claim, in the preface to the first volume of *London Labour and the London Poor*, that it was 'the first attempt to publish the history of a people, from the lips of the people themselves . . . in their own "unvarnished" language'.

Augustus helped in the interviewing, and used some of the evidence in his novel *Paved with Gold; or, The Romance and Reality of the London Streets* (1858). It tells the story of Phil Merton, who is born in a workhouse, educated in a workhouse school, escapes to go on the tramp and, after many adventures, comes into his inheritance. As the plot suggests, the novel owes a heavy debt to *Oliver Twist* except that, unlike Oliver, Phil is corrupted by living in the underworld—'his morality had become as muddy as his rags' (Bk. II, ch. 5). In the preface Augustus writes that the novel's purpose is to check vice by giving 'a truthful account . . . of the miseries of criminal life' and so proving to the wicked that virtue pays better. He insists on 'the extreme truthfulness with which this book has been written' and that 'the descriptions of boy-life in the streets . . . the peculiarities of tramp-dom and vagrancy, have all resulted from long and patient inquiries among the individuals them- selves . . . Indeed, some portions of this book (such as the chap- ters on the "crossing-sweepers" and the "Rat Match" . . .) were originally undertaken by me at the request of my brother, Mr. Henry Mayhew, and will, I believe, form part of his invaluable work on "London Labour and the Poor".' (See the chapter 'Crossing-Sweepers', *London Labour and the London Poor*, 4 vols., 1861–2, ii, and the section 'A Night at Rat-Killing' in the chapter 'The Destroyers of Vermin', vol. iii.)

It is very likely that the account of the watercress sellers in *London Labour and the London Poor*, i, is also by Augustus. In *Paved with Gold*, Ch. 2, he uses the editorial 'we' and claims that the account of the watercress-sellers' earnings is 'a fact of our own gathering' and refers to 'accounts rendered to us by the salesmen at the different green-markets of London'. Certainly the description of the watercress sellers in the novel is derived from material used in *London Labour and the London Poor*, and Phil Merton graduates from selling cresses to sweeping crossings, as does the crossing sweeper whose story was collected for *London Labour*, ii.

The preamble to the life of the Watercress Girl in *London Labour* illustrates Mayhew's attitude to his subject and shows why the passage convinces us that it is 'true to' her life, as distinct from simply recording facts about it. There is none of the arrogant self-confidence and self-righteousness so characteristic of contemporary middle-class response to the Other Nation. For example, G. J. Hall, M.A., won a prize in 1855 for his essay on 'Ragged Schools and Kindred Institutions' in which he asserted that children begged in the streets 'not at all because the parents are in destitute circumstances, or suffer from the pangs of hunger, but that they may have wherewith to gratify their indolent, besotted, and lustful propensities' (*Sought and Saved*, 1855, p. 188). Mayhew, instead of superimposing a preconceived stereotype on the eight-year-old cress-seller, puts into practice the advice T. H. Huxley later gave Charles Kingsley: 'sit down before fact as a little child, be prepared to give up every preconceived notion, follow humbly wherever and to whatever abysses nature leads, or you shall learn nothing' (*Life and Letters of Thomas Henry Huxley*, by his son Leonard Huxley, 2 vols., 1900, i. 219). And, far from being confident, he is nonplussed by the child: 'I did not know how to talk to her. At first I treated her as a child, speaking on childish subjects . . . I asked her about her toys and her games with her companions; but the look of amazement that answered me soon put an end to any attempt at fun on my part . . . All her knowledge seemed to begin and end with water-cresses, and what they fetched.' (*London Labour and the London Poor*, i. 151.)

He stops talking and lets the child speak, with the authentic voice of the Other Nation. Listening to her we realize what Dickens and Collins meant by their phrase 'strikes to the soul like reality'. From her words we get the same kind of direct impact of her life as we get from the remarkable photograph taken by Dr Barnardo of Sarah Burge, one of the girls in his care (see Plate 19), and as we do not get from, say, Dickens's Sissy Jupe. Mayhew is honest enough to record the child's corrections of what he says: 'I have to be down at Farringdon-market between four and five, or else I can't get any creases, because everyone almost—especially the Irish—is selling them, and they're picked up so quick. Some of the sales-women—we never calls 'em ladies—is very kind to us children, and some of them altogether spiteful.' (Ibid.) She stoutly refuses to pose as a pitiful creature: 'No; people never pities me in the street— excepting one gentleman, and he says, says he, "What do you do out so soon in the morning?" but he gave me nothink—he only walked away.' (Ibid.) And there is no self-pity in her words: 'When the snow is on the ground, there's no creases. I bears the cold—you must; so I puts my hands under my shawl, though it hurts 'em to take hold of the creases, especially when we takes 'em to the pump to wash 'em. No; I never see any children crying—it's no use.' (Ibid.)

Her objective description of the bitter cold in the few details she selects—her hands under the shawl, the pain of having to wash the cresses at the pump—and the direct, unexaggerated language in which she gives them, recreate the actuality of her life with startling clarity.

Augustus loses this clarity when he transfers her to *Paved with Gold*. Despite his direct reaction to her when recording her own words for *London Labour and the London Poor*, his fictional account is distorted by the quality of his imaginative response; the actuality is overwhelmed by what Medawar would describe as hypothesis, 'imaginative preconception of what might be true' (see above, p. 32). In the novel Ellen, the little cress seller, has a certain independence and shows Phil Merton how to sell when he sets up with cresses in London, but their relationship is sentimentalized in that Phil protects her, as a 'gentleman' should. Mayhew's informant would have scorned such protection:

On and off, I've been very near a twelvemonth in the streets . . . When I gets home, after selling creases, I stops at home. I puts the room to rights . . . I am a capital hand at bargaining . . . They can't take me in . . . I know the quantities very well . . . All my money I earns I puts in a club and draws it out to buy clothes with. It's better than spending it in sweet-stuff, for them as has a living to earn. Besides it's like a child to care for sugar-sticks, and not like one who's got a living and vittals to earn.

Also, like so many novelists of the period, he loses the impact of her individuality by generalizing about the group she represents:

These wretched cress-sellers belong to a class so terribly poor, that temptation must ever haunt them like an evil spirit; and yet they can be trusted without fear of their failing to pay the few pence they owe [that is, to the people from whom they buy the cresses in Farringdon Market], even though they hunger for it. It must require, too, no little energy of conscience on the part of the boys and girls frequenting this market to resist the luring advice of those they meet at the low lodging-houses. And yet they prefer the early rising—the walk to market with naked feet along the cold stones—the ten miles walk to earn the few halfpence—and the pinched meal when they *are* earned—to the thief's or wanton's easier life. (*Paved with Gold*, Bk. II, ch. 2.)

The heroic and evangelical concept 'energy of conscience' seems exaggerated and irrelevant when contrasted with the child's own acceptance of her way of life. The passage is, in fact, lifted almost verbatim from *London Labour and the London Poor*, a section in which his 'imaginative preconception' is also evident. Here he is no longer recording the Watercress Girl's words, but imposing his own interpretation on what he has seen of her life:

To visit Farringdon-market early on a Monday morning, is the only proper way to judge of the fortitude and courage and perseverance of the poor . . . These poor cress-sellers belong to a class so poor that their extreme want alone would almost be an excuse for theft, and they can be trusted paying the few pence they owe even though they hunger for it. It must require no little energy of conscience on the part of the lads to make them resist the temptations around them, and refuse the luring advice of the young thieves they meet at the low lodging house. And yet they prefer the early rising—the walk to market with naked feet along the cold stones— the pinched meal—and the day's hard labour to earn the few halfpence—to the thief's comparatively easy life. (i. 149.)

It is part of a general summary used to make a moral point, repeated in the novel:

The heroism of the unknown poor is a thing to set even the dullest marvelling, and in no place in all London is the virtue of the humblest . . . so conspicuous as among the watercress-buyers at Farringdon-market. (Loc. cit.)

Verily the heroism of the unknown poor is a thing to set the dullest marvelling; and in no place in all London is the virtue of the humblest, both young and old, so conspicuous as among the water-cress buyers of Farringdon-market. (*Paved with Gold*, Bk. II, ch. 2.)

Its transference to the novel gives it the air of a case-book at the expense of individual character. In both the documentary report and in the novel Mayhew idealizes the cress-sellers; the idealized image is based on reality but it falsifies their life and directs attention away from the people in favour of religious platitudes. Contemporary philanthropic desire to represent the poor as 'deserving' insisted on their virtue despite adverse circumstances and at the expense of their humanity. Dickens shares this attitude to the poor, especially in his early novels. And in *Hard Times* Stephen Blackpool is idealized to an absurd degree so that he can be presented as a suitable subject for philanthropy. Yet the pressure of opinion which Dickens attempted to sway by means of characters like Stephen can be deduced from their exaggerated virtue.

Mayhew's use, in his fiction, of statistics and tables from *London Labour* also detracts from individualization of the poor:

There are, we learned, from accounts rendered to us by the salesmen at the different green-markets of London, upwards of six millions and a half of bunches of water-cresses sold annually in London; and these, at the retail price of one halfpenny a bunch, gives a sum of nearly £14,000 for the amount spent annually in water-cresses throughout London; then, dividing this amount by the gross number of street-sellers, it shows a weekly receipt of 5*s*.5*d*., and a weekly profit of 3*s*.3*d*. accruing to each individual—a fact which proves, not only how small is the capital required by this trade, but how terribly limited are the earnings of the poor creatures engaged in it. (*Paved with Gold*, Bk. II, ch. 2.)

This is a transcript and expansion of: 'The total amount received is nearly £14,000, and this apportioned among 1,000 street-sellers, gives a weekly receipt of 5*s*.5*d*., with a profit of 3*s*.3*d*. per individual.' (*London Labour*, i. 153.)

As in Disraeli's use of the Blue book facts in Wodgate the facts collected for *London Labour* are not transmuted by the creative imagination so that they are acceptable in the novel. In the terms of Romantic aesthetic theory, Mayhew used his Primary Imagination to gather the facts for *London Labour* but failed to use the esemplastic, shaping power of the Secondary Imagination to make these facts part of his fiction. His 'imaginative preconception' makes the actuality subserve his ideas of morality and religion rather than perceiving the actuality with such intensity that it becomes 'truth' in the fiction. The passage about wages is a good example of reportage of facts in a novel which actually obscures the nature of the lives being described rather than revealing it. Contrast the impact of the child's own words, as reported by Mayhew:

'The creases is so bad now, that I haven't been out with 'em for three days. They're so cold, people won't buy 'em; for when I goes up to them, they say, "They'll freeze our bellies." . . . Sometimes I make a great deal of money. One day I took 1*s*.6*d*., and the creases cost 6*d*.; but it isn't often I get such luck as that. I oftener make 3*d*. or 4*d*. than 1*s*.; and then I'm at work, crying, "Creases, four bunches a penny, creases!" from six in the morning to about ten.' (*London Labour*, i. 151 f.)

The attempt to individualize the child in the novel by transferring a colloquial comment, 'They'll freeze our bellies', is not enough to prevent her becoming an example not a person.

London Labour and the London Poor reveals a contemporary preoccupation in its moral purpose. Henry Mayhew concluded the preface to the first volume:

My earnest hope is that the book may serve to give the rich a more intimate knowledge of the sufferings, and the frequent heroism under those sufferings, of the poor—that it may teach those who are beyond temptation to look with charity on the frailties of their less fortunate brethren—and cause those who are in 'high places,' and those of whom much is expected, to bestir themselves to improve the condition of a class of people whose misery, ignorance, and vice, amidst all the immense wealth and great knowledge of 'the first city in the world,' is, to say the very least, a national disgrace to us.

It is the familiar stereotype of the Two Nations, the one brutish and degraded, the other (beyond temptation!) to be taught to provide help and guidance; the stereotype appears in Tregarva's comment to Lancelot in *Yeast*: 'I should have thought those members of parliament, and statesmen, and university scholars have been set up in the high places, out of the wood where we are all struggling and scrambling, just that they might see their way out of it.' (Ch. 13.)

So, despite the Mayhews' excellent intentions to present the poor to the life in their own words, and despite the impact of much of this reported speech, the moral purpose of *London Labour* distorts the authentic life of the Other Nation; even further when it is represented in fiction, as in *Paved with Gold*.

IMAGES OF THE OTHER NATION IN NEWSPAPERS AND JOURNALS

Inevitably, in discussing the Blue books and the images of the poor which the novelists found in them, I have referred to newspaper reports of Blue book topics. Newspapers were the other great source of facts informing the middle-class 'consciousness' of the poor. Kingsley's chief source for *Alton Locke* is not Blue books but the *Morning Chronicle* letters on the London tailoring trade, which he also uses in 'Cheap Clothes and Nasty'. And 'Moses' in the novel (changed to 'Nebuchadnezzar' in 'Cheap Clothes and Nasty') is not a piece of gratuitous anti-Semitism, as might be supposed, but the name of a real shopkeeper discussed in *The Times* (see Plate 20): 'According to our Police Report of yesterday, a wretched-looking woman named BIDDELL, with a squalid half-starved infant at her breast, was placed at the bar of the Lambeth-street-office on Wednesday, and charged before Mr. HENRY with having unlawfully pawned several articles of wearing apparel which she had been employed to make up for Mr. MOSES, a slopseller on Tower-hill.' (27 October 1843.)

The previous January she had been widowed, with a child two years old and pregnant of the infant now in her arms:

she had attempted to support herself and the two children by her needle-work, principally in making trousers, for which she was paid SEVEN PENCE a pair, out of which she was obliged to buy the thread to make them; and, in order to provide *dry bread* for herself and her infants, she had been compelled to pawn a portion of the work which she had finished while she proceeded with the remainder . . . The slopseller's foreman . . . asserted that if she was honest and industrious she might make a 'good' living at her trade; and, on being questioned by the magistrate as to what he considered 'a good living for a woman who has herself and two infant children to support,' he explained it to be SEVEN SHILLINGS A WEEK.[7]

In the pamphlet and the novel Kingsley attacks this savage exploitation and the greed of a clientele who insist on cheap prices despite the undercutting and the human suffering involved.

Punch, which in its early years was a very Radical paper, seized on the name Moses and made it generic of the dishonourable slopseller, employing sweated labour to produce his cheap goods (see 'Moses and Son', 7 (1844), 228). There are several *Punch* cartoons which present in graphic form ideas which Kingsley made the subject of fiction in *Alton Locke* and *Yeast*, for example, the suggested patterns for shawls, which incorporate death's-heads (ibid., p. 221, see Plate 21); the Almanac for March 1845 entitled 'Cheap Clothing' and showing skeletons

[7] A blatant example of how the middle-class demands that the poor be virtuous could be used to exploit their labour.

working away at a tailors' bench (8, see Plate 22). Indeed, the
Two Nations theme recurs in the early numbers of *Punch*, for
example its comment on R. H. Horne's report for the Children's
Employment Commission, the cartoon 'Capital and Labour'
showing the poor toiling to support the luxuries of the rich
(5 (1843), facing 48; see Plate 23). Sometimes *Punch* makes
pictures of Dickens's attempts to make society aware of the
evils in its midst, which is not surprising as Dickens was a close
friend of the editor, Mark Lemon. Examples are, 'The Poor
Man's Friend' by Leech (8 (1845), 93), in which he shows the
destitute agricultural labourer's friend as Death and recalls in
the phrase Dickens's character Sir Joseph Bowley in *The Chimes*
(see particularly The Second Quarter and The Third Quarter),
and 'The Reconciliation; or, as it Ought to Be' (7 (1845), 123;
see Plates 24 and 25) showing the reconciliation of the rich man
and the agricultural labourer, with condescension on one side
and grateful deference on the other—the state for which
Dickens's Will Fern pleads in *The Chimes* (see The Third Quarter).

Certainly, the novels under discussion have much in common
with the Radical journalism of the period, and popularize by
fictionalizing abuses which had been aired by the press. One of
the pleasures in reading such fiction was the recognition of contemporary topics in imaginative form. Reade made the most use
of newspapers as he evolved his theory that facts had an undeniable artistic power, and of the group I am considering he
made the greatest use of the newspaper in his attempt to re-
create the Other Nation for his readers. Incidents reported in
the newspaper were often the sparks to fire his imagination. He
wrote to *The Times*, 26 August 1871, to say that to the paper
he owed the genesis of *It is Never Too Late to Mend*: 'A noble
passage in the *Times* of September 7 or 8, 1853, touched my
heart, inflamed my imagination, and was the germ of my first
important work, "It is Never Too Late to Mend".' He refers to
The Times 8 September 1853 which included a long extract
from the *Birmingham Journal* headed 'Commission of Inquiry
into the Alleged Abuses in the Birmingham Gaol' and is the substance of the prison section of the novel. But Reade also used
the newspaper to sanction his delight in a sensational yarn. As
The Times remarked, 15 September 1853, the recent events at
Birmingham Gaol were horrific enough to appeal to any reader

of fiction, in fact appeared stranger than fiction—'stories which
would have been thought exaggerations if perused in one of Mr.
DICKENS'S books are now related of a borough gaol in 1853'.
It was a story perfectly in accord with the fashionable sensation
fiction of the time; indeed, the paper's comment epitomizes the
appeal of sensation fiction—astounding events revealed in an
apparently well-ordered society. As Wilkie Collins, one of the
most popular sensation novelists, had his character Gabriel
Betteredge say in a later novel, *The Moonstone* (1868),

here was our quiet English house suddenly invaded by a devilish Indian
Diamond—bringing after it a conspiracy of living rogues, set loose on us by
the vengeance of a dead man . . . Whoever heard the like of it—in the nineteenth century, mind; in an age of progress, and in a country which rejoices
in the blessings of the British constitution? Nobody ever heard the like of
it, and, consequently, nobody can be expected to believe it. I shall go on
with my story, however, in spite of that. (First Period, Ch. 5.)

But Reade's novel differed from Collins's in that its subject
was not fantasy but an actual event of public importance. *The
Times*'s comment indicates the difficulty of representing such
horrific happenings without exaggeration, one of the difficulties
which beset Reade, and also the fascination of horrible events
which can be proved true; a delighted incredulity which can
feed its desire for sensation legitimately on facts without the
guilt of indulging in fantastic fiction. This pleasure in sensational
facts, to which Reade's novel certainly appealed, is like the
voyeur's pleasure in scrutinizing the horrible places in which the
poor lived, referred to at the beginning of Chapter 2. This is
given peculiar point by a report, in the *Birmingham Daily Mail*,
9 November 1891, on the retirement of the warder, William
Brown, from Winson Green Prison after forty years' service.
Apart from the corroborating details from Leicester Gaol, Winson Green is the Gaol of Reade's novel; and William Brown was
the prototype of Evans in *It is Never Too Late to Mend*. Brown
was 'the first-class warder in charge of the juvenile department'
in Birmingham Gaol when Austin was Governor and was the
only warder to be praised by the Commissioners as appearing
'to have exhibited in many cases considerable sympathy with
the prisoners under punishment, and to have not unfrequently
relaxed its severity, so far as to relieve them from the extremity
of suffering' (Birmingham *Report*, P.P. Session 1854 (XXXI),
xxxvi).

Reade wrote a play from the novel *It is Never Too Late to Mend*, and it provoked much discussion and adverse criticism of the realistic prison torture scenes, especially the use of the strait-jacket. Reade's 'character of Evans was taken from Mr. William Brown', commented the *Birmingham Daily Mail* (9 November 1891), and 'Mr. Brown is so well known in connection with these facts that he has more than once been offered a large remuneration to appear on the stage to play the part of himself in an adaptation of Reade's brilliant novel.' This same desire to have vulgar curiosity satisfied by the dramatic display of people who had recently been involved in remarkable events prompted the enticements held out to Grace Darling to act herself upon the stage, or to Betty Mouat (who survived alone a journey from Shetland to Norway in a drifting boat) if she would but sit for half an hour on the stage of an Edinburgh theatre. These people showed their calibre by refusing both the money and the opportunity to be the centre of attention. But the crude way in which Reade displays the characters of a recent *cause célèbre* in both novel and play makes it difficult to exonerate him from the charge of seeking to appeal to vulgar curiosity as well as to a sense of justice.

Moreover, in considering the realistic details of the torture in the Gaol, a recreation of process, like Van Gogh's evocation of the weaver's loom, can stimulate the imagination by generating interest in the way another man lives and works, in his skills, by extending human consciousness and sympathy. But process can also generate horrific sensation—Reade's accurate description, both in novel and play, of strapping a man into a strait-jacket and of his sufferings in it, evokes ephemeral indulgence in horror; and the human beings involved are subsidiary to this indulgence. Instead of concentrating on the re-creation of another individual's life, the writer has his attention fixed on his reader's or audience's sensations.

A realism which is specious because it is concerned with the superficial rather than with the essential can be created by inducing recognition of actual events. It can be found in Truman Capote's *In Cold Blood* (1966), the re-creation of a multiple murder in Kansas, or in the television re-enactment of President Kennedy's assassination, Felix Lützkendorf's 'Lee Oswald—Assassin' (BBC 1, 15 March 1966). Insight into the human im-

plications of the event is obscured by the cheap immediate thrill
of the illusion of being present while it all happened. Sincere as
was Reade's reforming zeal, undoubtedly he wanted to thrill
his readers in this way by his account of the extraordinary happenings in the Gaol.

In *Sybil* Disraeli uses a newspaper report to create an important scene showing the lives of the Other Nation. The description
of the homeless poor dossing down for the night in Hyde Park
(Bk. V, ch. 7) contrasts with the nearby 'saloons of Deloraine
House [which] blazed with a thousand lights to welcome the
world of power and fashion to a festival of almost unprecedented
magnificence'. He took this from *The Times* police report, 11
October 1843:

The Park-keepers and the police have recently brought several young girls
to this court [Marlborough-Street] who were found sleeping beneath the
trees in Hyde Park and Kensington-gardens . . .

From the statement of the Park-keepers it appears there is an average of
50 persons of both sexes and all ages who have no other shelter by night
than what the trees and hollows in the embankments afford . . . One poor
fellow, a Spanish refugee, has been there for months; and, judging from his
winter preparation of old matting and straw in a hollow part of one of the
pits, he appears to contemplate passing many months more in the same
locality.

The second leader in *The Times*, 12 October 1843, commented:

The condition of the poor is a subject which . . . must ever excite the
attention of thinking men. Above all, it should in London, where the condition of the poor is most strikingly appalling . . .

Poor there must be everywhere.[8] Indigence will find its way and set up
its hideous state in the heart of a great and luxurious city . . .

But let all men . . . remember this—that within the most courtly pre-
cincts of the richest city on GOD'S earth there may be found, night after
night, winter after winter, women—young in years—old in sin and suffering
—outcasts from society—ROTTING FROM FAMINE, FILTH AND
DISEASE. Let them remember this, and learn not to theorize, but to act.
GOD knows, there is much room for action now-a-days.

Disraeli might have hoped that some of his well-informed
readers would recall the news item, or at any rate that the well-
known location and situation would give verisimilitude to his
scene; although obviously, unlike Reade, he is not relying on

---

[8] Dickens agreed. 'Utilitarian economists, skeletons of schoolmasters, Commissioners of Fact . . . the poor you will have always with you.' (*Hard Times*, Bk. II,
ch. 6.)

the public interest of a recent scandal being transferred to his work of fiction. Engels quoted the passage from *The Times* in *The Condition of the Working Class in England* (op. cit., pp. 65 f.) as an example of acute poverty in London. Disraeli, who had not read Engels, dramatizes the scene to demonstrate the split between the Two Nations. Lads among the homeless crowd in the Park speculate on the life of 'the nobs' and discuss their own hopes:

'I think I should like to be a link, Jim,' said the young one.

'I wish you may get it,' was the response: 'it's the next best thing to a crossing: it's what every one looks to when he enters public life, but he soon finds 'tain't to be done without a deal of interest. They keeps it to themselves, and never lets anyone in unless he makes himself very troublesome and gets up a party agin 'em.'

This facetious transference of the jockeying for position in the political circles of high life (exemplified in the conversation at Deloraine House) to low life, is a good example of Disraeli's habit of describing the Other Nation with a knowing eye upon the public rather than an observing and penetrating eye upon his subject. In this passage the poor become a private joke between the author and his readers. Henry Mayhew's explanation why people become crossing sweepers exposes this facetious fantasy: 'People take to crossing-sweeping either on account of their bodily afflictions, depriving them of the power of performing ruder work, or because the occupation is the last resource left open to them of earning a living, and they considered even the scanty subsistence it yields preferable to that of the workhouse.' (*London Labour and the London Poor*, ii. 465.)

The boys' speech, recorded by Mayhew, also exposes Disraeli's artfully contrived dialogue:

'The boys call me Johnny . . . and I'm getting on for eleven, and I goes along with the Goose and Harry, a-sweeping at St. Martin's Church, and about there . . . The most of the boys has got no homes. Perhaps they've got the price of a lodging, but they're hungry, and they eats the money, and then they must lay out. There's some of 'em will stop out in the wet for perhaps the sake of a halfpenny, and get themselves sopping wet. I think all our chaps would like to get out of the work if they could . . .' (Ibid., pp. 501, 503.)

Paradoxically, Disraeli's one piece of verifiable factual evidence, that the boy crossing-sweepers banded together to monopolize a good crossing, appears suspect in its facetious context.

For the rest of the scene Disraeli displays a cross-section of the Other Nation—the widow with three children; the man distressed at being woken because, exhausted after having walked forty miles that day to find work, he had fallen asleep supperless and had been dreaming of roast pork; the Polish military veteran (presumably of the 1831 insurrection and therefore likely to be noble; he is a substitute for the 'Spanish refugee' of *The Times*) who keeps order amongst the group[9] and, like the Spaniard, manages to make himself comfortable in these unpromising conditions. There is an example of the generosity of the poor in the starving lad's offer of half his quid of tobacco to the hungry man who had walked forty miles. Disraeli carefully introduces authentic slang terms such as 'lushy' (drunk) into the speech to give it credibility. Their conversation centres on how to earn enough to stay alive, in contrast to the subsequent conversation in Deloraine House on political manoeuvring, the marriage and horse markets. Egremont withdraws from it on receiving the request for help from Sybil, caught up in the Chartist activities which are a protest at such a split in society. Disraeli uses the scene, as does *The Times*, to appeal to his readers to heal the split. His rhetoric in the novel often echoes the Thunderer's. For example, his passionate denunciation of the Reform Bill (see Bk. I, ch. 5) can be compared with *The Times* on the scene of destitution in Hyde Park:

There is wealth, there is skill, there is art, there is science, there is theory, —all these enough, and more than enough, in England. Most abundant are they in the heart of England. Yet does the life-blood rush in a more healthy stream? Does the pulse of the nation beat with a more generous rapture? Whom has its wealth made happier? Whom has its skill taught to shun the moral pestilence that consumes its tens of thousands? Whom has its theory taught the high and paramount duty which man owes to the infirmities of his brother man?

And, like Disraeli, *The Times'* leader-writer is anti-Utilitarian: 'There are men of many theories abroad . . . Some there are who, believing that society is hollow, false, and tottering, would restore long-forgotten rules, and bring the vague and casual charity of men under the cognizance and direction of the

---

[9] If he is meant to be an aristocrat down on his luck (and the way in which he is represented suggests this) it is interesting that this little scene echoes Disraeli's main thesis, that the enlightened aristocrat must lead and give guidance.

church. But these men are laughed at by the age. For is not the age utilitarian, and therefore wise?'

It is not surprising that Disraeli used the scene from *The Times* and the arguments drawn from it to further his own in *Sybil*. John Walter, the proprietor of *The Times*, had much sympathy with Young England, and occasionally, when the group was forming, allowed his house Bearwood to be their meeting place (see Robert Blake, *Disraeli*, 1966, p. 176). Walter might very well have drawn Disraeli's attention to this second leader, or discussed it with him. In the Hyde Park scene the novel and the newspaper are very close together both in subject-matter and technique.

The scene demonstrates a basic weakness in Disraeli's representation of the poor. The combination of factual event with fantasies of speech and subject-matter makes the whole scene improbable. It can be compared with the extravagant television production of *Hamlet* played in the castle of Elsinore, not against a fabricated set. This expensive exercise had the bizarre effect of making the play seem unreal, because theatrical convention warred with historical actuality. Similarly, the factual references in Disraeli's scene expose its falsities.

If, as Kant and Coleridge believed, the imagination is an instrument of perception, the lack of imagination in these depictions of the Other Nation betrays a failure of perception. In all the novels, except in parts of *Mary Barton*, preconception inevitably diminishes 'truth to' the life of the poor. Paradoxically, the sense of the gulf between the Two Nations is often strongest when the one is attempting to understand and describe the other. Kingsley's characteristically impulsive claim at a public meeting that he was a 'Chartist' is completely untenable. In fact there is evidence that Kingsley was embarrassed by congratulations on *Alton Locke* when they were offered by the active Chartist and poet John Bedford Leno, who contributed to the *Christian Socialist*. In his autobiography Leno writes:

The reading of 'Alton Locke' had led me to the belief that its author had genuine sympathy with the working class in their struggle for political independence. Hence it was, that on entering the printing office one day, I felt compelled to tender him my gratitude. Whether I committed a blunder in my mode of doing this, I know not; but, I know that his reply was the reverse of what I had expected. I know that I was urged on by my feelings, and that whatever I said was prompted by respect and genuine admiration. His reply was to the effect that I had misunderstood his motives in writing the work in question, and, in a word, that he did not require my thanks. I confess at the time I felt hurt, and puzzled. (Autobiography prefixed to his *Poems* (1892), p. 49.)

Leno, however, continued to have a great admiration for Kingsley, read his books, and made a pilgrimage to Eversley. It is obvious that Kingsley kept at a distance other Chartists, like Walter Cooper and Thomas Cooper. The friendship he had with them was a business friendship, or the friendship which provokes discussion of books, religion and politics, but does not create intimate personal knowledge. Significantly, Kingsley does not feature much in Thomas Cooper's autobiography. Undoubtedly the character Alton Locke owes something to Kingsley's knowledge of such men, although Thomas Cooper had parted company with Feargus O'Connor before the Kennington Common meeting of 10 April 1848, the turning point of Alton's fortunes, and was at that time vigorously denouncing the 'physical force' Chartists.

Certainly Disraeli was moved by the destitution he saw in the North before he wrote *Sybil* (see the preface to my *Mr. Disraeli's Readers*, Nottingham University, 1966), and undoubtedly scenes, like the great open-air meetings on the moors, impressed him and stayed in his mind, but he saw it all across the gulf between the ordinary man and the visiting politician. Dickens had indeed, for a few months in his boyhood, experienced desperate poverty in the London streets, and in the adventures of Oliver Twist and David Copperfield he recreated the isolation and desolation of those days. But in the description of this period which he wrote for John Forster the dominant emotion is one of relief that he had escaped becoming either 'a little robber or a little vagabond' (*Life of Dickens*, i. 27). The pity and the horror with which he describes such poverty come from his realization of the thin line dividing it from the apparent security of the prosperous classes. Possibly his most convincing poor are those desperately clinging to gentility like Bob Cratchit or Mr Dorrit, or those exposed to the cruelty of a pretentious and thoughtless middle class like Sally Brass's little servant girl. In either case, the creative imagination is apparently generated by fear of the depths rather than apprehension of the people experiencing them. And despite his interest in Urania Cottage and its rescued prostitutes, his attitude to the poor remained that of the philanthropist, the reformer, or the journalist seeing the horrors of the London slums through the eyes of the police. The course of his relationship with John Overs (see *Victorian Studies*, xviii (1974), 215-17) shows that he willingly helped and patronized him, but he could not be said to be his friend as he was Mark Lemon's or Wilkie Collins's friend. From the poor of the new industrial towns he was completely remote.

Reade conscientiously tried to imagine what the poor suffered and to bridge the gulf between the Two Nations by having their sufferings inflicted upon him; for example, he submitted to voluntary solitary confinement in the black hole of York Castle in order to experience a convict's feelings. (It could perhaps be argued that this reveals a weakness in his imagination in that it needed such a literal rehearsal of the event before it could re-create it.) At its best, this was the action of a responsible fact-finding journalist. It was a substitute for knowledge of the poor, in the sense of understanding.

Because of her first-hand and continuing knowledge of Manchester life among the Other Nation, Elizabeth Gaskell did not need Blue books, or books of political economy, or back numbers of newspapers to create *Mary Barton*, which is not to say that she did not work hard at getting the dialect correct and did not read James Kay's or Peter Gaskell's accounts of Manchester. But the incident which stands out of *Mary Barton* with the sensationalism of a horrible incident blazoned in a newspaper is the murder of Harry Carson by John Barton, who gets the job by the ballot organized by his Trade Union. Elizabeth Gaskell's imaginative re-creation of John's life is badly damaged by this sensational event. Anyone from the Manchester area who read the novel would have immediately associated the incident with the murder of Thomas Ashton, as did Thomas's sister Mary. In 1831 Thomas, son of Samuel Ashton of Pole Bank, Werneth, was twenty-four. He managed his father's new cotton-spinning mill at Woodley. His younger brother James managed Ashton's other mill at Apethorn. On 3 January at 7.0 p.m. Thomas set out for Apethorn to do his brother's work because James had gone out for the evening. Shortly afterwards Thomas was brought home, shot dead.

The trial of three men accused of the murder took place at

Chester Castle, 6 August 1834. They were William Mosley, who turned King's evidence, his brother Joseph, and James Garside, who had fired the shot. William Mosley, in the course of his evidence, said that one Schofield or Stansfield urged them on to do the murder for £10, on behalf of the Cotton Spinners' Union. When William asked his brother and Garside which of the brothers had been shot, ' "they said *it didn't matter which it was, it was one of them*" ' (Thomas Middleton, *Annals of Hyde and District*, Manchester, 1899, p. 92). William said that for his part in the crime he had got two sovereigns. The other two had had their share. They all signed a book saying that they had had the money, and had to swear to God that they would never tell, praying to be struck dead if they did. ' "We did it one after another. We everyone held a knife over the other while we said so." ' (Loc. cit.) James Garside and Joseph Mosley were executed at Horsemonger Lane Gaol, 25 November 1834. William wisely left the district, and reappeared after thirty years to die in the Stockport Workhouse 17 April 1865 at the age of 60. He had resided in the Workhouse only ten days.

The murder came at a time of desperation for the Manchester cotton-workers. John Doherty, an influential Trades Unionist and Owenite, told the Select Committee inquiring into Trades Unions in 1838, that there had been ten or twelve partial strikes in Manchester since 1824 (the Combination Laws were repealed 1824-5) 'but only one general one, in 1829. This was occasioned by the masters proposing a very heavy reduction of wages: the strike lasted six months . . . He was asked if, towards the end of the strike, the men became more exasperated and disposed to do mischief? He said they were in 1829; they had only 2.2¼d. a week to subsist on.' (*Combinations Defended; Being a Commentary Upon, and Analysis of the Evidence given before the Parliamentary Committee of Inquiry into Combinations of Employers and Workmen Appointed by the House of Commons, February 1838*, By the London Trades' Combination Committee, 1839, p. 29.)

Thomas Ashton, says Middleton, 'was noted far and wide for the kindness of his disposition'; but James Ashton gave a revealing piece of evidence at the trial: 'At this time there was considerable excitement amongst the workpeople in Ashton and Stalybridge. I had discharged one man the day before for belonging to the Union.' (Thomas Middleton, op. cit., p. 90.) In the novel John Barton discovers that no one wants to employ a Trades Unionist. On starvation wages and victimized if they joined a union to demand better wages, the Manchester cotton workers in 1830 were indeed in a desperate plight. Moreover, it was the strain of the Ashton-under-Lyne strike (referred to by James Ashton as 'considerable excitement amongst the work-people') which crippled the finances of the Grand General Union of all the Operative Spinners in the United Kingdom set up at the conference held at Ramsay, Isle of Man, in December 1829 and organized largely by John Doherty. (See G. D. H. Cole and A. W. Filson, *British Working Class Movements. Select Documents 1789-1875*, 1951, p. 247.) After this conference, 'In England a policy was pursued of attacking employers one by one for an advance in wages and giving help to each set of workers in turn . . .' (Ibid., p. 247.) The Ashton murder pre-sumably was an unusually violent demonstration of this policy.

Elizabeth Gaskell was distressed when Harry Carson's murder in *Mary Barton* was associated with Thomas Ashton's. Her ex-planation to Sir John Potter, Mary Ashton's brother-in-law, is somewhat disingenuous:

Of course, I had heard of young Mr. Ashton's murder at the time when it took place; but I knew none of the details, nothing about the family, never read the trial (if trial there were, which I do not to this day know): and that if the circumstance were present to my mind at the time of my writing Mary Barton it was so unconsciously; although it's [*sic*] occur-rence, and that of one or two similar cases at Glasgow at the time of a strike, were, I have no doubt, suggestive of the plot, as having shown me to what lengths the animosity of irritated workmen would go. (16 August 1852, *Letters*, p. 196.)

The enthusiasm with which the isolated incident was seized to blacken the unions is well illustrated by the remarks of Andrew Ure, the champion of *laissez-faire* industrialization: 'I paid an unexpected visit to Hyde, in order to view the factories of Thomas Ashton, Esq., uncle to the amiable youth who was shot dead some time ago near his father's door, by assassins who had hired themselves during the ferment of the spinners' strikes, to murder mill-owners at the rate of ten pounds for each.' (*Philosophy of Manufacturers*, 1835, p. 348.) The exaggeration in the final clause is typical.

Elizabeth Gaskell's inaccuracies about the Glasgow strike in her letter to Sir John Potter are important. Almost certainly she is referring to the strike of Glasgow cotton spinners in April 1837 to resist a reduction in wages. At Oakbank Cotton Mill a strike-breaker was shot dead. A member of the Cotton Spinners' Association was charged with the crime, and leaders of the Association were charged with hiring him to commit it. Only the fact that the murder was supposed to be instigated by union leaders connects the crime with that of John Barton. It was the murder of an operative, not of a factory owner. And at the trial the prosecution failed to prove the complicity of the Association in the murder, and the charge was withdrawn. Notwithstanding, the leaders of the Spinners' Union were sentenced to seven years' transportation for conspiracy. (See G. D. H. Cole and A. W. Filson, op. cit., pp. 291 f.; also *First Report of the Select Committee on Combinations of Workmen*, 1838; P.P. Session 1837-8 (VIII), especially 138-43.)

Both cases could be cited more convincingly as illustrating the implacable victimization of Trades Unionists in the first half of the nineteenth century rather than their bloodthirstiness. Andrew Ure remarked of Ashton's murder:

This lamented victim of violence was not a proprietor [which is bending the evidence; he was the son of the proprietor, managing his father's factory], was personally unknown to the assassins, and had never given offence to the operatives [but obviously his brother, for whom he was standing in, had]. It was an unprovoked murder, which impressed every heart with horror, and has cast upon unions a bloody stain which they will never wash away. (Op. cit., p. 348.)

It is an indication of Elizabeth Gaskell's superior understanding of the situation that in her novel she does make the attack provoked, and that the provocation is Carson's mockery of starvation and destitution. But although she does not make melodramatic hocus-pocus from the Trades Unionists' very real necessity for secrecy, as Disraeli does in *Sybil* (Bk. IV, ch. 4), she does use this incident to blacken union activity and to express the fears of her own class at the Other Nation's attempts to organize themselves and better their lot. It is obvious from her letter to Sir John Potter that, although she sympathized with starving men, she did not know the facts of strikes and their causes in Manchester, nor did she know much about the aims and organization of Trades Unions, and this weakens her novel because, as Trollope said, 'To be realistic you must know

accurately that which you describe.' But, lacking knowledge,
she asserted that the Unions were wrong, that they necessarily
encouraged physical violence, that they could have no part in
bettering the workpeople's conditions of labour, and that
'understanding' on both sides would allow the capitalist system
to proceed smoothly, and with fairness to the Two Nations. In
this she is in complete accord with Disraeli, Dickens, and Kingsley. Reade also agreed with this viewpoint, but it is not prominent in *It is Never Too Late to Mend*; rather in the later novel,
Put Yourself in His Place, provoked by the Sheffield Trade
Union outrages of 1866—which were, in fact, repudiated by the
Trades Unions. Such a distortion of actuality reduces the sensitive complexity of John Barton's life in the novel to the crude
sensationalism of 'Horrid Murder', a favourite heading for
broadside ballads (see Plates 26 and 27) and the headline which
announced Thomas Ashton's death in the *Stockport Advertiser*
7 January 1831.

Another contemporary social problem novelist treated the
Ashton murder—Elizabeth Stone in *William Langshawe, the
Cotton Lord* (1842), set in Manchester of the late 1820s and
early 1830s. She was the daughter of John Wheeler (died 1827),
who had owned the *Manchester Chronicle* (ceased publication
1842), a Tory newspaper—which explains her diatribe, in the
novel, against 'the scribes of the Radical newspaper press' who
declaimed 'on the slavery and the long-protracted toil of the
factory operative' and reported 'the much-exaggerated sorrows
of the manufacturing labourers' (*William Langshawe, the Cotton Lord*, 2 vols., 1842, vol. ii, ch. 15). By the end of the 1830s
she was married and living in London, and had begun to publish
popular books of a genteel kind: her *Art of Needlework, from
the earliest ages; including some notices of the Ancient Historical Tapestries*, edited by the Right Honourable the Countess of
Wilton and published by Henry Colburn, reached a third edition
in 1841. 1842 was the year of the great Lancashire cotton
strikes described by William Cooke Taylor in his tour through
Lancashire and in *William Langshawe* Elizabeth Stone obviously
seized the opportunity to capture middle-class attention with a
topical theme handled in a reassuring manner. Her Manchester
novel has an indescribably complicated plot, but basically tells
the story of Langshawe, who had risen from humble origin to

become a rich manufacturer of great probity and industry, of his one and only departure from safe trade for speculation in buying a great stock of material in the hope that prices would continue to rise; of the slump which nearly ruined him; but how, finally: 'his pleasurable anticipations, founded, as they had been, on acute calculation and extensive practical knowledge, were fully realized; he disposed of his heavy accumulation of goods at an immense profit, and, could money alone have repaid him for the anxiety he had undergone, he had been amply remunerated' (vol. ii, ch. 28).

The tone of the novel suggests that money goes a long way to repaying him. In fact its theme seems to be: ' "as a means, used unselfishly, riches can bring happiness to your heart" ' (vol. ii, ch. 23). The whole novel gives the impression of bits and pieces hastily assembled. For example, the scene in which Mr Ashworth visits a factory (vol. i, ch. 13) and finds that the 'exaggerated horrors' reported of work in the factories is without foundation, was, the novelist tells her readers in a footnote, 'intended merely as part of a slighter sketch' and 'written some time ago'. 'Manchester in the Race Week' (vol. i, ch. 15) and the description of Peel's visit to Manchester and the dinner given in his honour in the unfinished Town Hall[10] (vol. ii, ch. 10) also read like set pieces.

Her hysterical denunciations of the Cotton Spinners' Union should be set against Elizabeth Gaskell's scenes depicting the Unionists as rational but desperate men trying to solve the problem of keeping themselves and their families alive:

There has been murder,—not hasty slaying in hot blood, but cool, deliberate, well-'proven' murder, committed at the behest of the leaders of the 'Spinners' Union.'

For such deeds, which they hesitated not, for certain purposes, coolly to contemplate, fitting instruments were required. The multitude of the Unionists were honest well-disposed men; and though, by the laws of association, they swore to perform whatever their leaders might require of them, yet were those leaders far too shrewd to give the food of strong men to babes. But the secret rulers and delegates of this body, scattered through the mass of the population, (just as even now one trembles to think the 'familiars' of the Inquisition once were,) were always on the watch for tools suited to their purpose, and often showed no inconsiderable degree of shrewdness in selecting them. Jem Forshawe had long been

[10] The first Town Hall, King Street, Manchester, by Francis Goodwin, begun 1819. Work continued on the interior until 1834.

a marked man with them, for the very imbecility of mind which his countenance indicated rendered him a fit subject on whom to work. (Vol. ii, ch. 15.)

Like Andrew Ure, Elizabeth Stone generalizes from a unique, highly untypical event to charge the Union with making murder part of its policy. Jem Forshawe the factory hand has a grudge against his master's son, John Balshawe, because he has seduced Jem's lover, the factory girl Nancy Halliwell, and then given Jem twenty sovereigns to marry her. Before this Jem had nothing to do with the Union; he appears not to have been affected by the starvation wages which were the cause of the agitations:

Jem Forshawe, happy in his humble station, content with his wages, blessed with his Nancy, was impenetrable to their efforts. 'Th'Union might be well enough for other folk, but he wanted nought, not he.'

But, unhappily for Jem Forshawe, a notable instrument of the Union met him, as if commissioned by the Evil One himself, on the very night when, burning with agony and rage, he had flung the money, which was meant to be the reward of his shame, in the teeth of the base seducer.

In such a mood, Forshawe was easily worked upon, and his tempter had craft enough to make the most of his opportunity. Intimations of revenge, of chastisement on the selfish ruinator of his happiness and Nancy's honour, were greedily listened to by the excited wretch. Nay, his wily seducer did not content himself with general invectives on lustful and arbitrary masters, but he pointed at an especial vengeance which was to be directed against Mr. John Balshawe; a vengeance, by the way, which was but the coinage of his own brain at the moment of need. (Vol ii. ch. 15.)

Jem, however, becomes a raving lunatic from undergoing the terrifying initiation ceremonies demanded by the Union! None the less, the murder is committed. The victim is Henry Wolstenholme, son of a factory owner, spending Christmas in his father's beautiful new house built on a site which had been rural when the house was planned, but was now crowded round by 'poor manufacturing hovels' and the whole intervening area between it and the factory town 'broken into masses of cottage building, interspersed with brown bare fields, and here and there the glaring red-brick two-storied house of a "superintendent" or "overlooker" '[11] (vol. ii, ch. 27).

Henry is shown good-naturedly playing with the children,

[11] The best parts of this generally tedious and inferior novel are those describing the homes of the Manchester cotton-workers and masters: the house of the newly rich Balshawe, the handloom weaver's cottage (both vol. i, ch. 9 and ch. 11), Wolstenholme's new house. There is no sense of Manchester as a community and city but there are lively descriptions of some of its dwellings.

who adore him. He leaves them at his father's request to go to the factory. Ten minutes later there is a knock at the door and the news that he is lying injured. Then 'Mrs. Wolstenholme . . . saw her eldest son, Henry, borne in by the men—a corpse.' (Vol. ii, ch. 27.)

Elizabeth Stone tells her readers in a footnote: 'Let not my readers image this awful incident has been invented for the nonce. A few years ago a young cotton manufacturer of the highest respectability, and most excellent character, was murdered even so, and as suddenly, as we have described, by order of the Spinners' Union.' (Ibid.) And she comments,

Even this last blow had not the desired effect. The advance of wages, so boldly and wickedly sought, was not obtained; the 'strike' ended very nearly as and where it had commenced, save that it left its traces in the naked cottages of the work-people, the pallid and half-famished faces of mothers and children, the overladen shops of the pawn-brokers, and the almost broken heart of one unoffending lady. (Ibid.)

Henry Wolstenholme is a very minor character in the novel; he is suddenly singled out for this violent end to demonstrate the diabolical ways of the Trades Unions.

When *Mary Barton* first appeared, rumour went that Elizabeth Stone was the author (see Gaskell, *Letters*, pp. 62 f.). Elizabeth Gaskell's reference to it, 'some book called the "Cotton Lord" ', suggests that she had not read it when she wrote her own novel. The rumour did not proceed from discriminating readers. Any comparison of the novels shows Elizabeth Stone to be a bad political journalist and Elizabeth Gaskell a serious, imaginative novelist. But, if we compare their treatment of the murder, the very fact that Elizabeth Gaskell does not dismiss the Trade Unionists as 'ruffians' and does not record with satisfaction that their strike brought them to hunger and distress, gives authority to an incident which is false to the period and to its poor. She does not represent the impoverished Manchester factory workers as savages or monsters, but as human beings. But she shows these human beings engaged in a monstrous act which, although one such act occurred, is not representative of their behaviour at the time. The result is a misleading and falsifying distortion which offers trivial sensation instead of serious art. Engels, commenting on Margaret Harkness's novel of the East End, *A City Girl* (1887), wrote to her, 'Realism, to my mind, implies, besides truth of detail, the truthful reproduction of typical characters under typical circumstances.' (See Marx and Engels, *Literature and Art*, Bombay 1956, pp. 36 f.) Elizabeth Gaskell forfeits this realism when she engages John Barton in murder. This failure is symptomatic of the novel's greatest weakness. The 'life' of the Other Nation, as it is described in *Mary Barton*, is authentic in a way lacking in the other novels which I am considering, but its impact is lessened because the novelist does not see this life in a sufficiently wide context—she was not interested in politics ('I cannot manage politics', she wrote to George Smith, 26 August 1857, *Letters*, p. 469), or economics, or working-class organizations in which so much of this life found its expression. Even as she does not perceive the social attitudes which make Carson build his mansion on the outskirts of Manchester (see above, p. 96) she does not see that it is not enough to recreate John Barton's feelings, thoughts, and frustrations unless his activities as a Trades Unionist are known and established with a like seriousness because they are largely the source of his mental life. She cannot understand the man and so re-create his life without understanding his politics. Her eyes are steadily on the poor as are the eyes of no other novelist of the period, but that steady gaze is directed at only part of their life.

'THE POETRY OF COMMON LIFE': STREET BALLADS AND BROADSIDES

A source of information which helped form Elizabeth Gaskell's 'consciousness' of the poor and which was almost totally ignored by contemporary novelists seeking to bridge the gulf between the Two Nations is the ballads and songs of the period, many of them sung and sold as broadsides in the streets to get a few pennies for the workpeople striking to raise or maintain their wages. The Preston Lock-out, 1853–4, produced a large number of such songs:

> So now kind-hearted Christians, come forward with your hand,
> Give to us your shillings, pence, whilst round us you do stand;
> For masters they can all enjoy their luxuries with content,
> And we would have a share with them, by gaining Ten per Cent.
>   ('The Self-Actor Minders of Preston and the Ten Per Cent'.)

'Self-actor' is a self-acting mule in a spinning machine.

The cotton operatives had accepted a ten-per-cent cut in wages when the cotton trade was bad. Now the trade was prospering they wanted their wages raised to their former level. The masters had locked the workpeople out of the factories for demanding this, and for refusing to disband the union.

> Have you not heard the news of late,
> About some mighty men so great,
> I mean the swells of Fishergate,
>   The Cotton Lords of Preston.
> They are a set of stingy Blades,
> They've locked up all their Mills and Shades*
> So now we've nothing else to do,
> But come a singing songs for you,
> So with our ballads we've come out,
> To tramp the country round about,
> And try if we cannot live without
>   The Cotton Lords of Preston.
>   ('The Cotton Lords of Preston'.)
> *sheds

Sometimes the songs are hastily-composed doggerel, although the impact of the tune together with the words has to be taken into account. For example, the emphatic rhythm of the 'Song of the Preston Tyrants' makes it a powerful song even if the words, taken alone, are not very imaginative. It ends:

> There is a God above us all,—here truth inspires my song—
> He knows that you have not done right and we have not done wrong,
> You have stopt your Mills with tyranny too dreadful to unfold,
> And you again, like all such men, cry out for despot gold.
>   Chorus.   So you Tyrants of Proud Preston,
>   Your race is nearly run,
>   And you will have to answer too,
>   For all you've said and done.

But some of the songs have a neat wit expressing the operatives' plight concisely and strongly, like 'Ten Per Cent!! A New Song on the Preston Strike', 'Composed by Wm. Abbott, of Bamber Bridge':

> The winter it is coming on,
>   It will be very cold,
> But we'll stand out for our demand,
>   Like warriors so bold,
> But if the masters don't give way,
>   And firmly give consent,

> We'll stand out till their mills do fall,
> All for the Ten per cent,

with the play on 'standing' and 'falling' balanced in one line; or 'The Cotton Lord's Last Shift' which begins with a verse playing on three meanings of 'shift': 'trick'; 'shirt'; 'shroud':

> Cheer up you lads and lasses gay,
> The Cotton Lords will soon give way,
> They cannot stand the winter's drift,
> They're on the last and winding shift.

True wit, as opposed to mere word play, is acute perception of an idea or a situation in neat and arresting verbal form. Wit disturbs conventional or complacent thinking by offering for scrutiny an aspect of reality in place of prejudice or unawareness. When George Herbert writes at the end of 'Affliction'

> Ah, my dear God, though I be clean forgot,
> Let me not love thee, if I love thee not

the syntax of a colloquial oath, 'Let me be damned if . . .', that is, 'I'll be damned if . . .' takes on a new force as Herbert substitutes for the conventional curse the most appalling evil that he can call down upon himself, the state of not loving God. The conventional verbal form is revitalized in the process of sharply embodying Herbert's compelling need for God. This process in which an accepted verbal form is slightly changed to reveal the pressure of experience was obviously a feature of working-class speech in the nineteenth century, as it is today. The Revd A. Osborne Jay, vicar of the Holy Trinity, Shoreditch, who decided Arthur Morrison's choice of the Old Nichol, on the boundaries of Shoreditch and Bethnal Green, as the location of *A Child of the Jago* (1896) (see P. J. Keating, *The Working Classes in Victorian Fiction*, pp. 177–80) and who was the model for Father Sturt in that novel, observed:

Another result of poverty seems to be—if it does not seem far-fetched—the birth of a genuine spirit of comic originality. Those who are face to face with the very fundamental rules of existence speak often in no half-hearted or mincing way . . .

'The Lord is very good,' sometimes they say, bitterly, in allusion to the shape in which Providence comes to them, 'if He does not come Himself, He often sends two policemen for you.' . . .

'It's only for life,' many say, who work hard and get little; 'if it were for longer I should strike.' (A. O. Jay, *Life in Darkest London: A Hint to General Booth*, 1891, pp. 117 f.)

This tough, direct wit, born of the determined battle to exist, is rarely suggested in the novels which I am discussing. Disraeli's poor, as I have shown (see above, p. 139), speak a very artificial language. Kingsley's poor do not display any liveliness of wit; the country workers of *Yeast* say very little, and are represented as dull and debased; in *Alton Locke* Alton's own speech is neutral and unidiomatic, while the attempts to give the Chartists a lively speech are self-conscious and unconvincing, for example, Crossthwaite:

'that's my only comfort. It does make men of us, this bitter battle of life. We working men, when we do come out of the furnace, come out, not tinsel and papier maché, like those fops of red-tape statesmen, but steel and granite, Alton, my boy—that has been seven times tried in the fire: and woe to the papier maché gentleman that runs against us! But,' he went on sadly, 'for one who comes safe through the furnace, there are a hundred who crack in the burning. You are a young bear, my lad, with all your sorrows before you; and you'll find that a working man's training is like the Red Indian children's. The few who are strong enough to stand it grow up warriors; but all those who are not fire-and-water-proof by nature —just die, Alton, my lad, and the tribe thinks itself well rid of them.' (Vol. i, ch. 4 'Tailor and Poet'.)

Brevity is the soul of wit, and this is long-winded. In the novel pithiness of speech is reserved for Mackaye, the Scots bookseller who, like all Scotsmen, is allowed to be a 'character'. In the Chartist's language we do not feel the pressure of experience shaping language and wit to deal with it, but rather Kingsley's own literary artifice being applied to the ideas he supposes Crossthwaite would have. Both Josephs, the desperate boy-prisoner of Reade's novel, and Stephen Blackpool in *Hard Times* are characters depicted in terms of extreme pathos in which tough wit has no place. Their speech is stilted, if not maudlin. This lack of wit is symptomatic of the solemnity with which the novelists describe the poor in order to present them as pathetic sufferers. They are allowed endurance and resignation but not resilience or toughness.

Dickens comes nearest to suggesting tough lower class wit in two comic characters, Sam Weller and the Artful Dodger. But both are self-conscious Cockney 'characters', eccentrics in their communities. Sam's speech, especially, has the mechanical quality of a comic 'turn' and depends for much of its effect on exaggerated Cockney mannerisms which had become a convention of low comedy. Dickens again exploits this convention in his mutilated version of 'The Ballad of Lord Bateman', in which much of the comic effect depends on transmuting 'v's into 'w's. Sam is as much a 'picturesque' version of the Cockney as Rats' Castle is of St. Giles's.

Even Elizabeth Gaskell who, of these novelists is the most successful at reproducing the authentic speech of the working people she describes,[12] largely omits the characteristic wit, apart from occasional remarks, such as that of the factory worker listening to Margaret singing: 'She spun it reet fine!' (*Mary Barton*, ch. 8.) It is as though she feels that the scenes she describes are too harrowing for such wit; although in actuality the wit was a means of making an oppressive existence tolerable.

The steam printing press made mass production of broadsides possible. Like the printing of cheap literature for the barely literate, the printing of broadsides was commercially exploited and by the mid-century had become a lucrative business. Ballads on the Preston Lock-out were sold a long way from Lancashire. In George Augustus Sala's 'Bright Chanticleer', published in *Household Words*, a survey of the 'cocks' or broadsides printed and hawked in Seven Dials or taken into the West End to tempt the servants there, an example of a subject very popular in the West End is 'the Preston strike hended in blood, the hartillery called out' (*Household Words*, 11 (1855), 207). This is a typically facetious comment, precluding any serious discussion of the songs and their appeal.[13]

Dickens wrote up his visit to Preston in February 1854, during the Lock-out, for *Household Words*. In this essay 'On Strike' (*Household Words*, 8 (1854), 553-9) he says that his aim

---

[12] See a contemporary review of *Mary Barton*: 'its dialogues are managed with a degree of ease and naturalness rarely attained even by the most experienced writers of fiction. We believe that they approach very nearly, both in tone and style, to the conversations actually carried on in the dingy cottages of Lancashire.' (*Edinburgh Review*, 89 (1849), 403.)

[13] Although he briefly mentions the popularity of traditional ballads, Sala describes at great length the absurdities of the broadsides' sensational horrors. In fact, the traditional ballads were not only popular but the broadside printers often produced fine versions of them. Catnach, for example, had an attractive broadside containing 'The Welcome Sailor' and 'Bonnet so Blue' (Baring-Gould, *Ballads*, iv. 272). Moreover, he also printed eminently respectable songs—'Rule Britannia' (ibid. vi. 227) and 'God Save the Queen' (ibid. iv. 439). H. P. Such, another prolific printer and publisher of broadsides, based in Union-street, Borough, S.E., printed Hood's 'The Song of the Shirt' (ibid. vi. 211).

in visiting Preston is 'to see with my own eyes . . . how these
people acted under a mistaken impression, and what qualities
they showed, even at that disadvantage, which ought to be the
strength and peace—not the weakness and trouble—of the community'. During this quest he comes across some of the songs.
He quotes from the 'New Song of the Preston Strike' to prove
'that all masters were not indiscriminately unpopular', but in
fact the song as he quotes it extols certain employers from
neighbouring Blackburn—'Henry Hornby, of Blackburn, he is a
jolly brick'—at the expense of the 'Preston Cotton Lords' whom
the song warns 'to mind for future time', continuing:

> With peace and order too I hope we shall be clever,
> We sing success to Stockport and Blackburn for ever.

He quotes some of the verses on placards detailing the
amounts subscribed to the Preston workers that week, but no
other song is mentioned apart from the hymn sung at an open
air meeting, 'in long metre by the whole audience' and ending:

> Awake, ye sons of toil! nor sleep
> While millions starve, while millions weep;
> Demand your rights; let tyrants see
> You are resolved that you'll be free.

He records no reaction to this mass singing or to any of the
ballads which undoubtedly he would have heard sung in the
street. Although he thinks the struggle an unreasonable one, he
stresses the good humour, the solidarity, the sincerity and
decency, the energy of the workpeople engaged in it, and ends
by suggesting that the differences between masters and men
should be resolved by impartial arbitration.

Material gathered during his visit to Preston was obviously
used in *Hard Times*, begun in *Household Words* 1 April 1854.
The people of Coketown, imprisoned in their allegorical world,
are more remote from the reader than the determined factory
workers of Preston described in Dickens's report. Certainly they
do not react to their troubles with songs and hymns, not even
the undistinguished type quoted in 'On Strike'. Although
Dickens insists that the Coketown workpeople, despite the
efforts of Mr Gradgrind and the eighteen religious denomina-
tions in the town, 'persisted in wondering. They wondered
about human nature, human passions, human hopes and fears,
the struggles, triumphs and defeats, the cares and joys and sor-

rows, the lives and deaths of common men and women!' (Bk. I, ch. 8) they do not express any of these emotions in song. When Dickens utters his familiar note of warning:

Utilitarian economists, skeletons of schoolmasters, Commissioners of Fact, genteel and used-up infidels, gabblers of many little dog's-eared creeds, the poor you will have always with you. Cultivate in them, while there is yet time, the utmost graces of the fancies and affections to adorn their lives so much in need of ornament; or, in the day of your triumph, when romance is utterly driven out of their souls, and they and a bare existence stand face to face, Reality will take a wolfish turn, and make an end of you! (Bk. II, ch. 6),

those 'above' the poor are exhorted to develop feeling and imagination in them because they need it so badly; the implication is that they have little feeling or imagination at present, and cannot have them until they are helped to them. Dickens, presumably, was in sympathy with Sala's view that the street ballads were simply grotesquely comic and worth no further notice. This view is supported by Forster's description of Dickens's exploration of 'the ballad literature of Seven Dials', adding that he 'would occasionally sing, with an effect that justified his reputation for comic singing in his childhood, not a few of those wonderful productions' (*Life of Dickens*, i. 142). This suggests that he treated the ballads with the patronizing comedy that he and Cruikshank expended on 'The Ballad of Lord Bateman' in the original a very moving song. A 'straight' version of the ballad was printed and sold by Catnach (see Baring-Gould, *Ballads*, I(ii), 63).

In fact, Elizabeth Gaskell is the only Victorian novelist, of any stature, who is aware of the imaginative power of the best ballads and realizes how much they express of the Other Nation's life. Kingsley, in *Yeast*, regards the songs sung at the village wake as an example of the squalor and degradation of the rural labourer's life and, obsessed by his idea of the sanctity of married love, disapprovingly quotes the song of the soldier who returns to marry his sweetheart and cherish their child as one of 'lawless love', which he found to be the theme of 'a dozen different songs, more or less coarsely [embodied], but, in general, with a dash of pathetic sentiment' (ch. 13). One of the main reasons why writers like Kingsley rejected such songs and remained largely unmoved by them (although in the case of the love song he admits 'the sad melody of the air') is that they speak directly of situations, passions and emotions which the middle class denied, veiled, or referred to obliquely. Elizabeth Gaskell, always a direct and sensible woman, seems to have lacked this kind of prudery, to judge from a comment made to John Forster in a letter 17 May 1854, quoting part of the song 'Jess Macfarlane': 'I am rather afraid I've heard somebody say it is not a proper song; but I don't know why it should not be for all I know of it, and I am sure my two verses are charming & innocent.' (Gaskell, *Letters*, p. 286.)

Ironically, Kingsley achieves the directness and power, lacking elsewhere in the novel, in the ballad which Tregarva writes about the labourer's plight, and for which he is dismissed from the Squire's service (another reason why middle-class Victorians preferred not to know about the people's songs was that so many of them were subversive). It is a literary 'ballad' to be read, not sung, but despite its melodramatic ending, addressed to the Squire—

> In the season of shame and sadness,
>   In the dark and dreary day
> When scrofula, gout, and madness,
>   Are eating your race away;
>
> When to kennels and liveried varlets
>   You have cast your daughter's bread;
> And, worn out with liquor and harlots,
>   Your heir at your feet lies dead . . .—

some of the stanzas express, with more economy and force than the long-winded arguments between Lancelot and Tregarva, the contemporary plight of the rural labourer and the reason for the bitter division between the Two Nations:

> A labourer in Christian England,
>   Where they cant of a Saviour's name,
> And yet waste men's lives like the vermin's
>   For a few more brace of game . . .
>
> You have sold the labouring man, squire,
>   Body and soul to shame,
> To pay for your seat in the House, squire,
>   And to pay for the feed of your game.
>
> You made him a poacher yourself, squire,
>   When you'd give neither work nor meat;

> And your barley-fed hares robbed the garden
>   At our starving children's feet . . .
>
> Can your lady patch hearts that are breaking
>   With handfuls of coal and rice,
> Or by dealing out flannel and sheeting
>   A little below cost price?
>
> You may tire of the gaol and the workhouse,
>   And take to allotments and schools,
> But you've run up a debt that will never
>   Be repaid us by penny-club rules. (Ch. 11.)

But only Elizabeth Gaskell realized that the Romantic concern with 'the poetry of common life' could also include a concern with the poetry and the music of the common people. Wordsworth's poem 'The Solitary Reaper' expresses the universal appeal and the enduring poetic power of the labouring girl's Gaelic song:

> The music in my heart I bore
> Long after it was heard no more,

and he has a little-known poem, 'The Power of Music' (1806), in which he describes the compelling effect of a fiddler's music upon people in Oxford Street:

> As the Moon brightens round her the clouds of the night,
> So He, where he stands, is a centre of light;
> It gleams on the face, there, of dusky-browed Jack,
> And the pale-visaged Baker's, with basket on back.

It is not fanciful to suppose that one of the reasons why she knew that the parable of Dives and Lazarus haunted the minds of the poor (*Mary Barton*, ch. 9) was that she had heard unemployed workpeople singing versions of the magnificent ballad for pennies in the street. In the same novel she quotes an enduring Lancashire song created to voice the weavers' plight at the beginning of the nineteenth century. Margaret, the seamstress who lives in rooms above Alice Wilson's cellar and has a fine singing voice, sings 'The Oldham Weaver' at Alice's request on the occasion when Mary Barton comes to tea with Alice. Elizabeth Gaskell gives the song in full, in dialect, with the introductory query: 'Do you know "The Oldham Weaver"? Not unless you are Lancashire born and bred, for it is a complete Lancashire ditty. I will copy it for you.' (Ch. 4.)

The version in the novel can be set against that preserved in

Manchester Public Library under the title 'Jone o' Grinfield', that is, John of Greenfield, near Oldham, a character presented as a typical Lancashire workman whose adventures, such as those encountered in joining the army to fight Napoleon, are described in a group of ballads of the period:

Jone o' Grinfield

I'm a poor cotton weaver as many one knows,
I've nowt to eat i'th house on I've worn out my cloas,
You'd hardly give sixpence for all I have on,
My clugs they are brossen and stockings I've none,
You'd think it wur hard to be sent into th' world,
To clem and do th' best ot you con.

Our church parson kept telling us long,
We should have better times if we'd hold our tongues,
I've houden my tongue till I can hardly draw breath,
I think i' my heart he means to clem me to death;
I know he lives weel by backbiting the de'il,
But he never picked o'er in his life.

I tarried six week an thought every day wur t' last,
I tarried and shifted till now I'm quite fast;
I lived on nettles[14] while nettles were good,
An' Waterloo porridge* were best of my food;
I'm telling you true I can find folks enew,
That are living no better than me.
*oatmeal porridge made with water

Old Bill o' Dan's sent bailiffs one day,
For a shop score I owed him that I could not pay,
But he wur too late, for old Bill o' Bent,
Had sent tit and cart and taen goods for rent,
We had nou bur a stoo, that wur a seat for two,
And on it cowered Margit and me.

The bailiffs looked round as sly as a mouse,
When they saw aw things were taen out ot house,
Says one to the other all's gone thou may see,
Aw sed, Lads never fret you're welcome to me;
They made no more ado, but nipp'd up th' owd stoo',
And we both went wack upo' th' flags.

[14] 'Their is thousands unemployed and in a Starving State in Oldham you will (see) [inserted in brackets] Great numbers parading the streets in a starving state and numbers are rangeing the fields in search of nettles . . . docks . . . or anything green . . . wich the [they] boil and mix with oat meal of wich the [they] make a hearty meal.' (23 Apr. 1826, Rowbottom *Diaries*, v. 25 f.)

I geet howd of Margit for hoo wur strucken sick,
Hoo sed hoo ne'er had such a bang sin hoo wur wick†
†in her life

The bailiffs scoured off with owd stoo' on their backs,
They would not have cared had they brook our necks,
They're mad at owd Bent cos he's taen goods fur rent,
And wur ready to flee* us alive.
*flay

I sed to our Margit as we lay upo' th' floor,
We shall never be lower in this world I'm sure,
But if we alter I'm sure we mun mend,
For I think in my heart we are both at far end,
For meat we have none nor looms to weave on,
Egad they're as weel lost as found.

Then I geet up my piece and I took it em back
I scarcely dare speak mester looked so black,
He said, You wur o'erpaid last time you coom,
I said, If I wur 'twas for weaving bout loom;†
In a mind as I'm in I'll ne'er pick o'er again,
For I've woven mysel to th' fur end.
†without a loom

Then aw coom out and left him to chew that,
When aw thought again aw wur vext till aw sweat,
To think that we mun work to keep them and aw th' set,
All the day o' my life and still be in their debt;
So I'll give o'er trade an work with a spade,
Or go and break stones upo' th' road.

Our Margit declared if hoo'd cloas to put on,
Hoo'd go up to Lundun an see the big mon,
An if things didn't alter when hoo had been,
Hoo swears hoo'd feight, blood up to th' e'en,
Hoo's nought again th' Queen but likes a fair thing,
An hoo says hoo can tell when hoo's hurt.

(Manchester Ballads, I, Q398.8S9, p. 32A.)

This version in the Manchester Public Library is torn, and the printer's name has partly gone: 'Printed and Sold Wholesale and Retail, by ——ngton ——den-street, Oldham Road, Manchester'. This must have been John Bebbington.[15] A. L. Lloyd prints a Bebbington version of the ballad in his *Folk Song in England*,

[15] Roy Palmer tells me that the Manchester street directory for 1855 lists John Bebbington at 26 Goulden Street, Manchester; those for 1858 and 1861 list John Oliver Bebbington at 31 Oldham Road, Manchester. The defaced address on the Manchester broadside seems to be an amalgamation of the two addresses.

1967, pp. 324-6, which is almost the same as the version I have given and dates it about 1860. Certainly it is later than Elizabeth Gaskell's version—'t' king' has been replaced by 'th' Queen'. A. L. Lloyd's version is slightly different in that 'th' greet mon' or 'the big mon', that is, Wellington, has been replaced by 'the young Queen'. This ballad expresses the innocent belief, widely held among working people in the thirties and early forties, that if only those in authority knew about their plight something would be done to alleviate it; like 'a most excellent old Scotchwoman, Isabell Hogg', one of the witnesses in the *Children's Employment Commission* (1842), who was quoted by Lord Ashley in the House 7 June that year: 'You must just tell the Queen Victoria that we are quiet, loyal subjects; women-people here don't mind work; but they object to horse-work; and that she would have the blessings of all the Scotch coal-women if she would get them out of the pits, and send them to other labour.' (*Hansard*, 63, column 1329.)

The Chartists, encouraged by such a belief, took their petition to Parliament in 1839, and were bitterly disillusioned by its rejection. Elizabeth Gaskell convincingly embodies their hopes in John Barton's journey to London as a Chartist delegate (see *Mary Barton*, ch. 8) and their disappointment in his sullen return and silence, apart from the remark: ' "As long as I live, our rejection that day will bide in my heart; and as long as I live I shall curse them as so cruelly refused to hear us; but I'll not speak of it no more." ' (Ch. 9.)

'The Oldham Weaver' in *Mary Barton* appears to have been taken down from a singer. The correct sound of Lancashire speech is carefully reproduced in print. Elizabeth Gaskell shared with her husband a belief in the strength and dignity of the language spoken by ordinary Lancashire people against those who argued that such speech was uncouth and unrefined. Throughout the novel there are glosses on dialect words such as 'nesh', from the Anglo-Saxon 'nesc', 'tender' (ch. 1) or 'don' meaning 'do', as in Chaucer's 'But for th' entente to don this sinne' (ch. 6), to show that such usage is closer to the original language than the 'refined' modern forms and has the strength of Chaucer's and Shakespeare's language.[16] The fifth edition

---

[16] George Ewart Evans uses the same argument when discussing the strength of East Anglian dialect usage, *Where Beards Wag All*, 1970, ch. 15.

of *Mary Barton* (1854) included William Gaskell's *Two Lectures on the Lancashire Dialect* given to working-class audiences in Manchester and developing this same argument.

There are interesting differences between the version of the ballad given by Elizabeth Gaskell and that printed by Bebbington. In her version there is no criticism of the 'church parson' who, in Bebbington's version, gives pacifying advice which comes from complete lack of understanding of the weaver's plight. Nor is there the desperate meeting with the grinding 'master' which ends in the weaver's determination to give up his trade and become an unskilled labourer 'Or go and break stones upo' road', that is, become a pauper, given the exhausting labour of breaking stones to make the parish roads. The version in *Mary Barton* centres on the wryly comic situation of husband and wife literally reduced to a lowly station by the bailiffs' removal of their last piece of furniture, the stool on which they sit. It lacks the militancy of the other version, the bitter reflection

> To think that we mun work to keep them and aw th' set,
> All the day o' my life and still be in their debt . . .

and, more important, Marget resolves, if she gets no satisfaction from 'th' greet mon', to commit suicide, not 'feight, blood up to th' e'en'. It seems very unlikely that Elizabeth Gaskell printed a doctored version of the song in *Mary Barton*; it is much more likely that the singer gave her a gentler version out of respect for her and her station in life.

The tune is strong and expressive, and provides a powerful complement to the words. The novelist accurately describes the singing style: 'the air to which this is sung is a kind of droning recitative, depending much on expression and feeling', and the total absorption of the authentic folksinger: 'Margaret, with fixed eye, and earnest, dreamy look, seemed to become more and more absorbed in realising to herself the woe she had been describing, and which she felt might at that very moment be suffering and hopeless within a short distance of their comparative comfort.' But she implies that the song is an inferior vehicle for Margaret's beautiful voice. Margaret begins to sing 'with a faint smile, as if amused at Alice's choice of a song'; and, immediately after, 'suddenly she burst forth with all the power of her magnificent voice, as if a prayer from her very heart for all who were in distress, in the grand supplication, "Lord, remember David" '. She is then compared to Deborah Knyvett, once a factory girl, who was famous for her concert performances of Handel and sacred music (see Stephen Gill's Note 19, *Mary Barton*, Penguin, 1970, p. 476). Also, the novelist remarks on the song's humour, and comments: 'to those who have seen the distress it describes, it is a powerfully pathetic song', but she does not seem to realize that the song imaginatively creates the distress it describes, nor does she seem to be aware of its wit, for example in the aptness of the imagery 'oi think i' my heart we're booath at t' far eend' in which the weaving phrase for taking the shuttle to the end of the breadth of cloth means death; or the play on 'howd my tung'. The song's power comes from its sturdy independence in desperate circumstances; when there is nothing for the bailiffs to take it is the weaver who encourages the bailiff—' "Ne'er freet, mon, yeaur welcome ta' me." ' The situation is tragic rather than pathetic in that even such courageous independence must recognize 'we're booath at t' far eend'. The tone of the song is such that the determination to go out fighting seems more appropriate than the threat of suicide, as in Elizabeth Gaskell's version.

This independence and liveliness of mind are found in the portrait of Job Legh, the old weaver who is a keen amateur naturalist (E. P. Thompson comments on the authenticity of Job; see *The Making of the English Working Class*, p. 322). The self-reliance and desperation of the song are expressed in the story of the factory hand, John Barton, although as I have shown, the portrait is badly damaged by allowing his despair to take the highly untypical form of murder of one of the masters. But the interest which led Elizabeth Gaskell, in the first place, to listen to the speech and songs of the Lancashire working people and to transcribe at least one of the songs in dialect, enabled her to re-create the substance of lives such as Job Legh's and John Barton's, before the murder, in a way unequalled by any other Victorian novelist. This interest is born of her concern with the Other Nation as people. In a letter to Eliza Fox, 29 May 1849, she wrote that none of the characters or events in *Mary Barton* was based on real people or incidents except the character of John Barton; 'the circumstances are different, but the character and some of the speeches, are exactly a poor man I know'. From her letters, her biography and her novels, we get the impression that Elizabeth Gaskell approached the poor with something of the respect and humility of Augustus Mayhew talking with the little Watercress Girl. To a friend who was anxious to see the sights of Manchester she wrote: '*Whitworth*'s Machine{ry} Works, *Canal St, Brook St* or very near there. (The rifle works which have made Mr Whitworth so famous, are out of Manchester, and not easily shown.) But these works are very interesting, if you do not get a stupid *fine* young man to show you over—try rather for one of the *working* men.' (*Letters*, pp. 729 f.)

Here is respect for a working man's knowledge of his craft and for his intelligence expressed in his work which Van Gogh embodied in paint in his pictures of the handloom weavers.

As the poor became increasingly available to the novelists' 'consciousness' in the 1840s and 1850s through the medium of Blue books, newspapers, personal contacts, the most obvious reactions to the Other Nation were horror, disgust, or pity. Horror was accompanied by fear, either fear of disease or rebellion, or the enjoyable frisson induced by contemplating the horrible from a safe distance, a considerable element in Dickens's early work, as well as in *Alton Locke, Sybil*, and *It is Never Too Late to Mend*. Disgust or pity were accompanied by exhortation to readers to remove the matter for disgust or to share the novelist's pity—this is characteristic of Dickens's novels in his middle period, especially *Bleak House* and *Hard Times*. When they pity the poor the novelists tend to emphasize their sufferings to the exclusion of other feelings, in the name of philanthropy, as do Dickens, Kingsley, and Reade, or in the name of political ideology, as does Disraeli. Elizabeth Gaskell diminishes John Barton by representing him finally as a suitable case for Carson's Christian charity. The concentrated attention which the Romantic artist gave to detail thereby inducing 'vision' is diluted; scrutiny and attempt to 'know' the poor moves from the people to the problem. Elizabeth Gaskell is pre-eminently the novelist of the period who, in *Mary Barton*, imaginatively seizes on the details of the life of the poor to provide insight into it, but these insights are local and not sustained throughout the novel. The living continuity of John Barton's life congeals into a crude and falsifying emblem. The Romantic artist's 'vision' ceases to proceed from the substance of the Other Nation's life, imaginatively apprehended; rather, a spurious 'vision' of the future has been mechanically imposed upon it.

Ultimately John Barton's story demonstrates the poor's need for succour by the classes above them. The image of such succour is a placating one and embodies fear of the Other Nation as much as do the horrific images; it constantly recurs in the art and writings of the period, particularly in the work of Carlyle and the Evangelical philanthropists. Its presence in the novels I have been discussing accounts for their optimism despite their revelation of horrors. These novelists, although critical of 'civilization', believe in progress. Even in the stark world of *Hard Times* Dickens believes that things could be better were the Bounderbys to give a helping hand to the Black-pools and not leave them in their 'muddle'; Gradgrind's succour-ing of Sissy, which points the way for it, provides his salvation in more ways than one.

Paradoxically, this future progress depends on the reassertion of old values—traditional Christianity, feudalism, the alliance between monarch and people. And the novels depend on asser-tion rather than any new thinking proceeding from the engage-ment of traditional ideas with the contemporary situation, and the imagination which transmutes such thinking into compelling images. All the novelists are completely blind to the importance of Trade Unions in the new society because the concept of the lower classes organizing themselves to press their own claims is at variance with traditional values of loyalty, respect for the upper classes by the lower and aristocratic leadership, whether by the traditional aristocracy or the new aristocracy of mill-owners. Moreover, the ideas the novelists expound are at variance with their imaginative evocation of the Other Nation. The idealized ennobling of Sybil has no connection with the life of the colliers or the progress of Chartism; Lancelot's ideal quest at the end of *Yeast* takes him far from the misery of the agricultural labourers; in *Mary Barton* the self-sacrificing creed of the Christian is offered as workable in a society geared to competitive enterprise, as is the associationism of *Alton Locke*, in which novel starving Chartists are counselled to wait and prepare themselves for a Christian society after Kingsley has shown that hunger does not allow a man such leisure; the imaginative life which Dickens offers his readers in Sleary's Circus is nebulous and unconvincing contrasted with the enslavement of a life lived at the command of the factory bell, embodied in the relentlessly monotonous Coketown streets.

Despite his melodrama and his hectoring, only Reade, in grappling with the problem of justice for the poor, offers anything that can be described as constructive, new thinking about a contemporary problem, but even here not only does his thought get swamped in the novel's melodramatic plot and the charitable posturing of Mr Eden, but his perception of the problem is presented in argumentative rather than imaginative terms so that the reader remembers the menacing prison rather than the sensible ideas about how the criminal could be rehabilitated and even the poor receive justice.

The novels' optimism, then, proceeds not from the strength of ideas about future progress, but from confidence in the attitude which one Nation should adopt towards the Other, and which is embodied in the novels themselves—a charitable attitude. This concept of charity, its expression in the art and literature of the period, and its importance to the novels under discussion, I examine in the next chapter.

4
THE INEFFECTUAL
ANGEL OF CHARITY

We halt at the opening of a yard, alight, and in a few minutes are in a crowd of tattered and tired out creatures, who are being filtered into a refuge.

    Surely there can be only good in this minimum of relief, offered by spontaneous charity to the houseless, in a whole city-full of poor! (Blanchard Jerrold, *London. A Pilgrimage.*)

After the 1850s London became the nation's 'shock city' as Manchester had been in the 1840s. When Chartism collapsed, fear of the destruction of civilization built by the Industrial Revolution no longer centred on the industrial north but on London, where the casual trades, whose practitioners, according to Perkin, were among the last to feel any benefit from industrialized society, proliferated. London, not Manchester, became the key image of the Two Nations, and the particular territory of the Other Nation was the East End, created to establish the trade of the new Empire. Dickens's changing view of London, always a central theme in his work, reflects this new interest in the capital city. In *Edwin Drood* (1870) the East End dockland is described as a nightmare territory alien to order and peace. John Jasper penetrates its jungle in search of the false peace induced by opium.

    Journalists like Dickens and Yates had always enjoyed a 'slumming expedition' into the poor districts of London but now, as Yates said, such expeditions were 'done to death' (see above, p. 55). Gareth Stedman Jones writes, 'The poor districts became an immense *terra incognita* periodically mapped out by intrepid missionaries and explorers who catered to an insatiable middle-class demand for travellers' tales', and points to the work of James Greenwood in the 1870s, citing *In Strange Company* (1873) and *Low Life Deeps and an account of the strange fish to be found there* (1876). (*Outcast London. A Study in the Relationship between Classes in Victorian Society,*

31. Henry Wallis, 'The Stonebreaker', 1857

32. Gustave Courbet, 'Les Demoiselles de Village', 1851 (preliminary oil sketch)

33. Gustave Courbet, 'Les Demoiselles de Village', 1851 (The Metropolitan Museum of Art, New York, Gift of Harry Payne Bingham, 1940)

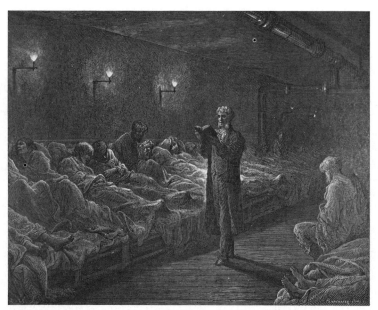

34. Gustave Doré, 'Scripture Reader in a Night Refuge', 1872

'DISTRIBUTION OF HER MAJESTY'S NEW YEAR'S ALMS ON THE 1ST OF JANUARY, 1846.'

35. 'Distribution of Her Majesty's New Year's Alms on the 1st of January, 1846.'

36. Interior of Columbia Market, 1869

37. Reynolds, 1882

Peregrine Books, 1976, p. 14 and note.) *London. A Pilgrimage* (1872) is to be seen in the context of such publications.

Published two years after Dickens's death, it is conceived and written in his shadow. It is the record of a 'pilgrimage' through the world's greatest and largest city of commerce and trade, undertaken by the French artist Gustave Doré, who did the copious illustrations, and Blanchard Jerrold, who provided the text. Blanchard's father, Douglas Jerrold, dramatist, journalist, writer for *Punch*, had been a friend of Dickens; his son makes no secret of Dickens's influence on his description of London. The urchins, following the cabs coming back from the Boat Race or the Derby in the hope of sixpences, are 'Tom Allalones' (p. 64) 'in all the rich picturesqueness of rags' (p. 62); on the way to the Derby 'the vilest of Fagin's pupils' (p. 68) mingle with 'all the company of Pickwick—Sam Weller and his father a hundred times: Mr. Pickwick benevolent and bibulous: Jingle on the top of many a coach and omnibus . . . The brothers Cheeryble pass in a handsome barouche . . . Mr. Jonas Chuzzlewit has travelled in the congenial company of Scrooge to mark their prey. Mr. Dombey is here . . . Barkiss [*sic*] is as willing as ever . . .' (pp. 69 f.) In visiting the London slums Jerrold and Doré put themselves into the protection of the police and follow the trail, blazed by Dickens and Inspector Field, and in Whitechapel 'were introduced to the room in which "Edwin Drood" opens' (p. 147). The whole scheme of the book, recording 'excursions in quest of the picturesque and the typical' (p. 2), 'a grand mass of suggestive bits' (as Jerrold describes pictures of the old London Bridge, p. 13) culled from the Docks, the West End, Newgate, Hyde Park, Seven Dials, Westminster, the Devil's Acre, reveals its debt to Boz, not least in the dramatic contrast between rich and poor.

The final chapter deals with London Charities. In it Dickens, 'the prince of charity dinner speakers', has a prominent place. The chapter heading is an engraving of Doré's drawing of the houseless poor sitting out a cold, starry night on the stone benches in an alcove on London Bridge; inset into the text of the first two paragraphs is Doré's Angel of Charity (see Plate 28), illustrating the first sentence: 'Charity knocks at nearly every house-hold door in this, England's capital, and is not turned away empty-handed from many.' (p. 179.) In Doré's

picture the night sky over the city is dramatic—a full moon
swinging clear of the clouds and providing that theatrical lighting so favoured by the artist. Here it throws into relief the
Angel and its burden, the Orphan Child. The Angel has great
swan's wings, parted as if ready for flight, and hair floating in
loose curls, radiant in the moonlight. The face, half in shadow,
has a thoughtful yearning expression as it looks down at the
child, held safe in a muscular arm. The Angel's flowing garments,
diaphanous towards the hem, reveal bear sturdy legs and feet,
mounting the steps to a substantial house door. The Angel's left
hand lifts the massive knocker to rouse the inhabitants. The
little that can be seen of the street and of the other houses is
made more dark and forbidding by the contrast of the moonlight streaming upon the Angel and the Child. The house steps
and the street flags, from which the Child is being rescued, look
very cold and stony, partly because the Angel's bare feet are set
upon them.

The image is used to suggest the charity with which Jerrold
closely associates Dickens in this chapter. It seems to me to be a
very important image partly because it is so familiar in Victorian
iconography, partly because it perfectly expresses an attitude to
the Other Nation which is fatal to an imaginative re-creation of
their life, to a sensuous apprehension of the poor inducing a
Romantic vision of their 'truth'. It is no chance that Dickens is
associated with the image; it describes his attitude to the poor
in *Hard Times* and elsewhere in his fiction, and explains his
failure as an artist to re-create them as people. The same attitude, and the same artistic failure, can be found in differing
degrees in the other novels which I am discussing.

Doré's picture is characteristically anti-Utilitarian in its implications. Here is one angel impulsively knocking at one door on
behalf of one child found in the street. The Utilitarians believed
that an action is right if it achieves the greatest good of the
greatest number. Reformers, like Chadwick and Southwood
Smith, who translated the Utilitarian philosophy and psychology
into social terms, believed in affording relief to the needy in
society by means of institutions like the new workhouses, by
legislation such as the Public Health Act (1848), and by institut-
ing officers, such as the Poor Law Commissioners, who would
control organized relief within the community. They wanted to

structure society so that it could deal impartially with all distress or need, and their work reflected a growing confidence in the science of government. Their great error, as Dickens saw in *Hard Times*, was to reduce people to quantities.

The Industrial Revolution was accompanied by poverty in Britain on an unprecedented scale. It was hoped that the new scientific methods would control it; they ran counter to traditional ideas of charity, which had its source in the Bible and found expression in the eighteenth century in Pope's Man of Ross (*Moral Essays*, III) or in Henry Brooke's novel *The Fool of Quality*[1] which analyses the virtues expected of a gentleman, charity being the chief. This traditional charity is the spontaneous feeling for the poor which Dives so conspicuously lacked when Lazarus appealed to him for food; the individual impulse of love (*caritas*) towards the poor man finds expression in the giving of alms. Such charity won the approval of God. This is the charity which Doré symbolizes in his picture of the Angel and the Orphan.

Political economy did not depend on the vagaries of individual impulse. It prided itself on being an objective science, a science of wealth. As such it faced with equanimity the fact that some people in society would be dismissed as 'useless'. In 1878 Stanley Jevons summed up the ideas of the political economists in a 'primer'; he wrote:

Dwarfs and giants are always much less common than men of average size; if there happened to be any work of importance which could only be done by dwarfs and giants, they could demand high wages. Dwarfs, however, are of no special use except to exhibit as curiosities; very large strong men, too, are not generally speaking of any particular use, because most heavy work is now done by machinery. They can, however, still get very high wages hewing coal, or puddling iron, because this is work, requiring great strength and endurance, which is not yet commonly done by machinery. Iron puddlers sometimes earn as much as £250 a year. (*Political Economy*, W. Stanley Jevons, 2nd edn. 1878, p. 57.)

He makes it clear that political economy is the science supporting competitive capitalism. Charity is put in its place in this scheme:

There are many good-hearted people who think that it is virtuous to give alms to poor people who ask for them, without considering the effect produced upon the people. They see the pleasure of the beggar on getting the alms, but they do not see the after effects, namely, that beggars

[1] Kingsley wrote a biographical preface for the 1859 edition.

become more numerous than before. Much of the poverty and crime which now exist have been caused by mistaken charity in past times, which has caused a large part of the population to grow up careless, and improvident, and idle. Political economy proves that, instead of giving casual ill-considered alms, we should educate people, teach them to work and earn their own livings, and save up something to live upon in old age. If they continue idle and improvident, they must suffer the results of it. But as this seems hard-hearted treatment, political economists are condemned by soft-hearted and mistaken people. The science is said to be a dismal, cold-blooded one, and it is implied that the object of the science is to make the rich richer, and to leave the poor to perish. All this is quite mistaken.

The political economist, when he inquires how people may more easily acquire riches, does not teach that the rich man should keep his wealth like a miser, nor spend it in luxurious living like a spendthrift. There is absolutely nothing in the science to dissuade the rich man from spending his wealth generously and yet wisely. He may prudently help his relatives and friends; he may establish useful public institutions, such as free public libraries, museums, public parks, dispensaries, &c.; he may assist in educating the poor, or promoting institutions for higher education; he may relieve any who are suffering from misfortunes which could not have been provided against; cripples, blind people, and all who are absolutely disabled from helping themselves, are proper objects of the rich man's charity. All that the political economist insists upon is that [here he adopts the heavier and larger type reserved to make the 'points' in his book] charity shall be really charity, and shall not injure those whom it is intended to aid. (Ibid., pp. 9 f.)

With a hit at Carlyle, who dubbed political economy 'the dismal science', Jevons comfortably ignores John Overs's point that there were many people who worked desperately hard and yet could not earn enough to support themselves and their families.

Sybil, Yeast, Alton Locke, Mary Barton, Hard Times, and *It is Never Too Late to Mend* are all anti-Utilitarian in the sense that they all appeal to individual feeling for the poor, among those in the middle classes and upper classes, to bring about a happier society rather than trust to the scientific application of the 'laws' discerned by political economists in man's pursuit of wealth. *Hard Times*, indeed, sets out to satirize those who believe such laws exist and can be discerned.

Louis Cazamian who, in *Le Roman social en Angleterre 1830–1850*, discusses all these novels except *It is Never Too Late to Mend*, saw them as examples of 'la naissance entre 1830 et 1850, d'un interventionnisme sentimental et conservateur, où l'émotion humaine ou religieuse, alliée à l'intérêt, suggère la notion d'une solidarité sociale' (first published 1903; 2 vols. in 1, Paris, 1934, p. 4). In fact, they represent the reactionary religious heart protesting against the progressive Utilitarian head.

Continually in Dickens's novels the tableau of the poor gratefully acknowledging the attention of the rich is presented approvingly: Oliver Twist, raised from the gutter by Mr Brownlow, experiencing the greatest agony of mind, when the thieves reclaim him, in the idea that his benefactor will think him ungrateful; Will Fern pleading at Sir Joseph Bowley's banquet 'gentlemen, gentlemen . . . Give us, in mercy, better homes . . . give us better food . . . give us kinder laws . . . There an't a condescension you can show the Labourer then, that he won't take, as ready and as grateful as a man can be; for he has a patient, peaceful, willing heart' (*The Chimes*, the Third Quarter); Jo the Crossing Sweeper who 'never knowd what it wos all about' but 'wery thankful' to Allan Woodcourt that he has taken him out of Tom-all-Alone's (*Bleak House*, ch. 47). They are all held out as objects of pity to arouse the reader's compassion. As Dickens writes of Jo: 'Dead, your Majesty. Dead, my lords and gentlemen. Dead, Right Reverends and Wrong Reverends of every order. Dead, men and women, born with Heavenly compassion in your hearts. And dying thus around us every day.' (Ibid., ch. 47.)

In *Hard Times* the mystery of Stephen Blackpool's disappearance, his association, in public rumour, with the bank robbery, the dramatic discovery by his lover and her friend that he is lying, fatally injured, at the bottom of a disused mine-shaft, build up to the climax of his death scene where he is exhibited as, 'a poor crushed human creature' who elicits 'a low murmur of pity' from 'the throng' (Bk. III, ch. 6) and whose pitiable condition is to shock Gradgrind and Louisa into more humane thoughts about the factory workers.

This desirable tableau of the rich bent in pity to succour the poor can be found in *Yeast*—it is Lancelot's attitude to the rural labourers and to Crawy (he guiltily gives the man money, defying the theories of the political economists); Alton Locke, an ex-convict, ill, an outcast in society, is presented prostrate at the end of the novel so that Eleanor can minister to him and raise him up; in *It is Never Too Late to Mend* Eden is the ministering angel who saves Robinson and pities Josephs in the dark world of the Gaol.

Contemporary paintings and drawings also seek sympathetic approval for this relationship between the Two Nations. In *Punch* a solution to the agricultural labourer's plight was offered in the cartoon 'The Reconciliation' (see above, p. 173, and Plate 25) showing the rich titled man and his son condescending to the farm-worker and his child. Richard Dadd's water-colour, 'Crossing Sweeper', done some time after 1864 (Plate 29 and see catalogue of 'The Late Richard Dadd', Tate Gallery 1974, exhibit no. 230) shows a ragged boy with a broom; he touches his forelock in deference. It is the graphic equivalent to Dickens's Jo. It appeals to the same feelings of pity, condescension, and gratification that the boy is so grateful for what he receives. On the other hand, W. P. Frith's oil-painting 'The Crossing Sweeper' (1863. Loaned by a private owner to 'The Camera and Dr. Barnardo', 1974; Plate 30) apparently rebukes those of the middle classes and upper classes who do not feel such emotions. It shows a boy sweeper touching his forelock to a wealthy young lady coming from a porticoed house; she turns away from him and has given him nothing. Here the image is further trivialized by making the sweeper very clean and pink-faced, and setting him on a road which patently does not need sweeping. Jo in *Bleak House* at least smells bad—Allan Woodcourt has to force himself not to recoil when he bends over the boy. However, these unpleasant details are concealed during the climactic deathbed scene.

But this recurring and cherished image of the rich condescendingly succouring the poor is bred of an enviable confidence in rectitude (of the kind that Shaftesbury, Gladstone, and Dr Barnardo had) and in the possibility of encompassing all humanity in that relationship. And although both Dickens and Kingsley mock Young England with its bogus medievalism, the image is also feudal, expressive of the relationship of lord and retainer; this is the image which supports the optimism of *Sybil*; Egremont, representative of the enlightened responsible aristocracy,[2] is the modern equivalent of the feudal overlord, a fiction which

[2] Embodying Carlyle's idea, 'For this now is our sad lot, that we must find a *real* Aristocracy, that an apparent Aristocracy, how plausible soever, has become inadequate for us.' (*Chartism*, ch. 6, Carlyle, *Works*, x. 374.)

many a Victorian aristocrat played out in his own village and acres (see, for example, George Ewart Evans on the Tollemache family in Helmingham, Suffolk, *Where Beards Wag All*, op. cit., pp. 122 f.). For Disraeli the image also carries the traditional authority of the Church before the Reformation. Not least among the attractions of the image of rich condescending to poor was its adaptability—it could be used with effect by Disraeli, in 1845 sympathetic towards the ancient Roman Catholic faith, and by Kingsley, who, by the time he wrote *Yeast*, was an emotional opponent of Catholicism.

Cazamian felt that 'l'émotion humaine ou religieuse' of the social philosophy embodied in these novels was 'alliée à l'intérêt'. Implicit in the tableau of the one Nation extending charity to the Other is control. James Kay observed that the Provident Charitable Society in Liverpool felt that almsgiving gave its members the indisputable right to control the lives of the people to whom they gave help: 'they acquire by their charity, the right of inquiring into their arrangements—of instructing them in domestic economy—of recommending sobriety, cleanliness, forethought, and method' (*Moral and Physical Condition of the Working Classes Employed in the Cotton Manufacture in Manchester*, p. 99).

Education in the cause of better health and a more rational way of life was, and is, very necessary; but not only amongst the poor. Well-born Victorian women endangered their unborn children's health and lives by tight-lacing; manufacturers were polluting the rivers, as Peacock points out in *Gryll Grange*. The two different sets of social and economic norms applied to the Two Nations by the upper Nation included an impossibly high standard of moral behaviour exacted from the Other Nation in return for condescension and charity. Witness the rousing peroration of Peter Gaskell's *Manufacturing Population of England its Moral, Social and Physical Conditions* (1833):

Thus it will be, if the manufacturing population can be roused from their present evil habits; if they will make home what it should be; if the earnings of families are brought into a joint fund;[3] if domestic discipline is re-established; and if they become good husbands, fathers, brothers, and wives; if they will limit the demands of their appetites to their means of

[3] Certainly not the practice in middle-class homes. The first Married Women's Property Act was not passed until 1870.

supply; throw aside ruinous combinations; become peaceable, orderly, and well-behaved citizens; devote their earnings to legitimate purposes, and eschew alike evil and folly, they have within their power—means to be comfortable, happy, and perfectly independent; and to defer, or perhaps do away with the chance of the frightful consummation of their misfortunes, which their present modes [*sic*] of life is so rapidly and so fatally accelerating. (p. 361.)

As Hopkins, the gardener, says feelingly in Trollope's *The Small House at Allington*, 'a poor man mustn't never lie, nor yet drink, nor yet do nothing' (ch. 57).

Such hectoring complacency helped to cause the gulf between the Two Nations rather than bridge it. At its root was fear that the poor, by their demands, might upset the status quo. Such fear has its place in the riots in *Alton Locke* and at the end of *Sybil*, or in the 'wolfish turn' Dickens dreads in the 'reality' of Coketown. If the poor are under obligations to the rich then they are powerless. In *Jane Rutherford; or, The Miners' Strike*, serialized in her journal the *True Briton* directed at improving the labourer, Fanny Mayne describes Lord Westerland, the coalowner, who builds 'model lodging-houses for families as well as single men' and, 'as a strong means of binding the workpeople to the soil, and to the love of order', he gives his men the opportunity to buy the freeholds of allotments near the town,

rightly judging that the man who has strength of mind, forethought, and self-denial sufficient to enable him to lay by out of his weekly wages enough to make himself a proprietor of a free-hold, and the power of voting in parliamentary elections consequent upon it, will be the last, even though he should continue a labourer at weekly wages, to try to overthrow the true rights of property. (Ch. 34; the *True Briton*, New Series II (22 September 1853).)

The tableau is also static; there is no suggestion that the relationship will ever change. There is a case for applying Marx's comment on the Utopian Socialists such as Owen and Fourier to the Victorian writers and artists who depicted the Other Nation: 'Only from the point of view of being the most suffering class does the proletariat exist for them.' (*Manifesto of the Communist Party*, 1848, III, 'Socialist and Communist Literature', Karl Marx and Frederick Engels, *Selected Works*, p. 60.) Henry Wallis's painting 'The Stonebreaker' (1857) is the perfect expression of this vision of the Other Nation (see Plate 31). It shows a pauper who has died at his task of breaking stones. It was first exhibited at the Royal Academy 1858. Accompanying its entry in the exhibition catalogue was a quotation from Carlyle's *Sartor Resartus*: 'For us was thy back so bent, for us were thy straight limbs and fingers so deformed', revealing the guilt expressed by the pathos.

In Elizabeth Stone's novel *William Langshawe, the Cotton Lord* there is a detailed description of the kind of command which charity conferred upon the charitable. Edith, daughter of the cotton lord, has brought charity to a fine art and she snuffs up the heady incense of gratitude:

And Edith was blessed. The blessing of the widow and the fatherless; the blessing of the stricken, the desolate, and the poor, came upon her. Her father, though liberal, was somewhat ostentatious in his charities; they had reference to societies, not individuals: her mother's was a great, but un-discriminating generosity; but Edith's was like the gentle dew from heaven, irrigating and refreshing with perpetual moisture.[4] She gave away to no very great amount; she would have had no difficulty in obtaining five times as much from her father, but she did not want it. She knew that perpetual *giving* is apt to deaden those feelings of independence which are the pledge of the well doing of poor people. (Vol. i, ch. 5.)

How Jevons would have approved of Edith! She has the sanction of Heaven (the Biblical cadences of the first sentences) and the blessing of political economists. Moreover, as Jevons stipulates, she deprives herself of nothing. It is only the pleasurable exertion of training pet animals, a diversion suitable for a young lady: 'She stimulated them to exertion by occasional and well-timed aid; but especially by taking an obvious interest in their pursuits.' However, some ladies felt that by giving alms they had paid the Other Nation to keep out of their sight and felt cheated when this part of the bargain was not kept. Engels quotes a letter written to the editor of the *Manchester Guardian* complaining of beggars in the streets who display their sores and mutilations for alms: 'I should think that when one not only pays the poor-rate, but also contributes largely to the charitable institutions, one had done enough to earn a right to be spared such disagreeable and impertinent molestations.' (*The Condition of the Working Class in England*, p. 303.)[5] But whether

[4] A singularly inappropriate simile; the dew, like the rain, falls upon the just and the unjust.

[5] A note by W. O. Henderson and W. H. Chaloner in their edition of *The Condition of the Working Class in England* (Oxford, 1958), p. 314, says that they have not been able to find the original version of the letter in the *Manchester Guardian*, but that one from 'A Female Sufferer', 20 Dec. 1843, expresses somewhat similar sentiments. This letter is quoted in the note.

you enjoyed watching the Other Nation at its exertions or preferred to have them decently out of the way was really a matter of temperament. Either way you were not actually involved with them.

Gustave Courbet painted a picture of his sisters dispensing charity to a bare-foot cowherd which perfectly expresses the gulf created between the Two Nations by this transaction. 'Demoiselles de la Village' was painted in 1851. There are two versions: a small preliminary oil-sketch with tiny figures dwarfed by the landscape (now in Leeds City Art Gallery; reproduced as Plate 21 in *Courbet*, Alessandra Pinto, Dolphin Art Books, 1971) and the larger finished painting (in the Metropolitan Museum, New York, reproduced as plate 37 in *Image of the People; Gustave Courbet and the 1848 Revolution*, T. J. Clark, 1973) in which Courbet's three sisters, their dog, the girl cowherd and her cows are much more distinct and in the foreground of the picture. (See Plates 32 and 33.) But in both the implications are the same. The cowherd is subdued, submissive, deferent, her head bowed in gratitude. The well-dressed young lady who is offering the food is sweetly condescending, head graciously bent. (Courbet's skill implies such a world of difference in the reasons for those two bent heads.) Another sister, holding a parasol, looks on complacently, holding herself remote. The third sister's back is arched in a movement away from the cowherd as she watches the transaction. Both consciously separate themselves from the girl and her need. The well-fed dog turns his back on the group and barks at the cows. There is a different detail in the earlier sketch in that the girl and the ladies stand on each side of the trodden path so that they seem to confront each other over a dividing line. T. J. Clark rightly remarks on the ambiguity of the painting (op. cit., p. 114). The artist recognizes that his own sisters are engaged charmingly in an activity which emphasizes the gulf between the Two Nations and reduces the humanity of both. Such a painting calls to mind the remark of a London lawyer expounding Owen's theories in the 1830s, that charity purchases 'the submission of the poor by the payment of a debt' (see T. Wayland, *National Advancement and Happiness Considered in Reference to the Equalization of Property, and the formation of Communities*, 1832, p. 7), and the 'trading in' 'benevolence, and generosity, and liberality', which the *Athenaeum* reviewer detected in Disraeli's *Sybil* (see above, p. 6). Indeed, the posture of Courbet's sister in the painting does suggest that she is buying something from the cowherd.

This posture of self-conscious benevolence also, of course, draws attention to the giver and puts him—or her—into a histrionic light, sometimes charming and gracious, sometimes heroic. In Doré's picture we can see little of the Orphan; the eye is caught by the Angel and his flamboyant gesture. Similarly, self-conscious heroic gesture is implied by Dickens's determination in 1844 to strike a 'sledge-hammer blow' on behalf of the poor planting at the same time 'an indignant right-hander on the eye of certain wicked cant that makes my blood boil' (to Macready; Nonesuch *Letters*, i. 646) or by his reaction to the *Second Report* of the Children's Employment Commission (1843):

> since I wrote to you last, reasons have presented themselves for deferring the production of that pamphlet [he had thought of writing a pamphlet, 'An Appeal to the People of England on behalf of the Poor Man's Child'] till the end of the year . . . when you know them, and see what I do, and where, and how, you will certainly feel that a sledge-hammer blow has come down with twenty times the force—twenty thousand times the force I could exert by following out my first idea. Even so recently as when I wrote to you the other day I had not contemplated the means I shall now, please God, use. But they have been suggested to me; and I have girded myself for its seizure. (Ibid., i. 512.)

Dickens's fondness for melodrama sometimes led him to cast himself as the chief character. *The Chimes* was one of the results of his excited benevolence in 1844; some of his letters on *Hard Times*, written ten years later, have an echo of this tone of heroic endeavour, for example the famous letter, 17 March 1854 to Charles Knight, expostulating: 'The English are, so far as I know, the hardest-worked people on whom the sun shines. Be content, if, in their wretched intervals of pleasure, they read for amusement and do no worse. They are born at the oar, and they live and die at it. Good God, what would we have of them!' This becomes in the novel the exhortation to 'Utilitarian economists, skeletons of schoolmasters' to cultivate in the poor 'fancies and affections' before the time comes when 'Reality will take a wolfish turn, and make an end of you.' (Bk. II, ch. 6.)

'The poor' are lost in the generous gesture towards them. In

Dickens's treatment of Stephen the benefactor rather than the beneficiary is the more prominent. The continued insistence on the pathos of his lot—in terms of dialogue, event, characterization, gesture, and posture—stifles our sense of the man but increases our admiration for the director of the pathos. Stephen becomes a receptacle for Dickens's publicly-shed tears. In the same way, interest is deflected from the man Crawy to his pathetic situation in *Yeast*; Alton Locke is treated similarly at the end of the novel, and Josephs and Robinson during the prison scenes of *It is Never Too Late to Mend*; as is Warner in *Sybil*.

At first sight Elizabeth Gaskell, with her steadier vision of the Manchester poor, seems to avoid diminishing in pathos characters from the Other Nation. In her letters she is very critical of charity and its implications. When on 12 November 1850 she sends Lady Kay-Shuttleworth some papers by Dr West, who was then intent on establishing the Hospital for poor children in Great Ormond Street, London (on behalf of which Dickens made a highly emotional speech, quoted admiringly by Jerrold in *London*), she adds: 'You will [be] glad to hear that before Christmas a trial-public nursery will be established in Manchester; the subject is taken up very warmly. I hope they will make it as nearly self-supporting as they can, and as little of a charity as possible; but I am afraid the latter is the error they are likely to fall into.' (Gaskell, *Letters*, p. 135.) And in the year of the establishment of the Great Ormond Street Hospital she amplifies her idea that charitable giving is a matter of laziness, of putting the poor out of mind:

you don't understand how in Manchester when you want a little good hearty personal individual exertion from any one they are apt to say in deeds if not in words 'Spare my time, but take my money'—a sort of 'leave me, leave me to repose' way, handing you their purse in order to be spared any trouble themselves, although by taking a little trouble they may benefit any person in a far more wholesome & durable way than by lazy handing over the money they don't want. It is the fault *of the place*. (To Mary Cowden Clarke, 23? May 1852, Gaskell, *Letters*, p. 192.)

I have already quoted John Barton's savage 'Damn their charity!' ratifying William Cooke Taylor's observation that the Lancashire operative regards alms as an insult if there is any chance of work. (See above, pp. 94-5.) But John's refusal to receive charity does not separate *Mary Barton* from the other novels. The charity he spurns is institutional, 'relief from the town' granted by the local board of guardians taking their instructions from the Poor Law Commissioners. This is the charity provided by the Utilitarian philosophy. Disraeli criticizes it in *Sybil* when he, like Pugin, contrasts the modern workhouses and jails with the hospitality of the ancient monasteries; it is the charity which Lancelot defies when he gives Crawy a sovereign, or Mackaye when he gives the seamstress money to buy coals to warm her sisters, one of whom is dying, and the old mother:

'Doesn't the parish allow the old lady anything?' I ventured to ask.

'They used to allow half-a-crown for a bit; and the doctor ordered Ellen things from the parish, but it isn't half of 'em she ever got; and when the meat came, it was half times not fit to eat, and when it was her stomach turned against it . . . And the hospital wouldn't take her in because she was incurable; and, besides, the old un wouldn't let her go—nor into the union neither . . . she won't hear of the workhouse; so now, these last three weeks, they takes off all her pay, because they says she must go into the house, and not kill her daughter by keeping her out—as if they warn't a killing her themselves.' (*Alton Locke*, vol. i, ch. 8 'Light in a Dark Place'.)

Satire on such charity runs all through Dickens's novels. It is a central theme of *Oliver Twist* where the inhumanity of the workhouse scenes is emphasized by countless small ironic details, such as Mr Bumble's pride in his uniform's buttons which carry the device of the Good Samaritan. The nature of this charity is implied in the desperation of the charity school boy, Rob the Grinder, in *Dombey and Son* (see chs. 5, 6, and 22), or Betty Higden's obsessive terror at the workhouse in *Our Mutual Friend* (ch. 16).

And Reade's sustained attack on the Utilitarian system for restoring spiritual health to the criminal population includes a protest that such a 'scientific' scheme faithfully carried out leaves no room for the impulse of feeling for suffering; that only a man of superlatively fine character and courage would dare to respond to the needs of the criminals supposedly being helped by the scheme (Robinson, in the punishment jacket, appeals to the chaplain of the prison, Mr Jones):

'You can't soften *their* hearts, for they haven't such a thing about them; but only just you open your mouth and speak your mind in right-down earnest, and you will shame them into treating us openly like human beings, let them hate us and scorn us at bottom as they will. We have no friend here, sir, but you, not one; have pity on us! have pity on us!'

And the thief stretched out his hands, and fixed his ardent glistening eyes upon the successor of the apostles.

The successor of the apostles hung his head, and showed plainly that he was not unmoved. A moment of suspense followed—Robinson hung upon his answer. At length Mr. Jones raised his head, and said with icy coldness—

'Mr. Hawes is the governor of this gaol. I have no power to interfere with his acts supported as they are by the visiting justices; and I have but one advice to give you: Submit to the discipline and to Mr. Hawes in everything; it will be the worse for you if you don't.'

So saying he went out abruptly, leaving his petitioner with his eyes fixed ruefully upon the door by which his last hope had left him. (*It is Never Too Late to Mend*, vol. i, ch. 12.)

The Biblical echoes, the suggestion that this penitent thief meets with no response, emphasizes the nature of the charity excluded from the Utilitarian 'penal hospital for diseased and contagious souls' (vol. i, ch. 10).

John Barton finds no succour in Utilitarian charity but his needs are met by the spiritual alms proffered by Mr Carson at the end of the novel. As he lies dying, guilty of the murder of Carson's son, he meditates on the help for which he has yearned but has never received. Elizabeth Gaskell agrees with Carlyle that the cry of the Other Nation is 'Guide me, govern me! I am mad and miserable, and cannot guide myself!' (*Chartism*, ch. 6, Carlyle, *Works*, x. 371)—in fact, she writes in the preface to the novel that it was written 'to give some utterance to the agony which . . . convulses this dumb people; the agony of suffering without the sympathy of the happy . . .', which is an echo of Carlyle's words, 'Bellowings, *in*articulate cries as of a dumb creature in rage and pain; to the ear of wisdom they are inarticulate prayers' (*Chartism*, ch. 6, Carlyle, *Works*, x. 371):

'You see I've so often been hankering after the right way; and it's a hard one for a poor man to find . . . No one learned me, and no one told me. When I was a little chap they taught me to read, and then they never gave no books; only I heard say the Bible was a good book . . . In those days I would ha' gone about wi' my Bible, like a little child, my finger in th' place, and asking the meaning of this or that text, and no one told me . . .

All along it came natural to love folk, though now I am what I am. I think one time I could e'en have loved the masters if they'd ha' letten me; that was in my Gospel-days, afore my child died o' hunger. I was tore in two oftentimes, between my sorrow for poor suffering folk, and my trying to love them as caused their sufferings (to my mind).

At last I gave it up in despair, trying to make folks' actions square wi' th' Bible; and I thought I'd no longer labour at following th' Bible mysel . . . But from that time I've dropped down, down—down.' (Ch. 35.)

And so, displaying the pageant of his bleeding heart, he asks for pity, like Stephen Blackpool. Mr Carson appears opportunely in a spirit of forgiveness, and the appropriate tableau is formed. His strong arms support John as the Angel's support the Orphan: 'He raised up the powerless frame; and the departing soul looked out of the eyes with gratitude. He held the dying man propped in his arms. John Barton folded his hands as if in prayer.'

Elizabeth Gaskell's imaginative recreation of John Barton's life in the earlier part of the novel was sufficient to bring down upon her a storm of criticism that she was favouring the working people at the expense of the masters. But her failure of vision, noticed in the previous chapter, evident in the way she implicates John in a totally untypical murder, becomes even more apparent when he shrinks to a figure in this consolatory moral tableau.

The social control and superiority implied in such an image proceeds from its moral control, which is of the same rigid, limiting, unimaginative kind suggested by Doré's Angel. It reduces 'Love one another' to a moral tag rather than imaginatively re-creating the human experience which makes it a profound moral philosophy.

All these novelists see hope for the regeneration of society in the personal impulse of pity from the rich for the poor. They all support traditional personal charity and deny the efficacy of institutions in satisfying personal need. As Dickens writes in *Hard Times*:

Mr. Gradgrind was at home for the vacation.

He sat writing in the room with the deadly statistical clock, proving something no doubt—probably, in the main, that the Good Samaritan was a Bad Economist. (Bk. II, ch. 12.)

But they fail to see that their interpretation of the Bible's charity is as degrading and dehumanizing to the recipient as the institutional variety. When the Good Samaritan provided medical aid and shelter for the traveller he did not insist that he then listen to a moral reading, as did the Victorians who provided 'model lodging houses' for the London homeless—Doré has a full-page illustration of the practice in *London*. Obviously he was unaware of the irony of the prosperously-dressed reader, his patriarchal hair and whiskers neatly arranged, standing upright

and confident, listening with admiration to his own declama-
tion while the wretched exhausted shapes with despairing or
anguished faces turn on their hard crowded beds and try to get
some sleep. (See Plate 34.) It is a perfect example of the artist's
accurate record of the scene defying the moral message imposed
upon it. Dickens criticized George Cruikshank for the crude
moralizing in his series of plates and captions 'The Bottle' with
which he hoped to persuade the poor to espouse the temperance cause, and satirized his own Mrs Pardiggle who took her
victims into 'moral custody', but was unaware that the tableau
of Stephen Blackpool longing for the condescension of those in
the classes above him preaches a morality which is just as crude.
Alexander Welsh, in his discussion of Dickens and charity (see
The City of Dickens, 1971, pp. 86–100) fails to differentiate
between individual impulse towards the poor, 'and institutional
charity. It escapes his notice that although, in a character like
Betty Higden, Dickens pays lip-service to the independent poor,
he much prefers them in an attitude of grateful deference. In
real life, this was his attitude to John Overs. Welsh rightly says
that Dickens 'cannot readily conceive of any self-respecting
person accepting charity'; and yet Dickens oppresses Stephen
Blackpool with charity, as Henry Wallis oppresses the Stonebreaker. The poor, to be acceptable, had to lose their self-
respect.

Like Doré's Angel, the kind of tableau in which Stephen
takes part at the end of *Hard Times* appeals not to the responsive feeling, the deep emotion which evoked Romantic 'vision'
but to sentimentality. The distinction is obvious if we compare
Thackeray's description of the charity children at their annual
service in St. Paul's and his complacent remark (quoted approvingly in *London*, p. 96) that London had no grander sight to
show the stranger, with Blake's sparse lines in the 'Holy Thursday' of *Songs of Experience* describing the children's public
ritual of gratitude for food given with 'a usurous hand'. At the
beginning of my discussion (see above, pp. 22–3) I referred to
George Eliot's concern with the 'sacred task' of the artist who
takes as subject 'the life of our more heavily-laden fellow-men'
and her distaste that 'our sympathy with the perennial joys and
struggles, the toil, the tragedy, and the humour' in this life
should be 'turned towards a false object instead of the true one.'

39. The Wakling children, 1891

38. William Daniels, 'Two Children Selling Matches', 1851

41. Albert Martin, 1902

40. A. E. Mulready, 'A London Crossing Sweeper and Flower Girl', 1861

42. Louisa Butin, 1882

43. Minnie Reynolds, 1886

44. 'The Holders', 1874

45. Emma Cook, 1887

THE EMIGRANT.

46. 'The Emigrant', 1847

47. Gustave Doré, drawing for Hood's 'Bridge of Sighs'

The Angel of Charity, and its equivalents in the novels I have been discussing, is sentimental rather than genuinely compassionate because it is 'a false object'; a static cliché has been substituted for the intense awareness of reality which results in the Romantic vision of truth. So the reader or spectator is exhorted to lavish emotion on an image which cannot of its nature evoke it. Therefore the Angel needs its theatrical lighting and flamboyant gesture to insist on this emotion, even as the novelists need the carefully stage-managed tableau and the over-emphatic rhetoric to establish the Other Nation as objects of charity. And so these gestures and words call attention to themselves because the 'false object' is incapable of sustaining such attention. The apparently simple line of the Oldham weaver, 'I've woven myself t' far end', is moving because the listener responds to the implications of the image which recreates in his imagination the poverty it describes. The words are the vehicle, not the end, which is the recreation and sharing of the weaver's experience of poverty. It is therefore of its nature disturbing and challenging; it changes and expands the listener's experience, extends his awareness, in George Eliot's phrase. This is the essential nature of Romantic art as Wordsworth, Keats, Shelley, and Coleridge expounded it. Doré's Angel of Charity has precisely the opposite effect. A bland image has been substituted for reality; it is therefore soothing and consoling. It evokes not emotion but complacency, that deathly complacency which Blake sets in the ironic perspective of youthful trust and innocence in the 'Holy Thursday' of *Songs of Innocence*. In an aesthetic sense it leaves 'the matter just where it was', to quote John Overs on Carlyle's *Chartism* (*Victorian Studies*, 13 (December 1974), p. 197), not because it does not provide solutions for society's ills, which is not the artist's job, but because it has not enriched the spectator's imagination, which is. This accounts for the feeling of dissatisfaction at the endings of these novels purporting to describe the Other Nation, particularly *Mary Barton* because so much of the book succeeds in re-creating the life of the Manchester poor in the 1840s.

One of the recurring themes in *London* is the overwhelming number of the Other Nation to be encountered in this prosperous city: 'The aged, the orphan, the halt, the blind, of London, would fill an ordinary city' (p. 179); 'The mighty capital

comprehends whole townships of the almost hopeless poor'
(p. 188). Doré's drawings are a record of his own nightmare as
he encountered these swarms as well as an attempt to describe
their lives. Undoubtedly these multitudes are menacing, and
therefore something must be done; again self-interest mingles
with the compassion. But even while Jerrold is extolling personal
charity there is a note of uncertainty, sometimes appearing in a
revealing over-emphasis—'Surely there can be only good in this
minimum of relief . . .' (p. 143); or in his defensive descriptions
of charity dinners ('The appetite, for almsgiving at any rate,
comes with eating. It would be absurd to ask a man for a sub-
scription while he is waiting for his dinner . . . The why the
diners give, let us not too narrowly seek to know; above all, let
us not inquire in a cynical mood . . .' pp. 181 f.); and of aristocratic charity bazaars ('Shall the Boys' Home, for the bread-and-
butter fund of which Her Royal Highness deigns to make tea;
reject the grace, because it is tendered from the heart of Vanity
Fair?' p. 188). Once he dolefully recounts a great charitable
venture, undertaken by Dickens's friend and helper, the bank-
ing heiress Angela Burdett Coutts. She is 'the Lady Bountiful
of our time—at once wise and gentle and charitable: the Lady of
the open hand; among her countless benefactions to her poor
brothers and sisters, [she] gave them Columbia Market, which
she reared in the thickest of London squalor . . .' (p. 152). He
goes on:

Her design was to bring cheap and good food within the reach of those
who could least afford to be cheated of a farthing's worth. And so in
1868, under liberal regulations unknown in the old markets, the spacious
avenues of a fine architectural edifice were given up to the marketing of
the ragged, the unfortunate, and the guilty. It was a merciful and provident idea, most liberally carried out: yet so sunk were those for whom the
good was intended in ignorance and the wantonness of vice, that they
would not use the gift. The costermonger drove his barrow past the gates
to the byeways of Covent Garden or the alleys about overcrowded Billings-
gate, as of old; the hosts of half-fed creatures massed far and wide around
the building would not take the comfort and economy the new market
offered, but went to the street shambles and road-side barrows as of old.
Columbia Market—like many other places disposed by Charity for the
improvement of the unfortunate—was a failure. (pp. 151 f.)

Columbia Market was in Bethnal Green where, as the *Builder*
put it, 'Miss Burdett Coutts, prompted by head as well as heart,
became possessed of a considerable tract of land' (27 (1869),

137). The same journal gives a full account of the opening cere-
mony (in 1869, not 1868 as Jerrold says) in which Miss Burdett
Coutts appeared as an apotheosis of Charity. She

was received by a guard of honour composed of about 300 of the Tower
Hamlets Volunteers. She was afterwards conducted . . . to a dais which had
been erected in the centre of the quadrangle; and various formal introduc-
tions having taken place, the company present received the addition of the
Duchess of Cambridge, Princess Mary of Teck, the Prince of Teck, the
Duchess of Argyll, the Marquis of Lorne, the Duke of Wellington . . . the
Bishop of London, the Earl of Harrowby, the Marquis of Salisbury, Lord
Redesdale, the Lord Mayor and the Sheriffs of London and Middlesex, &c.
A procession was then formed to meet the Archbishop of Canterbury.
(27 (1869), 345.)

The workmen who had built the market presented Miss
Coutts with a suitably grateful address:

The care and solicitude you have continuously shown on behalf of the
moral and social elevation of our class emboldens us to join in the congratulations of to-day, and we feel assured that the magnificent and beautiful structure now completed, and which your bounty has provided, will be
another proof, added to many, of a rare generosity united with practical
wisdom . . . We earnestly hope and pray that this edifice may . . . remain a
monument to a remote posterity of a loving spirit, a fostering care, and a
bounteous benevolence.

Miss Coutts gave the Archbishop of Canterbury a letter for
him to read out in reply to the men: 'Miss Coutts, he said,
thanked the workmen for the address they had delivered to her.
It was a satisfaction for her to know that by their conduct while
the works were in progress they had shown a good example to
the neighbourhood.'

It was a suitably spectacular gesture. Rich and poor had
played their accustomed roles to perfection. It was the sort of
'lovely spectacle' celebrated by the *Pictorial Times* (7 (1846), 1)
in its New Year article on 'Charity', illustrated by a picture of
Queen Victoria and Prince Albert presiding over the distribution
of meat, bread, and blankets to the poor at Windsor (see Plate
35). Describing the scene, the writer again uses the word 'spectacle': 'The spectacle was grand and imposing, and embraced all
that could be wished for in the exercise of Christian charity.'

The fiasco of Columbia Market shows that Jerrold, despite
his celebration of charity, was right to be uncertain that it could
deal with the casualties of the fiercely competitive system
which the political economists had taught was necessary to the

pursuit of wealth, that it was adequate to meet the needs of the
poor 'when the struggle for life is so severe as it is in England'.
Columbia Market in fact failed because of this competitive system not because of the depravity and ignorance of those for
whom it was built. It cost £200,000. The architect was Henry
Darbishire. There was a quadrangle with surrounding market
buildings, of which the galleried market hall was one. There
were permanent shops in the neighbouring arcades, and a
warden who lived on the site. No tolls were charged. There are
pictures of it in the *Builder*, 27 (1869), 147, 347. The style is
pointed Gothic, 'Christian architecture', as Pugin and Disraeli
might have described it. The market hall had great soaring
pillars and a lofty aisle. It looked just like a church (see Plate
36). But, according to Hermione Hobhouse, the 'whole elaborate
and well-organized scheme was frustrated by the opposition of
dealers established elsewhere, afraid for their trade, who prevented wholesalers from supplying the market' (*Lost London*,
1971, p. 184). The charitable enterprise was no match for the
competitive contemporary society.[6] This typical attempt to
encompass the cut-throat competition of the market-place
within a structure reared by piety and reminiscent of the House
of God met with total failure. The novelists' failure is similar
when they advance personal charity as the solace to the casualties of the society they have described. They reject the Utilitarian
philosophy which sanctions the competitive society, yet extol
the charity which Jevons describes as perfectly in accord with
the ethos of that society. His description of the approved activities of the rich man could be a description of the activities of
Baroness Burdett Coutts—or Dickens.

The fears and aspirations which shaped and cherished the
Angel of Charity are obviously of their time. It expresses confidence in energy and will, in widely-held moral beliefs, and in

[6] See the article, 'The Unseen Charities of London', *Fraser's Magazine* (39 (1849),
639–47). The writer describes the almshouse, St. Anne's House, Compton Street,
Soho, provided by the rector of St. Anne's and a small number of private gentlemen
to house one hundred and thirty single working-men ('No smoking, no spiritous
liquors, no cards, are allowed. Quarrelling, uncleanly habits, profane or abusive language, are punished by expulsion.'); an asylum for the Houseless Poor opened in
London Wall; the Model Lodging-house in Glasshouse Yard, East Smithfield; and the
adjacent Refuge for the Homeless Poor; but admits, 'Admirable are these endeavours,
and much may they effect; but the mighty mass of human misery remains, comparatively unassuaged.'

the blessedness of affording others the opportunity for such energy and morality. It is not surprising that Disraeli, Kingsley, Dickens, Elizabeth Gaskell, and Reade found it an attractive image and used it, in their several ways, to contain the threatening presence of the Other Nation. But it is fatal to their achievement as artists supposedly re-creating the experience of contemporary poverty. How fatal was perfectly demonstrated in the 1974 exhibition of the photographs Dr Barnardo took as records of the children who entered his Home. They were taken between 1874 and 1905. So the first were taken two years after the publication of *London*, and the photographs which were taken when the children first entered his refuge are a valuable factual record of the Other Nation. The main hall of the exhibition was hung with three thousand photographs of the children. It was approached by a corridor hung with contemporary paintings of the kind of children Dr Barnardo photographed and housed. Although the thinking which created Doré's Angel of Charity was evident in some of the photographs, such as those taken 'before' and 'after', transforming waifs into scrubbed servant girls and 'little workmen', or those of Barnardo himself, short and stocky but confident, ebullient, adopting a commanding attitude with folded arms, there was a startling difference between the direct impact of the photographs and the evasive sentimentality of the paintings. Barnardo occasionally used picturesque rags to achieve pathos (as William Bell Scott said, 'beggary is the most picturesque condition of social life') and attract the money of charitable Victorians, but usually the face above the rags has a startling actuality (see Plate 37); the faces of these children strike to the soul like the reality they are. William Daniels's painting, 'Two Children Selling Matches' (1851; see Plate 38), included in the exhibition, shows a boy and girl in picturesque rags. Like Doré's Angel they are lit theatrically—the girl holds a lamp which gives a histrionic interest to the two faces, which are rounded, clean and well-fed. The boy's throat is bared romantically; he rests his head on the girl's shoulder and looks downward dreamily, staring into space; her eyes, raised to heaven, stream with tears. As always in the picturesque, the pose is dominant; its moral import is made clear by the large sheet of crumpled paper painted in front of the children and on which can be deciphered 'Benevolent kind

. . . take pity . . .' The painting contrasts violently with the photograph 'Wakling Group' (No. 19499, taken 30 January 1891; see Plate 39) showing a small girl and a boy clinging together. Destitution and alarm are in their faces, but no trace of the match-sellers' self-conscious pathos. Another painting, A. E. Mulready's 'A London Crossing Sweeper and Flower Girl' (see Plate 40), shows one of the stone benches on London Bridge which Doré used in his heading to the chapter 'London Charities'. Stars shine in the sky and pretty lights along the river; on the bench kneels a boy, eating a hunch of bread, staring into the distance and absently selling matches. A girl holds up her flowers for sale. Again, their expressions crave pity; the children seem to be playing at work in order to form a pathetic tableau. Certainly they lack the energy which Mayhew's Watercress Girl had to exert in order to exist in her hostile society. Set these paintings against their real counterparts, either in Mayhew's account or in Barnardo's photographs, and the obvious difference is that the real children did not cry for help. The pathos is heaped upon them by their social superiors. A small ragged boy with one leg and a crutch has an impudent grin and an unmistakable sense of fun—no hint of Tiny Tim here (Plate 41); Sarah Burge has desperation in her eyes, but it is controlled and there is no hint of self-pity (Plate 19); a small girl's face recalls Mayhew's Watercress Girl, it shows the early maturity and confident determination bred of adversity (Plate 42); a girl's face is vulnerable and wary, but her gaze is withdrawn, not cast upwards in self-displaying pathos (Plate 43); two girls standing close together are obviously distressed, defensive, but have dignity (Plate 44).

Margaret Oliphant, in her essay on Dickens, shrewdly queries 'the utter forlornness and desolation of childhood' displayed by the children freed from Dotheboys Hall:

Is it real? Is a child ever so thoroughly broken in spirit by any amount of ill usage? We doubt it greatly . . . The more we are acquainted with children—with the simplicity which takes everything as it comes, and with that vivid interest and curiosity which is caught by every novel sight or thought —the less we are prepared to receive such plaintive little martyrs as little Dick in *Oliver Twist*, or the host of saintly little Dicks which abound in less able books than those of Mr. Dickens. ('Charles Dickens', *Blackwood's Edinburgh Magazine*, 77 (1855), 457 f.)

When they indulge in such images the painters and novelists

dwindle to patrons and spectators of the Other Nation, not artists patiently re-creating their experience. If the bland image of Daniels's match-seller is compared with the photograph of Emma Cook (Plate 45), evidently driven to the limits of her endurance but showing in her face and gesture the utmost determination to cling to her frail wisp of life, the artist appears impertinent to pretend to express such experience in such terms. Indeed, the Angel of Charity has no contact with reality; it is, to quote Arnold on Shelley but with more reason, an 'ineffectual angel, beating in the void his luminous wings in vain'.[7]

[7] Alan Woods, in 'Doré's *London*: Art and Evidence' (*Art History*, 1 (1978), 341–359), puts a contrary view, 'Doré . . . makes no complacent moral statements, refuses to rely on sentiment', arguing that although 'Doré liked monsters' (with which I agree, see above p. 60) and used a 'vocabulary of Gothic romanticism' his 'images are radically different from those of mainstream Victorian culture' because his dark pictures of London's poor suggest resentment of upper-class intrusion, resistance to authority and the force implicit in social control. One of the 'key illustrations' in this argument is 'The Bull's Eye' (Doré's plate 30) showing three policemen confronting six vagrants caught in the light of a lantern held by one of the police. 'Doré avoids the customary Victorian distortions, and states the nature of the problem clearly.' But this scene is the exact graphic equivalent to Dickens's view of Rats' Castle when he was escorted there by Inspector Field—'Rogers to the front with the light, and let us look!'—see my discussion of his essay in *Household Words* on pp. 54–5 above; a view shared by the journalist Edmund Yates on a similar slumming expedition (see above, p. 55). Doré's 'Gothic romanticism' is the familiar Victorian sensationalism exploiting the frisson of horror afforded by the poor yet confident that social forces can reveal and control it. Woods argues that Doré 'does not rule out charity' but that some of his illustrations query its efficacy. But it seems to me that the irony in some of Doré's illustrations is unconscious (see my discussion of his 'Scripture Reader in a Night Refuge', pp. 221–2 above) and that there is a danger of modern sensibility erroneously ascribing conscious intentions to Doré's work. Of 'The Angel and the Orphan' Woods simply remarks, 'Doré was constantly drawing angels, so it comes as no surprise that he should include one in this chapter', which evades the issue.

5
NEW WINE IN OLD BOTTLES

A Damocles' sword of *Respectability* hangs forever over the poor English Life-writer (as it does over poor English Life in general), and reduces him to the verge of paralysis.
(Carlyle, 'Sir Walter Scott', 1838.)

It is sometimes difficult to determine whether what we find in a work of art reflects the life or only the dreams of a period.
(E. S. Dallas, *The Gay Science*, 1866.)

The novels on which I have concentrated in this book were written largely because the novelists were shocked by the intransigent fact of the poor. Even Disraeli, ambitious for political power and concerned to give a panoramic rather than domestic view of society, was not merely the aloof, note-taking politician; Edmund Gosse recorded that Lord John Manners told him 'that he accompanied Disraeli on the journey [to Manchester and the North, 1844] which led to the composition of "Sybil," and that he never, in long years of intimacy, saw him so profoundly moved as he was at the aspect of the miserable dwellings of the hand-loom workers' ('The Novels of Benjamin Disraeli', *Transactions of the Royal Society of Literature*, 36 (1918), 18). Kingsley felt himself driven by God to describe the conditions of the poor in *Yeast*—'He has made "the Word of the Lord like fire within my bones," giving me no peace till I have spoken out.' (Letter to J. M. Ludlow, 17 July 1848, *Charles Kingsley. Letters and Memories*, i. 180.) While, in another letter to Ludlow, discussing his friend's article 'Labour and the Poor', *Fraser's Magazine*, January 1850, on Mayhew's revelations in the *Morning Chronicle*, the germ of *Alton Locke*, he wrote, 'I am shamed[1] and sickened by the revelations in your article in Fraser's . . . I have a wild longing to do *something*' (ibid., i.

---

[1] 'Stunned' in the manuscript. See R. B. Martin, 'Correspondence of Charles Kingsley', p. 195, cited below, pp. 232–3.

221 f.). Elizabeth Gaskell, distressed at the reception of *Mary Barton*, wrote to her friend Catherine Winkworth, 23 December 1848: 'It is a painful subject and *must* be painful, and I felt it all so deeply myself I could hardly be lighthearted any part of the time I was writing it.' (Gaskell, *Letters*, p. 66.) When Reade wrote to *The Times*, 26 August 1871, recalling the passage in that newspaper which had inspired him to publicize in a novel the wrongs of the prisoners in Birmingham Gaol, he remembered that it had touched his heart and inflamed his imagination. But, characteristically, Dickens is the most vigorous in describing how the subject of his novel assailed him, compelled him to write, and exhausted him: 'Why I found myself so "used up" after Hard Times I scarcely know, perhaps because I intended to do nothing in that way for a year, when the idea laid hold of me by the throat in a very violent manner . . . But I really was tired, which is a result so very incomprehensible that I can't forget it.' (Letter to the Hon. Mrs Richard Watson, 1 November 1854, Nonesuch *Letters*, ii. 602.)

The novelists' problem was to re-create the life of the Other Nation, which had so moved them, in novels which would extend the imagination of their readers so as to include this life. For this purpose the novel could not be trivial amusement, it had to be art of the kind defined by George Eliot: 'Art is the nearest thing to life; it is a mode of amplifying experience and extending our contact with our fellow-men beyond the bounds of our personal lot.' ('The Natural History of German Life', *Westminster Review*, 66 (1856), quoted T. Pinney, *Essays of George Eliot*, p. 271.) Her words recall Wordsworth's view of poetry in the 1800 Preface to the *Lyrical Ballads*: 'the Poet binds together by passion and knowledge the vast empire of human society'.

She was writing at the end of the period which I am considering, and her comment indicates the rediscovery of the novel as an art-form since the time when the *Athenaeum* critic dismissed it as 'tinsel' (see above, p. 6). In the 1840s the stereotypes of the popular novel proliferated in cheap publications made possible by the steam printing press and broadcast by the circulating libraries. Later, writers like George Eliot and George Meredith, concerned with the serious 'philosophy' embodied in a novel, with language as a subtle means of expression, who were in touch with European culture and responsive to it, helped, both in practice and by critical analysis, to effect a change in the novel's status. They were aided by the established novel with a social purpose which, as Kathleen Tillotson shows in *Novels of the Eighteen-Forties*, helped to make the novel more serious. It also contributed to its thematic structure. The contrast between the rich and the poor helps give shape, other than that of a contrived plot, to all the novels which I have been considering. Even the loosest of these 'baggy monsters', Disraeli's *Sybil*, has a theme, 'The Two Nations', as well as a heroine.

However, the very strength of the novelists' feelings about the poor and the need to share them with their readers could lead to over-emphasis and crudity of characterization and event. Such crudity is evident in contemporary journalism, also publicizing the gulf between the Two Nations, for example, the large engraving 'Condition of the Poor' on the front page of the *Pictorial Times*, 8 (1846), 225, showing a filthy child on the squalid rubbish near the Thames, and forcing the reader to acknowledge the difference between the lives of those inhabiting this region of London and those of the inhabitants of Lambeth Palace close by (see *The Victorian City*, ii, Plate 405).

Moreover, novels are read for enjoyment. They would fail in their purpose of publicizing the plight of the Other Nation if their readers abandoned them because they assaulted contemporary ideas of propriety and offered none of the pleasure associated with romance. Hence the attraction of reconciling the Two Nations in the image of the Angel of Charity, and of inducing the pleasurable frisson afforded by contemplating distant horrors.

The novelists' greatest innovation was to take the poor into account in a serious study of society. That by so doing they sometimes destroyed the popular novel's stereotypes is evident from the reviewers' complaints that exposure of destitution was no part of the novelist's business. But it is also apparent that when the novelists conformed to these stereotypes their depiction of the Other Nation was falsified.

In November 1848 Kingsley wrote to the publisher of *Fraser's* enclosing part of the current instalment of *Yeast* and remarking 'don't be frightened about peoples' [*sic*] not understanding them. There is love and murder enough in the no. to satisfy "sweet-toothed" readers.' (R. B. Martin, 'An Edition of the

Correspondence and Private Papers of Charles Kingsley 1819–1856' (unpublished D.Phil. dissertation, University of Oxford, 1950), p. 107; hereafter cited as R. B. Martin, 'Correspondence of Charles Kingsley'.)

In all the novels under discussion the convention that a love story must be central to a novel's plot is disastrous to a serious re-creation of the Other Nation. Lancelot's ecstasies about Argemone deflect attention from the village of Whitford Priors, and, as the reviewer in *Blackwood's* pointed out (see 68 (1850), 593), Alton's improbable infatuation with Lillian and his courting her call in question the truths of his life as a working tailor and a Chartist. Egremont's operatic love affair with Sybil relegates the poor to a subsidiary position, and Jem's romance with Mary displaces the previous interest in John Barton. Reade recognized that the love story of Susan Merton is 'the stale and conventional part' of *It is Never Too Late to Mend*. And in *Hard Times* Stephen Blackpool's unhappy marriage and his hopeless love for Rachael, despite Dickens's use of the situation to exemplify the difference between the Two Nations in ease of divorce, makes his problems untypical of those of the urban poor. Dickens's transference of problems of Trades Union allegiance to the realms of aristocratic medieval romance (Stephen has, in effect, sworn an oath to his 'ladye' that he will not join, and therefore nothing can induce him to break it) precludes any serious representation of Trades Union activity in the novel.

The heroine is the key figure of the love story. In the 1840s she had to be endowed with the technical 'purity' and modesty which we have seen to have been impossible for the poor, and to be idealized and remote from real life. Hence the difficulty of a novelist's establishing 'truth to' the life of the poor in a heroine. 'I am glad you like Mary, I do:' wrote Elizabeth Gaskell to Eliza Fox, 29 May 1849, 'but people are angry with her just because she is not perfect.' Yet Mary is a neutral and insufficiently realized character compared with her father in the early part of the novel, or with Alice Wilson or Job Legh.

Of the other heroines, Sybil is supposedly a 'daughter of the people' but is really an aristocrat and behaves throughout in a remotely regal manner; Argemone in *Yeast* and Eleanor in *Alton Locke* are also aristocratic heroines in accord with Kingsley's admiration for idealized womanhood. Reade's Susan

Merton is described as a country girl but this is asserted rather than established; her part in the novel is to be trusting and patient, while her pure regard for Mr Eden enables her to support him in his struggle for justice in the prison. Sissy Jupe in *Hard Times* is a subsidiary character and has no love adventures of her own. She plays a supporting role to Louisa and, although at times her childish directness, like that of many of Dickens's characters such as Paul Dombey and the young David Copperfield, exposes the inhumanity and egotism of the adult world, as in her response to M'Choakumchild's 'stutterings' (Bk. I, ch. 9), she lacks individuality and is chiefly important for her obstinate belief, contrary to all appearances, that her father will return thereby proving the power of faith as against the power of fact; and as the embodiment of innocence's strength confounding and vanquishing the diabolical Harthouse. Rachael, the object of Stephen's enduring devotion and the heroine of the novel's love-story of the poor, is a totally static character, an Agnes Whitfield in poor circumstances and, like her, associated with suitably pious and rigid images. As Agnes is seen as the guardian angel in the stained-glass window (see my essay 'Anti-Mechanism and the Comic in the Writings of Charles Dickens', *Renaissance and Modern Studies*, 3 (1959), 136–8) Rachael is given a halo: 'Seen across the dim candle with his moistened eyes, she looked as if she had a glory shining round her head. He could have believed she had.' (Bk. I, ch. 13.) Appropriately, she is the chief figure assisting at the pietà of the martyred Stephen. (Bk. III, ch. 6.)

Caroline Helstone in *Shirley* (ch. 22) connects the poor and single women as deprived and ignored categories in her society. In the case of both, evasion of their true situation appears as idealization in fiction. Exploration of the actuality of women's lives gave the novel increased sensitivity to areas of experience hitherto ignored, and this furthered its development. In *Jane Eyre* Charlotte Brontë showed that a plain governess earning her bread could be an interesting heroine; George Eliot depicted the tragedy and triumph of a woman's outwardly uneventful life in 'Janet's Repentance' (*Scenes of Clerical Life*, 1858). But these unconventional 'heroines' are not of the Other Nation. It was possible to re-create the consciousness of women in, or aspiring to the middle class, but not of those below. This is an understandable limitation of the period but it means that the lower-class heroines of fiction are denied the interest and complexity which would have established them as characters rather than ciphers.

The other ingredient which Kingsley felt his 'sweet-toothed' readers would require is 'murder'. An exciting plot, with sensational incidents, was essential. The murder in *Yeast* is that of the illegitimate child of the country girl seduced by Bracebridge, who later commits suicide. It would need a novelist of George Eliot's apprehension of psychology to make this situation convincing fiction (as she does the murder of Hetty's child in *Adam Bede*). Kingsley's melodramatic treatment of the characters, particularly the girl, weakens his description of rural life, even as Elizabeth Gaskell's involvement of John Barton in murder damages her re-creation of his life as a factory worker.

Sensational incident both emphasizes the distorting, horrific image of the poor as savages, and dissipates patient exploration of their ordinary lives in spurious excitement. When the fight for justice in the gaol is reduced to a melodramatic struggle between the angel Eden and the devil Hawes, Reade's creative imagination ceases to engage with reality, as does Dickens's when he involves Stephen in the complicated mystery of the bank robbery, or Disraeli's when he offers as acceptable solution to the Chartist disturbances the masterful appearance of Egremont with a sabre. The mechanical use of conventions betrays the failure of imagination.

Conventions, whether of art or behaviour, are forms accepted by a particular society as appropriate for communication. Any artistic convention, if used with sufficient imagination and feeling, is effective and retains its power to communicate even when the society which evolved it has gone. The formal gestures and tableaux, the stylized poetry of the medieval Crucifixion drama in the York Cycle are still profoundly moving because of the dramatist's imagination and passion. As Louis James writes, 'Conventions only destroy when they become a substitute for creativity.' (*Fiction for the Working Man 1830–1850*, 1963, p. 112.) Conventions lacking such feeling and imagination have an ephemeral life as long as they are supported by the society which evolved them. To later generations they appear empty and faded. Many of the stereotypes in which the novelists sought

refuge from the actuality of the life of the Other Nation have
their counterparts in the contemporary melodrama which was,
like the novel, popular and equally dependent upon repeated
and obvious formulae for its public acclaim. Its conventions
repeatedly celebrate qualities—sexual purity, filial affection,
courage, energy, industry—which its period publicly approved
and congratulated itself on possessing. This is why men as intelligent as Dickens enjoyed melodrama (although he could guy
its absurdities) because he wholeheartedly shared this celebration. He thought Westland Marston's *A Hard Struggle* 'an
excellent play' and 'confessed that he cried over [it] . . . till he
sobbed again' (see Dutton Cook, 'Charles Dickens as a Dramatic
Critic', *Longman's Magazine*, 2 (1883), 40). It was first performed at the Lyceum, 1858. Today it reads as an undistinguished, not to say maudlin, little play with an improbable plot
in which the bluff but good-hearted Reuben, childhood sweetheart and accepted fiancé of Lillian Trevor, makes the great
sacrifice of relinquishing her to Fergus Graham, the doctor who
saved her life and whom she now loves; but he resists the
temptation to emigrate because of his affection for Amy,
Lillian's orphan niece. Apart from the fact that Dickens was
very susceptible to tales of heroic self-sacrifice (witness his
imaginative involvement in Wilkie Collins's melodrama *The
Frozen Deep* and his handling of the theme in *A Tale of Two
Cities*), this play extols the purity and fidelity of Lillian Trevor
(she tries to conceal her love for Graham and intends to honour
her engagement to Reuben), Reuben's strength of love and
honour, and emphasizes the pathos and tenderness of the
relationship between Reuben and Amy. In Scene 3 he takes his
lesson in sacrifice from her:

Reuben	. . . suppose I was to choose another pet—to find some other little face that would make me happier to look on than my Amy's.
Amy	That would make you happier?
Reuben	Suppose so.
Amy	If it did make you happier—
Reuben	Well, go on, darling.
Amy	Oh, that would hurt me!—but—
Reuben	Yes, yes!
Amy	(*Stifling her sobs.*) I should pray to God; I should try to think how good you had been to me, how you ought to be happy.

And if—if another pet made you so, I should give you up, and
try—to love her for your sake. (*She weeps silently, and covers
her face with her hands.*)

Reuben   (*Kissing her fervently.*) Bless you, darling! No fear! no fear!

The feeble language, the obviously-contrived situation we now
find absurd and lifeless. Dickens found it moving because he
imaginatively assented to the idea of self-sacrifice and supplied
the emotions which the words and actions cannot of themselves
generate because the dramatist presupposed the kind of response
which Dickens gave and merely provided a framework for it. Moreover, in an age much more given to the public expression of emotion than our own, such a scene provided a suitable outlet for it,
even as the death of Stephen Blackpool afforded a welcome
indulgence in tears. ('The story of their unfulfilled love, and its
sad catastrophe, is a truly pathetic episode of humble life',
wrote the reviewer in the *Westminster Review* (62 (1854), 606).)
The consciously-struck attitude, the tableau, the flamboyant
gesture could be held and savoured because publicly approved.

On the other hand, Kingsley uses the convention of exciting
incident effectively in *Alton Locke* when he describes the terror
of the agricultural riot because he has previously established
Alton's concern with the agricultural labourers' poverty and
imaginatively established their desperation in scenes such as the
desolate landscape in which Alton and his guide encounter the
turnip-cutters. The riot is the logical conclusion of the concern
and the desperation.

Much of the sensational excitement popularly supposed to be
indispensable to the novel had its counterpart in the melodrama
and made a similar appeal. The carefully-prepared scene at the
end of Book III of *Sybil* repeats many of the stereotypes of the
'dog-drama' popular in the 1830s and 1840s and established by
The Forest of Bondy; or, The Dog of Montargis, *c.* 1830. In
this melodrama, based on an ancient tale, the dog, Dragon,
avenges his master's murder by bringing the murderer to justice.
But in many of the plays the dog prevents rather than avenges
murder, as in *The Mirror of Fate or the Gnome of the Gold
Mine and the Demon and his Dog*, which was to be produced
'on or before Easter Monday, April 8th, 1844' at the Albert
Saloon, Shepherdess Walk, City Road (see the Lord Chamberlain's Plays, BL MS, f. 74). Act I ends: 'Music. The Mirror lights

up and the figure of Leopold is seen reclining on a couch. Paulo
enters stealthily and is about to slay him when the Dog fastens
on his throat—he falls and dies.'

In *Sybil* the mysterious circumstances, the mist concealing
the assailant, the thrill of terror, all suggest the melodrama, as
does the language in which Disraeli describes the incident: 'Suddenly he was seized; an iron grasp assailed his throat, a hand of
steel gripped his arm.' Even the details of the scene—the ledge
of pointed rocks, the rapids, the heroic dog—are stereotypes
repeated from the dog-drama. For example, in Dibdin's version
of *The Forest of Bondy* Dragon pursues the murderer Macaire
among rocks: 'Macaire is seen to fly up the rocks, and appears
on a high one that overhangs the water-fall—here he is met by
the Dog.'

As M. R. Booth points out, the melodrama provides easy
thrills and sensations.

Another important reason for popularity is that melodrama is easy and
asks nothing from the spectator except identification with what happens
on the stage. This fact, too, was understood early; the *Theatrical Inquisitor*
comments that the taste for melodrama 'must arise from an inertness in
the minds of the spectators and a wish to be amused without the slightest
exertion on their own parts or any exercise whatever of their intellectual
powers'. (M. R. Booth, *English Melodrama*, 1965, p. 188. He gives the
reference to the *Theatrical Inquisitor*, 'On Melo-Drama', March 1818,
pp. 160 f.)

Also, part of the enjoyment of melodrama lies in the witnessing
of wicked actions in the full knowledge that all will come right;
the irresponsibility of the thrill of evil without its consequences.

A novelist who includes such empty excitements among his
effects cannot hope to do justice to the life of the Oldham
Weaver, or the collier-girl Ann Eggley, or the miner's wife who
described her experiences at the Tommy-shop, because he
necessarily reduces them to this level. He is using the wrong
tools to give adequate expression to their humanity, their reticence and their vitality.

The way in which melodrama could reduce Elizabeth Gaskell's
patiently observed and imaginatively re-created poor of Manchester to ciphers and puppets can be seen in Dion Boucicault's
The Long Strike, a drama based on *Mary Barton* and first produced at the Lyceum, 15 September 1866. (See George Dolby's
account of the production in *Charles Dickens as I Knew Him*,

1912, p. 63; also the illustration of the production, *The Victorian City*, op. cit., i, Plate 65.) Boucicault was an actor and a sensation dramatist who made it fashionable to exploit the Victorian theatre's technical resources for thrills and spectacle. (He collaborated with Reade in *Foul Play*, exposing malpractice in insurance of ships but concentrating mainly on sensational stage effects, first produced at the Holborn Theatre, 28 May 1868.) Boucicault laid heavy hands on Elizabeth Gaskell's 'tragedy'; it is as well that she was dead before it was produced. The play is centred on the romance between Jem Starkee (*sic*) and Jane Learoyd (Jem and Mary in the novel). Its climax is the scene in the telegraph office in which the wonderful invention is used to recall the sailor, John Reilly, prove Jem's alibi and so save his life. The Manchester workmen and their troubles simply provide background and, in Act II Scene 2, when the millhands are demanding the release of their delegates from prison, Jem denounces violence, gives them all the money he can spare, and remarks, 'Poor lads, how bright their sorrow seems beside mine.' The plot, like that of *Mary Barton*, is complicated. Noah, Jane's father, shoots and kills the manufacturer Readley when he overhears him offering to abandon prosecution against Noah for plotting to fire mills if Jane will be his mistress. The wadding used in the pistol is a letter addressed to Jem, which throws suspicion on him. In Act III all the millhands go back to work to show that they have no part in the murder. Noah goes crazy, and from his ravings Jane learns that he is guilty. Helped by Moneypenny, the crusty old lawyer with a kind heart, she telegraphs asking John Reilly to come back and give evidence at the trial. John's Captain will not allow him to leave the ship, but he jumps overboard and arrives at the court in time to clear Jem. The play ends in rejoicing, Noah and his guilt forgotten.

Dickens read *The Long Strike* as it was being constructed. On 4 September 1866 he wrote to Fechter, the producer: 'This morning ᴵ received the play to the end of the telegraph scene, and I have since read it twice.' He then goes on to counter two criticisms evidently made by Boucicault as to how the play was shaping:

I clearly see the *ground* of Mr. Boucicault's two objections; but I do not see their *force*.

First, as to the writing. If the characters did not speak in a terse and homely way, their idea and language would be inconsistent with their dress and station, and they would lose, as characters, before the audience. The dialogue seems to be exactly what is wanted. Its simplicity . . . is often very effective; and throughout there is an honest, straight-to-the-purpose ruggedness in it, like the real life and the real people.

Secondly, as to the absence of the comic element, I really do not see how more of it could be got into the story, and I think Mr. Boucicault underrates the pleasant effect of his own part [Johnny Reilly]. The very notion of a sailor, whose life is not among those little courts and streets, and whose business does not lie with the monotonous machinery, but with the four wild winds, is a relief to me in reading the play. I am quite confident of its being an immense relief to the audience when they see the sailor before them, with an entirely different bearing, action, dress, complexion even, from the rest of the men. I would make him the freshest and airiest sailor that ever was seen; and through him I can distinctly see my way out of 'the Black Country' into clearer air. (I speak as one of the audience, mind.) . . . I feel Widdicomb's part [H. Widdicombe played Moneypenny, the lawyer] (which is charming, and ought to make the whole house cry) most agreeable and welcome, much better than any amount in such a story, of mere comicality. (Nonesuch *Letters*, iii. 482 f.)

This letter shows Dickens's tact and sensitivity to theme by his resistance to the apparent suggestion that the Manchester people should speak 'elevated' language, and by his objection to the introduction of gratuitous comic action and by-play into the drama. But it seems extraordinary that he should think the play's dialogue 'terse and homely', having 'honest, straight-to-the-purpose ruggedness in it, like the real life and the real people'.[2] The following is an example of the dialogue in Act III, Scene 2:

Maggie . . . I don't mind throwin' a brick through a pane o' glass or destroyin' a man's jacket in a nob stick [*sic*], but when it comes to shootin' or stabin', I don't hand wi' thee. For my part, I be going back to work, whether I get paid or not.

Omnes So be I—so be I!

Tom o' Bills and 4 Male Operatives enter.

Jack (o' Bobs) Where be thee going, lads?

Tom We be going back to work. The strike be at an end, and we be main glad of it. Come, lads, let's to work. (Exit all but Jack)

(*French's Standard Drama*, No. CCCLX, New York, p. 24.)

[2] Compare the impoverished language representing the poor working-man's speech in Dickens's 'A Poor Man's Tale of a Patent' (*Reprinted Pieces*, pp. 461–6). We are never told what it is that the man has invented; and F. Walker's illustration, showing the man and his wife looking at the invention, sets it half off the page and makes it equally indistinct. Dickens is concerned not with the machine and the man's craftsmanship, but with the frustration and pathos of the situation.

This speech, without rhythm or vigour, was never spoken in Lancashire or anywhere else. That Dickens should think it the language spoken by 'real people' shows his complete ignorance of the speech of the Other Nation in manufacturing towns, as is obvious from the language spoken by Stephen Blackpool in *Hard Times*. His comment also shows how melodrama—and its stereotypes repeated in the novel—ratified prejudice, returned to the audience the ideas it wanted to find even as it supported the emotions it wanted to indulge. Dickens thinks that Lancashire mill-hands speak like the puppet characters of *The Long Strike*, and therefore for him their speech is 'real'. Similarly, Margaret Oliphant in her essay on Dickens describes John Browdie in *Nicholas Nickleby* as 'a true Yorkshire original' (*Blackwood's Edinburgh Magazine*, 77 (1855), 457) not because she knows Yorkshiremen but because Browdie accords with her idea of them; and the *Saturday Review* writes of Reade's miners in the Australian gold fields in *It is Never Too Late to Mend* 'Mr. Reade makes his miners talk as miners would talk' because the reviewer feels they ought to talk like this (*Saturday Review*, 2 (1856), 361). The same review makes a very revealing comment on Jacky, the stagey aborigine who befriends George in Australia, 'Although we may not have known what an Australian savage was before we read the book, we are sure, as we read, that Jacky is a faithful sketch.'

Characteristically, Dickens is confident that the audience watching *The Long Strike* will welcome 'relief' from the people in the 'little courts and streets' of Manchester; the sailor offers a welcome 'way out of "the Black Country" into clearer air'. This ratifies my argument in Chapter 3 that Dickens does not 'know' Coketown but, rather, he escapes from it, sometimes in obvious physical images of smoke and oil, sometimes in images more directly expressing his own prejudices, like that of the red and black painted savage, sometimes in tableaux of pathos and guilt, like the death of Stephen Blackpool.

Often, as in the incidents in *The Long Strike* when the mill-hands return to work to show that they have no part in the murder, plot deflects attention from the real issues of the lives of the Other Nation, or to further a specious argument about them. For example, Alton's love for Lillian is seen as a delusion which is paralleled by his delusion of the Charter. Christian

Socialism, in the person of Eleanor, is the philosophy which will dispel both delusions. Fiction is used to simplify and distort a serious actuality. It is a device much used by nineteenth-century novelists anxious to demonstrate Carlyle's insistence that the lower classes are foolish, wayward, and requiring strong guidance from above. In Mary Howitt's *Little Coin, Much Care* (1842), on the poverty of the Nottingham lace-workers, Ford attends an open air meeting of the People's Association on the Forest where he contracts rheumatic fever and all his wife's savings disappear in doctor's bills. This fictional disaster is used to demonstrate the evil of Trades Unions. Similarly, Jonathan Rutherford in *Jane Rutherford; or, The Miners' Strike* is unable to prolong the strike because Lord Westerland, the coal-owner, sees to it that the men get the wage increases promised them, and is refused employment because of his reputation as an agitator. In vengeance he cuts the rope of the mine's winding apparatus and twelve people are killed as a group of men descend. ('Zum villain, zum villain worze nor the devil himself huz dun thiz', remarks one of the bystanders.) Nothing is proved against him, but he is forced to emigrate and eventually dies raving of his evil deed and terrified at the thought of divine retribution after death. A sensational woodcut of the deathbed accompanies the narrative (the *True Briton*, 2 (13 October 1853)). This lurid fiction is meant to prove the iniquity of Trade Union activity. In *Demos* Gissing later uses the fiction of Mutimer's unexpected fortune and his consequent selfishness and irresponsibility to blacken the Other Nation's attempts to better itself by political action.

The stereotypes of novel and melodrama encouraged evasion of the Other Nation most of all in the demands of the 'happy ending', what George Eliot described as 'the vulgar coercion of conventional plot', adding that 'effective truths' in art required freedom from it (see 'Leaves from a Notebook', *Essays* ed. T. Pinney, p. 301, and the *Westminster Review*, 65 (1856), 626). Reade succumbs to this vulgar coercion when he turns his reader away from the horrors of the Gaol to the 'pure air among the daisies' and the happy ending of the love affair between George and Susan. As *Mary Barton* dwindles into a conventional love story the novel has an appropriately conventional ending— the emigration of Jem and Mary to Canada. Even here, Elizabeth

Gaskell does something to make the stereotype an organic part of the novel by making the emigration the result of the coldness with which Jem is treated by his former workmates after his trial for murder. The concern with social pressures continues even until the happy ending. But, despite this, the ending of *Mary Barton* is stereotyped and reflects contemporary ideas about the alleviation of poverty—emigration was believed by many to offer a new life to the poor, but by 1848 it had become a cliché of social thinking. J. A. V. Chapple, in his reprint of Elizabeth Gaskell's story 'Life in Manchester: Libbie Marsh's Three Eras', first published in *Howitt's Journal of Literature and Popular Progress*, 5, 12, and 19 June 1847, points out the close resemblance between her description of Jem's life in Canada and the engraving 'The Emigrant' (see his reprint for The Lancashire and Cheshire Antiquarian Society, Manchester, 1968 and my Plate 46, which appeared in *Howitt's Journal*, 12 June 1847). The lifelessness of her description suggests mechanically repeated stereotype rather than an imaginative response to actuality. Kingsley uses the same solution at the end of *Alton Locke*, although Alton's case has the added appeal of pathos, for he dies within sight of America. Kingsley was dismayed when he heard that Walter Cooper, one of the men on whom Alton is based, was thinking of emigrating to America: 'I am quite shocked about Cooper . . . and shall at the risk of rudeness, write my whole heart to [him]' (unpublished letter, probably 5 July 1849, to Ludlow. R. B. Martin, 'Correspondence of Charles Kingsley', p. 158). Martin suggests that Kingsley might have been instrumental in preventing Cooper from emigrating. A situation acceptable as social policy (in which he supported Sidney Godolphin Osborne who helped many rural labourers to emigrate) and as an ending to his fiction about the Other Nation, dismayed him when it involved someone he knew personally.

The emigration literary stereotype, like its counterpart in social philosophy, evaded rather than confronted the problem of poverty. *Yeast* lacks the stereotyped happy ending but is equally evasive. It is a very muddled ending, partly because Kingsley had ideas, later abandoned, of continuing the novel (see Charles Kingsley, *Letters and Memories*, i. 219), partly because he was under pressure from Parker, publisher of *Fraser's*, because readers were protesting at the attacks on the Game Laws, and partly because he was ill and had to hurry the book to its close. The farm labourers' hovels and low wages are abandoned in favour of Barnakill's vague visions of utopia.[3]

The strength of contemporary pressure upon novelists to supply a happy ending can be gauged by the editorial note to the parody of *Hard Times* 'Hard Times Refinished', which appeared in *Our Miscellany* (new edition, 1857, pp. 142–56) and which P. A. W. Collins (*Dickens, The Critical Heritage*, 1971, p. 309) ascribes to one of the editors, Robert Brough:[4]

[3] Barnakill's strange name appears first in the one volume edition of *Yeast*, 1851. In the serialized novel in *Fraser's Magazine* July–December 1848 he has no name. The 1851 edition adds that he saved Claude Mellot's life during the 1830 Paris Revolution: ' "he picked me out of a gutter, a boy of fifteen, with a musket-ball through my body; mended me, and sent me to a painter's studio" ' (p. 317). There are important differences between the original ending in *Fraser's* and in the 1851 version. In *Fraser's* Argemone, watched over by Lancelot, has a death-bed vision in which she chants Biblical prophecies—

' "He shall judge the people with judgment, and the poor with righteousness."

"He shall save the children of the needy, and break in pieces the oppressor." ...

"For he shall deliver the needy when he crieth; the poor also, and him that hath no helper!" ...

I have bought the vision with my life-blood, for myself, and for you. Every letter of it will be fulfilled, Beloved! will you not bear your part in the glorious battle?' (*Fraser's*, 38 (1848), 704.)

This is omitted in 1851. In the serialized version there is hope for Lancelot alone to find 'some everlasting rock-stratum whereon to build, utterly careless what the building may be ... provided God and Nature help him in its construction' (ibid., p. 711). Yet between him and the promised land 'are waste, raging waters, foul mud-banks, thick with dragons and syrens'. Tregarva has gone away and 'is fast turning into a Chartist lecturer'. He will go on to be a field-preacher and probably a Mormonite! The 1851 ending is amplified by discussions between Lancelot and his cousin Luke to demonstrate the folly of Roman Catholicism.

[4] Brough was an outspoken Radical, who dared to advocate revolution—see his dedication of his *Songs of the Governing Classes* (1855), poems which, he wrote in the preface, express his 'deeply-rooted belief that to the institution of aristocracy in this country ... is mainly attributable all the political injustice ... and moral debasement, we have to deplore'. One of his poems, 'The Marquis of Carabas', ends:

> They've got him in—he's gone to vote
> Your rights and mine away;
> Perchance our lives, should men be scarce,
> To fight his cause for pay.
> We are his slaves! he owns our lands,
> Our woods, our seas, and skies;
> He'd have us shot like vicious dogs,
> Should we in murm'ring rise!
> Chapeau bas!
> Chapeau bas!
> Gloire au Marquis de Carabas!

'the striking want of poetical justice in the usually-received termination of this otherwise excellent story, wherein none of the good people were made happy, and the wicked were most inadequately punished, had caused the author to tremble for his popularity among the female portion of the community—

Carabas is a character in Perrault's tale 'Chat botté', 'Puss in Boots', and the subject of a song by Pierre-Jean de Béranger (1780–1857), 'Le Marquis de Carabas', November 1816, a satire on the arrogance of a reinstated French aristocrat. Brough's poem is an adaptation of Béranger's, using not only the title but the refrain; this is also quoted at the end of Bk. II, ch. 1 of Disraeli's *Vivian Grey*, in which the Marquis de Carabas is a wealthy aristocrat ambitious for political power.

Another of the *Songs* is 'Lord Charles Cleverly', a wicked description of Disraeli's enlightened aristocrat:

> Lord Charles is the hope of the Peerage;
> No fears of a wreck need o'erwhelm
> The passengers down in the steerage,
> With men like Lord Charles at the helm.
> A publisher's shop full of blue books
> Is this budding senator's head;
> He has also written a few books,
> Much noticed, and some of them read . . .
> To him, legislation's a pleasure;
> (Though by it so many are bored!)
> Last session, he brought in a measure
> To have the old Maypoles restored;
> And, then, with the people so kindly
> He mixes—their meetings attends—
> Advises them not to rush blindly
> In face of their masters and friends!—
> . . . His charity, too, so disarming
> To malice—he's founded some schools,
> (The costume and badge are most charming!)
> Himself, he has framed all the rules.
> With scriptural texts (*his* selecting)
> The walls round are tastily hung:
> Content and submission directing,
> As virtues most fit for the young . . .
> 'Tis cheering and really delightful
> To see such a promising gem—
> A Lord—of Democracy frightful,
> The tide, who has talent to stem!
> The Peers, they say, care but for plenty,
> And won't even work for their pelf!
> Here's one who has scarcely turned twenty,
> Will manage the nation himself!

Brough's co-editor of *Our Miscellany* was Edmund Yates who, in his autobiography, wrote of *Songs of the Governing Classes*, 'it had scarcely any sale, and has been un-procurable for many years . . . it was a very remarkable production; but neither its sentiments nor its statements would bear analysis, and its teachings were dangerous and uncalled for' (*Edmund Yates: his Recollections and Experiences*, i. 316).

who, it is well known, will stand no liberties of that description'.[5]

Evidently Dickens felt it inappropriate to end the novel with the stereotype of happy marriage and cosy contentment concluding *Oliver Twist* or *The Chimes*. He was moving away from the idea that social evil can be forgotten if the evil characters are punished and the good rewarded to a more profound conception of evil existing in society itself. The lack of happy ending to *Hard Times* must have contributed to the critics' nostalgic lament for the congenial amusement of *Pickwick* (see Margaret Oliphant's 'Charles Dickens' in *Blackwood's Edinburgh Magazine* 77 (April 1855), or E. B. Hamley's 'Remonstrance with Dickens', *Blackwood's*, 81 (April 1857)). Rachael's love is unfulfilled because Stephen dies; Louisa remains unmarried. Nevertheless, Mr Sleary appears, like an asthmatic Pickwick with one roving eye, to act the good fairy and prevent Tom from having to suffer his crime's legal consequences. And, in its own way, the novel's conclusion is just as evasive as that of *The Chimes* or *Oliver Twist*. Louisa has

happy Sissy's happy children loving her; all children loving her; she, grown learned in childish lore; thinking no innocent and pretty fancy ever to be despised; trying hard to know her humbler fellow-creatures, and to beautify their lives of machinery and reality with those imaginative graces and delights without which the heart of infancy will wither up, the sturdiest physical manhood will be morally stark death, and the plainest national prosperity figures can show, will be the Writing on the Wall. (Bk. III, ch. 9.)

Ostensibly Dickens is advocating the life-giving Imagination of the Romantics. This passage reveals it instead to be Fancy, the associative faculty which plays with images and provides ephemeral amusement but, as Keats says in 'Ode to the Nightingale', 'cheats' and 'deceives' leaving emptiness and desolation. Here 'pretty fancy' has to 'beautify' 'machinery and reality'—it is applied to them, like paint, from without. The imagination does not 'seize upon' machinery and reality to make them 'truth', to use Keats's phrase, as Van Gogh responded to the worker at his loom, or the Oldham Weaver to his destitution, to

---

[5] For melodrama's insistence on a cosy happy ending see Frederick Fox Cooper's dramatization of *Hard Times* (done without Dickens's permission or approval) at the Strand Theatre in August 1854. In this version the hardness of the times is mitigated by Stephen's marriage with Rachael (his drunken wife forgotten), Louisa's return to Bounderby and the discovery that Tom, after all, did not steal the money. (See Malcolm Morley, '*Hard Times* on the Stage', the *Dickensian*, 50 (1954), 70.)

make them poetry which extends our consciousness of man and his condition. Imagination, as preached in *Hard Times*, is not the Romantic instrument of perception, 'vision', but of evasion and escape.[6]

The belief that the 'pleasure' of a novel consisted in placating the reader proceeded from a conception of art quite different from the Romantic belief that aesthetic pleasure is the extension and enrichment of the imaginative life. Matthew Arnold's question 'To George Cruikshank On Seeing, in the country, his picture of "The Bottle" ',

> Artist, whose hand, with horror winged, hath torn
> From the rank life of towns this leaf! and flung
> The prodigy of full-blown crime among
> Valleys and men to middle fortune born,

was

> Say, what shall calm us when such guests intrude?

Harriet Beecher Stowe, visiting England in 1853, remarked 'the matter of coziness and home comfort has been so studied, and matured, and reduced to system, that they really have it in their power to effect more, towards making their guests comfortable, than perhaps any other people' (*Sunny Memories of Foreign Lands*, p. 13). The middle-class genius for making itself comfortable had a stultifying effect on its taste in art which debarred anything uncomfortable or challenging, so even if the novel were accepted as 'art' the implications for the majority of middle-class readers would be very different from those for George Eliot, upon whose thought and art Wordsworth had a profound effect. In 1853 the reviewer in the *North American Review* deplored fiction 'with a purpose' of the kind which I have been discussing and declared that it had parted company from 'Beauty':

It were folly to deny that the novel has become more *respectable* in its modern form; we say only that it is less *pleasing*. It has not attempted to stem the utilitarian current of the time, like painting and sculpture, and music—(would we could add poetry, but that, alas! has become didactic, in order that it may be read)—Painting, Sculpture, and Music—blessings on them for standing proudly up, unmodified by all the press of the world-tendencies—unaccommodated to the encroachments of vulgarity,

[6] For a study of the meanings of Fancy and of its divorce from feeling in *Hard Times*, see David Sonstroem, 'Fettered Fancy in *Hard Times*', *Publications of the Modern Language Association of America*, 84 (1969), 520–9.

however specious or popular—faithful witnesses to the high uses of Beauty!
Fiction has confessed its inferiority as an art; it has sought not to lead, but
to follow; not to inspire, but to persuade. It no longer claims to have an
end within itself; it labors, and to an ultimate purpose. (76 (1853), 109.)

Art should be above the mundane affairs of life. The reviewer
describes his journey from

> Italy, where Art has been the handmaid of beauty, elegance, and grandeur,
> till it seems to the delighted traveller vexing and vulgar to be obliged to
> devote part of every precious day to eating and sleeping,—into Holland,
> where the exquisite skill of Teniers and his compeers has been expended
> upon objects so mean and unpleasing that, if they came in our way in real
> life, the first thought would be a speedy retreat. To exchange the Trans-
> figuration for Boors drinking—the Madonna della Seggiola for Paul Potter's
> Bull—the Apollo for the Subject for Dissection,—what perfection of execu-
> tion would console us? Nay, the very perfection with which these mean
> and graceless things are rendered, added to our vexation in contemplating
> them, for it was just so much deducted from the illustration of the true
> and ennobling realm of Art. (Ibid., pp. 104 f.)

It was against such criticism that George Eliot wrote Chapter
17 of *Adam Bede* in which she agrees that the artist should paint
madonnas but urges that his range of objects should include the
ordinary and the ugly, the 'old women scraping carrots'. In the
passage from the *North American Review* the aesthetic pleasure
which the Romantics found in the sensuous apprehension of
people and things, in which the imaginative life is extended and
found 'pleasurable' in the sense of satisfying and invigorating, is
reduced to approving recognition of agreeable situations.[7] In a
sense, all the novelists at the centre of my discussion challenge
this view of beauty and art. As Kingsley wrote to Fanny after
S.G.O. had introduced him to the horrors of life in rural Dorset,
'I will never believe that a man has a real love for the good and
beautiful, except he attacks the evil and the disgusting the
moment he sees it! . . . It is very easy to turn our eyes away
from ugly sights, and so consider ourselves refined. The refined
man to me is he who cannot rest in peace with a coal mine, or a
factory, or a Dorsetshire peasant's house near him, in the state

---

[7] See Ruskin's comment on John Brett's 'Val d'Aosta': 'here . . . we have by help
of art, the power of visiting a place, reasoning about it, and knowing it, just as if we
were there . . . standing before this picture is just as good as standing on that spot in
Val d'Aosta, so far as gaining of knowledge is concerned; and perhaps in some degree
pleasanter, for it would be very hot on that rock today, and there would probably be
a disagreeable smell of Juniper plants growing on the slopes above' (*Works*, xiv. 234).

in which they are.' (Quoted R. B. Martin, *The Dust of Combat*, p. 59.) Brave words. But pressure of contrary opinion was strong and helps to explain why those who depicted the Other Nation in the 1840s and 1850s, and those who criticized their representations, so often stopped at the revulsion caused by dirty, perhaps diseased, bodies and smelly habitations; dramatized the personal discomfort and the horror they felt, and used them to support arguments for action to alleviate such circumstances, but penetrated no further into the lives of those living in such conditions. Dickens's Coketown is bred of this kind of reaction; as is Disraeli's Marney and Wodgate; Kingsley's Ashy and Bermondsey. And in all these descriptions the 'refinement' which decreed that certain subjects were 'unmentionable' discouraged direct representation. For example, the *North British Review*, 15 (May 1851), reviewing a batch of books including Chadwick's *Report* said that England must demonstrate the practical effect of her boasted civilization by supplying the needs of an increasing population and by cleansing 'from her fair face such plague-spots as we have been—not describing, for too many of them are past description, but—hinting at, as delicately as the nature of the subject will allow' (p. 252). If a serious review discussing a scientific survey of the Other Nation's habitations were so inhibited, far more were the novels, aiming at middle-class readers of whom a large proportion were women.

Kingsley himself found *The Tenant of Wildfell Hall* and *Shirley* 'coarse' before he knew the identity of the authors (see R. B. Martin, *The Dust of Combat*, p. 108). It was a charge often levelled at Charlotte Brontë. J. Cordy Jeaffreson wrote of her, in his discussion of *Jane Eyre*, 'she acquired from her companions a coarse, as well as a vigorous vocabulary. She thought of things not positively unchaste—but such as no delicate woman nurtured in refined society would like to acknowledge she had considered.' (*Novels and Novelists, from Elizabeth to Victoria*, 1858, ii. 300.)

The frustration of a writer who wanted to be both a serious artist and a popular novelist in such a climate of opinion is expressed by Dickens in a letter to Forster, a year after *Hard Times*: 'Don't think it a part of my despondency about public affairs, and my fear that our national glory is on the decline, when I say that mere form and conventionalities usurp, in

English art, as in English government and social relations, the place of living force and truth.' (Quoted Forster's *Life*, ii. 191.)

Many critics found ideal artistic refinement in Classical art, expressive of a culture thought to be the traditional equipment of the gentleman. The writer in the *North American Review* who was so upset by the Dutch painters, looked back with regret to 'Italy, where Art has been the handmaid of beauty, elegance, and grandeur'. This debate between the ideal and the real lasted throughout the century and in the 1840s and 1850s many of those who were striving to make 'real life' the artist's subject succumbed to falsifying idealization which was not confined to the depiction of heroines, discussed above. Dickens, who in the preface to the 1841 edition of *Oliver Twist* attacked the false glamour of Gay's and Ainsworth's criminals and insisted, in the preface to *Bleak House*, that his romance was that of 'familiar things', was upset by Millais's early PRB picture 'Christ in the House of his Parents' (1849), and found his depiction of the Holy Family 'vulgar'. (See his attack on the painting in *Household Words* (1 (1850), 265 f.) For Dickens, and for many of his contemporaries, religious experience had to be separated from ordinary life and expressed in conventional stereotyped images—the angels who carry Little Nell to heaven are evidently first cousins to the Angel of Charity. He was outraged that the painter could depict the Mother of God as a woman to be seen in the poor streets of London. Alan Bowness has suggested that the outcry against the painting was primarily a class reaction (see 'Art and Society in England and France in the Mid-Nineteenth Century: Two Paintings Before the Public', *Transactions of the Royal Historical Society*, 22 (1972), 119-39); certainly Dickens's gibe of vulgarity emphasizes the social conventions which sustained the artistic conventions of the period, even for one of its most original writers and one who generally disliked Classical art and culture for its pretensions and remoteness. In *Hard Times* his satire of Mrs Sparsit's snobbery and deathly formality is expressed in her 'Coriolanean nose'.

Clough, using architectural metaphors, congratulated the novelist on his attempt to express the real rather than the ideal: 'The novelist does try to build us a real house to be lived in; and this common builder, with no notion of the orders [the Classical orders of architecture], is more to our purpose than the student of ancient art who proposes to lodge us under an Ionic portico. We are, unhappily, not gods, not even marble statues.' ('Recent English Poetry', *North American Review*, 77 (1853), 3 f.) But the tendency towards idealization and the heroic gesture associated with Classical sculpture is so strong that even when he urges the poet to look for his subject among the urban poor (as Mackaye urged Alton to do) he arrays them inappropriately in the garb of conventional Classical art, like Disraeli parading his personified abstractions at the end of the detailed description of Marney:

There are moods when one is prone to believe that, in these last days, no longer by 'clear spring or shady grove,' no more upon any Pindus or Parnassus, or by the side of any Castaly, are the true and lawful haunts of the poetic powers: but, we could believe it, if anywhere, in the blank and desolate streets, and upon the solitary bridges of the midnight city, where Guilt is, and wild Temptation, and the dire Compulsion of what has once been done—there, with these tragic sisters around him, and with Pity also, and pure Compassion, and pale Hope, that looks like Despair, and Faith in the garb of Doubt, there walks the discrowned Apollo, with unstrung lyre; nay, and could he sound it, those mournful Muses would scarcely be able as of old, to respond and 'sing in turn with their beautiful voices'. (p. 4.)

With a similar irony, the early PRB insistence on fidelity to the actuality of detail is at times combined inappropriately with the heroic gesture of the Classical painting they criticized, as in Ford Madox Brown's 'Work' (1852–65). This is the graphic equivalent to George Eliot's idealization of the working man in *Felix Holt*. Brown's painting can be compared with John Tupper's discussion 'The Subject in Art' in the first and second issues of the PRB journal *The Germ* (January and March 1850), in which he urges the painter to find his subject in his own period but offers, as the province of 'Fine Art', subjects traditionally those of the Classical epic which 'excite the activity of men's rational and benevolent powers . . . all subjects from such parts of history as are morally or intellectually instructive or attractive' (no. 1, p. 18). It could be Sir Philip Sidney's definition of the epic in 1583: 'not only a kind, but the best and most accomplished kind of poetry. For, as the image of each action stirreth and instructeth the mind, so the lofty image of such worthies most inflameth the mind with desire to be worthy, and informs with counsel how to be worthy.'

Moreover, in the Victorian period there is a close relationship between melodramatic gesture and heroic Classical idealization. This can be seen in Doré's illustration to Hood's 'Bridge of Sighs' (see Plate 47). The picture is the exact graphic equivalent to Clough's 'solitary bridges of the midnight city, where Guilt is, and wild Temptation'. Treated in this way, the Other Nation was inflated beyond all recognition.

Carlyle, amplifying the Romantic doctrine of the 'vision' which proceeds from intense sensuous experience of environment and society, insisted on the essential 'truth' of Shakespeare's plays and distinguished this from verisimilitude—'Are these dramas of his not verisimilar only, but true; nay, truer than reality itself, since the essence of unmixed reality is bodied forth in them under more expressive symbols?' (*Works*, vi. 61.) Here he uses 'reality' to mean 'actuality'. Accuracy of representation subserves the greater artistic purpose of the essential truth about human feelings and the human condition in these particular terms, just as Turner's acute perception of sea, light and ship in 'Slavers throwing overboard the Dead and Dying—Typhon coming on' (exhibited at the Royal Academy Exhibition, 1840; see catalogue of the Royal Academy exhibition 1974-5, 'Turner 1775-1851', no. 518) subserves his vision of natural and human energy, the latter including both endeavour and resource in the face of the elements; and man's inhumanity to man in his greed for gain. The immediate cause of the painting was probably the publication, in 1839, of the second edition of Thomas Clarkson's *History of the Slave Trade* which included the story of the slave ship 'Zong' whose captain in 1783 ordered his cargo of slaves, dying of an epidemic, to be thrown overboard so that insurance, payable for loss at sea, could be claimed. (See Turner catalogue, pp. 144 f. and 188 f.) But the picture can be seen as a great imaginative evocation of contemporary society's rejection of the Other Nation. It records a terrible deed done for money. The quotation accompanying the entry of the picture in the Royal Academy catalogue, 1840, is from Turner's 'Fallacies of Hope':

> Aloft all hands, strike the top-masts and belay;
> Yon angry setting sun and fierce-edged clouds
> Declare the Typhon's coming.

Before it sweep your decks, throw overboard
The dead and dying—n'er heed their chains.
Hope, Hope, fallacious Hope!
Where is thy market now?

These lines refer the painting to the wider theme of contemporary competitive society, the scramble for existence heedless of those weaker or more encumbered, which is the context of the divided Nations in the novels I have been discussing. Turner's ironic reference to Hope as a marketable commodity reflects on the commercial society which puts human life below its insurance value. The column of light from top to bottom of the painting is a brilliant metaphoric evocation of the Two Nations because it emphasizes the inexorable movement of the lurching ship, intent on its own safety, away from the drowning slaves. In a moment of time it suggests the process of this society, its becoming as well as its being, which Lukács sees as the province of the great novelists: 'The essential aim of the novel is the representation of the way society moves.' (*The Historical Novel*, p. 144.) Nor is this division heavy-handed and literal, the ship on one side and all the slaves on the other, rather the ship's movement particularly exposes the fate of the group in the bottom right-hand corner, separated from the ship by the path of the sun. The lurid sky, a closely observed natural phenomenon, also suggests impending divine judgement. The association of slaves with the English poor was common; as we have seen, when Ashley wanted an image to describe the lives of children working in the mines, he referred to the African slave trade. Turner's painting is the pictorial expression of Cobbett's 'masters and slaves' or Carlyle's 'Dandies and Poor Slaves', those early metaphors of the Two Nations with which I began this book. And its aesthetic appeal and moral statement are indivisible because recognition of the moral challenge depends on response to the aesthetic pleasure.

Carlyle believed that 'all true Works of Art' were symbols of intrinsic meaning, 'in them . . . wilt thou discern Eternity looking through Time; the Godlike rendered visible' (*Sartor Resartus*, Bk. III, ch. 3, Carlyle, *Works*, i. 216). He mistrusted fiction but he believed that in fictions shaped from acute observation of contemporary life could be symbolized the essential truths of human existence. In this way the real expressed not an

inappropriate ideal remote from man but one of vital importance to him. (Ruskin said of Turner's 'Slavers', 'Its daring
conception, ideal in the highest sense of the word, is based on
the purest truth, and wrought out with the concentrated knowledge of a life,' Ruskin, *Works*, iii. 572.)

Yeast is heavily indebted to Carlyle, and the mysterious
'prophet' obviously owes much to him. He says: 'Art was never
Art till it was more than Art; that the Finite only existed as a
body of the Infinite; and that the man of genius must first
know the Infinite, unless he wished to become not a poet, but
a maker of idols.' (Ch. 17.)

But often, in the novels I have been discussing, the appearance
and environment of the Other Nation are recorded with detailed
accuracy yet fail to create symbols expressive of the elusive
essential reality. Quentin Bell, discussing Holman Hunt, comments on the disturbing effect of his fidelity to detail combined
with his lack of imagination. Of 'The Triumph of the Innocents'
he writes, 'the very sincerity of Holman Hunt's desire to believe
and the ruthlessness with which he does in fact observe, makes
the failure more painful and more obvious' (*Victorian Artists*,
1967, p. 30). The same is true, in varying degrees, of all the
novels under discussion, apart from *Hard Times*. Despite the
enumeration of factual details in Wodgate, Disraeli lacks the
shaping spirit of the Romantic imagination to give it symbolic
significance revealing the life of the Other Nation; despite his
skill, it remains an aggregate of details. In *Yeast* and *Alton
Locke* there are only fleeting symbolic metaphors based on
observation of landscape—the sparkling water-meadows embodying the deceptive idyll of rural Arcadia or the lowering landscape symbolic of the labourer's desolate life. In *It is Never Too
Late to Mend* Reade fails to sustain the imaginative symbol of
Birmingham Gaol's façade; and Elizabeth Gaskell's failure to use
physical actuality to give metaphoric intensity to her re-creation
of Manchester is partly the reason why she is a very good novelist rather than a great one. Despite her aspirations, her novel
cannot be accounted a 'poem'. But *Hard Times* is full of symbols
expressive of the life of the Other Nation; they are part of the
novel's shorthand. The two main symbols are Coketown, expressive of the arid, mechanical life created for the Other Nation by
the Utilitarians, and the Horse Riding, embodying the health-

giving life of the imagination which Bentham so despised and so conspicuously lacked. Neither has the quality of 'visible embodiment' which Carlyle saw as characteristic of a symbol. The image of the painted savage, denoting the red and black of Coketown, proceeds as I have shown, from prejudice not from penetrating observation. As prejudice it is necessarily limited; in this case, to the grinding routine of factory life to the exclusion of any other aspect. Being Dickens, he represents the deadening monotony in arresting terms which, nevertheless, do less than justice to the actuality they are meant to describe. The 'melancholy-mad elephant' denotes the machinery used by the Coketown factory hands and the monotony and repetitiveness of mechanical labour. Again, it does not result from accurate observation. It suggests a quick glance at the piston of a steam-powered machine. It need not have anything to do with the manufacture of cotton; it could describe the repeated action of a 'donkey' extracting oil from the ground in small quantities. Together with the 'serpents of smoke' which hang over Coketown, Dickens creates from it his own cliché in the novel. The 'keynote' is simply repeated, not developed as a motif. Therefore the book has a pattern but not a structure. Not only does Coketown lack the observed substance of Carlyle's symbols; it fails to embody 'the Infinite'—instead of releasing the reader's imagination in the profundity suggested by the term, preaching what Carlyle calls the 'Gospel of Freedom', Dickens simply establishes a crude and, by 1854, well-worn idea of Benthamism. *Hard Times* is dedicated to Carlyle, and fittingly, for the ideas expressed by its symbols are contained in a sentence or two from his chapter 'Symbols' in *Sartor Resartus* (Bk. III, ch. 3, Carlyle, *Works*, i. 213 f.):

'Fantastic tricks enough man has played, in his time; has fancied himself to be most things . . . but to fancy himself a dead Iron-Balance for weighing Pains and Pleasures on [the reference is to Bentham], was reserved for this his latter era . . . now the Genius of Mechanism smothers him worse than any Nightmare did; till the Soul is nigh choked out of him, and only a kind of Digestive, Mechanic life remains . . .

'Yes, Friends,' elsewhere observes the Professor, 'not our Logical, Mensurative faculty, but our Imaginative one is King over us.'

Fifteen years later a reviewer of J. S. Mill's *Principles of Political Economy* began his essay: 'At the present moment, Political Economy may be considered an unpopular science. Its professors are deemed fair game by all the small wits of every class; and in popular assemblies, abuse of what is termed the *cold-blooded* sect of political economists has become a regular commonplace for vulgar rhetoric.' (*Fraser's Magazine*, 38 (1848), 245.)

I am not denying that Bentham's habit of quantifying society was sinister and dangerous; it left a sorry legacy to our own century. But Dickens's symbol of Coketown lacks substance and conviction because it expresses not experience, observation, and feeling, but only a 'commonplace for vulgar rhetoric'. Throughout the book Dickens repeats it with characteristic energy, but it does not develop and acquire new meaning as the repeated symbol of the leg-iron and file develops in *Great Expectations* (see my essay 'Anti-Mechanism and the Comic in the Writings of Charles Dickens', op. cit., 139 f.), it remains static. By its frequent recurrence it hypnotizes the reader into believing that it represents the essential life of a factory town, but its insistence embodies Dickens's fear of Bentham's philosophy, expressed in well-worn terms, rather than the life of the industrial poor.

Despite Dickens's enjoyment of circuses—Yates said that 'he delighted in the *ir*regular drama, the shows and booths and circuses' (Edmund Yates, op. cit., ii. 108)—and his diligent search for authentic circus talk (see his letter to Mark Lemon 20 February 1854 asking for 'any slang terms among the tumblers and circus-people')—the Horse Riding is obviously inadequate as a symbol of the imaginative life. Thomas Frost quotes the acrobat who pointed out the inaccuracies of Dickens's account (see *Reminiscences of a Country Journalist*, 1886, pp. 152 f.) and although, as Carlyle insisted, verisimilitude is not the truth of 'vision', in this case the inaccuracies are symptomatic of the lack of substance in Dickens's account of the circus. The sense of 'visible embodiment' is lacking. A literary symbol, like a painter's symbol, is most powerful when it re-creates (often with great economy) the substance of an acutely perceived object and then extends its significance. Bunyan's Slough of Despond embodies the inertia of depression because he re-creates the clinging stickiness of the mud and connects it with a spiritual state; barley 'borne on the bier with white and bristly beard' symbolizes old age because Shakespeare has so closely observed and imaginatively re-created a sheaf of barley and found an apt connection between details of its appearance and that of an old man. His apprehension of the physical details of old age, and of the details of harvest which connect with it and illuminate it, transform the cliché of Death the Reaper into a profound truth about man's condition. It is not surprising that Dickens's symbol for the imaginative life is unsatisfying when the novel reduces such life to the dictum 'people muth be amuthed'.

Christopher Ricks has written 'Dickens's knowledge of the truth was deepest when its medium was comicality.' (Review of the Pilgrim *Letters of Charles Dickens*, vol. iii, *Sunday Times* 8 September 1974.) I have shown how Stephen Blackpool is protected from the comedy in *Hard Times*, and how the laboured symbols, Coketown and the Horse Riding, which give the novel its pattern, express little of the life of the poor but, rather, Dickens's satire on Benthamism and his limited ideas on the nature of the imagination. Some of the finest comic symbolic writing in the book is in the first chapter in which the aridity of the educational system (including the training of teachers) is perfectly embodied in Gradgrind:

The scene was a plain, bare, monotonous vault of a schoolroom, and the speaker's square forefinger emphasized his observations by underscoring every sentence with a line on the schoolmaster's sleeve. The emphasis was helped by the speaker's square wall of a forehead . . . The emphasis was helped by the speaker's mouth . . . The emphasis was helped by the speaker's voice . . . The emphasis was helped by the speaker's hair, which bristled on the skirts of his bald head, a plantation of firs to keep the wind from its shining surface, all covered with knobs, like the crust of a plum pie, as if the head had scarcely warehouse-room for the hard facts stored inside.

The repetition is constructive because it embodies the character's essential mental life, whereas the repetitive images of Coketown establish only part of the operatives' lives; the whimsical images of firs and plum pie establish a visual connection between themselves and Gradgrind and a meaningful symbol of his vulnerability—fancy challenges fact despite all prohibitions, fancy (of the proliferating Victorian kind beloved of Dickens and Cruikshank) *will* play on the most forbidding fact. Here Dickens's perception of absurdity and incongruity reveals in Gradgrind the limitations bred by the middle-class will to succeed. And although the fancy *is* whimsical and far removed from the strenuous and life-giving Romantic imagination, the symbol appeals to the reader's creative imagination for it opens up possibilities of comedy and menace in this character. Sinyavsky, defending himself against the charges that he had refused to write Russian propaganda, said at his trial 'It is the nature of a literary image to be complex' (see the *Listener*, 78 (1967), 665). The initial image of Gradgrind has a complexity of implication totally lacking in the repetitive symbols of Coketown and the Horse Riding.

Unsuccessful as these symbols are, they are used to shape the narrative in *Hard Times*. The novel is the most important Victorian literary form because the finest novelists realized that narrative is a profoundly serious art not, as E. M. Forster suggests in his *Aspects of the Novel*, a tedious convention which the novelist must tolerate. Traditional folk-tales, like the gipsies' many stories about Jack, of which Jack the Giant-killer is one, are told so that a close bond is established between narrator and audience; they express the values of the community which creates them—admiration for quick wit, courage, resourcefulness —and help to foster these values. (Frank Kermode, in *The Sense of an Ending*, New York (1967), has examined the relationship between Victorian novels and the values of the society which produced them.) In any novel the reader is aware of a speaking voice, the literary equivalent of the traditional story-teller addressing his group, his community. In these six novels the tone of voice is inevitably middle-class, appealing to middle-class readers to tackle the problem of the Other Nation, because the novel is essentially a middle-class form born of middle-class self-consciousness in the eighteenth century and continuing into the nineteenth when the power, leisure, and prestige of the middle class substantially increased. All these novelists were confronted with the necessity of using middle-class fictions, appealing to middle-class prejudices and social attitudes, to convey the reality of the life of the poor, the Other Nation who, for the most part, did not share these prejudices and social attitudes. So, although there are occasional glimpses of the actuality of the Other Nation, the novels are inevitably what the Victorian middle class thinks and fears of the Other Nation rather than an imaginative re-creation of its life. Their profoundly serious attitude to the novel can be gauged by their efforts to incorporate the new material of the Other Nation into a continuing creative process; in their view the novelist had to deal with the Other Nation because it was a fact of his society. If we judge their novels by the greatest—*War and Peace, Crime and Punishment*—they are failures, but they are vigorous and challenging if at times distorting, and my attempted analysis of their failure has, I hope, revealed some of its reasons and some of the lessons which succeeding writers and artists should learn from them. Their awareness that the serious artist had to concern himself with the Other Nation did not include realization that the new material demanded new forms. For all their interest in narrative they did not, for example, recognize that many of the Other Nation were profoundly skilled in the art—Disraeli uses the woman complaining of truck to the Midland Mining Commission but he does not learn from her how to tell her tale; Elizabeth Gaskell responds to the desperate plight which bred 'The Oldham Weaver' but she does not imitate its wit or its metaphoric intensity. All these writers, however fleetingly, had some comprehension of the actuality of the Other Nation, and as soon as they combine it with the fanciful conventions of tortuous love stories and sensational events these conventions are shown up for the pasteboard they are. Reality does not only 'strike to the soul', it also kicks to bits the flimsy trellises and the paper roses of soothing make-believe. Moreover, their own social class, for whom they wrote, prejudiced them against seeing the reality of the work processes in which those of the Other Nation who were lucky enough to have work were engaged. Van Gogh's direct apprehension of the reality of weaving or digging or carrying coal, that this involvement in labour is of itself poetic and dramatic because it engages man's or woman's skill, resource, or strength and does not need the decoration of a love affair or a sensational event to make it interesting, is almost impossible to a class whose ideal is either the achievement of leisure to cultivate refinement and sensibility, or the relinquishing of manual labour in order to achieve command over others. Trollope's popularity waned more than ever when his posthumous *Autobiography* revealed that he had worked like a craftsman at his novels. Van Gogh, on the other hand, believed that 'A painter should live like a workman'. The idea that work has to be deplored or decorated to be included in 'art' has

resulted in the modern division between 'art' and 'documentary', seen particularly in film and television, and only now
beginning to close. It starts in the Victorian belief that novels
dealing with the actuality of the Other Nation should be 'artless'. The lack of 'art' was, according to *Fraser's Magazine*
(42 (1850), 574), 'the distinctive mark of modern fiction'—
'leaving art to shift for itself, it seeks to express and embody
what may be described as the wants and yearnings of the time'.
Kingsley defiantly set the tone in the heading to the first instalment of *Yeast* (*Fraser's Magazine*, 38 (1848), 102): 'N.B.—
This work is composed according to no rules of art whatsoever,
except the cardinal one,—That the artist knowing best what he
wants to say, is also likely to know best how to say it.'

This is a courageous and understandable rejection of the
idealizing art of the kind demanded by the writer in the *North
American Review*, but the lack of confidence that 'art' could
deal with the actuality of the Other Nation, or that the life of
the poor contained within itself both poetry and drama, led to
the 'oratory', to use Carlyle's word, which is so evident in *Yeast*
and *Alton Locke*, in *Sybil* and *It is Never Too Late to Mend*
and, to a lesser degree, in *Hard Times* and *Mary Barton*. Scattered through Carlyle's writing is a discussion of the crisis in the
Romantic imagination which I think is relevant to these novelists' treatment of the poor. On 10 October 1831 Carlyle recorded
in his notebook that his ambition was to 'spread abroad Reverence over the hearts of men'. He asks, 'Is it to be done by Art;
or are men's minds as yet shut to Art, and open only at best to
oratory; not fit for a *Meister*, but only for a better and better
Teufelsdreck'. (*Two Note Books of Thomas Carlyle: From 23d
March 1822 to 16th May 1832*, ed. C. E. Norton, New York,
1898, pp. 203 f.) By 'Reverence' I think he means the joyful recognition of men, objects, environment outside the
artist's individuality but sustaining it which constituted the
prime artistic activity for Wordsworth, Coleridge, and Keats.
But Carlyle doubts if men are now capable of an imaginative
response to the poetic symbolism of Goëthe's *Wilhelm Meister*;
perhaps they can only respond to the harangues of the fictional
Teufelsdröckh in *Sartor Resartus*. When the novelists are dealing with the Other Nation imaginative re-creation often gives
way to enumeration of facts, representation of literal details,

excessive exhortation. And this tendency to exhort rather than to re-create is related to the persistent belief—again evident in Carlyle's writing—that good deeds are superior to great works of art. In the realm of ethics this is a tenable proposition and, ironically, the idea connects with the seriousness with which the novelists regarded their writing; moreover, it is understandable in the work of writers who are trying to influence their society. But for the creating artist the idea is fatal because it destroys his concentration and disturbs his imagination. On the title page of *Mary Barton* Elizabeth Gaskell grasped at the small comfort Carlyle allowed the novelist seeking justification of his craft:

'How knowest thou,' may the distressed Novel-wright exclaim, 'that I, here where I sit, am the Foolishest of existing mortals; that this my Long-ear of a fictitious Biography shall not find one and the other, into whose still longer ears it may be the means, under Providence, of instilling somewhat?' We answer, 'None knows, none can certainly know; therefore, write on, worthy Brother, even as thou canst, even as it is given thee.' (The quotation comes from Carlyle's essay 'Biography', 1832, Carlyle, *Works*, ix. 8.)

And, in her distress at the reception of the book, she comforted herself with a sentence in Carlyle's congratulatory letter to her, ' "May you live long to write good books, or *do silently good actions which in my sight is far more indispensable.*" ' Letter to Miss Lamont, 5 January 1849, *Letters*, p. 70.)

At the end of *Yeast* as it was first serialized, Kingsley attempts to defend the novel from the charge of formlessness by arguing that it has to be completed by the reader's own life: 'If any reader shall complain that I have left Lancelot's history unfinished, let me entreat him manfully to set about finishing his own history—a far more important one to him than Lancelot's.' (*Fraser's Magazine*, 38 (1848), 710.) This is repeated, with slight alteration, in the 1851 edition.

The lack of confidence that fiction can be 'worthwhile' unless it breeds an immediate practical result disturbs the concentration on the Other Nation which could be hoped for in the social and artistic climate of the period and, paradoxically, shows that these novels to some extent share the utilitarian temper of the time. The Romantic belief in the artist's appeal to the imagination, the source of moral life, has become the crude desire to exhort to moral action. The Romantic conception of art feeding life has become the idea that life should supplant art.

In the treatment of the Other Nation in all these novels there

are fitful glimpses—and a more sustained vision in *Mary Barton*
—of the truth expressed by Margaret Oliphant in her essay on
Dickens: 'the art which works its results by means of common
men and women, the ordinary everyday creatures, who are
neither odd nor eccentric, is certainly the highest art' (op. cit.,
p. 457).

But, for the social and aesthetic reasons I have examined,
none of them fully achieved it.

6
THE POET AND THE MAN OF SCIENCE

Poetry is the breath and finer spirit of all knowledge; it is the impassioned expression which is in the countenance of all Science. (Wordsworth, Preface to *Lyrical Ballads*, 1800.)

I have quoted at length from these novelists, compared their fiction with its sources to determine its insights, and discussed the efficacy of the literary tool afforded them by the novel in their attempts to re-create the Other Nation in the 1840s and 1850s, because their work exemplifies imaginative writers grappling both with the urgent problems of their society and with the exigencies of a developing literary form. I have tried to provide a better understanding of their work by relating both its content and method to its artistic, intellectual, and social context. In the statistical reports of the 1830s and 1840s which attempted to reveal the facts about contemporary poverty the Benthamite plan of accumulating facts about society, seen as an aggregate of individuals, combined with political economy derived from Adam Smith's science of wealth to produce what Philip Abrams calls 'aggregated data about the circumstances and behaviour of individuals' (*The Origins of British Sociology: 1834-1914*, Chicago and London, 1968, p. 11). So some novelists, notably Kingsley, Disraeli, and Reade, found sources of character and environment in them. Cazamian has argued that the novelists substituted the feeling heart for the cold heads of the political economists, and certainly the novelists sometimes urge this view of themselves, especially Dickens in *Hard Times*. But, as I have tried to show, in these novels imagination based on feeling is an instrument of perception, insight, albeit this imaginative engagement with the poor is rare, and possibly it is more helpful to an understanding of this fiction to see it not as opposed to the Statistical Society of London, for example, but as its imaginative counterpart. Because, in these novelists' representation of the poor, while their weakness is to diminish people to data, they are most powerful and most perceptive when the synthesizing method of the Romantic imagination is combined with the empirical method of the natural and social scientists. Although the novels' arguments are well-worn, some of their images and scenes are revelatory: a flat, desolate landscape peopled only by two children struggling with a frozen turnip-cutter while fat sheep wait for their food; a child, resolute to live, grateful to the factory which provides him with identity and status; a mill-hand's familiar room made desolate by his wife's death, the desolation confirming him in his Chartism; the monotony of a mill-town's streets evoking the relentless demands of industrial routine; a new model prison, impregnable as a medieval fortress. When Romantic response to the sensuous plays on the empirical fact of the poor the result is aesthetically-satisfying 'vision', a revelatory image generating 'knowledge' in the Romantic sense, that is, imaginative understanding.

But the novel is a narrative, and has a beginning, a middle and an end. In the 1840s and 1850s both the nature of the readers' expectations, and the novelists' values and standpoint, made it inevitable that the 'understanding' promoted by imaginative feeling for the poor would be rationalized into argument. Despite the darkness of the poverty they depict, despite the warnings given, all the novels which I discuss are optimistic because the novelists believed that their revelations would dispel ignorance and so effect a reconciliation between the Two Nations. Even *Hard Times* offers a hope that the warning will be heeded; after all, Mr Gradgrind himself experiences a salutary change of heart. Reade's tone implies confidence that the perpetrators of injustice will quail before his onslaught. Kingsley sees Christian Socialism as an effective creed in place of Chartism. Elizabeth Gaskell believes that Christian understanding will reconcile the Two Nations in Manchester. This optimism is characteristic of many contemporary social surveys, and for the same reasons. Abrams points out that the statistical inquiries of the 1830s were based on the belief that 'Conflict had to spring from ignorance or unreason, since it could not spring from real incompatibilities.' (Ibid., p. 9.) The facts, once discovered, necessarily destroyed ignorance and established reason, thereby resolving the conflict. This view was not exclusive to political economists. The early Chartists believed that working-class poverty would be alleviated once Parliament knew the facts. Many of the poor who had nothing to do with political organization thought the same. 'You must just tell the Queen Victoria', said the old Scottish collier-woman to the Sub-Commissioner collecting evidence for the Children's Employment Commission. And with similar optimism the novelists of the 1840s and 1850s popularized the state of the poor.

The novelists also demonstrated how from exploration of the empirical facts of poverty grows concern for the moral state of the individual in the context of society. Abrams, discussing the aims and philosophy of the National Association for the Promotion of Social Science (inaugurated 1856), shows that the social problem of the earliest inquiries and reports soon became a moral problem, and points to the concern with 'poverty as a context for drunkenness, prostitution, depravity'—imaginatively described, for example, in Dickens's 'Gin-Shops' or *Oliver Twist*, or in any of the novels at the centre of this study—with 'poverty as an obstacle to the moral development of the individual' (ibid., p. 37). This increasingly becomes the novelist's subject—it can be seen in Kingsley's concern with Alton's moral regeneration in which he sees salvation rather than in political agitation, or in Reade's conviction that contemporary prisons prevent rather than encourage moral reform. Paralleling the development of contemporary social science, the novel becomes increasingly preoccupied with individual morality in the larger context of society. Abrams points out that one of the social scientist's roles delineated by Lord Brougham in his first presidential address to the National Association in 1857 is that of philosopher generating new understanding of the close-woven mesh of the social network (George Eliot thought the novelist's task the same and used a similar image, the web, to describe society's interrelationships), and that 'the most frequently used units of social analysis in the *Transactions* of the Association are those of the state, the individual (moral or immoral) and occasionally, the classes' (ibid., p. 48). Raymond Williams writes: 'The problem of the knowable community, with its deep implications for the novelist, is . . . clearly a part of the social history of early nineteenth-century England and of the imaginative penetration and recoil which was the creative response.' (*The English Novel. From Dickens to Lawrence*, p. 17.) That novelists did respond creatively to the Other Nation, an undeniable part of their community, I have tried to show while acknowledging the flaws of their novels. After this there is a 'recoil'; the poor recede from the novels of the 1860s and early 1870s in the sense that the physical, urgent confrontation with them is lost, and the plea for compassion on their behalf is no longer a central theme. This can only partly be explained by the social pressures which turned Elizabeth Gaskell's attention to the mill-owners in *North and South*, or by the increasing prosperity of the country. Images of confrontation of the Two Nations or reconciliation between them are superseded by questions of morality, both individual and social, and of the individual's relationships to the society of which he is a part. The eighteenth-century novelists had explored such topics, but they were given a new emphasis in a more detailed social setting, and a new psychological complexity, in the 1860s and 1870s. *Felix Holt* repeats the old stereotype of the savage poor in the Sproxton miners, but Felix himself, however wooden, is a poor man much concerned with questions of individual and social morality. In Dickens's later novels society's interrelatedness helps determine their structure; and poverty poses moral questions—the moral degeneracy of lengthy, corrosive poverty in *Little Dorrit*, the predatory nature of poverty in an acquisitive society in *Our Mutual Friend*.

In the face of the economic depression of the 1870s faith was lost in the remedies of the traditional political economists. Despite Cazamian's pioneering work on the social problem novels of the 1830s and 1840s it has limited value because he shared the early Victorians' optimism in society's inevitable progress towards material and spiritual benefits. Obviously, Perkin is correct in arguing that industrialization caused a general rise in living conditions and quality of life for many during the nineteenth century, yet publications like John Burnett's *Report to the Board of Trade on the Sweating System of the East End of London* (1887) and the *Report of the Select Committee on Sweating* (1888) reveal that tailors and seamstresses were still working long hours in appalling conditions for starvation rates of pay; Charles Booth's *Life and Labour of the People in London* (1889) was undertaken because he could not believe the stories of destitution he had heard, and he found that it was possible for industrious, skilled workmen to be haunted by the spectre of destitution; in the rural areas Joseph Arch, who worked to create the Labourers' Union in 1870, was concerned to better agricultural workers' conditions which had not improved much since Kingsley wrote *Yeast*. The social philanthropy of the National Association was challenged as the franchise was extended, the Independent Labour Party formed and the Other Nation acquired a voice in the legislation intended to alleviate its plight. It is not until the poor become articulate about their exploitation and militant in their claims to a better life that they again become of central interest to the novelists, for example, Hardy, Gissing, Besant, and Morrison.

Dickens shows his imaginative insight into his society in the increasing pessimism of his later novels, darkened by the perception that personal charity and isolated social reforms cannot cure the malaise. Kingsley, on the other hand, while continuing to urge sanitary reform, gradually accepted current optimistic notions of Empire, British supremacy and prosperity. Yet the despair of powerful novels like *Little Dorrit* (immediately following *Hard Times*) and *Our Mutual Friend* (Dickens's last completed novel) also diminishes them, for his later radical insight is not fully integrated into the imaginative world he creates. Arthur Clennam's moral triumph, for instance, depends on the power of private, individual love, as does Bella Wilfer's, and both exist apart from the dark world of the London poor. The personal and the social worlds are divided, not part of the same imaginative vision. Hence the despair, resulting from the realization (also uneasily present in the eulogy on charity in Jerrold's *London*) that traditional charitable philanthropy, of the kind fostered by the National Association, was powerless in the face of such social malaise and such suffering, and that the personal morality, central to Dickens's fictional world, had to be nurtured in isolation from the unjust social structure. This gulf between social reality and the personal morality of a small number of individuals is reflected in many of the debates and political struggles of the later Victorian period. In such ways the work of the social scientist and that of the imaginative artist complement and illuminate each other.

BIBLIOGRAPHY

...al MSS 41297, Kingsley
, Vol. I.
...dditional MSS 42974, Lord Cham-
...erlain's Plays, Vol. CX.
Free Library of Philadelphia, Rare Book
Department, D. Jacques Benoliel Col-
lection, letter from John Overs to
Charles Dickens, 20 July 1840.
Martin, R. B., 'An Edition of the Cor-
respondence and Private Papers of
Charles Kingsley 1819–1856', un-
published D.Phil. dissertation, Uni-
versity of Oxford, 1950.
Oldham Local History Library, The
Rowbottom Diaries, 5 vols., 1787–
1830.
Trinity College Library, Cambridge,
Munby MSS 97, Notebooks 4, 6.

Secondary Sources

Novels

(Dates given are those of first publica-
tion in volume form. Where the edition
quoted in the text is of a later date this
has been indicated in the body of the
book.)
Brooke, H., *The Fool of Quality*, 1766–
70.
Dickens, C., *Bleak House*, 1853.
—, *The Chimes*, 1844.
—, *Dombey and Son*, 1848.
—, *Hard Times*, 1854.
—, *Little Dorrit*, 1857.
—, *Oliver Twist*, 1838.
—, *The Old Curiosity Shop*, 1840.
—, *Sketches by Boz*, 1836–7.
Disraeli, B., *Sybil*, 1845.
Ferrier, S., *Marriage*, 1818.
Frost, T., *Paul the Poacher*, 1848.
Gaskell, E. C., *Mary Barton*, 1848.
—, *North and South*, 1855.
Jerrold, D., *St. Giles and St. James*,
1851.
Kingsley, C., *Alton Locke*, 1850.
—, *Yeast*, 1851.
Mayhew, A., *Paved with Gold*, 1858.
Mayne, F., *Jane Rutherford; or, The
Miners' Strike*, 1854.
Miller, T., *Gideon Giles the Roper*, 1841.
Reade, C., *It is Never Too Late to Mend*,
1856.

Stone, E., *William Langshawe, the Cotton Lord*, 1842.

Broadside Ballads

B.L. *Collection of Ballads, Chiefly printed
in London by Catnach, J. Pitts and
others, mostly between 1800 and
1870, but with a few of earlier date
and with a few prose broadsides. Col-
lected by the Rev. Sabine Baring
Gould. With manuscript indexes.*
B.L. *Collection of Broadsides on Crimi-
nal Trials and Executions 1801–58.*
Birmingham Public Libraries, Local
Studies Department, *Broadsides* (Poli-
tical).
Cambridge University Library, *Ballads*,
Madden Collection, XVIII.
Manchester Central Library, *Manchester
Ballads*, Q398, 8S9.

Reports and Commissions

*The Assistant Poor Law Commissioners'
Reports on the Employment of
Women and Children in Agriculture*,
P.P. Session 1843, XII.
Children's Employment Commission.
*First Report of the Commissioners,
Mines*, P.P. Session 1842, XV.
Children's Employment Commission.
*Appendix to First Report of Com-
missioners, Mines. Part I*, P.P. Session
1842, XVI.
Children's Employment Commission.
*Appendix to First Report of Com-
missioners, Mines. Part II. Reports
and Evidence from Sub-Commis-
sioners*, P.P. Session 1842, XVII.
Children's Employment Commission.
*Appendix to the Second Report of
the Commissioners. Trades and
Manufactures. Part I. Reports and
Evidence from Sub-Commissioners*,
P.P. Session 1843, XIV.
Children's Employment Commission.
*Appendix to the Second Report of
the Commissioners. Trades and
Manufactures. Part II. Reports and
Evidence from Sub-Commissioners*,
P.P. Session 1843, XV.
*Combinations Defended; Being a Com-
mentary Upon, and Analysis of the*

Evidence given before the Parliamentary Committee of Inquiry into Combinations of Employers and Workmen Appointed by the House of Commons, February 1838, by the London Trades' Combination Committee, 1839.

First Report of the Select Committee on Combinations of Workmen, P.P. Session 1837–8, VIII.

Report of the Commissioners appointed to inquire into the Condition and Treatment of the Prisoners confined in Birmingham Borough Prison, and the Conduct, Management, and Discipline of the said Prison; together with the Minutes of Evidence, P.P. Session 1854, XXXI.

Report of the Commissioners appointed to inquire into the Condition and Treatment of the Prisoners confined in Leicester County Gaol and House of Correction; together with the Minutes of Evidence, P.P. Session 1854, XXXIV.

Report of the Commissioners on Handloom Weavers, P.P. Session 1841, X.

Report from the Select Committee on the Game Laws, P.P. Session 1846, IX, i.

Report from the Select Committee on the Bill to regulate the Labour of Children in Mills and Factories of the United Kingdom, P.P. Session 1831–2, XV.

Midland Mining Commission. *Appendix to First Report*, P.P. Session 1843, XIII.

Report from the Select Committee on the Payment of Wages, P.P. Session 1842, IX.

Report on the Sanitary Condition of the Labouring Population of Great Britain (Chadwick's *Report*, 1842), ed. M. Flinn, Edinburgh, 1965.

Exhibition Catalogues

'The Camera and Dr. Barnardo', National Portrait Gallery, 1974.

'From Today Painting is Dead', Victoria and Albert Museum, 1972.

'Landscape in Britain c.1750–1850', Tate Gallery, 1973.

'The Late Richard Dadd', Tate Gallery, 1974.

'Primitives to Picasso', Royal Academy, 1962.

'The Romantic Movement', Tate Gallery and Arts Council Gallery, 1959.

'The Shock of Recognition', Tate Gallery, 1971.

'Turner 1775–1851', Royal Academy, 1974.

Literary and Dramatic Sources; and Literary Criticism

Boucicault, D., 'The Long Strike', first performed Lyceum Theatre, 15 September 1866.

Carlyle, T., *Two Note Books of Thomas Carlyle: from 23d March 1822 to 16th May 1832*, ed. C. E. Norton, New York, 1898.

—, *Collected Works*, Library Edn., 30 vols., 1870.

Cazamian, L., *Le Roman Social en Angleterre 1830–1850*, new edn., 2 vols. in 1, Paris, 1934.

Chapple, J. A. V. and Pollard, A., eds., *The Letters of Mrs. Gaskell*, Manchester, 1966.

Clough, A. H., 'Recent English Poetry', *North American Review*, LXXVII, 1853.

Coleridge, S. T., *Biographia Literaria*, Everyman edn., 1956.

Collins, P. A. W., *Dickens and Crime*, 1962.

— ed., Dickens, *The Critical Heritage*, 1971.

Dexter, W., ed., *Letters of Charles Dickens*, 2 vols., 1938.

Eliot, G., 'The Natural History of German Life', *Westminster Review*, LXVI, 1856.

Fielding, K. J. ed., *The Speeches of Charles Dickens*, Oxford, 1960.

Forster, J., *The Life of Charles Dickens*, 2 vols., 1908.

Keating, P. J., *The Working Classes in Victorian Fiction*, 1971.

Kingsley, F. E., ed., *Charles Kingsley: His Letters and Memories of His Life*, 2 vols., 1877.

Lukács, G., *The Historical Novel*, 1962.

...d Struggle', first per-
...yceum Theatre, 1858.
..., *The Dust of Combat: A*
... Charles Kingsley, 1959.
..., T., ed., *Essays of George Eliot*,
1963.

Rollins, H. E., ed., *The Letters of John Keats*, 2 vols., Cambridge, 1958.

Ruskin, J., *Complete Works*, ed. E. T. Cook and A. Wedderburn, 39 vols., 1904-12.

Sala, G. A., 'Bright Chanticleer', *Household Words*, XI, 1855.

Smith, S. M., 'Blue Books and Victorian Novelists', *Review of English Studies*, XXI, 1970.

—, ed., *Mr. Disraeli's Readers*, Nottingham, 1966.

—, 'Willenhall and Wodgate: Disraeli's Use of Blue Book Evidence', *Review of English Studies*, XIII, 1962.

Sonstroem, D., 'Fettered Fancy in *Hard Times*', *Publications of the Modern Language Association of America*, LXXXIV, 1969.

Welsh, A., *The City of Dickens*, 1971.

Williams, R., *The Country and the City*, London and Toronto, 1973.

Wordsworth, W., Preface to the *Lyrical Ballads*, 1800.

Yates, E., *Edmund Yates: his Recollections and Experiences*, 2 vols., 1884.

History; Economic and Social History

Adshead, J., *Distress in Manchester*, 1842.

Alexander, S., *St. Giles's Fair, 1830–1914*, Oxford, 1970.

Allday, J., *True Account of the Proceedings Leading to, and a Full and Authentic Report of, The Searching Inquiry, by Her Majesty's Commissioners, into the Horrible System of Discipline practised at the Borough Gaol of Birmingham*, Birmingham and London, 1853.

Ashby, M. K., *Joseph Ashby of Tysoe, 1859-1919: a study of English village life*, Cambridge, 1961.

Aspin, C., *Lancashire, the First Industrial Society*, Helmshore Local History Society, 1969.

—, *Manchester and the Textile Districts in 1849*, Helmshore Local History Society, 1972.

Bloomfield, B. C., ed., *The Autobiography of Sir James Kay Shuttleworth*, 1964.

Bunce, J. T., *History of the Corporation of Birmingham; with a Sketch of the Earlier Government of the Town*, 2 vols., Birmingham, 1885.

Cobbett, W., *A History of the Protestant Reformation*, 2 vols., 1829.

Cole, G. D. H. and Filson, A. W., eds., *British Working Class Movements, Select Documents 1789-1875*, 1951.

Dickens, C., 'On Strike', *Household Words*, VIII, 1854.

Doré, G. and Jerrold, B., *London. A Pilgrimage*, 1872.

Dyos, H. J. and Wolff, M., eds., *The Victorian City*, 2 vols., London and Boston, 1973.

Engels, F., *The Condition of the Working Class in England*, Leipzig, 1845, English translation introduced by E. Hobsbawm, 1969.

Fay, C. R., *Life and Labour in the Nineteenth Century*, Cambridge, 1947.

Gaskell, P., *Manufacturing Population of England, its Moral, Social and Physical Conditions*, 1833.

Gavin, H., *Sanitary Ramblings, Being Sketches and Illustrations, of Bethnal Green. A Type of the Condition of the Metropolis and Other Large Towns*, 1848.

Gordon, S., 'The London *Economist* and the High Tide of Laissez Faire', *Journal of Political Economy*, LXIII, 1955.

Hansard's Parliamentary Debates, Third Series, LV, 1840; LXIII, 1842; LXIV, 1842.

Hardy, T., 'The Dorsetshire Labourer', *Longman's Magazine*, II, 1883.

Hartwell, R. M., *The Long Debate on Poverty*, 1972.

Howitt, W., *Rural Life of England*, 2 vols., 1838.

Hudson, D., *Munby Man of Two Worlds*, 1972.

Kay, J. (later James Kay-Shuttleworth), *Moral and Physical Condition of the*

Working Classes Employed in the Cotton Manufacture in Manchester, 2nd edn., 1832.

Mayhew, H., 'The Cholera Districts of Bermondsey', the *Morning Chronicle*, 24 September 1849.

—, 'Labour and the Poor. The Metropolitan Districts', Letters XVII and XVIII, the *Morning Chronicle*, 14 and 18 December 1849.

— et al., *London Labour and the London Poor*, 4 vols., 1861–2.

Middleton, T., *Annals of Hyde and District*, Manchester, 1899.

Miller, T., *Pictures of Country Life, and Summer Rambles in Green and Shady Places*, 1847.

—, *Picturesque Sketches of London, Past and Present*, 1851.

Reach, A. B., 'Labour and the Poor. The Manufacturing Districts. Ashton-under-Lyne', Letter VII, the *Morning Chronicle*, 8 November 1849.

Southey, R., *Sir Thomas More; or, Colloquies on the Progress and Prospects of Society*, 1829.

Talbot, C. J. C. (Viscount Ingestre), ed., *Meliora; or, Better Times to Come*, 1852.

Taylor, W. C., *Notes of a Tour in the Manufacturing Districts of Lancashire in a Series of Letters to His Grace the Archbishop of Dublin*, 2nd edn., 1842.

Thompson, E. P., *The Making of the English Working Class*, 1963.

Unwin, J. C., *The Hungry Forties*, 1904.

Wakefield, E. G., *Swing Unmasked; or,*

The Causes of Rural Incendiarism, 1831.

Art. Architecture, and Photography

Boys, T. S., *Original Views of London as it is*, 1842.

Gowing, L., *Turner: Imagination and Reality*, New York, 1966.

Pugin, A. W., *The True Principles of Pointed or Christian Architecture*, 1841.

Scott, W. B., *Half-Hour Lectures on the History and Practice of the Fine and Ornamental Arts*, 1861.

Talbot, H. F., *The Pencil of Nature*, 1844.

Philosophy

Kant, E., *Critique of Pure Reason*, trans. N. K. Smith, 1933.

Medawar, P. B., *The Art of the Soluble*, 1967.

Strawson, P. F., 'Imagination and Perception', *Experience and Theory*, ed. L. Foster and J. W. Swanson, Massachusetts, 1970.

Miscellaneous

Dickens, C., 'The Noble Savage', *Household Words*, VII, 1853.

Gaskell, W., 'Two Lectures on the Lancashire Dialect', *Mary Barton*, E. C. Gaskell, 5th edn., 1854.

Lloyd, A. L., *Folk Song in England*, 1967.

Stowe, H. B., *Sunny Memories of Foreign Lands*, 1854.

INDEX